FIBREGLASS BOATS
FITTING OUT, MAINTENANCE AND REPAIR

Fibreglass Boats

FITTING OUT
MAINTENANCE
AND REPAIR

Hugo du Plessis

Associate of the Royal Institution of Naval Architects
Senior Member of the Society of Plastic Engineers

ADLARD COLES LIMITED

LONDON

Granada Publishing Limited
First published in Great Britain 1964 by Adlard Coles
in association with Rupert Hart-Davis Limited
Frogmore, St Albans, Hertfordshire AL2 2NF and
3 Upper James Street, London W1R 4BP

Copyright © 1964, 1973 Hugo du Plessis
Second impression 1966
Second edition 1973
Reprinted 1974

ISBN 0 229 11521 7
Printed in Great Britain by
Fletcher & Son Ltd, Norwich

CONTENTS

APPENDICES

Introduction

THE purpose of this book is to turn good mouldings into good boats. Sound moulding is, of course, very important, and so is a good basic shape, for the boat will never be any good if the hull shape is wrong. But sound moulding and a good shape are not enough in themselves. The shell must still be fitted out properly before it can honestly be called a boat. This demands intelligent appreciation of the nature of the moulding, a knowledge of how to attach fittings so that they do not pull off chunks of boat, and experience of boats and the conditions they have to put up with. The large number of boat-shaped mouldings, which have so many elementary faults that they can hardly be called boats, shows that many moulders and boatbuilders still do not appreciate this.

Yet it is only by attention to proper fitting out that a boatbuilder can turn out safe, seaworthy boats, free from stupid annoying little faults, as well as dangerous major bloomers, and which will retain their initial pristine appearance with the minimum of maintenance for years to come.

This book is aimed at everybody who builds or uses boats, wooden boats as well as fibreglass ones, for the two are drawing close together. It will be of use to moulders, both professional and amateur, designers, owners, surveyors and the conventional yard normally handling wooden boats, for a lot of the ideas can be applied to wooden boats as well.

First, the moulders and designers of fibreglass boats: the good ones will know a lot of what I have to say already—for I have copied extensively from the best of them—but even they will pick up some worthwhile tips, particularly the moulders of smaller boats who decide to advance to larger sizes. Some of their ears may burn, for several of the faults which I have condemned roundly are still being repeated by well-respected, pioneering companies. The less experienced moulders, and especially that large band of moulders who are not by tradition boatbuilders, can well make it their Bible. Most of the mistakes quoted have been based on what they have done that they should not have done.

Designers, too, will find much that is helpful, for with a fibreglass boat it is essential to indicate a lot of detailed design which on a wooden boat could confidently be left to the yard's usual practice. Quite apart from the fact that many moulders will have no traditional practice to fall back on, a great deal of the detailed design of a fibreglass boat must be decided at a very early stage when making the mould or master pattern. Forethought here will save much expense later; it is often possible to design the boat to take a standard fitting or to mould in a bulge or dent, instead of having to obtain expensive specially made fittings later. Forethought or good planning is one of the keys to a good fibreglass boat.

Secondly the conventional boatyard, which is probably backed by generations of experience and is often very progressive—so long as it is working with wood: These yards have a growing tendency, a very sound tendency, to buy standard moulded hulls to fit out on largely conventional lines in wood. How are the two materials married safely and reliably? This book tells how, with mention of methods which use "dry" methods as opposed to the "wet" methods of moulding (or "clean" as opposed to "messy" methods). However, because of their superiority, no one should consider fitting out GRP cruisers seriously unless prepared to learn how to use enough GRP for essential attachments.

This aspect will also appeal to the amateur, for moulding a one-off boat is a far bigger proposition than fitting out a ready-moulded shell, whether the job is done entirely in wood or with a series of small mouldings. Again many of these ideas for fitting out can be applied successfully to fitting out a wooden boat, or alterations to an old one, with a considerable saving in trouble and cost, and often enable an amateur to do alterations himself which otherwise would require a yard.

Thirdly the owner and also the surveyor: what does one look for when buying? What are good points and, more important, what are bad? What details will give persistent trouble? What will involve a lot of maintenance? What are latent defects, sources of danger and possible premature failure. I have quoted many cases of bad design—all of which have been taken from actual boats, although not all have been fibreglass boats—to illustrate as much what should not be done as what should be.

Fourthly there is a section on maintenance and repair appealing to everybody. There has been far too much emphasis on "no maintenance." "Low maintenance" is certainly true, and with sensible design it may be "very low maintenance," but never "no maintenance." This can only lead to fibreglass boats having a generally scruffy appearance and a low secondhand value, a state of affairs which certainly exists already in the small boat field. This compares badly with a wooden boat which depreciates in value fairly slowly, if well maintained, and can always be kept smart albeit at considerable trouble and expense. Sensible design can cut down many of the places which obviously are going to get worn and thus help to maintain a good appearance.

Designing for low maintenance has been given special attention throughout this book, as it is another point which seldom gets enough consideration. Many moulders would be shocked if they could see their nice shiny boats after a few years; others, I fear, could not care less; but there are certain types of boat, chiefly runabouts but also in some racing classes, where planned obsolescence is a factor recognised by both owners and builders. Wooden boats are traditionally supposed to last for ever. This is, of course, an exaggeration, for rot will claim all but the staunchest long before the century is near, and fifty years is longer than most will see. The oldest boat in *Lloyd's Register* is in its eighties (and iron-built at that) and only a handful are over seventy. Strange to say the list was headed by almost the same yachts fifteen years earlier.

A good fibreglass boat has a better claim to last for ever, for it is at least proof against rot. The cynics will say that twenty years or so, the age of the oldest fibreglass boats, is not long enough to judge, and they can probably dig up some bad boats to prove it. I know of a number of wooden boats which have not lasted ten years and plenty more which are not much older, but which run up an annual maintenance bill of half their original cost in an effort to delay the approaching end. I have not heard of a single *soundly made* GRP boat which has yet fallen to pieces. But it is important to realise that early boats were not typical: materials were crude, unreliable and very expensive. The temptation, often a necessity, to economise was strong. There was no experience and few guidelines. Enthusiasts worked by trial and error. But in some ways they were better, too. It was before the era of the cut-price, low quality mass-producer.

However, there is one serious consideration which is often forgotten. If the boat really is going to last for ever there are likely to be plenty of conventional parts of it, such as almost everything connected with the engines, mast, rigging and accommodation. These are certainly going to get worn out or broken and it must be possible to renew them at no great expense. It could happen that a good boat would have to be written off because some comparatively small fitting was moulded in and impossible to replace. As Pooh-Bah sings in *The Mikado* "Long life to you—till then."

Plenty of yards have been reluctant to lay up fibreglass boats because they know nothing about them and perhaps fear that with this "no maintenance" idea there will be no work and therefore no money in it. This is not so. Anything that floats, regardless of construction, mops up money like a sponge. Many moulded boats are gin-palaces, and all of them are in the newer and more expensive class. This implies an owner with money to spend, although it must be emphasised that some have put their money into a fibreglass boat with the idea of spending less on annual painting. However, cleaning, polishing, antifouling, together with conventional interior and engine work will cover the yard's overheads satisfactorily. Alterations and repairs, too, will be needed, and they are not difficult, nothing like so difficult as moulding a complete boat; a yard which rightly is shy about moulding complete boats will find it worthwhile to learn enough to tackle ordinary repairs and alterations to fibreglass boats. A good repair is a rarity. Most repairs are crude and unsightly. Few moulders even can fill their common little moulding flaws inconspicuously. Every boat needs chandlery and fittings, and they are more likely to be ordered through the yard where the boat is laid up. Therefore laying up fibreglass boats is still good business, even if there is little painting to be done; and any yard which can make a name for itself as a specialist in this field can be sure of plenty of business for years to come.

Much of this book will be elementary to an experienced and conscientious moulder or boatbuilder. That is inevitable, because it has to cover a wide field, starting with the man to whom a boat is just another moulding and who has possibly never been in a boat in his life. But the experienced should not scorn it on that account, for it describes faults and pitfalls which have been seen on boats from moulders who should know better.

The reader must pick and choose what he needs. If it is too elementary, skip that part; there is worthwhile reading further on. There will be few who need to read it from cover to cover; few, too, who know it all.

For those completely new to moulding there are a series of Appendices at the back summarising the general moulding techniques together with a lot of useful hints covering working under actual yard conditions as opposed to a well-equipped laboratory. These hints can usually be taken as overriding the suppliers' recommendations, particularly as regards that stock obstacle, the working temperature. The meaning of unfamiliar terms will be found in Appendix 7.

This is not a book on general moulding; there is another to come which will cover that, and these appendices are only intended as a general description to cover an initial gap, say in the planning or design stage before any experience has been gained by actually trying and using the materials. Once they have been used and one has got the feel of them a lot will be self-evident. The suppliers' instructions will contain more detailed information in particular detailed information on mixing the resins, etc. In the main part of the book it is always assumed that when resin, moulding or lay-up is mentioned, that the resins have been mixed in the appropriate way and the piece will be moulded by the proper techniques. Detailed step-by-step descriptions every time would be tedious and confusing.

Suppliers' instructions and advisory services are often contradictory and biased in favour of their particular material, not only their own brand, which is understandable in a commercial world, but also the type of material, *e.g.* resin, glass or even some unimportant ancillary like a filler. None can view the moulding as a whole, yet that is the most important aspect of all. What is it like as a boat? That is all that interests that important fellow, the owner.

Certain firms have brought disrepute on the industry by turning out shoddy mouldings; such firms are popularly supposed to be garages and backyard builders who have jumped on the bandwagon of a small-boat boom. In fact there have been plenty of bad boats turned out by large firms, as well, and some very good ones by the smallest. But there is no doubt that some of these bad boats have been really useless, and not only useless but dangerous. Fate has caught up with many of the small firms, and they have faded from the scene, although more often from lack of capital and business experience than because of their shoddy boats. Large companies selling bad boats seem to thrive, and as long as high pressure salesmanship and a large advertising budget can reach an even more gullible public I fear they will continue to do so. But it is not too late for them to mend their ways and find out that a good boat can be just as flashy and sell better.

However, many excellent boats are moulded in backyards or by small non-marine firms, indeed some of the best dinghies I know come from what was originally a most unpromising background. On the other hand some old-established and well-known boatyards have turned out bad boats because of lack of moulding experience and insufficient appreciation of how to design for the new materials. I know of other cases where high-class yards have dropped a good moulded project, with their fingers burnt, but have had enough sense to cut their losses and keep it dark rather than put their good name on a boat which, through inexperience, did not come up to their usual standard.

The size of firm does not necessarily determine the quality of the boat. It is the men in the firm who count. As well as knowing how to mould, do they know what a boat has to put up with? Do they appreciate the standard of finish which a yachtsman expects not only today but after five, ten, twenty or even fifty years of use?

Selecting a name for this book has been rather a problem. The common name for these boats is fibreglass boats, or fiberglass if our illogical English spelling is too much for you. Glass fibre (or fiber) is the same thing, but unassociated with any trade name. The more correct name is reinforced plastics, a much better description of a boat which is only 25 per cent or less of fibreglass. Moreover it looks and feels like a moulded plastic, not fibreglass. Does a fibreglass boat look like a moulded plastic washing-up bowl or a bundle of loose fibreglass jacketing a hot water tank or lining a roof?

My patient publisher and I have therefore reached a compromise. He has had his way in the title and we have called it *Fibreglass Boats* to attract the right sort of attention, but inside I have used "moulded" or "plastic" boats, because this is a better description and technically more correct. It also avoids confusion with the actual fibreglass material. The term moulded boats may be confused with moulded plywood boats, but this is not important because the requirements for both are very similar. Indeed moulded plywood is far more akin to reinforced plastic than to conventional boatbuilding and may be considered a wood-reinforced plastic—the glues being certainly a plastic material.

I could have used the full technical name "silane-treated alkali-free fibreglass-reinforced unsaturated polyester resin peroxide catalysed"—but I cannot think of a quicker way to send the reader dashing off to buy a wooden boat; and if anyone quoted him the chemical name for wood, that wonderful, highly complex natural product he would jump in the river, for these clever man-made synthetic materials which are hailed as being so new and revolutionary are really very simple compared with familiar natural products which have been taken for granted since time began.

Lymington
October 1963

Introduction to Second Edition

THERE have naturally been many developments since this book was first written. It would be surprising if there had not, for it was written at the beginning of the era of the GRP cruiser, when wood was still the traditional boatbuilding material. Nevertheless, it is practice which has developed rather than principles, and sound practice must still be based on sound principles. Some boatbuilders may produce some decent boats one day when they remember this.

It will be some time yet before these new developments and the experience of good and bad points revealed by my many surveys on GRP boats can be brought out as a completely new and expanded book. But there has been continued demand for this new edition so I have revised and updated what I can within the severe limitations of the existing format.

The most outstanding lesson has been the importance of quality. This is nothing new. It is only remarkable that anyone would assume that modern technology was a substitute for high quality or, by itself, should guarantee it. Quality starts fairly and squarely right at the top, with the management. Nowhere else. Their attitude to quality sets the standard. The custom of fitting out hulls moulded by another company means that quality must extend all down the chain. What is the point of fitting out to a high standard a badly moulded hull?

Price is the worst guide to quality. Of course there have been bad, cheap boats, lots of them and often very dangerous, just as there have been plenty of very good expensive boats. But the most nearly perfect GRP boat I have surveyed was a Hurley 20 and Hurley Marine Ltd were pioneers of cheap, small, mass-produced cruisers. On the other hand most of the worst boats I have encountered (and some of them have been positively murderous) have not been cheap ones. For example I once narrowly escaped serious injury on a test sail when a substantial part of a very expensive new boat just disintegrated under quite unexceptional conditions of sailing. This boat bore the name of an established company of very high repute.

In recent years the term GRP, standing for glass reinforced plastics, has become widely accepted. It is a far better term than fibreglass for these *are* plastics boats in appearance, texture and behaviour. It is also devoid of trade connections. For continuity I have retained the original title but now use the term GRP in the text.

Bantry, Ireland
March 1973

CHAPTER ONE

How to Attach Fittings
and Join Mouldings

A COMMON objection to a fibreglass boat, particularly from the gadgeteer or ship's husband type of owner, is the supposed difficulty of attaching things to the boat. This same fear discourages many professional boatbuilders from fitting out hull shells moulded by other firms, and even from carrying out simple alterations and repairs to fibreglass boats laid up in their yards. Yet fixing things to a moulded hull is really quite easy and secure if the *right* techniques are used. Armed with some of the plastic materials it is quite easy to fix anything anywhere, and also many conventional or "dry" methods of fastening can be used.

It is true that on a stout old wooden boat you can hammer nails or drive screws almost anywhere (if she is sound enough), but this is by no means so on light plywood or even double-diagonal planking, and steel and aluminium present severe problems to anyone but a skilled welder.

SUMMARY OF FIXING METHODS   The main fixing methods are:

1. Moulded fillets, "matting-in" or "glass" angles, and moulded butt-straps.
2. Blocks, battens, or plates, embedded or open.
3. Through-fastenings, bolts or rivets.
4. Selt-tapping screws.
5. Tapped inserts.
6. Self-locking "push-in" inserts.
7. Gluing.

Every join between mouldings, every join between a moulding and woodwork or metal, or attachment of fittings makes use of one or more of these methods.

The section on Hard Spots and Stress Concentrations on pages 60–62 is also highly relevant to the question of fixing, because all unfair stress concentrations arise from joins or attachments of some kind.

PREPARATION   Proper preparation is important, and bad results are inevitable if it is skimped. Indeed this is the commonest cause of trouble, much commoner than mere inexperience.

No special preparation is needed when bolting or screwing together other than ensuring a good mating fit, but a good sanding will help to remove high spots and ensure a better seat.

Before moulding anything extra on to the hull the surface must be cleaned up. Sand thoroughly all over the areas where the fitting is to be attached, allowing for generous overlaps. This sanding will break up the glossy surface to provide a key, remove high spots and take off any surface layer of paint or muck.

If the surface is painted, dirty or oily the bond will be unreliable or may not take at all. Therefore the cleaner the moulding and the more it is sanded to expose clean material the better the bond will be. The same applies to the preparation for gluing, which is much the same as for moulding, and is equally necessary.

In the bilges be particularly careful to clean and degrease thoroughly. If it is not a new boat they may be covered with oil and muck which will prevent proper bonding, and even a new boat will have collected dirty footprints, dust and débris.

Acetone can be used to soften and degrease the surface, and also to improve the chemical bond. It dries the surface, and is useful in damp weather, particularly cold damp weather, when condensation is bad. But acetone dissolves the resin and must be used with discretion. It must be applied sparingly and all wiped off the surface after about fifteen minutes. It will cause damage if allowed to collect and lie in a puddle, and for that reason its use is often condemned. If the surface is clean acetone is better avoided, but if it is dirty the disadvantages of using acetone, with discretion, are less than the risk of a bad bond if it is not used. It is more suitable for old boats than new.

In a confined space the fumes are sickly, although reasonably harmless, but they are inflammable and should be treated with as much respect as petrol fumes or bottled gas.

The bond is always better on the rough "inside" of the moulding than on the smooth "outside" which was laid up against the mould. Apart from being smooth this side may still have traces of release agent or polish from routine maintenance which will affect the bond.

If there is any doubt about the bond, and the fitting is important and highly stressed, fastenings should be used as well.

DELAMINATION AND DESIGN OF JOINTS All reinforced plastic mouldings are made as laminates, i.e. as a series of layers one on top of the other. Considered as a whole the glass fibre provides the strength, and the resin binds it together to give the form and texture, the two acting together as a homogeneous material. But considered more closely as a laminate, it is only separate layers of strong glass-fibre bonded together with a resin of much lower strength (Fig. 1.1).

1.1: *A reinforced plastic moulding is made basically of layers or laminations of strong glass-fibre, 1, with layers of weaker resin in between, 2. The outer faces, 3, are also of resin only.*

It is of fundamental importance that fittings and joints are attached in such a way that there is no tendency to pull the laminate apart and cause delamination. This can occur if a tensile load is applied to a joint or a fitting which is secured only by bonding (Figs. 1.2, 1.3).

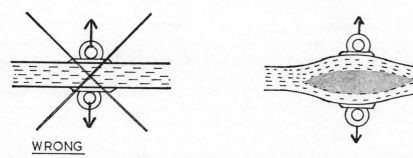

WRONG
Tensile loads applied to bonded attachments will cause delamination.

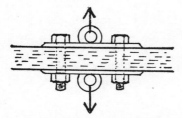

RIGHT
Fitting through fastened; load carried by the moulding as a whole.

1.2: *Tensile loads applied to opposite faces of a moulding will cause delamination.*

Therefore all attachments subject to a tensile load must be through-fastened so that the load is carried by the laminate as a whole and no strain is taken by the bonds between the layers of the laminate. This applies almost as much to any attachment or joint normally in compression, but which may be put in tension accidentally. In moments of stress, surprise or in plain ignorance ropes may pull in quite the wrong direction, and there is absolutely no excuse if part of the boat follows a cleat and rope's end over the side.

All attachments must be designed in such a way that no matter whether the strain is fair or unfair, predicted or unpredicted, it is the fitting or its fastenings which fail, NEVER the boat.

This is such obvious good practice that it should not need special mention—but unfortunately it does; too many boats have had to be patched up (and not only moulded ones) which should have needed only a new cleat.

Any joint between two mouldings or between a moulding and woodwork must be as strong as the parts being joined together. Again bonded joints should be in shear or compression, never in tension which would cause delamination. If it is possible to put the joint substantially in tension under any circumstances, through-fastenings should be used as well as plain bonding. Bending may put part of the joint in tension, and the effects of loading other parts of the structure, including possible unfair loading or overloading should be considered also.

The strength of the moulding lies in the glass-fibres, so as far as possible every joint must represent a continuity of glass-fibres. It is impracticable to knit the glass fibres together, therefore the next best thing is a lap joint, so that at least there is a generous area of overlapping fibres. A butt-joint gives no continuity of glass fibres and is quite unsuitable. If a flush-joint is essential, a butt-strap, or two lap joints, must be used (Fig. 1.4).

JOINING TWO MEMBERS The configurations for joining two mouldings are much the same whether joining two hard and cured mouldings or laying up a second moulding (a "wet" moulding) in contact with an earlier hard one.

An overlap made with a "wet" moulding on top of a cured one will normally hold well enough due to a degree of chemical bond and intimate contact, but two hard mouldings are better fastened mechanically. Joining two hard mouldings by means of a layer of "wet" glass-fibre and resin sandwiched between them is often recommended, but is not satisfactory because ordinary polyester moulding resins are poor structural adhesives and there is no continuity of glass. If used it should be in conjunction with mechanical fastenings.

All joints must be made as lap-joints to give a continuity of strength. Butt-joints cannot be used except in conjunction with butt-straps. Figs. 1.5 and 1.6 show some typical joints. The single lap-joints on the whole are suitable for "wet" or "dry" joints; double lap-joints and moulded angles are more suitable for "wet" joints as the "wet" glass-fibre is so easy to form to the exact shape and intimate contact, but strips or sections of other materials can also be used where the shape permits.

The edges of the lap-joint should be chamfered. A "step"-joint is bad practice. If one piece is appreciably thicker than the other (Fig. 1.7), the join must taper to avoid abrupt change of thickness. An abrupt change causes stress concentration. Often it is more convenient to thicken the thinner piece at the join or back it with a piece of plywood.

A scarfed joint (Fig. 1.8) is not strong by itself unless properly glued or through-fastened. Very accurate cutting is needed if a "dry" joint is to mate properly over a long length—as it usually must on a boat moulding. The filled "V"-joint and butt-strap, or a stepped lap-joint, as in Fig. 1.5, is easier to use where a flush finish is wanted over a long length. They are more reliable, too, for a joint which is easier to make is less likely to go wrong.

It is very seldom that the dimensions or the "inside" appearance of a moulding is so critical that the slight bulge of a well tapered lap-joint is unacceptable. In the few cases where it might interfere it is usually over a short portion of the length only, and if a scarf or butt-joint is inevitable here it will be supported by adjoining lap joints. The part which causes the interference, possibly a frame or a bulkhead, may also give support.

A join made by laying up one member "wet" will bond well, fit intimately and not need sealing. But joins between two hard mouldings or between a moulding and woodwork must be well sealed. "Wet" mat goes hard and is useless as a sealer. Use high quality elastomeric sealants such as polysulphide (Thiokol), silicone, polybutadiene or a neoprene gasket. For cheaper sealants use permanently flexible bedding compounds. GRP is a flexible material. All sealants must be permanently flexible too, and not age harden. However a joint which is moulded over inside for strength may be considered immobile, and a harder, less flexible sealant such as resin putty can be used.

"Wet" polyester will bond to hard polyester because of chemical affinity. But the older the GRP the less the bond and the more likely that the surface will be dirty and contaminated. Therefore unless new and "green" clean the surface thoroughly and sand

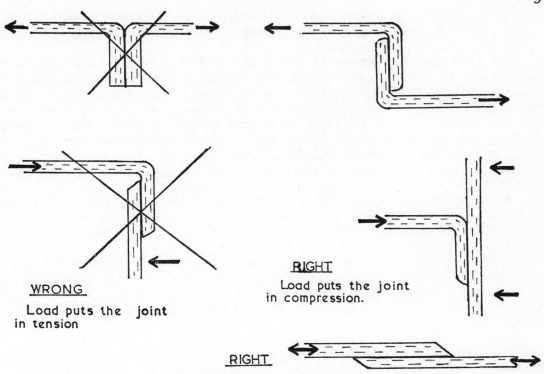

WRONG

Load puts the joint
in tension

RIGHT

Load puts the joint
in compression.

RIGHT

Load puts the joint in shear
on both tensile and compressive loads.

1.3: *Joint design: direction of loading.*

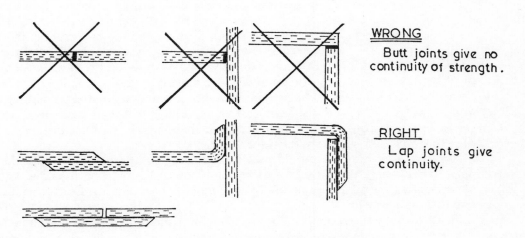

WRONG

Butt joints give no
continuity of strength.

RIGHT

Lap joints give
continuity.

1.4 *Joint design: use lap joints not butt joints.*

well. Wipe with acetone to clean and condition it. Bonding will always be better to the rough side rather than the gel coat side. If in doubt use epoxy not polyester as this is a strong glue yet laminates like polyester.

The gap is often wide because it is impossible to hold two substantial mouldings, such as a hull and a moulded gunwale or deck, to an exact fit all round. There will inevitably be some uneven contraction during cure. By using fastenings these discrepancies can often be corrected, because the natural flexibility of the mouldings allows them to be drawn together, whereas layers of "wet" mat intended for bonding would only force the semi-flexible mouldings further apart. Pulling together with fastenings should only be done within narrow limits as the moulding must not be forced.

The shapes for joining to wood or metal are, in general, similar to joining two mouldings. Butt-joints must be avoided and a lap-joint of some kind used every time.

A "wet" joint must be preceded by a primer suitable for the material; and it is best where an ample area of contact, ideally a locking contact, can be secured. A good "grip" around the other material is much stronger than flat adhesion, and it is often possible to design for it to be embedded.

When the proper primers for wood or metal, as described in the next sections, are not available, bonding is not likely to be reliable and mechanical fastenings or gluing should be used instead. Gluing and conventional methods of fastening are usually satisfactory if done sensibly and, being familiar, may be more reliable in inexperienced hands—an important factor.

DO NOT FORCE TO FIT   Do not force a moulding to fit, whether you are joining two hard, cured, mouldings or joining a hard moulding to preformed woodwork. Forcing the moulding to fit pre-stresses the joint, and not only the joint but a lot of the moulding too, so that it will be more susceptible to damage. This can well upset calculations for strength and will certainly reduce the factor of safety. Similarly no internal part should be a force fit inside the hull. In particular rigid incompressible members such as bulkheads can cause considerable prestressing and severe hard spots if forced or even just tight.

In many cases some padding in the form of a resin-glass putty can be used to fill in minor discrepancies. Always shape or pad woodwork to fit the moulding, never force the moulding to fit the woodwork. Two mouldings should be designed to mate exactly. However, they will not maintain close tolerances during cure unless well supported, and they may warp too. If badly out, one of the mouldings should be scrapped rather than both forced to fit. Where tolerances are critical mouldings should cure in jigs.

It is always better for two mouldings to be joined together as soon after moulding as possible, while still "green" and fairly flexible. The mouldings will then accommodate a much larger movement without being forced. Also if they cure in position distortion is impossible because any "set" will be to the right shape.

Quick-cure resins cure in the mould and do not have a "green" stage. Therefore unless both parts will mate perfectly it is as well for one of them to be moulded with ordinary, slower curing resins, and joined soon after moulding so that it is flexible enough to accommodate misalignment.

It is difficult to hold the rough or "inside" face of a moulding to close tolerances. Some unevenness is inevitable where there is no mould face to control the dimensions and surface. Accurate fitting is impossible and sufficient clearance must be allowed. The varia-

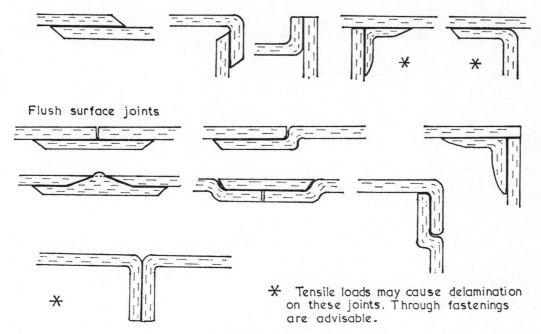

Flush surface joints

✳ Tensile loads may cause delamination on these joints. Through fastenings are advisable.

1.5: *Single-lap joints.*

tions in thickness may be of the order of 10 per cent on a thick moulding, to 50 per cent on a thin or badly moulded one.

If close fitting which involves an "inside" face is essential, it will be necessary to file down high spots, and probably a lot of the moulding, too. This can be avoided if the two parts are mated together while one is still "wet". An alternative is to leave a clearance and fit them together with sealant between.

BENDS Bends and angles may vary a lot in thickness. When an inside bend is moulded, the various successive layers tend to remain parallel, each following the same radius but with different centre-points. Compare this with a sheet of metal which bends evenly about its neutral axis with each part following a different radius about a common centre-point. This is shown in Fig. 6.2 (page 86).

In actual practice this effect is aggravated, because the layers will tend to bridge the hollow, and it will be found that the bend tends to fill up, with the last layers following a considerably greater radius than the first layer or the mould. Also resin often drains down to form a puddle on the bend. As a result the bend becomes thicker than the general thickness of the moulding.

The opposite tendency occurs where the lay-up is on the outside of a bend or angle. On a sharp bend there is a risk that the glass mat will pull down, and even break up a little so that the bend may be thinner than the rest of the moulding. Moreover resin tends to drain away from such bends, which also makes them thinner and weaker than the rest

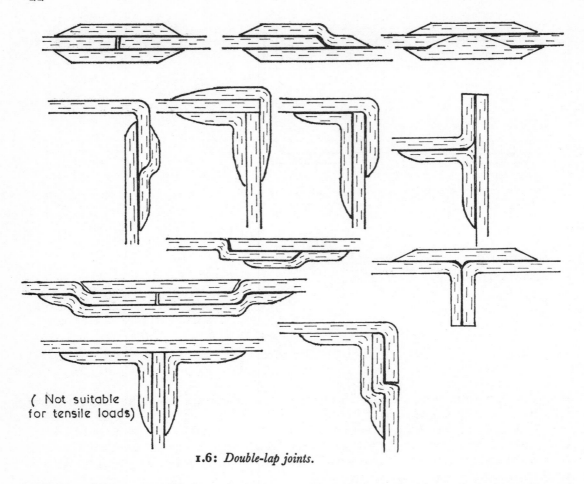

(Not suitable
for tensile loads)

1.6: *Double-lap joints.*

of the moulding, with a likelihood of flaws. Successive layers are likely to repeat the weakness along the same line, so that a line of weakness develops along the bend.

Where it is suspected that this is happening, extra strips should be moulded along sharp outside bends to compensate. Narrow strips will not break up on a bend like part of a wide piece.

BONDING TO WOOD This must be considered seriously. Debonding of glass angles securing main structural members such as bulkheads and frames is a common fault. Polyester resins are not good adhesives and are not meant to be. However a reasonable bond can be achieved by getting the resin to soak into the wood, ensuring a generous area of contact, making sure it is clean and dry, using a suitable species and rough sanding to give a key. The wood must be unpainted.

Ordinary laminating resins are usually too thick and thixotropic to soak in. It is necessary to prime the wood with a thin resin which readily soaks in and keys to the wood, as in painting. The thicker laminating resins then bond by chemical action to the primer

NOT RECOMMENDED   RECOMMENDED PRACTICE

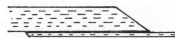   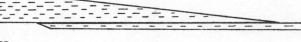

'Step' joint causes stress concentration. Always chamfer edges.

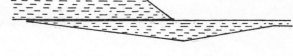

Avoid substantial change in thickness
unless well tapered. Alternatively
ease transition by thickening the
thinner member locally. A butt
strap will have a similar effect.

Round off re-entrant angle to avoid stress concentration.
  N B It is difficult to get a good fit over long lengths of join unless
one part is 'wet'

1.7: *Avoiding stress concentrations.*

1.8: *Scarfed joint. Difficult to ensure a good fit on a long run of joint. It gives a flush surface but a weak joint. It may be riveted for security.*

resin. If thin primer resins cannot be obtained they can be made by thinning down ordinary clear polyester resin, preferably non-thixotropic, with 10 per cent of styrene. Styrene is the best thinning agent but if unavailable (which is likely as it cannot be bought locally and must be ordered from resin suppliers) acetone can be used instead. As acetone does not form part of the reaction, as styrene does, it should be reduced to 5 per cent.

A polyester resin quickly gets thinner as it is warmed so warm resin can be used as a primer. Note that cold resins get thick and much bad bonding may be due to careless use of thick, cold resins. Do not overheat. The flashpoint is low, 88° F. (24° C.), and it may ignite. The temperature can be controlled by heating the tin in a pan of water which should not be hotter than a moderately warm bath. Warm resin will set much more quickly. Catalyst should be reduced to a half or quarter of the usual amount otherwise it may be uncontrollable. Warm before adding catalyst, otherwise it will set as the resin gets hot.

Wood preservative must be used with great discretion. Most preservatives have a deadly effect on polyester resin, especially on the bonding surface, an insidious effect as it is not apparent for some time until a damp rot-growing atmosphere releases the active constituents of the preservative. It is safer to avoid preservatives altogether, but if required particularly, or if already in the wood, do not rely at all on bonding. Use "dry" joints or fasten the "wet" overlap with screws when dry. Anyway polyester resins themselves have some preservative properties.

Sometimes epoxy resins are recommended for laying up in contact with wood because of their better properties as adhesives. They too should first be used as a thin primer to soak in. Acetone is the commonest thinning agent but it should be used sparingly, say 5 per cent. Excess can be trapped and it reduces tackiness. Epoxy resins also get thinner when warmed, but as no variation in the proportion of the hardener is permitted there is no control over the setting time. Reactive thinners which combine with the resins are now available. Certainly epoxies, used properly, are better adhesives, but given a generous area of contact and fair loading, the extra cost of epoxy and the complications of using a separate resin are not justified on wood.

Woods vary in the amount of resin they will absorb. The bond will be worst on hard, non-absorbent woods, or on teak, iroko and other naturally oily woods. Oily woods should be degreased with solvent, e.g. acetone, BCF, etc., to remove oil from the surface. If there is any doubt the bond should be supplemented with ordinary fastenings, but more to maintain the friction of contact and grip than to hold by themselves.

BONDING TO METAL Most metals have some effect on "wet" polyester resins; some accelerate the setting time, some delay it. Of the common metals, only the delaying effect of copper is of any importance, and even this can often be ignored if the area is small or of no structural importance, as in a well-embedded insert, or individual brass fastenings. Large or important parts of copper, or of materials containing copper, should be avoided or plated.

An embedded insert of copper or brass can be coated with a layer of polyester resin first, and the resin allowed to set so that it forms a barrier to reduce the effect on the "wet" structural resin surrounding it.

However, epoxy is not affected by copper, so it is better for any really important copper fittings, and this includes anything like brass or bronze which contains copper, to be primed with epoxy rather than polyester, and allowed to set before coming into contact with polyester. The epoxy resin barrier should certainly be used on high-class work, and must be well cured.

It is said that ideally such coatings should be stove-cured, but this is not essential and in most cases proper controlled stoving is impracticable. Stoving in the kitchen oven is likely to do more harm than good.

A good bond can be obtained on to steel and aluminium if it is primed with an etch primer of the phosphoric acid type to make a key. Suitable primers are made by Croda, Ltd., and Pyrene, Ltd. These must be washed off after a short time or the effect will continue, possibly even under the resin. A rust-inhibiting etch primer has obvious advantages.

All metal must be thoroughly degreased with a good degreasing solvent such as carbon tetrachloride, but subsequent careless handling and fingermarks will undo the degreasing.

In general the bond to properly treated steel and aluminium is good but only moderate to copper, brass and bronze. Bonding is better to rough surfaces like rusty or galvanised iron and steel, than to smooth, polished surfaces. Bonding to polished stainless steel or bright plating will be unreliable.

BONDING TO OTHER MATERIALS Porous materials, such as cardboard, hardboard, plaster, cement and canvas, can be treated like wood with a thin primer resin. Rubber should be wiped with dilute sulphuric acid; battery acid is of suitable strength. This makes minute hair-cracks on the surface to provide a key.

Most of the better sheet plastic materials are too waxy for either polyester or epoxy resins to bond on to, but it is possible to bond on to some grades of PVC by using special polyester resins made for this purpose. They should not be used without a trial first.

Foam polystyrene is very quickly attacked by polyester resins. An epoxy sealer will protect it, as also will bitumen and bitumen epoxy paints which are cheaper. Another convenient method where the material is to be embedded is to wrap the foam polystyrene in a polythene bag. Foam PVC may be softened, but usually if the resin sets quickly little harm will be done. The more flexible the foam the less resistant it is to softening.

There is no easy way to get reliable adhesion to ordinary sheet glass. (Glass-fibres are specially treated in the factory). For this reason sheets of glass are ideal for flat moulds.

A bond to Tufnol and to similar materials can be obtained if the suraface is well roughened. A machined or sawn surface is better than the hard, smooth outside finish.

"DRY" JOINTS A "dry" joint in this case has nothing to do with radio breakdowns but means a joint between two members which is not made with any "wet" glass-fibre or liquid resin, e.g. fastening two hard mouldings together with glue or bolts, or fastening woodwork to a moulding with screws. It is the sort of problem encountered by a conventional yard fitting out a GRP boat, or an amateur with no glass or resin to hand, who wants to attach something, or perhaps do an emergency repair at sea.

Fig. 1.9 shows some typical methods equally suitable for joining moulded sections to wood and metal, or for joining two mouldings. Remember that good workmanship is just as important as when joining wood to wood in conventional work.

The curves associated with moulded construction are not always easy to follow with wood. Steaming makes wood bend more easily, but it has its limits. Carving from solid needs careful fitting with a lot of waste. Laminating and gluing thin strips in difficult places is an easier alternative; it is also lighter and stronger, more in keeping with moulded construction.

The time has passed when a GRP boat of cruiser size could be fitted out entirely "dry". Unless all structural work is done first by the moulder anyone fitting out a cruiser ought to know enough about simple moulding to make at least the ubiquitous glass angle—but this is no more than should be expected today from any competent boatbuilder or boat-owning handyman.

NO FITTINGS MUST BE ATTACHED TO AN UNSTIFFENED MOULD-ING Stressed attachments must not be made to a moulding unless the moulding is strong enough at that point to take them. This is obvious, of course; but too many fittings have been pulled right through unthickened and unstiffened mouldings—and through light plywood and even good planking, too, because thoughtless, unimaginative workmanship is not confined to some builders of fibreglass boats.

26

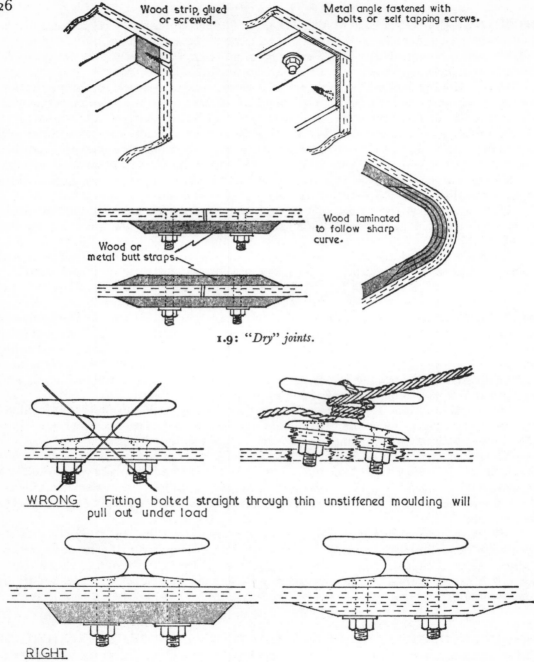

Wood strip, glued or screwed.

Metal angle fastened with bolts or self tapping screws.

Wood laminated to follow sharp curve.

Wood or metal butt straps.

1.9: *"Dry" joints.*

WRONG   Fitting bolted straight through thin unstiffened moulding will pull out under load

RIGHT

Bolt through a block on the under side, or thicken the moulding substantially, to spread the load.

1.10: *Fittings must never be bolted through an unstiffened moulding.*

Yet it is so easy to thicken up and strengthen a moulding wherever a fitting is to be attached, or to put in a block of wood to spread the load. No thin skin can be expected to withstand a heavy localised load. It would not be good practice on a wood or metal boat, even a stoutly built one. There is no excuse on a moulded boat. Fig. 1.10 shows the nasty sort of thing which happens when this is ignored. It is much cheaper to replace a cleat than to repair a tattered moulding.

MOULDED ANGLES Two mouldings, a moulding and wood, or even two pieces of woodwork can be joined by moulding an angle or strip between them. This method is commonly known as "matting-in" or simply "glassing-in." It is an extremely versatile method of fastening parts to a GRP shell, or two parts together. It is strong, quick, light, cheap, stress distributing and very easy. The angle fits intimately, no matter how difficult, because it is moulded "wet" right in position. On a clean GRP surface the bond will be excellent owing to chemical interaction. It is the basis of most of the joints and attachments described throughout this book. It is so fundamental that it is taken for granted.

The method is delightfully simple. Shape the piece or pieces to fit. Offer them up to make sure. There will be no time for further alterations once work starts. Prepare the surfaces. Hold the pieces in position temporarily with clamps, struts or sticky tape if not held naturally. Mould the glass angle or strip between the pieces using them as a former and build up to thickness. Do not release the supports until the resin has set and the pieces are locked in position firmly. Sometimes they can be "tacked" in position first with a few short quick-setting pieces which are allowed to set to hold them in position, like tack welds. If possible mould an angle on both sides of the join except on light non-structural parts, although as it cannot match it is seldom done on gel coat faces.

The pieces must not be allowed to move until they have set properly, or flaws and cavities are probable and the joint will be weak. However a light, well balanced piece may sometimes be held by hand relying on the stickiness of the resin to hold it in position afterwards, but this must never be done with a heavy member or something whose position is critical.

Check the position again before the resin sets in case it has moved (clear resin allows marks to show through). Once the angle has set the part will be very difficult to move without causing damage. Jigs should be used on production. Successful prefabrication and use of large submouldings depends greatly on accurate positioning of main structural members and attachment points. Repositioning will be expensive and play havoc with a production schedule.

EMBEDDING BLOCKS Wherever a fitting is to be attached, a moulding will require reinforcing. A common way to do this is to fit or embed a block. As well as providing something more substantial to fix into, the block spreads the load over a wider area of the moulding. Most commonly the block will be of wood because this is the most convenient, cheapest and easiest to shape, but metal or Tufnol can be used, too. In better class work, shaped perforated metal plates are used (Fig. 1.11).

To fix the block, sand the surface to remove high spots and shape the block to fit snugly. Drill the holes. Bed the block on bedding compound, sealant or "wet" mat. The size of the block should be chosen sensibly to suit the purpose of the fitting, the load and its direction. The moulding thickness is relevant too, so is the space available and near**by**

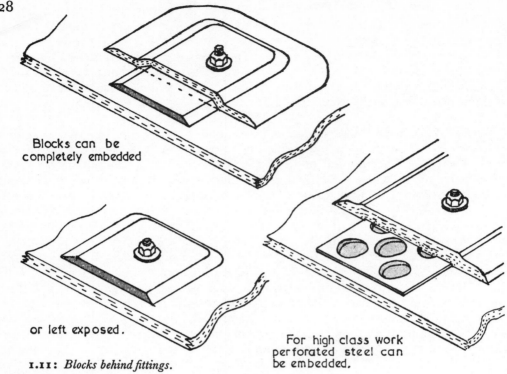

Blocks can be completely embedded

or left exposed.

For high class work perforated steel can be embedded.

1.11: *Blocks behind fittings.*

strong features. The block for a heavily loaded fitting should be large to spread the load widely and extend to link with strong members or be backed by stiffening frames. The moulding may need to be stiffened first for extra strength. All corners must be well rounded and edges bevelled to reduce stress concentrations.

The block can be embedded by moulding over it. This should be structural, not just sealing, and thick enough for worthwhile strength. It is better for the block to be open than lightly and badly embedded with seepage paths, pockets to collect water, and possibly porous too. Blocks are often embedded during moulding—but be sure they are in the right place. Large blocks allow some latitude in positioning, and in the position of the fitting. It is not essential to embed the block. The through-fastenings of the fitting ought to hold it, but it is likely to leak if not bedded.

As long as the load is in compression or shear, simple embedding will be satisfactory; but if the load is substantial and in tension, or ever likely to be in tension, i.e. in a direction which will pull the block away from the moulding, through fastenings are essential to avoid delamination. This is only likely when the block is on the same side of the moulding as the fitting. It is much more satisfactory for the block to be on the opposite side of the moulding, as in Fig. 1.10 and in this case, of course, delamination is impossible.

As long as there is no tendency to pull away, wood screws into a wooden block are satisfactory, but where there is any possibility of substantial tensile loads, bolts are essential. It is advisable to bolt all major cleats, stanchions, fairleads, eyes, shroud plates and coamings. Toe rails, floorboards, thwarts and most woodwork can normally be screwed. The size and purpose of the boat, of course, will be a major influence; correct practice on a large cruiser may be superfluous on a knock-about dinghy, and a method adequate on the dinghy will be dangerous on a larger boat. Obviously common sense must be used too.

BATTENS Long battens for fixing a shelf or a bunk can be embedded, but it is not necessary to embed the whole length. Certainly it looks neater to embed the lot, but if cost is important they can be secured with a few moulded straps or tacking pieces at intervals along the length (Fig. 1.12).

Straps, instead of full embedding, look untidy and "cheap," so they are best used where they will not be seen, and will be hidden by the woodwork attached to them.

BOLTING The rough appearance of a GRP angle looks out of place when joining the smooth gel coat side of a moulding. It is neater to bolt right through especially where the bolts also secure woodwork. Bolting is essential where a tension load could cause delamination. Bolts are often used to back up a bonded joint and act in some respects as an insurance, especially where bonding to a gel coat face, which cannot be as sound as to the inner face.

Where a block is not used it is sound practice to thicken the skin by moulding on a few extra layers where anything is to be bolted. Bolts apply very localised stresses which the thicker moulding is better able to withstand. Large washers are essential to spread the area of contact and they need to be oversize.

Care is needed not to crush the moulding when using bolts. A bolt can apply considerable pressure when tightened enthusiastically. It is very important not to overtighten, for the harder the bolt is tightened the more the resin is crushed, and the bolt, instead of becoming tighter, in fact gets looser. Nylon, neoprene or rubber washers and gaskets will cushion the moulding, and prevent it being crushed by ham-fisted hands on the end of a large spanner. In smaller cases nylon or polythene washers could be used alone instead of metal.

A hard metal fitting, particularly a heavy or highly stressed one, needs to be insulated from the moulding with a thin gasket to avoid crushing the resin-rich gel coat or high spots on the inner surface. Bedding compound is sufficient on smaller fittings, but an engine, mast step or winch needs a rubber gasket, preferably neoprene. A rubbery paint can be used instead of a gasket for light use.

SPACING OF FASTENINGS Bolts, rivets and screws should not be nearer the edge than two and a half times their diameter, and spacing between them should be three times the diameter (Fig. 1.14).

Edges, unless trimmed back, or cut out openings, are often rather badly moulded. It is not easy, particularly for beginners, to mould soundly right up to the edge of the mould. It is a good plan to increase the spacing from a moulded edge, and allow a minimum of 1 in. The spacing should also be increased if using small fastenings where the diameter is less than twice the thickness of the moulding.

RIVETS Rivets can be used to join pieces together, or to wood or metal. It is most important that the resin is not crushed when riveting and large washers or **roves are**

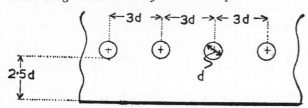

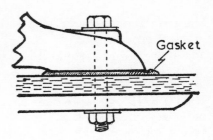

1.12: *Long batten secured by moulded straps.*

1.13: *When bolting a heavy metal fitting to a moulded surface use a soft gasket, 1, to avoid crushing the surface, 2, under the pressure of the bolts and loading of the fitting.*

1.14: *Minimum spacing of fastenings. Fastenings must not be spaced closer together than three times their diameter or nearer the edge than two and a half times their diameter.*

essential to spread the strain. Hammering will tend to shatter the hard, non-ductile resin. The rivets must be soft and easily flattened. Hot rivets are impracticable because of the temperature limitations of the resin. Riveting is only suitable for small fittings, and it is not advisable below the water-line, particularly on bilge-keels and other parts liable to wear. Rivets used in these positions will work loose and cause troublesome leaks. Riveting wood/GRP/wood is better than riveting on a GRP face. In general pop-rivets are preferable because they are flattened by a steady controlled pull from a special tool, not by sharp hammer blows, and ordinary rivets or clenched fastenings are not advised if any other fastening can be used instead.

POP-RIVETS A pop-rivet is a hollow rivet with a loose centre spindle. A special tool grips the spindle and pulls it; a knob or head on the spindle flattens out the rivet and squeezes it tight. On further pulling the head breaks off and falls away (Fig. 1.15). It is a cheap method of fastening and, with the appropriate rivets, can be used blind from one side only. A hollow rivet will leak, of course, and must be used with discretion. Some pop-rivets have a closed end, but the retained head may rust and cause stains.

   The moulding should be thickened where the pop-rivets are to come, although this may not be necessary with very small ones. The strain of pulling tight and breaking off the spindle can sometimes crush a thin or weak moulding so that the rivet pulls through. The size of the hole is critical. A special tool is needed, but for small scale use this is a hand-tool and is not expensive. It will almost pay for itself in fitting the fender on a single dinghy.

   Pop-rivets and their special pliers can now be obtained from local stores in handyman-sized quantities.

SELF-TAPPING SCREWS (PK SCREWS) Small fittings such as name-plates, lights or instruments which are subject to very little strain can be fixed with self-tapping screws straight into the moulding. They must not be used on large fittings or anything subject to stress, tension, movement or repeated refastening.

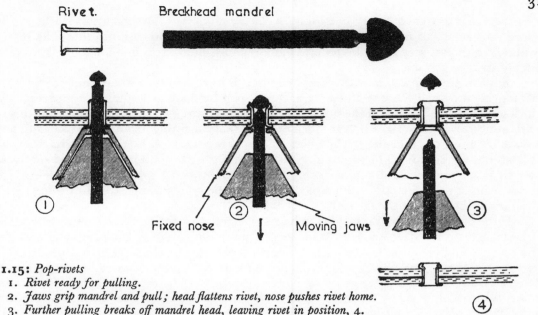

Rivet. Breakhead mandrel

Fixed nose   Moving jaws

1.15: *Pop-rivets*
  1. *Rivet ready for pulling.*
  2. *Jaws grip mandrel and pull; head flattens rivet, nose pushes rivet home.*
  3. *Further pulling breaks off mandrel head, leaving rivet in position, 4.*

A self-tapping screw, also known as a PK screw, is a screw with a hardened thread which, as its name implies, will cut its own thread as it is driven home. For reinforced plastics they must be the thread-cutting type not the thread-forming. In Britain the Guest, Keen and Nettlefold type "Z" (blunt end) should be used, rather than type "A" (pointed end). Hammer-drive screws (type "U") are likely to damage the moulding. They must, of course, be marine screws. All self-tapping screws are made of hardened steel, but they can be obtained plated or in stainless steel.

The size of pilot-hole is critical, and the exact size of drill recommended by the manufacturers must be used. This is important. Moreover, the hole must be drilled, not punched. No self-tapping screw, or any screw or fastening for that matter, should be driven into the edge of a moulding, because this will cause the moulding to delaminate. The screw will work loose, and the centre of the laminate will be exposed to moisture (Fig. 1.16). Self-tapping screws should not be driven into material thinner than one and a half times their diameter. Sizes smaller than $\frac{1}{8}$ in. do not hold well, because the thread is too near the size of the strands of glass-fibre. Screws projecting through can scratch hands.

TAPPING AND TAPPED INSERTS Being of a composite nature, reinforced plastic does not readily take a screw-thread. Consequently it is unsatisfactory to tap it, but this is sometimes done if the moulding is substantially thickened at that point and a coarse-threaded screw used, e.g. a Whitworth, U.N.C., etc.

The screw-thread must be coarse compared with the size of the strands of glass-fibre and the spaces between them; nothing much less than a $\frac{3}{8}$ in. screw into a $\frac{3}{8}$ in. laminate will hold reliably, and even then the size of screw needs to be well oversize for the load it is to bear. Tapping should only be done when bolting or a tapped insert are impossible.

Where it is known before moulding that a screw-thread must be tapped, it is much more satisfactory to mould in an insert of metal or Tufnol and tap into this. The insert will hold a thread very much better and more reliably, and it is safe to use a smaller, more highly stressed screw.

But the simplest way to make a tapped insert is to embed an ordinary nut (Fig. 1.17). Moreover, provided there is adequate access, it can be done at any time, not necessarily during moulding. To embed the nut by itself would require precise positioning, but this is seldom necessary because it is very much easier to bolt the fitting down in the conventional way and embed the nuts then, while held in the correct position by the bolts. In this way it is absolutely certain to fit accurately without any trouble. It does not spread the load so well as a large insert, although it is usually adequate with generous washers; if critical it can be used in conjunction with a block or insert, the bolts passing straight through and the nuts embedded on the far side.

Nuts should not be embedded when subjected to continual reversing rotational stresses such as on a steering-gear. A hexagonal nut is likely to twist and gradually enlarge the hole. A square nut at least or something with a better mechanical grip is needed.

A very simple and cheap compromise is to mould in a piece of wood and use a wood screw. This is not suitable for anything which must be undone repeatedly, but if it is only taken off every few years, or better still is a permanent fixture, then it will be perfectly satisfactory. Moreover if the screw-hole does get worn it would be a simple matter to drill another nearby into the same piece of wood. Embedding wood is dealt with in the next chapter.

INSERTS There are various patent "push-in" inserts, e.g. "Banc-lok." This is a short split brass tube with a knurled or finned outside to grip the hole and a thread inside for a screw (Fig. 1.18). Fitting is simple. Drill a hole slightly undersize, push the insert into the hole and tighten the screw. The screw expands the insert so that it grips the hole. The purely push-in kind should not be heavily stressed because the ridges are forced, not cut, into the moulding. Most inserts are made for ductile materials: GRP is not ductile and tends to crack. They should, if possible, be inserted soon after moulding when the GRP is still "green." The preferred kind of Banc-lok has a collar behind to take the pressure, with the serrations just to stop it twisting, but it requires access from the back and may leak. It is more suitable for inside mouldings.

Most of these inserts are difficult to obtain in small quantities. They are not stocked by local ironmongers. Manufacturers prefer to supply them by the thousand, not the dozen. Builders' wall plugs, e.g. Rawlplug, Thorsman, etc., can be used but are more suitable for deep holes in thick mouldings. Various patent expanding plugs are used for fastening to sheet metal or panels, including toggles for larger fittings. Many are unsuitable or do not have marine finish. However, they are obtainable in every town in small quantities.

"Bigheads" are threaded metal studs welded to large perforated feet and designed to be embedded in GRP. They can also be bonded on. They should normally be loaded mainly in shear but there is a temptation to use them for tensile loads. This will do little harm if light but there is a risk of delamination if highly stressed.

There are other inserts which might be acquired in small numbers through friendly local factories. However, most are designed for ductile materials and should not be suit-

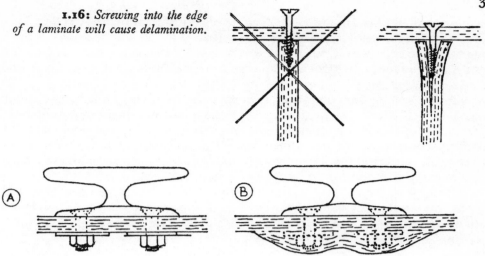

1.16: *Screwing into the edge of a laminate will cause delamination.*

1.17: *Attaching a cleat by embedding nuts.*
A. *Bolt down the cleat using oversize washers.*
B. *Embed the nuts by moulding over them.*

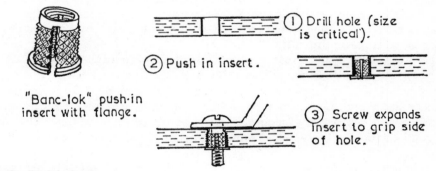

"Banc-lok" push-in insert with flange.

① Drill hole (size is critical).

② Push in insert.

③ Screw expands insert to grip side of hole.

1.18: *Push-in inserts.*

able for GRP, although they might hold after a fashion. Try them first where they will do no harm.

COUNTERSINKING The average moulding is too thin to allow a proper depth of countersinking. Countersink only very small screws where the depth is small relative to thickness and the stresses low. Countersinking exposes the glass, which must be sealed before the screw goes in. There is no depth to spare for the luxury of filling the screwhead. Washers cannot be used and countersunk screws often pull through or cause cracks. After a few years decay starts around the heads. Stainless steel or plated round or mushroom head screws with washers are the correct choice and need not look unsightly.

BEDDING DOWN All fittings and woodwork on the outside must be firmly bedded down to seat firmly and seal the holes. This is most important as otherwise they are sure to leak, especially if through-fastened. Even if sealed inside, water may collect in pockets or run, find seepage paths and cause decay. Fastenings too should be sealed. A method often suggested is to dip them in resin, but as it is unlikely that ready catalysed resin will be to hand a more practical method is to squeeze some sealant into the hole. Treat wood screws in the same way.

Flexible sealing compounds and neoprene gaskets are very much better than bedding down on "wet" mat. They retain some give and allow movement in use without breaking the seal. "Wet" mat may appear to seal perfectly at first, but the resin sets hard and has no give. It cannot take up subsequent movement of the fitting or moulding under load, or loosening or settling of the fastenings. Flexibility is needed to accommodate movement of wood or metal with thermal or humidity changes.

The appearance of "wet" glass is quite out of place on the gel coat side, and it is not easy to trim neatly. Therefore on the grounds of appearance alone only a soft sealing compound or gasket which can be trimmed with a knife is appropriate. If "wet" mat has to be used limit its spread with masking tape.

GLUING Where there are no facilities for attaching by moulding or "matting-in," —perhaps materials are not available—or moulding is feared to be dangerous Terra Incognita, then wood trim or blocks, structural members, fittings or even two cured mouldings can be joined by gluing. Gluing may be more familiar, but there is in fact a a lot more to go wrong, and it is more chancy than using the comparatively foolproof polyester resins. (As the sage remarked: "It is easy enough to make a thing fool-proof, but clever-proof is really difficult.")

Prepare the surfaces in the same way as for joining mouldings on page 18. Sand the surfaces clean and smooth, degrease them and shape the parts to fit snugly.

Use a good quality gap-filling marine glue accompanied by pressure. Reliable structural gluing cannot be satisfactory without adequate pressure. If clamps are impractical use struts and wedges, or glue and screw. Light fittings can be fixed without pressure using a good contact adhesive or common tube blue provided it is water and mould resistant.

On a light boat there may be difficulty in exerting enough pressure because the sides bulge and are not stiff enough to wedge against. A Spanish windlass around the boat will hold the sides in and take the outward thrust of the wedges. It can even be used to exert pressure. Be very careful to protect the hull with pads, particularly around the gunwales or the rope will chafe and mark them. (Fig. 1.20.)

With glued fittings there is a considerable danger of delamination. Loads should not be applied in a direction which pulls the block away from the surface, unless backed up with bolts, for the strength of the glue will be greater than the strength of the resin bonding the layers of the laminate together—a point to be remembered also if a glued fitting has to be taken off.

ATTACHMENTS TO SANDWICH MOULDINGS The basic construction of a sandwich moulding is two GRP skins bonded to a light core. Over a wide area the whole sandwich behaves as a strong, stiff girder and the core need be no stronger than necessary to hold the two skins together. This is the attractive theory. In practice it cannot be considered simply over a wide area. Local details and loads are very important. The light

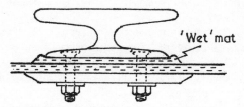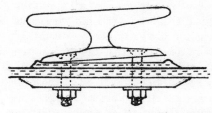

'Wet' mat

Not Recommended. *Bedding down on a layer of "wet" mat.*

Effect (exaggerated) Leaks are likely later because the hard mat has no give and flexibility.

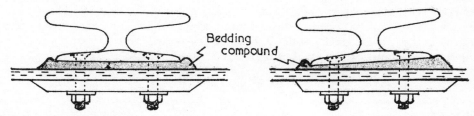

Bedding compound

Recommended. *Bed down on a flexible bedding compound which will give and retain its sealing properties.*

1.19: *Bedding down.*

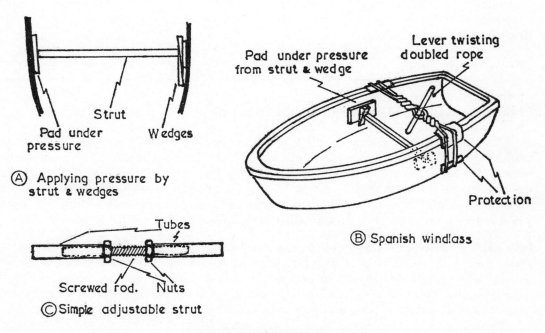

Strut

Pad under pressure

Wedges

Ⓐ Applying pressure by strut & wedges

Tubes

Screwed rod. Nuts

Ⓒ Simple adjustable strut

Pad under pressure from strut & wedge

Lever twisting doubled rope

Protection

Ⓑ Spanish windlass

1.20: *Applying pressure.*

core is easily crushed and all attachments must be made carefully. Fig. 1.21 shows what happens if this is ignored, and it is seen commonly.

Table 1.1 shows typical compressive strengths for common core materials. The figures are ultimate strengths, given by various manufacturers. They should be treated with considerable reserve. The force exerted by a $\frac{3}{16}$ in. brass screw can be about 400 lb., a $\frac{1}{4}$ in. screw about 800 lb., (200 kg. for 5 mm. screw, 360 kg. for 6 mm.). Stainless steel is 2–3 times greater. This is at breaking point—yet often a brass screw breaks simply in tightening. In small sizes a large part of this force is distributed by the stiffness of the GRP, but note that each skin is only half the thickness or less of single-skin GRP. Clearly even normal working levels will crush most cores. Polyurethane foam is brittle. It fails progressively with no recovery. Light grades are very weak. "Airex" PVC is resilient and can be compressed substantially without damage although under fastenings strength is reduced by creep. It softens at moderately hot deck temperatures. Balsa is weakened by prolonged wetness and can get waterlogged.

Table 1.1

Material	Density lb./cu. ft.	S.G.	Ultimate compressive strength	
			lb./sq. in.	kg./m.²
Foam polyurethane (rigid)	2	0·03	15–30	100–200
	4	0·06	90	620
	6*	0·09	150	1,000
Foam PVC (Airex)				
at 60° F. (16° C.)	5*	0·07	60 (45**)	400 (300**)
at 104° F. (40° C.)	5*	0·07	29 (13**)	200 (90**)
End-grain balsa	6	0·09	500	3,500
	11*	0·17	1,400	9,500
	15	0·24	2,200	15,000

* Preferred grades.
** Sustained loads liable to creep, e.g. under fastenings.

Also avoid delaminating attachments. Even on a good sandwich the bond to the core is weak. Moreover a core can shear beneath the bond. Attachments by bonding or self-tapping screws to one skin only are wrong even for small fittings. Wood screws into an insert will also be delaminating if subject to pull. Always through-fasten even with an insert. If through-fastenings are small, not tightened hard, and the core is strong, it may be possible to use no insert, but delaminating fastenings should never be used.

INSERTS It is most important to use incompressible inserts in way of all fastenings through sandwich mouldings. When the positions are known, wood inserts can be let into the core during moulding. Provided they are in the right places (also the fittings!) there is little difficulty. Wood should be a low movement species. Marine plywood is far the best (page 58). Avoid oak and poor quality woods. A rotten insert is worse than no insert.

Difficulty arises when there are no inserts either because the fittings are afterthoughts or inserts have been forgotten or misplaced. Inserts *must* still be formed. What is done

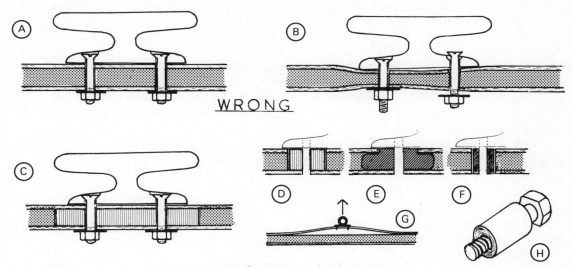

1.21: *Attachments to sandwich moulding.*

A. **Wrong.** *Fitting through bolted with no inserts.*

B. *This is what happens. The bolts crush the core, fastenings work loose, water leaks through into both boat and core.*

C. **Right.** *The core is replaced by a solid insert in way of the fitting. Screws can be tightened without crushing the core.*

D. *Unplanned insert using wood plug or resin putty.*

E. *As method D but core scooped out to make putty more effective. Note how the hole is still concealed by the fitting.*

F. *As method D but using metal tube.*

G. *Avoid delaminating attachments. Even small fittings can do this.*

H. *Thick GRP tubes for inserts are easily moulded over a waxed bolt.*

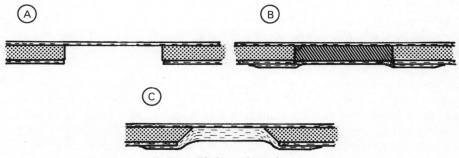

1.22: *Fitting a large insert.*

A. *Cut away one skin (the inner is generally less conspicuous) and the core.*

B. *Fit a wooden block and mould over. Note the overlap on to the original skin.*

C. *If the core is thin the insert can be moulded solid.*

depends on the circumstances, but note that the crushing force of the fastenings matters as much as the size and load of the fitting.

One way is to drill the hole oversize and fill it with resin putty or a wooden plug. Putty is made more effective by scooping away the core inside the hole. This enlarges the insert yet the hole is still concealed by the fitting. For important fittings cut away one skin (the inner is usually the less conspicuous) and fit a substantial wooden insert or mould it solid. Alternatively fit metal tubes combined with wooden pads to reduce movement and bearing pressure. Thick GRP tubes are easily moulded using tape or strips of cloth over a waxed bolt and bond in readily.

All inserts must be very well sealed to stop water seeping into the core. This is difficult with metal tubes. Epoxy bonds better than polyester.

JOINING SANDWICH MOULDINGS
Sandwich mouldings require joining to other sandwiches, single-skin GRP, or woodwork. The requirements are:

1. Continuity of strength.
2. No abrupt changes of thickness and consequent hard spots.
3. No crushing of the core.

When joining two sandwiches the two GRP skins and the core should be treated as separate entities. The GRP should be lap jointed to give continuity and the joins staggered. The cores should be butted or scarfed because of their thickness.

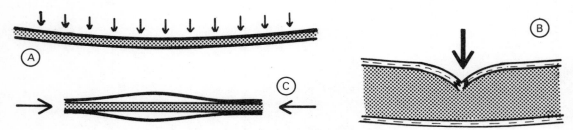

1.23: *Behaviour of a sandwich moulding.*
A. *With well-distributed, well-cushioned loads the sandwich behaves as a composite structure.*
B. *But under sharp, point impact it is only a single very thin skin backed by a soft core with little resistance.*
C. *Sandwiches are also vulnerable to buckling. This often happens under impact, especially to decks, following a bump on the hull or even just squeezing.*

The commoner case is for a sandwich to join to a single skin. It makes little difference whether it is between two separate mouldings or the transition from sandwich to single skin in the same moulding. Similar considerations apply when joining to wood.

The change must be gradual and the core well tapered. An abrupt step from rigid sandwich to more flexible single skin will cause a severe stress concentration at the step and a marked hinge effect. This applies just as much, but less obviously, at an angle, e.g. the common case of sandwich deck to single skin hull or cabin top side. A hull/deck join is stiffened anyway, but not a cabin top angle. Taper off the sandwich before reaching the angle. Alternatively use a tapered fillet in the angle. Do not butt the sandwich right into the angle. A filling of syntactic foam may be easier than tapering a slab core.

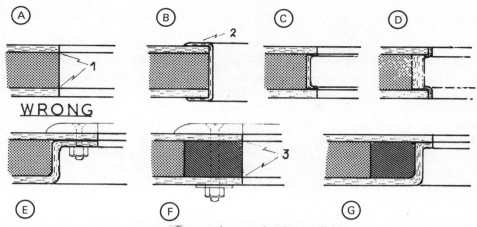

1.24: *Cut-outs in a sandwich moulding.*

A. **Wrong.** *Hole cut out and left unsealed. Core and moulding edge exposed. N.B. The action of cutting usually causes delamination at 1.*

B. *Exposed edges moulded over. This seals but is unsightly, and it is difficult to bed a fitting down properly due to the raised flange, 2.*

C. *A neater method is to scoop out some of the core and keep the seal inside. The edge of the moulding is still exposed.*

N.B. *None of these provide an insert to prevent crushing.*

D. *C can be thickened to act as an insert (probably not quite in the right place but it may be near enough). The GRP lip now seals the moulding edge.*

Planned cut-outs

E. *Leave out the core in way of the cut-out and mould as single skin. Sealing will probably be perfect and by bolting through the flange no insert is needed.*

F. *Insert put in during moulding, cut out later. Fastenings are sound but sawing will probably have caused delamination at 3. Seepage is possible even though the fastenings will clamp it together. Edges should still be sealed.*

G. *The ideal case is a ring insert, put in during moulding and sealed by the inner skin.*

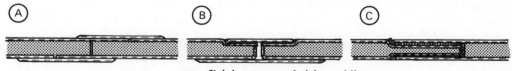

1.25: *Joining two sandwich mouldings.*

A. *The simple case: core butted, skins joined by staggered butt straps.*

B. *Where a flush surface is needed, rabbets can be moulded in so that the butt strap is flush.*

C. *A neater, more elaborate, tongue and groove joint. The tongue is moulded and fits into a groove where the ore has been left out. Jointing should be with epoxy, not polyester.*

SEALING It is most important that water does not enter a sandwich core. Cutouts must have their edges sealed, preferably by moulding. Screw holes are difficult to seal but no less important. Fastenings should be well smothered in sealant before insertion. All fittings must be very well bedded to reduce the possibility of seepage underneath.

The way to prevent a leak is to stop water getting in, not through. This is absolutely essential with a sandwich. Once water gets past the outer skin into the core deterioration and decay are inevitable. Always seal the wet sides very carefully.

WATER IN THE CORE Once water gets into the core it is virtually certain the core will never dry out. Its presence makes sound repair impossible. Only in theory is the core formed of separate cells which limit water travel. Water has other ideas. In practice it finds innumerable seepage paths, waterways and porous material. I surveyed one boat where the water travelled from one end to the other by multiple paths entirely within the core. The core will generally be wet far inside, out of sight and beyond hope of ever drying out, long before there are any clear signs or it is even suspected. Even if water cannot migrate immediately it will start decay and will spread further as time passes. Frost and hot sunshine will be powerful allies.

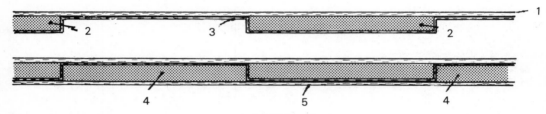

1.26: *Web cores.*
A web core is made by laying up the first layer, 1, and putting down the core in alternate strips, 2, 2. The interconnecting web layer is laid up, zigzag fashion, 3, over these strips. The remaining strips are now put down, 4, 4, and the inner skin laid up overall, 5.
    Regardless of how good or bad the bond to the core, either initially or after use and misuse, the skins will remain tied together by the GRP webs.
    A refinement is to put down the core in alternate blocks, not strips, so that the webs run in two directions.

Water can enter in various ways. The commonest route is via poorly sealed fastenings and fittings. One effect of not using inserts is that it is impossible to seal fittings properly, as tightening the fastenings only crushes the core, distorts the surface, and makes the seal worse not better. Consequently there is an open pathway for water.

Damage is an obvious cause. Sandwich mouldings are very vulnerable. A point impact meets only the one thin GRP skin backed by a structurally weak core which affords little support. The second skin is too far away to help and is isolated by the weak core. Impact which a single-skin moulding would brush aside with hardly a scratch can pierce the skin of a sandwich. The damage may be no more than a small crack which seems unimportant and is ignored or not even noticed. But water will find it (Fig. 1.23).

GRP is slightly permeable, and enough moisture will be absorbed over the years, even with no direct seepage or damage, to start decay, rot or waterlogging. (This is disputed by balsa suppliers but long term experience suggests otherwise.) Permeability will be more severe with a sandwich because the outer skin, which keeps water away from the core, is so much thinner.

Trapped water from any cause is inviting decay not only in the core but in the GRP too. Unlike the outer gel coat surfaces the inner GRP faces of a sandwich are unprotected by resin and are vulnerable. How to dry out a core when one cannot tell how far moisture has gone—or even if it is wet at all—is one of the nasty practical problems associated with sandwich mouldings. My personal opinion is that they are a bad long-term bet.

Arguments can rage as to whether a delaminating sandwich is structurally weak or not. (I consider that if the design specifies a sandwich it must be properly made regardless of excuses that anything less is as good.) But the secondary effect of water in the core will, in the long run, be far more serious. Delamination may be corrected to some extent, albeit with difficulty. Internal decay cannot, even if its extent could be discovered. Moreover that is only the start of trouble. Waterways may lead to vital structural parts, such as the hull-deck join, where hidden decay will be disastrous.

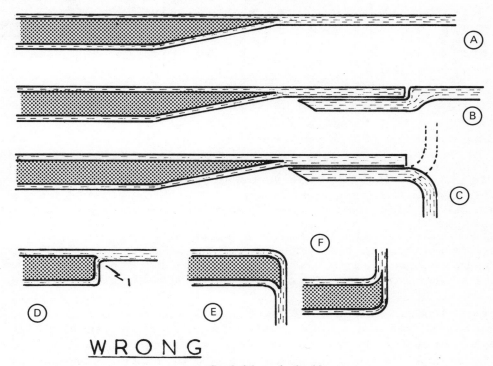

WRONG

1.27: *Sandwich to single skin.*
It is essential to taper the core to give a gradual transition from thick sandwich to thin single skin. It is immaterial whether this is, A, change from sandwich to single skin in the same moulding, B, separate mouldings, C, at an angle.
Wrong. *Abrupt change will form a severe hard spot at 1, and applies just as much to an angle, E, F.*

SANDWICH MOULDING   Spacing the two skins apart gives the high stiffness of a girder with little extra weight. A rough rule is to split the single skin into two, the extra weight is then only the light core. In theory it sounds very attractive. In practice it causes more trouble than any other single feature. It seems so easy—yet to make a sound, reliable sandwich is harder than anything else in GRP moulding. As this section is, of necessity, squeezed into a limited space in this revised edition I can only offer a few hints. It warrants a book on its own.

My principle recommendation is to avoid sandwich moulding altogether. Leave it

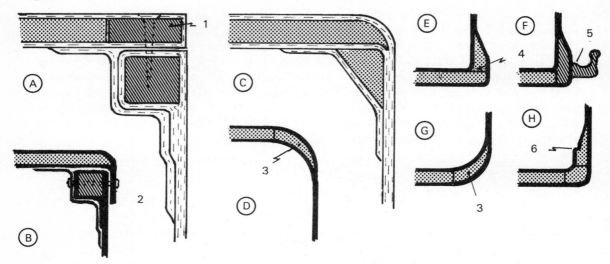

1.28: *Sandwich to single skin at an angle.*

A. *Abrupt ending is acceptable if the other member is very strong, e.g. hull/deck join.* N.B. *It is usual to fasten such joints as well as bonding (which anyway is delaminating). The sandwich must have a solid insert along the edge,* 1.

B. *A better join is to bolt through the flange or down (or up) turned lip,* 2, *formed at the edge.*

C. *A tapered fillet in the angle gives gradual transition.*

D. *More sophisticated design tapers in the curve. Slab core would be impracticable on this curve,* 3. *Plaster on syntactic foam.*

E. *Outward angles are more difficult. Method C creates a peculiar bulge,* 4.

F. *This bulge could be used for the insert for a grab-rail,* 5.

G. *Tapering in the curve is neat if the large radius is acceptable.*

H. *Hide by making conspicuous. Mould the taper in the outer skin and make it a decorative feature,* 6.

for the experts or those with plenty of money to lose. Certainly it can be done—but become highly proficient on a small scale first. Boat-sized mistakes are very expensive. Even then leave open a way of escape. Larger size raises fresh problems.

The principal defect is delamination between the outer GRP skin and the core. The inner skin is normally applied "wet" and fails much less often (see mouldless construction, Appendix 3).

Laying down the core should be treated as a gluing operation between a set GRP moulding and a core of totally different material, not as part of the ordinary lay-up. "Wet" mat or thixotropic polyester are poor adhesives. Use a proper glue, e.g. epoxy, and enough pressure to ensure intimate contact at all points. The core must be in small sections, or bend enough, to follow the shape readily.

The core must be absolutely dry, particularly balsa.

Fill gaps with resin or putty, to reduce waterways.

Handle sandwiches with care. Strains when turning a sandwich deck often start delamination.

Do not rely solely on bonding to the core. The most reliable sandwiches have GRP webs at intervals, to tie the skins together and limit delamination.

Ninety per cent of sandwiches delaminate, many extensively and very early, even while under construction. Probably they were never bonded properly in the first place. Detecting delamination is tedious and requires skill. Many more areas can remain undetected or have a weak, spotty bond. The detectable delamination should be assumed to be only part of the actual or potential area. A bad bond will never improve. Use and age will spread delamination, e.g. normal sailing stresses, thermal stress, damage, decay, swelling of the core due to water, etc. A side bump can start delamination of the deck by buckling, even with no obvious damage.

A delaminating sandwich can only deteriorate, the newer the quicker. Once water gets in—and only luck or a miracle will stop it—decay will follow. A competent surveyor will not miss it so the resale value will be low and selling at all may be difficult, another reason for suing the builder if new.

A delaminating deck is bad enough, but a hull is very serious. Stresses are higher and varied, water entry is certain by permeability if not by seepage, and the crew's lives are at stake. A sandwich hull should be only for a short-life racing machine carefully stored ashore. Exceptions are close-spaced web sandwich where the structural element is the GRP web not the bonded core, and mouldless foam sandwich where the attraction of a one-off boat outweighs many disadvantages. Both are still vulnerable to point impact and seepage, especially the web.

THERMAL STRESS Single skin GRP seldom delaminates under thermal or mechanical stress because the interlaminar bond is good, and it behaves as a homogeneous material (except as page 16). But a sandwich is not homogeneous. The core is weak. It can shear fairly easily and its bond is crucial.

The core is a good insulator so there is a temperature differential across the sandwich and hence internal thermal stresses. On a wide deck such as a catamaran the expansion of the upper skin exposed to hot sun can be $\frac{1}{4}$ in. (6 mm) more than the shaded skin beneath. The sandwich must absorb this large relative movement or delaminate. It is a tall order, impossible with a rigid or brittle core and a severe strain even on a semi-flexible foam.

A catamaran surveyed two years running and not used meanwhile had severe delamination where none had been detected the year before. The summer had been hot. Signs of similar stresses have been noticed under catamaran bridge decks too, due to the temperature differential between the exposed upper deck and shaded underside.

Thermal expansion is suspected to be one initiator of delamination and the stresses are something to be reckoned with. They will add to normal sailing stresses and the probable outcome is spreading invisible damage (page 281). It is therefore questionable if a deck is a suitable application for sandwich moulding at all, particularly in the tropics and those popular sunny holiday resorts. The wider or longer the deck the greater the problem.

CHAPTER TWO

Stiffening

As a reinforced plastic moulding is essentially a thin shell—the materials are too expensive to waste in building up unnecessary thickness—it will require extra support and stiffening in all but the simplest cases. The natural shape, together with compound curves, corrugations, swedging, and "decorative dents" will all add considerable stiffness, but they are not enough in themselves for a hull or upperworks beyond the size of a dinghy, or indeed for any largish load-bearing structure.

A polyester resin/glass-fibre laminate is a more flexible material than most metals, twenty times more flexible than steel, six times more than aluminium—yet of comparable strength. (Do not confuse strength and rigidity: a steel wire is strong, but flexible; an eggshell rigid, but weak.) However, stiffness is usually the primary requirement rather than absolute maximum strength.

Yet it must not be assumed that it is a "rubbery" material. The flexibility is, in fact, much the same as that of wood, and it behaves like springy plywood, not soft, flexible rubber. The flexibility is of more serious concern because, being stronger and more costly than wood, it is always much thinner. In short, it has the strength and thickness of a metal but the flexibility of wood, with a weight much nearer that of wood than any metal.

No cost comparison is valid unless it takes into account the cost of forming to shape. Wood and steel may be cheaper in material cost but need a lot of fabrication to get the right shape. Reinforced plastic more than compensates for its higher material cost by the extreme ease of fabrication and low wastage.

SUMMARY OF STIFFENING METHODS Similar methods to those used in stiffening or stabilising sheet metal can be used, but in addition there are other methods denied to sheet metal.

The methods are:

1. Use of shape, curvature, corrugations, swedging, "decorative dents," etc.
2. Extra thickness.
3. Moulded or added frames and ribs.
4. Bulkheads.
5. Beading and flanges, particularly at edges.
6. Angles and webs.
7. Sandwich construction.

In general a moulded boat is much more akin in concept to pressed steel, e.g. a car body, than to traditional wooden construction.

Table 2.1 Ultimate Strengths

Material		Weight lb./cu. ft.	S.G.	Tensile strength		Compressive strength		Elastic modulus E	
				lb./sq. in. $\times 10^3$	kN/m.² $\times 10^3$	lb./sq. in. $\times 10^3$	kN/m.² $\times 10^3$	lb./sq. in. $\times 10^6$	kg./m.² $\times 10^6$
GRP	mat	94	1·5	15	100	15	100	0·9	6
	woven rovings	106	1·7	35	240	25	170	2	14
Wood	with grain	30–55	0·5–0·9	8	55	6	40	1·2	8
e.g. spruce	across grain			0·5	3·5	0·7	5		
Plywood	dry	40	0·65	2·5*	16*	1·7*	12*	1·6*	11*
	wet			2·0*	13*	1·4*	9·6*	1·3*	8·5*
Aluminium		170	2·7	6–30	40–200	10–15	70–100	10	70
Steel		485	7·8	29–33	200–225	28	190	30	200
Stainless steel		495	7·9	30–35	200–250	30	200	28	190
Nylon		69	1·1	7–12	50–80	5–13	34–90	0·2–0·5	14–28
Carbon fibre reinforced plastics (CRP)		106	1·7	90	620			40	280

* Working levels, not ultimate strength.

Note 1: These are average figures. Data varies considerably between different authorities.

Note 2: Invisible internal damage can reduce the figures for GRP and CRP substantially. Watch design weaknesses.

CURVATURE   Clever use of curvature will give tremendous extra stiffness with no increase in weight or cost. Flat panels should be avoided. On the whole curvature must be brought in at the design stage, although it is often possible to work in dents and grooves at a later date by using simple, detachable projections in the mould. These can usually be arranged to come away with the moulding and so avoid jamming the release, if they are attached lightly with pins or screws through the mould, or by a spot of weak adhesive.

As they can be introduced after the mould has been made they are suitable for modifications, if it is found that extra stiffness is needed, without having to go to all the considerable expense and trouble of making a new pattern and mould.

EXTRA THICKNESS   A sheet of metal or plywood is of uniform thickness, and the thickness chosen must be determined by the maximum stress any part of it has to withstand. The rest of it is too thick and represents waste, but that is unavoidable with a sheet of uniform thickness.

A reinforced plastic moulding can be of graded thickness, thicker where extra stiffness or strength is needed, thinner where just a bare shell is sufficient. This gives wonderful versatility in the hands of a clever designer and affords scope for tremendous economy in cost and weight, for with a fairly expensive material like this, where little is wasted in offcuts, there is a direct relationship between material and money.

Extra thickness is an extremely easy and simple way to gain extra stiffness over a localised area, for instance to reinforce behind a fitting or to emphasise the effect of a naturally stiff feature such as the channel shape formed by the keel, stem, coaming, or any natural or cunningly contrived angle, ridge or dent. Over a large area it is of limited value, and it is often more economical to use other means.

The extra thickness need not be added only during moulding, but can be applied at any time that some local thickening is considered necessary; moreover no special equipment is needed.

AVOID ABRUPT CHANGES IN THICKNESS   Any abrupt change in thickness produces a large stress concentration at that point. In bad cases this can lead to unexpected premature failure.

For instance, an abrupt increase from a thickness of three layers in a basic lay-up to six layers for a local reinforcement will give a weak line along the join where stress is concentrated, and under load this will be seen as an abrupt deformation instead of a smooth deflection (Fig. 2.1).

All changes in thickness must be done gradually one layer at a time, e.g.

Glass weight	*Minimum separation per layer*	*Preferred separation*
1½ oz./sq. ft. (450 g./m.²)	1 in. (25 mm.)	1½ in. (40 mm.)
2 oz./sq. ft. (600 g./m.²)	1¼ in. (30 mm.)	2 in. (50 mm.)

These apply whether it is local or general thickening, or an angle, etc. Other glass weights and reinforcements *pro-rata*. Of necessity they are approximate: measurement while moulding is impracticable (Fig. 2.1).

As a general rule it is good moulding practice to do nothing abruptly. Changes of

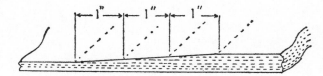

Allow at least 1 in. (2·5 cm.) per layer of 1½ oz. mat, preferably 1½ in. (4 cm.) or more.

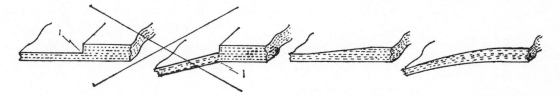

Wrong. *Abrupt change of thickness causes severe stress along edge 1 and sharp deflection.*

Right. *Gradual change of thickness gives even deflection.*

2.1: *Change of thickness.*

thickness taper gradually, angles and corners are rounded, stiffening members end on another or fade out evenly. The only unavoidable sharp change is the trimmed edge of the moulding, and even this should mate up with another moulding or woodwork.

"TOP-HAT" SECTION RIBS The commonest stiffening member is the top-hat" section moulded channel (Fig. 2.2). "Top-hat" is an unduly dignified description of what is more often a common bowler (derby) or "billycock" shape, or even some "creation" from the millinery department.

The basic idea is to mould "wet" fibreglass over a core to form a channel section, with flanges (the brim of the "topper") to bond it to the moulding. It can be formed during moulding, or after the basic shell is complete or even at a later date; it can be incorporated as part of the shell by laying up the later layers over the core, or as an addition to the basic shell. For optimum strength it should be done during, or soon after moulding, before the main moulding has cured, but this is not vital as any shortcoming should be amply allowed for by the normal factor of safety. The contraction of a top hat member as it cures may distort a light moulding which should be supported or braced to prevent this.

The usual practice is to consider the core solely as a former over which to mould the structural top hat section. Therefore it need have no strength or durability, for the strength lies in the moulded "top hat" section and it is only needed until the "wet" "top-hat" moulding sets. After that its purpose is finished, but it cannot be got out again, so it must be considered expendable. Obviously it needs to be cheap, and it needs to be light too, because it will form a considerable mass. (In the keel area, however, it may usefully be heavy to avoid wasting ballast space.)

It is important to appreciate that the strength lies in the moulded "top-hat" section, not the core, for that is the fundamental principle. All that is needed is a core sufficiently flexible or disjointed to follow the contours, and cheap enough to be expendable. The top hat section is formed "wet", so it is very easy to fit and to make it follow any sort of complicated and individual shape. Moreover it is right first time. There is no steaming,

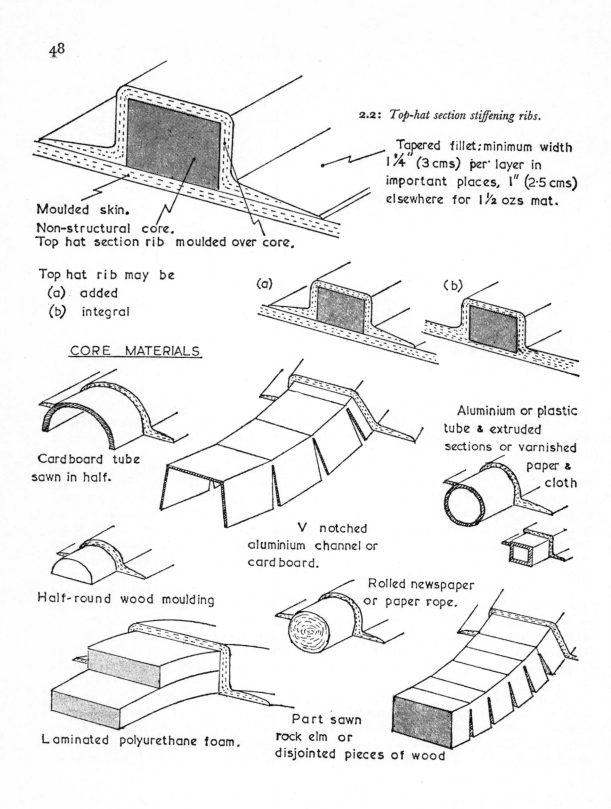

48

2.2: *Top-hat section stiffening ribs.*

Tapered fillet: minimum width 1¼" (3 cms) per layer in important places, 1" (2·5 cms) elsewhere for 1½ ozs mat.

Moulded skin.
Non-structural core.
Top hat section rib moulded over core.

Top hat rib may be
(a) added
(b) integral

(a)

(b)

CORE MATERIALS

Cardboard tube sawn in half.

V notched aluminium channel or cardboard.

Aluminium or plastic tube & extruded sections or varnished paper & cloth

Half-round wood moulding

Rolled newspaper or paper rope.

Laminated polyurethane foam.

Part sawn rock elm or disjointed pieces of wood

bending, trying, fitting and trying again which can absorb such a large labour cost with other materials which are basically much cheaper.

The core can be of any material, provided it is not harmful to the resins. Ideally it should be light, cheap, easily formed to shape and attached, and should age harmlessly. Ease of forming rules out most fabricated sections; if extensive fabrication is needed for the core one might as well fabricate the lot.

Typical examples of materials which can and have been used are:

Disjointed sections, or part-sawn strips of wood.
Half-round wooden moulding.
Paper "rope".
Rolled newspaper.
Cardboard bent to a channel shape or rolled into a tube.
Cardboard mailing tubes or formers cut in half.
V-slotted aluminium channel.
Strips of polyurethane foam.
Polythene pipe, and extruded plastic sections.
Varnished paper or cloth tubes ("Sistoflex").
Expanded metal or wire netting.

Wood is the commonest core material because it holds screws well and can be used for attachment points for the accommodation. It is cheap, readily obtainable, familiar and easily formed. Sawn into short lengths or just sawn nearly through so that it bends, it will approximate to any curve.

Light gauge aluminium channel with edges notched so that it bends readily is expensive but cannot produce harmful deterioration products.

Rolled paper or folded cardboard is cheap, but it goes pulpy if there is any leakage; it will do little harm if it does—but one does not like the thought of it. Kraft paper and waterproof cardboards are preferable. A paper "rope" is now available which is cheap and very flexible. Many drapers are only too pleased to get rid of the accumulation of cardboard tubes on which cloth is rolled. Cut in half they make handy cores, and if V-notched or disjointed they will follow curves.

A simple method is to stick down strips of polyurethane foam. They can be rigidised by coating with resin and laminated to any thickness. They can be easily shaped and profiled. Polystyrene foam is unsuitable as it is dissolved.

In the keel area, where weight is no handicap but empty or light space is, strips of lead or metal filled concrete make good cores, so does polythene tubing filled with shot or sand.

While moulding the top-hat section hold the core in place temporarily with resin or masking tape. The cores need to be positioned accurately and symmetrically if they are to look neat and professional (a point which many builders do not yet appreciate). Accuracy is absolutely vital if the frames are to be used as attachment points for the deck, large submouldings or anything prefabricated. In production, positioning jigs are advisable; their cost is more than offset by the difficulties encountered in correcting one frame out of position.

As the core is sealed in, away from moisture and air, deterioration is unlikely, but, in the event of damage, seepage or flaws, it is desirable that decomposition should not set up

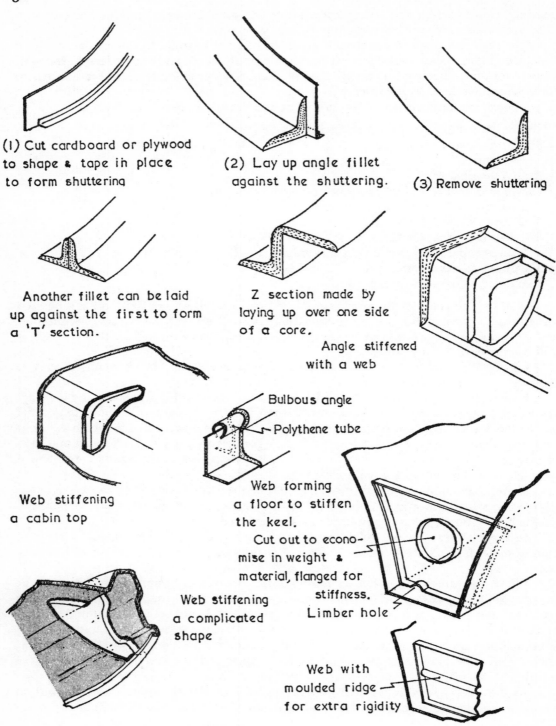

(1) Cut cardboard or plywood to shape & tape in place to form shuttering

(2) Lay up angle fillet against the shuttering.

(3) Remove shuttering

Another fillet can be laid up against the first to form a 'T' section.

Z section made by laying up over one side of a core.

Angle stiffened with a web

Web stiffening a cabin top

Bulbous angle

Polythene tube

Web forming a floor to stiffen the keel.

Cut out to economise in weight & material, flanged for stiffness.

Limber hole

Web stiffening a complicated shape

Web with moulded ridge for extra rigidity

2.3: *Webs and angles.*

gas pressures, swelling, or anything harmful to the plastic. In most cases the very damage or flaw provides an outlet for any gases from decomposition and minor swelling. (See also under "Embedding Wood" below.)

Moulding "top-hat" section frames will make a shell considerably stiffer, at much lower cost than building up the thickness to give an equivalent effect. But they must be strongly moulded. Some look massive but are thin and weak. Wooden cores may sometimes be structural but the GRP must be strong enough to hold them down and be non-porous. The wood must be durable because rot could not be detected.

ANGLES Many aircraft in the last war used a stressed skin construction of angle sections riveted to the aluminium skin. The same principle can be used in moulding. An angle section is easier to mould than a "top-hat" section, and has the advantage that the former can be reclaimed. It must be remembered, however, that it is not so stiff.

To make a moulded angle cut a piece of plywood or cardboard to the correct profile, fasten it in position with sticky tape and mould the angle against it using it like a shuttering when pouring concrete; if treated for release it can be used again (Fig. 2.3). A second angle can be moulded against the first to form a T-section.

Z-SECTIONS A Z-section is another useful stiffening member which has the advantage that the core can be used again. It is really one half of a "top-hat" section with one side left open so that the core can be removed. It is not so stiff as a "top-hat" section, but it is stiffer than a plain angle or T-section. The flange is convenient to bolt through.

BULBOUS ANGLE An ordinary angle can be made much stronger by forming a bulb on the free side. This type of section has been used in shipbuilding and was used extensively on the old "Queens." It is in effect a "top-hat" section with the core mounted on a stalk or a thin web.

A bulbous angle is made by laying up an ordinary angle and allowing it to set. A single layer would be sufficient as at this stage it has only to support the bulb. Now split a length of polythene hosepipe down one side and clip it over the upstanding angle to form the bulb. Lay up the bulbous angle over the tube, continuing down on both sides of the web and forming flanges on both sides if possible. The bulb may well be thicker than the web, because this is the part which really does the work.

WEBS A web (Fig. 2.3) is a convenient way to stiffen an angle, a channel or a deep section. It may be used to support an angle bracket for mounting a heavy shelf, to stiffen a large angled moulding like a dashboard or cabin top, or as floors to strengthen a keel section. It is made in the same way as an angle by cutting cardboard to the profile and moulding the web against it. It is joined to the moulding by forming an angle around the edge. Sometimes the web is moulded on both sides of the former, making in effect a very deep "top-hat" section.

A plain web is more suitable as a tension member, unless it is very short. If it has also to be in compression it will need to be more elaborate. An angle or flange moulded along the open edge is the first step. "Top-hat" sections moulded across the web can also be used, although these really need only be grooves or "dents" in the moulding. Few large webs need be continuous. Most can have large holes cut out for economy in material and

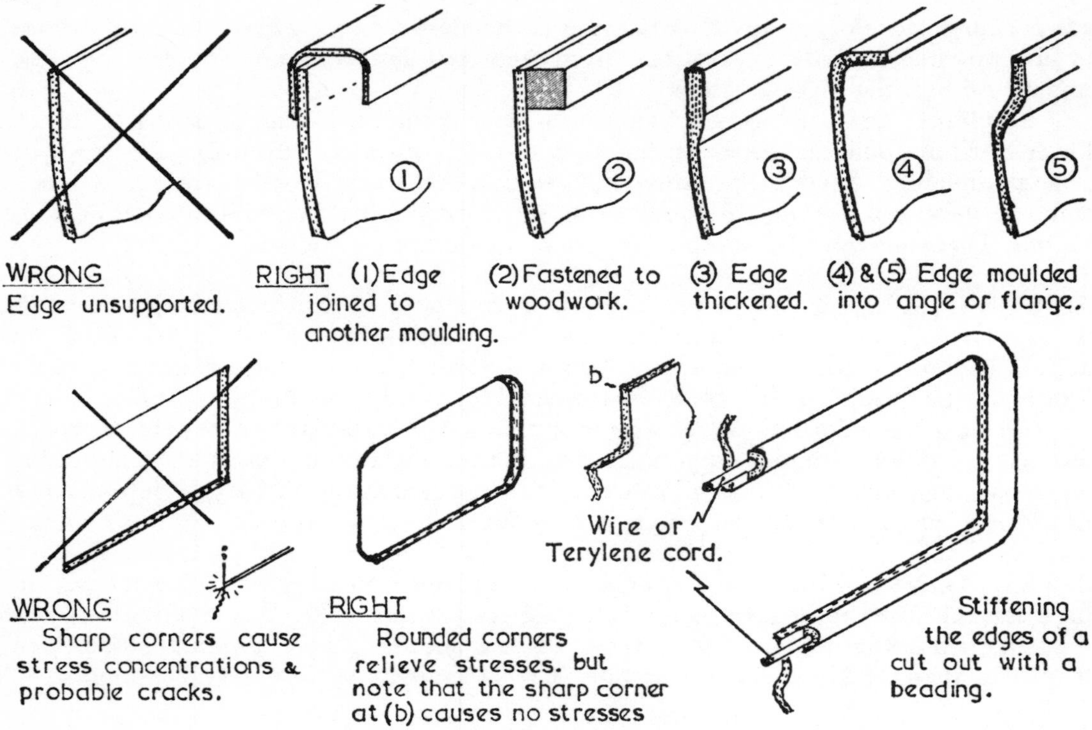

WRONG
Edge unsupported.

RIGHT (1) Edge
joined to
another moulding.

(2) Fastened to
woodwork.

(3) Edge
thickened.

(4) & (5) Edge moulded
into angle or flange.

WRONG
Sharp corners cause
stress concentrations &
probable cracks.

RIGHT
Rounded corners
relieve stresses. but
note that the sharp corner
at (b) causes no stresses

Wire or
Terylene cord.

Stiffening
the edges of a
cut out with a
beading.

2.4: *Outside edges and cut-outs.*

weight, and in a situation like the floors of a sailing cruiser, these spaces allow an easier flow of bilge-water. If moulded round a projection such as a piece of wood or a tin lid these cut-outs can have flanges and actually add to the stiffness (Fig. 2.3).

EDGE-STIFFENING AND BEADING

An opening cut in a panel will need support, or the edge will be weak and may get damaged, particularly if the opening is used for access. The trimmed outside edge of the moulding (Fig. 2.4) is very vulnerable.

Examples are cut-out hatches, pockets, handholes, in fact wherever the edge is not attached to something else such as a window-frame, hatch surround, gunwale, another moulding or woodwork.

When you know that there is to be an opening it is usually simple to work in an angle or flange around it while moulding. A piece of wood stuck on the mould will make the necessary indentation. Where this would interfere with release it can be made detachable, located by simple pins or a spot of weak glue, so that it comes away easily with the moulding and is released separately. The angle or flange should be thickened.

If the cut-out was not foreseen before moulding, the edge can be stiffened with an angle, wood or a beading. A beading is really a small "top-hat" moulding and performs the same function as a rolled or wired edge in sheet metal. Most strains put the edge in tension rather than compression, so there is considerable advantage in using wire or terylene cord for the core, and so making the core material do some work.

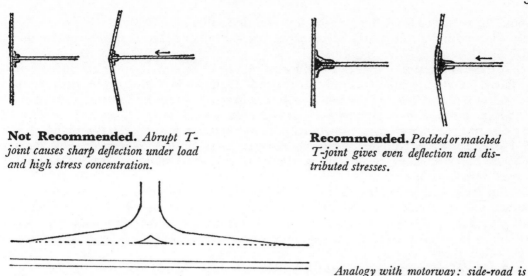

Not Recommended. *Abrupt T-joint causes sharp deflection under load and high stress concentration.*

Recommended. *Padded or matched T-joint gives even deflection and distributed stresses.*

Analogy with motorway: side-road is "matched" into carriageway.

2.5: *Joining a bulkhead to the hull skin.*

Cut-outs, and also trimmed edges, should not have square or sharp re-entrant angles because these cause severe stress concentrations. As a result cracks are likely to develop at the corners after some use, but these will seldom occur if the corners are rounded (Fig. 2.4). On the other hand a protruding point or angle is acceptable because it does not cause a stress concentration. It is only a re-entrant or inside angle which is serious.

The outside trimmed edges of a moulding (e.g. the gunwale) are not usually strong enough by themselves. Unless moulded with flanges, angles or substantial extra thickness they should always be supported by joining to another moulding such as a moulded gunwale or deck, or to woodwork. It is a sound plan to thicken the edge, too, in every case. It is not so easy to mould well right up to the edge of the mould, so edges are often badly moulded and weak. An edge such as a gunwale is subject to severe abuse, like bumping and even being rammed by other boats.

A moulded boat must expect to be treated in exactly the same way as a wooden boat and to withstand everything a wooden boat will withstand without strain and preferably without a mark, and if it is to justify its high repute it must withstand such conditions even better than wood and preferably for ever.

Finally all sawn edges should be sealed with resin, or, if no resin is available, with paint or varnish to keep out moisture which would otherwise enter the laminate through the sawn and slightly shattered edges and result in gradual deterioration and erosion.

BULKHEADS On larger boats bulkheads are used as main stiffening members. They are the cheapest and strongest form of transverse support, a practice now also used extensively in wooden construction.

Bulkheads are attached to the hull by moulding angle fillets, or matting-in angles, along the join between the bulkhead and the hull. For greatest strength they should be moulded on both sides of the bulkhead with generous overlaps onto the hull. The angles should be at least half as thick as the hull skin if double, or equally thick if single (Figs. 2.6). The width depends on the thickness and must be enough to allow for proper tapering off.

An incompressible bulkhead—and any bulkhead mounted at right angles can be considered incompressible—will distort the hull as shown in Fig. 2.5 if in direct contact. It needs to be "matched" to the hull skin, just as in radio or physics a line must be matched to an impedance; a more general analogy is the way a side-road is "matched" to a motorway or turnpike by feeding in slowly with an acceleration and deceleration lane. A side-road leading straight on to a busy motorway as an abrupt T-junction will cause a considerable "distortion" of the traffic pattern. Similarly in reinforced plastics concentrated stresses must be avoided.

The bulkhead is "matched" to the hull by leaving a space so that it is not in direct contact, and the strain is taken on the moulded angles, which taper off to blend with the hull (Fig. 2.6). In practice it is easier to mould if instead of having a space, a strip or pad of soft material such as polyurethane foam or balsa wood is used. A bulkhead should never be a tight fit.

A strip of masking tape round the bulkhead, where the edge of the moulded angle is to be, will give a well defined sharp border. It gives a professional finish, much neater than the usual straggling edge, even if painted over, and is less trouble than sanding. A varnished wood bulkhead and a sharp-edged coloured moulded angle look very smart.

WOOD FRAMES Moulded frames are so easy to fit that they are the obvious choice, but wood frames can be used and the boat fitted out like a conventional hull if moulded frames are impossible. This is sometimes done when a builder of conventional wooden boats or an amateur buys a shell from a specialist moulding company and fits it out.

A serious objection is the large number of through-fastenings needed, and it would be rash to claim a leak-proof hull, for every through-fastening is a potential leak. There is no doubt that fastening through a thin GRP shell is not as satisfactory as riveting or screwing through stout timber. The GRP tends to shatter locally when riveted, and, being thin, it has less ability to spread the load. There is little depth for countersinking so fastenings are almost bound to be proud and unsightly, and the hull will need painting afterwards like a conventional boat. Wood swells to seal a fastening, GRP cannot.

In general, therefore, if the boat is large enough to need frames it is much better if they are either moulded in by the builder together with engine-bearers and other main structural members, or attached by the fitting-out yard by moulding rather than riveting. This will preserve a smooth and watertight hull. In short, any yard fitting out a GRP hull must learn something about GRP and its use, even if they still do not venture on the more perilous and unfamiliar ground of moulding complete boats.

Fitting out a custom-moulded shell (i.e. a shell moulded by someone else, usually a specialist moulder) on conventional boatbuilding lines has advantages for both the yard and the owner, and even more for the amateur. It enables a local yard to satisfy an owner's demand for a fibreglass boat and at the same time provide work for their own men. For the owner it can mean a considerable saving on the cost of the boat, for a small yard in a remote area can fit out a boat much more cheaply than a fashionable yard competing for scarce labour with local union-squeezed manufacturing giants. The major cost and labour on a cruiser is not the moulded hull but the fitting out.

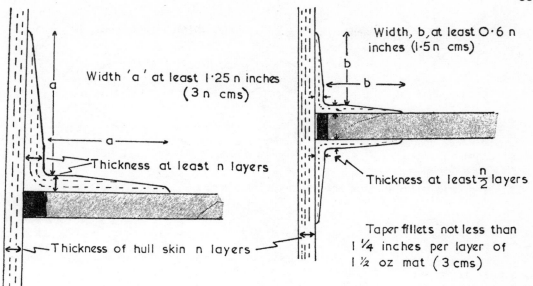

Width 'a' at least 1·25 n inches (3 n cms)

Width, b, at least O·6 n inches (1·5 n cms)

Thickness at least n layers

Thickness at least $\frac{n}{2}$ layers

Thickness of hull skin n layers

Taper fillets not less than 1 ¼ inches per layer of 1 ½ oz mat (3 cms)

2.6: *Proportions of fillets or matting in angles for securing bulkheads.*

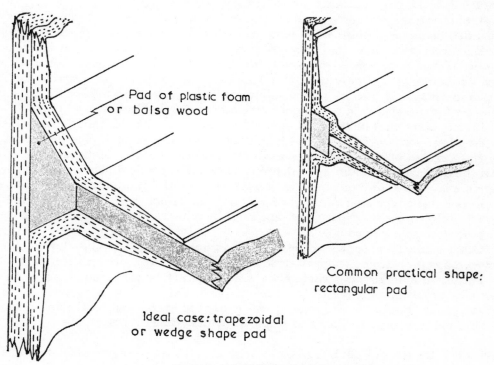

Pad of plastic foam or balsa wood

Common practical shape: rectangular pad

Ideal case: trapezoidal or wedge shape pad

2.7: *Padded or "matched" bulkhead connection.*

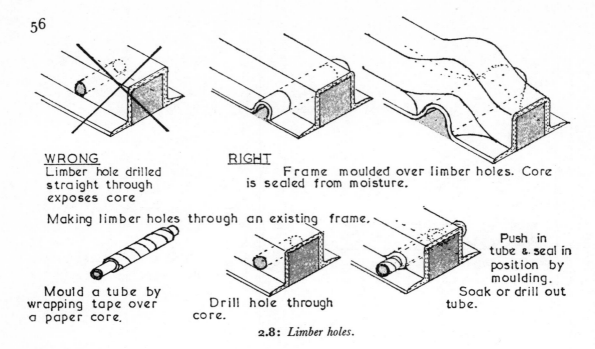

WRONG
Limber hole drilled
straight through
exposes core

RIGHT
Frame moulded over limber holes. Core
is sealed from moisture.

Making limber holes through an existing frame.

Mould a tube by
wrapping tape over
a paper core.

Drill hole through
core.

Push in
tube & seal in
position by
moulding.
Soak or drill out
tube.

2.8: *Limber holes.*

LIMBER HOLES   On any boat limber holes are essential to allow bilge-water a clear run aft to the pump; even on a small dinghy pockets of water are a nuisance. The bilges of a moulded boat will get just as full of match-sticks, fluff and general muck as any other. Manufacturers often claim that only a dustpan and brush are needed, but accidents will happen. Water, particularly sea water, has a knack of finding that carelessly opened hatch or scuttle, or a clumsy crew may knock over the skipper's beer and worse things happen in the galley. The driest boat still needs limber holes, and the less the bilge-water the larger the proportion of muck and so the more unchokable they need to be.

Limber holes must be moulded in, not drilled through, for this would expose the core of a "top-hat" section (Fig. 2.8). A reliable way is to use a piece of polythene pipe, long enough to extend beyond the flanges as well as the centre of the top-hat section, and lay down the frame, core and all, over the pipe. It will make little difference to the strength if the core is grooved or interrupted to fit over the pipe. It will usually be possible to drive out the polythene pipe afterwards leaving a lined limber hole and a core sealed from contact with bilge-water. Obviously the pipe must be moulded over before laying down the core to form the GRP-lined hole.

Other materials to use are paper or cardboard tubes, wooden plugs, lumps of plaster or even soap; they can be chopped or scooped out afterwards, or just left to dissolve.

Putting in a limber hole where none was thought of, or enlarging an existing one, is more of a problem, as it must not be left unlined. One method is to cut out the hole oversize, mould a tube by wrapping "wet" glass tape over a paper tube and allow it to set. Push the tube into the hole and seal it in by moulding over the joins.

SANDWICH CONSTRUCTION   It is a well-known engineering principle that two members some distance apart, but linked firmly together, are very much stiffer than the same two members side by side. This is the principle of the lattice girder. Similarly two moulded skins, separated but linked together to form a sandwich construction, are stiffer than the two skins side by side.

In a GRP boat this can be done by using a core of lightweight plastic foam, balsa, or a honeycomb of paper or glass-fibre, bonded to both skins to form the "jam" in the sandwich; but this is a technique for use during moulding rather than when fitting out or at a later date, and sandwich structures are a subject in themselves (Chapter 1).

SYNTACTIC FOAM It is often necessary to fill up small pockets and awkward places. Solid GRP is fairly heavy, about 95 lb./cu. ft. (S.G. 1·5) and expensive. Ordinary resin putties are cheaper but heavier, about 120 lb./cu. ft. (S.G. 2·0). Both have high exotherm in large lumps, i.e. they get hot soon after setting. The thermal stresses can cause bad cracking and also damage the adjoining GRP.

Syntactic foam is a resin putty made with very lightweight filler. These are generally minute bubbles of phenolic "Microballons", or glass "Eccospheres", and others. Foam polystyrene granules can be used with epoxy. Light materials like vermiculite, pumice, diatomaceous earth, sawdust, etc., can also be used, but spongy materials soak up resin and become heavy and expensive. For lightness and economy they must be in bubble form. Large bubbles make a heavy putty. Small bubbles are needed to lighten the mass of infilling resin. Mixing proportions are fairly critical. Too much resin makes it slushy and heavy, too little makes it dry and not cohesive.

Compared with other plastics foams syntactic foam is fairly heavy, 20–25 lb./cu. ft. (S.G. 0·3–0·4) with Microballons, but it is very convenient, quick and formable as it is simply plastered on. For large volumes foam-in-situ polyurethane is lighter, cheaper and more convenient.

A typical application is the tapered edge of the core of a sandwich moulding, especially if on a curve (Fig. 1.25). The compressive strength is generally high and it can be used for inserts added later in a sandwich.

EMBEDDING WOOD Opinions are mixed about embedding wood. Horror stories say it will swell and burst open the hull, or rot and develop gases which will blow the moulding asunder like Steamboat Bill's fate. Experience, however, has proved otherwise.

Certain precautions must be observed, most of them normal sensible practice.

1. Use only sound, dry, good quality wood in a fit state for embedding.
2. Embed soundly.
3. Use low-movement woods or plywood.
4. Bond-in the wood (page 22).
5. Avoid preservatives (page 23).
6. Make the wood an easy shape to mould over.

Obviously it is asking for trouble to use rotten or damp wood. This has always been so. "Out-of-sight, out-of-mind" is no excuse for embedding any old cheap timber.

Wood cannot rot without air, moisture and rot spores. So it is commonly argued that as the wood is sealed in away from moisture and air, rot is impossible. This is not valid.

Even good GRP is slightly permeable and will allow enough air and moisture to pass for rot to develop, admittedly slowly and after many years, and no wood is really free of rot spores, which can be very long lived. Preservatives might seem the answer but they have a very bad effect on polyester.

In practice wood is very, very seldom embedded perfectly. The shape is generally awkward and the moulding thin, even skimped. Porosity and pinholes are very common. Waterways due to poor bonding and the GRP not following the wood properly are found on almost every boat. Embedded wood is generally associated with fastenings and seepage is a strong possibility. Damage can never be discounted. Consequently it is highly probable that sooner or later water will seep into embedded wood somewhere and run along inside to affect a much larger area.

Sound moulding is essential however awkward the shape. Moulding over wood will not of itself seal it. It needs care and the right methods. A single layer of GRP is usually porous. Always use two layers, preferably three. Two layers of thin mat are less porous than one layer of heavier. Woven rovings, especially if coarse, nearly always have pinholes in the interstices and should never be used alone for embedding. Obviously sound moulding is more important in wet places like the bilges, but note that seepage, condensation and just high humidity can make theoretically dry places damp. Water gets into embedded wood far more easily than it gets out, indeed once in it probably never will get out.

Wood must be dry when embedded. The safety level below which it will not rot is about 20 per cent moisture content. Wood stored in a dry workshop will be 15–18 per cent and is reasonably stable. Wood can be too dry (5–8 per cent is possible by heating) but this would be quite unstable under boat conditions. Even permeation would increase it. Wood swells when it gets wet. This possibility should not be ignored. A strong embedding will contain it and, by exerting counter pressure, will limit the water absorbed. A light embedding will split.

Dense woods absorb water slowly but exert powerful pressure if they do. Soft woods absorb quickly with extensive migration within the wood, but exert a lower and more easily contained pressure. But this is oversimplifying: the initial dryness, i.e. the starting level, is most important. The saturation level and swelling per 1 per cent change in moisture content vary according to species. The total movement of a dense wood may actually be small.

The wood with the least movement is plywood. The cross-ply construction and barrier layers of glue give high stability. Of the solid woods, iroko, teak and afrormosia have low movement but are expensive for embedding. (When builders use an expensive wood they like it to be seen to be used!) Most mahogany types, spruce (whitewood), Douglas fir (Oregon pine) and cedar have larger movement but are still acceptable. Unsuitable large movement woods are oak, scots pine (redwood or common deal), elm, pitch pine, parana pine, beech and ash. One of the problems is knowing just what a wood is. "Teak," "mahogany," "pine," etc., cover a range of species with exotic names which leave the average man none the wiser. Although they may be of similar appearance and strength, movement and water absorption can vary.

Bonding to wood is difficult with lay-up resins: it needs to be primed (page 23). Bonding is unreliable to woods that are hard and dense like oak and iroko, oily like teak, resinous like pitch pine or wet like greenheart. Cedar and some other durable woods contain a natural preservative which affects polyester. It may be simpler to abandon ideas of keeping water out and use a naturally durable, low movement wood.

Marine plywood is outstanding as the most suitable wood for embedding. Where mass is needed, e.g. engine bearers, it is better not to embed at all. Then a less suitable wood like oak can be used without the troubles associated with embedding.

Insect attack is unlikely unless infected wood is embedded (some larvae can live forty years), but damage or pinholes could give entry. Boats stored upside down, or even right way up, could be food for termites if they can find a hole into embedded wood.

Rot is quicker under hot conditions. Embedded wood is more vulnerable under the deck or in engine spaces, also when boats are stored upside down.

Wood has its drawbacks. But against these must be set its advantages. It is the only material which is cheap, readily available, familiar, easily worked, light, takes simple fastenings and holds them well. The advantages far outweigh the admitted disadvantages, which anyway can be minimised by sensible design and good quality control. Stainless steel, galvanised steel, Tufnol, etc., can be used but also have serious disadvantages. Their cost is far higher and making attachments is more difficult. For average quality boats what else is there but wood?

ELECTROLYTIC CORROSION Although some authorities have their suspicions, electrolytic corrosion seems unknown with GRP, but secondary effects can be damaging. Metal fastenings, especially steel (including stainless steel), can corrode in wet wood. The corrosion products are soaked up and retained in the wood. These can get moderately strong and attack the GRP, both polyester and glass. The glass is particularly vulnerable because the inner surface of any embedding has no protective layers of resin and moulding is commonly poor. Such corrosion will only happen in wet wood, but as seepage occurs mainly around fastenings, wet wooden inserts are distinctly possible.

To put this in perspective, decay in the GRP will be limited in area, much as is the electrolysis in the wood. But it can affect the basic moulding as well as the embedding and, if at a bolt hole, can attack the full thickness.

SUPPORT A GRP boat distorts more readily than wood or steel. In the short term, if not overstrained, it returns to its original shape at once because of its springy nature, but long maintained distortion can become permanent due to creep.

The most critical stage is when newly moulded and "green." It will be very flexible then, the extent depending on the materials used, time taken, size, thickness, methods, moulding expertise and the framing fitted in the mould. Often it can bend like a banana..

The important thing to note is that during this early stage the GRP is hardening and becoming rigid quickly. Whatever shape it is in while curing will become the natural shape regardless of whether that was the moulded shape. Distortion will become permanent. The sooner major parts can be joined together the less risk of misalignment and forcing to fit.

It is essential that mouldings are supported in the right shape during this very critical period while they are hardening rapidly. They must not be left lying around carelessly, allowed to become full of water, roll over onto their bilges, or twist. Obviously the more framing fitted while in the mould the less vulnerable the moulding. It is most vulnerable for the first few days but still needs special care for months.

Distortion can occur later due to creep. A common case is prolonged bad support, e.g. badly fitting trailer chocks, or a tight shore left all winter, generally because these are placed where there is no frame or bulkhead to resist their pressure. The tighter the shore is wedged the more the hull indents, rather like pushing against an inflatable. Actually it is not so simple because the hull may resist at first: the dents occur later as the prolonged stress leads to creep.

GRP softens when hot, which can cause distortion and accelerated creep. The heat distortion point of average marine resins is 140° F. (60° C.) which, allowing for decreasing strength as this temperature is approached, is below the tropical temperature of a deck or hull stored upside down.

PRESTRESSING   All distortion causes stress. Permanent distortion causes permanent stress, otherwise known as prestressing or locked-in stress. This must always be assumed to add to both normal working stresses and abnormal stresses due to overload or accident. Prestressing therefore weakens the GRP, makes it damage prone, and seriously erodes the designed factor of safety.

Forcing to fit will cause prestressing whether because the mouldings have distorted or the moulds were inaccurate. To force a distorted moulding out of the "natural" shape in which it has cured or partly cured back into the moulded shape it *ought* to be will stress it just as surely as forcibly distorting a right shaped moulding. This is of crucial importance where the moulding must mate with other mouldings, e.g. hull and deck, or with large unalterable fittings like keels (which could themselves be out of true).

Easy distortion while "green" will cause little stress as the moulding is so flexible, but later deformation due to creep must cause permanent internal damage (page 281). Creep will partly relieve prestressing caused by forcing to fit, but only at the expense of weakening the GRP.

HARD SPOTS   Hard spots or stress concentrations are a little understood and grossly neglected feature of GRP design and construction. Hard spots are not new or peculiar to GRP boats. They are well known in engineering. They were certainly not absent on traditionally constructed wooden boats, but their thickness offset the effects. They are very common on plywood boats—and for less appreciated.

Distortion causes stress. The sharper the angle of distortion the higher the stress. A moulding can distort widely without high stress provided it is smooth distortion, but a small distortion which produces sharp bending at some feature can cause high stress. Hard spots are interference with the smooth pattern of bending producing high local stress concentration.

A baby sitting on a balloon causes gross distortion but little stress concentration because its bottom is well padded. But nasty brother's pin causes acute stress concentration with dire results.

In Fig. 2.1 there is an abrupt step. Bending causes a sharp change of line at this step showing that stress is concentrated there. In contrast the tapered transition gives a smooth curve and low stress. Fig. 2.5 shows how a bulkhead can cause discontinuity of line when the hull distorts, generally under impact nearby but sometimes in ordinary use.

It is common to see a line of cracks at a bulkhead indicating a stress concentration there where the hull has bent sharply. Note that the impact or pressure is not *at* the bulk-

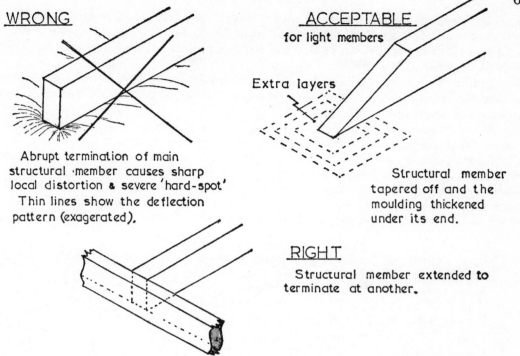

WRONG

Abrupt termination of main
structural member causes sharp
local distortion & severe 'hard-spot'
Thin lines show the deflection
pattern (exagerated).

ACCEPTABLE
for light members

Extra layers

Structural member
tapered off and the
moulding thickened
under its end.

RIGHT

Structural member extended to
terminate at another.

2.9: *Avoiding hard spots: structural members.*

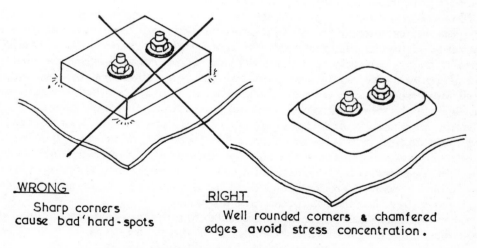

WRONG

Sharp corners
cause bad 'hard-spots'

RIGHT

Well rounded corners & chamfered
edges avoid stress concentration.

2.10: *Avoiding hard spots: block behind a fitting.*

head but beyond—where a padded impact might leave hardly a scratch. The bulkhead acts as a knife edge across which the hull must bend. This happens wherever there is a hard spot. Damage occurs not only at the point of impact but also at nearby hard spots, often at the hard spots alone.

Traffic flow provides an analogy. A smooth traffic flow is "stress-free"—the essential principle of a motorway or turnpike. In towns "stress concentrations" occur at every crossing or side turning.

Any structure will fail at the point of highest stress. The more this is concentrated in one part the earlier that part will fail. Normal working stresses are magnified there.

Because of a stress concentration damage often occurs when a boat without it would escape unscathed. This point is generally ignored, the damage being blamed entirely on whatever caused it. Few question whether the boat *ought* to have suffered damage. With GRP invisible damage can occur due to overstrain at a hard spot which can cause unexpected failure later (page 281). The following rules will reduce if not eliminate the hard spots.

1. End one structural member at another or taper away to blend into the GRP skin, thickened at that point. Never end abruptly (Fig. 2.9).
2. Make changes of thickness gradual and staggered.
3. Round off sharp corners and angles (Fig. 2.10).
4. Do not fit bulkheads in direct contact with the hull (Figs. 2.5, 2.7).
5. Radius the corners of cut-outs (Fig. 2.4).
6. Use pads or thickened moulding behind fastenings.
7. Do not force the moulding to fit: pad if necessary.
8. Make woodwork and fittings to fit the boat. Mouldings must mate accurately.
9. Be especially careful with monocoque construction.

Intelligent application of these rules will make a stronger boat with economy of materials, for why make a moulding strong to resist a stress which need not be there? It may help to visualise the distortion patterns by picturing the boat as an inflatable.

Monocoque, also known as frameless or stressed skin construction, is very sensitive to hard spots because movement must be unrestrained. Small details can alter the pattern disastrously. Designers often leave the details of fitting out to the builder. A builder who ignores hard spots can seriously weaken the boat. I once counted 65 serious hard spots on one high-performance, sophisticated monocoque hull, all added by the builder and entirely unforeseen in the eminent designer's calculations. Similarly owners—or their yards—can inadvertently introduce weakening features when adding fittings.

Common places to find hard spots are: the abrupt ends of floor bearers, engine bearers and frames; the sharp corners of half bulkheads, shelf brackets, web floors, bunk supports, bunks, lockers and embedded woodwork; the transition from sandwich to single skin. The most vulnerable areas are: the forward topsides of sailing cruisers (especially if liable to "pant"), around fin keels, between twin keels, the bottom of power boats and all parts already subject to considerable stress.

Every crack tells a story. Never dismiss them simply as gel coat cracks. Their patterns are the first, often the only signs, of damaging stress concentrations.

CHAPTER THREE

Using Tools on GRP Mouldings

No special tools are needed for work on reinforced plastic after it has set and is hard, but metal-working, rather than wood-working, tools should be used.

It can be drilled, filed, sawn, sanded and polished but not hammered or bent, and not easily punched or sheared. The basic shape cannot be altered, and the resin component is brittle and inclined to chip.

It should be remembered that apart from trimming and drilling very little work is usually required, because all the shaping and forming is done while the plastic is soft and "wet" in the mould. In this respect it is like concrete. It is this business of shaping and forming stock planks, sheets and sections which is responsible for so much work and waste with conventional materials.

The glass content makes the material slightly abrasive and it takes the edge off any cutting tool, not quickly enough to be a serious inconvenience on a small scale, but diamond tools are advisable for mass production.

The resin component cracks and shatters if overstressed. It has little ductility, and it does not deform and yield like a metal, or even like wood. Any fastening which depends on deforming or denting the material will not hold satisfactorily, e.g. a wood screw or a nail, and bending is as impracticable as bending concrete. Although the basic shape cannot be altered the natural springiness allows a certain degree of minor distortion. The extent of this will depend on the framework (added to resist bending) and the age of the moulding. It is much more flexible when newly moulded and still "green" than it is when fully cured. It can be turned on a lathe but tends to chip and must not overheat. A sawn, turned, ground or sanded surface will have a matt finish and cannot be polished until recoated with resin. A "green" moulding will be too sticky to work properly.

DRILLING   Holes can be drilled easily with ordinary twist drills. Wherever possible drill from the smooth, "good" face towards the rough, "inside" face. This prevents chipping of the resin-rich gel coat on the smooth side. If it is essential to drill the other way, from the rough inside towards the smooth outside, the outer face should be protected by holding or clamping a block of wood tightly against it.

Obviously care must be taken to prevent the drill slipping and scratching the smooth face, just as when drilling a car wing. A piece of masking tape will save a lot of anguish.

For repeated drilling, or when drilling into a moulding with a large content of abrasive filler, a tipped masonry drill will last longer.

It is possible to drill a few large holes with a wood bit, but do not use one's best. It is better to use a large twist drill. For larger round cut-outs use a trepanning bit, washer cutter, tank cutter or hole-saw.

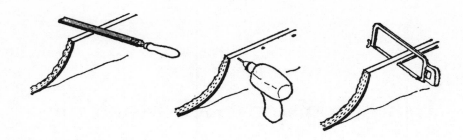

3.1: *File, drill and saw in the direction away from the smooth face to avoid chipping the resin-rich, brittle surface.*

SAWING A hacksaw, padsaw or jigsaw, 26–32 teeth/in. (10–12/cm.), should be used for hand sawing and trimming. Always saw in the direction away from the gel coat face to avoid chipping. A woodsaw will cause delamination. Power driven jigsaws, portable routers or abrasive discs are effective for production sawing. Better, but more expensive, are diamond wheels, which are usually air powered because high speeds are essential. On a small scale use a jigsaw attachment on a popular type electric drill. Proper jigsaw blades will wear quickly and are expensive. Pieces of small hacksaw blades are cheap enough to be expendable.

FILING Reinforced plastic files readily, much like aluminium. An open pattern file is less liable to clog, particularly when the resin is "green" or new and still somewhat sticky. The thin serrated steel files of the Surform and Stanley File type are very good. They cut well and do not clog so much; moreover they are easily cleaned from the reverse side if they do clog. Some models can be used like a plane on flat surfaces.

On edges the cutting stroke should always be away from the "good" face to avoid chipping the resin-rich gel coat and breaking away at the edge; just as when planing wood, extra care is needed at corners to prevent them breaking away (Fig. 3.1).

HAMMERING Reinforced plastic cannot be bent by hammering or any other method. Hammering will only shatter the resin, just as hammering concrete shatters the concrete. Care is therefore needed in any process like riveting or nailing which entails hammering close to the plastic surface. One slip or miss can cause damage, and it is almost impossible for the rivet or nail to be a tight fastening. Soft washers are advisable.

In general any fastening which needs hammering is bad practice and should not be used without very good reason and elaborate precautions.

SANDING Glasspaper will clog badly particularly if the resin is new. "Wet and dry" is the only suitable kind, and it must be used with plenty of water. White spirit may be preferred, as it gives better lubricating properties, but it must not be stinted, and must be washed off very thoroughly afterwards with plenty of water. Traces of white spirit will affect the adhesion of subsequent resin or paint.

When you know that extensive sanding will be necessary, for instance, in rubbing down the "rough" side of a moulding to get a presentable finish, or in sheathing, put ten per cent of talc or French chalk in the resin. This acts as a lubricant and reduces clogging very considerably. It will have little effect on the other properties of the resin. Modern resins seem easier to sand than the earlier ones.

For power sanding a very open grade of disc will clog least. Resin-bonded discs must be used. The cheap paper discs are useless; the 4 in. or 5 in. paper discs used on the popular ¼ in. electric drills will clog, drag and tear in a few minutes. Unfortunately the resin-bonded discs are not usually available under the 7 in. size, but some of the tougher small electric drills will drive a full 7 in. disc. It is not recommended by the makers, of course, and it will not do the drill any good, but for a moderate time it should not wreck one of the tougher ones. I used this practice extensively in my works because girls could handle the small drills all day without getting tired. The proper 7 in. high-speed disc sanders are so heavy and fierce that few girls could lift them let alone control them; indeed they are quite tiring for a strong man to use all day. A big disc sander in unskilled hands is a devastating instrument. It can make deep scars, too deep to polish out, and also do serious damage cutting deep into the moulding quickly before the operator realises what is happening.

However, if the drill is your own, buy the 7-in. discs and cut them down to size. They are a lot more expensive, but they will outlast dozens of cheap paper discs, and when they do clog up they can be cleaned quite easily by soaking them in acetone. If reduced in size, of course, they will not cut so well, for speed is essential for proper cutting, but the bearings of the drill will be happier.

These resin-bonded discs can be obtained with grit of very varied size and density. The ideal is a very open pattern which looks like a gravel path; but unless obtained direct from the manufacturer usually to a minimum order of a hundred or so, or "through the firm", you will have to take whatever your best local tool store can offer.

An orbital sander should be used for fine sanding or finishing, such as working up a really good surface on the "rough" side, the inevitable result of using a male mould for a boat. It is easier to control and gives a more even finish. It will not scar as a disc sander will in a moment's carelessness, but it can only be used for finishing, and it is not much good when you really want to grind off material.

When you are sanding wear a mask or handkerchief over your face and a scarf round your neck. Fine chips of glass-fibre and resin are very itchy.

CLEANING   Clean files, drills, saw-blades and sanding discs in acetone after use, and during use when clogged. If left for long the resin will harden and ruin the tool.

Chloro-bromethane fire-extinguisher fluid can be used in really serious cases where the tool is worth the expense, but keep this well away from the boat at all costs or the Chloro-bromethane will dissolve it. It must *not* be used as a solvent when working, only for the occasional serious cases to reclaim a good but hard clogged tool, and afterwards the tool must be cleaned very thoroughly in water or acetone before being used again.

EFFECT OF FILLERS   The workability of resins can be affected to a large extent by fillers. French chalk or talc has a lubricating and anti-clogging effect. For extensive sanding it is almost essential. Hard fillers such as quartz, silica flour, powdered slate or carborundum make the resin so abrasive as to be almost unworkable. With a high proportion of such filler, tools will wear away rapidly leaving little impression on the resin. Try drilling a hole through a grindstone, the effect is much the same.

Hard fillers impart valuable properties to the resin, particularly resistance to wear, and they are well worth using in the right place, but there must be some thought for holes and trimming, A tipped masonry drill will tackle resins filled with normal quantities of abrasive filler, but sawing will be expensive on hacksaw blades. Cutting must be done with a knife while the moulding is rubbery; if extensive cutting is considered a diamond cutter will be worthwhile.

TRIMMING   The easiest stage to trim is just after the resin has set, when the moulding is still rubbery and can be cut with a sharp knife. A large moulding must be trimmed in stages as each layer sets. The rubbery stage lasts only about half an hour depending on the resin used. Do not trim too soon or the resin will not have set enough and the edge will be disturbed and delaminated.

However, in fitting out the more likely case is a hard untrimmed moulding. Hand sawing all round a large thick boat will be very hard work. Use a power jigsaw or abrasive disc. For production invest in a diamond wheel trimmer: 60 grit is suitable. The high speeds necessary usually require an air tool and may entail investing in a compressor. Small wheels can be used for cut-outs.

SEALING EDGES   All sawing, drilling, filing, drilling, etc., will leave a rough, rather shattered edge with ends of glass-fibres exposed. This edge has no natural protection against water and weather, and moisture will enter. As a result the moulding will tend to decay around the edge or hole. Moulding is often bad near the edge of the mould, allowing moisture to penetrate quite a distance into the heart of the moulding. All edges must be sealed with resin. An underwater fitting is generally well sealed but often a deck fitting is not. The sealing must not just stop the water getting through: it must be on the outside to protect the edges of the moulding too.

SANDWICH MOULDINGS   Working on sandwich mouldings demands special care. Whenever sawing, filing or drilling there will be a likelihood of causing delamination between the opposite face and the core. This will be so from whichever side one is working, but owing to the worse bond, it is most likely when the opposite face is the gel coat face. Therefore, when possible work from the gel coat side and make sure the opposite face is supported with a block. Coarse tools must be avoided. Drilling must be done gently and with the minimum of pressure when the opposite face is reached.

It is most important to seal edges, even bolt holes, to keep water out of the core.

TESTING   This needs a book. The common way is tapping with a coin, a crude method of which surveyors and moulders should now be ashamed. Tapping will only detect the common little gel coat flaws and rare large deeper ones if within $\frac{1}{4}$ in. (6 mm) or so. Rubbing covers more ground and misses less. It will not usually detect deep or small flaws, dry moulding, undercure, invisible damage (page 281), thin patches or most serious defects. The tapper is easily confused by thickness changes, frames, lockers, tanks, soft linings and things which rattle, and thwarted by noise, traffic and jet planes. He needs a piano tuner's ear.

Use a magnifier for examining gel coats, preferably a microscope. Staining shows up defects. Its absorption is a guide to porosity and weathering.

CHAPTER FOUR

Designing for Low Maintenance and Protection from Chafe

THE NEED FOR PROTECTION Strong though it is, a moulded hull is essentially a thin shell and it can wear through. The places where this is likely to happen are few, and small in area, and all well-made boats should be protected from the worst effects if the long trouble-free life which is claimed to be such a valuable feature of a moulded boat is to be achieved. Most of these places are perfectly obvious to anyone who knows what happens to a boat in use, and it is more a question of common sense than anything else.

The finish of a moulded boat is durable, and although not actually maintenance-free as is often claimed, it can certainly be kept in reasonable condition for quite a long time. But this presupposes that it can be kept free from scratches, chafe, bumps and minor damage —all those vague effects known as fair wear and tear. Scratches and wear will ruin the appearance of a fibreglass boat quicker than anything else—they are the Enemy No. 1 of a smart boat. True they can be touched up, but it is not at all easy to do this invisibly and get an exact colour match.

The risk of scratches and wear can be reduced by intelligent design and protection where they will obviously occur. Unfortunately the present trend is exactly the opposite and most moulded boats seem to be designed so that the most conspicuous places are most vulnerable to wear.

There are two approaches to the problem:

1. Protect vulnerable areas with other materials which are more resistant to wear.
2. Make sure that vulnerable areas can be easily touched up or renewed.

All areas subject to chafe and wear need to be protected with other materials, which should preferably be thick, cheap and hard-wearing. Moreover these pieces must be considered expendable, intended to get worn and designed to be replaced when necessary. Fastenings should be screws or bolts; clenching is just acceptable, but gluing is not. These points must be considered right at the design stage—not as modifications incorporated in the Mark III version only after complaints by disappointed buyers.

Some builders rightly assume that a boat's life is a tough one and make some provisions for it, but too often this is inadequate or only available as an overpriced extra. Most dinghies are completely defenceless.

The average cruiser has little built-in protection and is seldom supplied with even a set of fenders. Better design could often eliminate the obviously vulnerable points which are a source of worry and disfigurement. Although despised on "smart" yachts, a rubbing strake will keep away at least 90 per cent of those expensive crunching sounds.

Most runabouts seem designed to spend their lives looking decorative in a showroom—as divorced from the harsh realities of life as the "pop" song impression of marriage. Very little protection is given as a rule for normal bumping and fair wear. Yet more than most boats, runabouts have to come ashore frequently, whether it is to a beach, pontoon or harbour wall. Few are in really experienced hands; they do not handle like a dinghy, nor like a car—or a motor-bike either—and to come alongside "without cracking an eggshell" is really quite an art. Even then a swell is more common than a millpond calm, even in a sheltered harbour, and they must still be kept from bumping.

Provision is made for every conceivable luxury, reclining seats, sunbathing cushions, cocktail cabinets, vanity mirror, cigar lighter, radio, trafficators—but not fenders for harbour walls!

Fishing-boats, work-boats, contractors' launches, pilot cutters, patrol-boats, and suchlike craft which work all the year round need durable tough surfaces. Their crews will have little use for the niceties of soft-soled yachting shoes; in winter weather stout sea-boots are warmer.

Hard-wearing surfaces which can take a lot of punishment are essential. It is better to keep the moulding itself out of immediate contact. Use it for the hull, deck and superstructure but protect the deck with Trakmark, or a renewable non-slip coating, and use a generous thickness of wood for the gunwales, rails, bottom boards, hatch surrounds, seats, and other places which are going to take a hammering. If any of these parts are moulded and not protected, make them at least twice as thick to allow for wear, and start with a matt finish, so that the inevitable scratches are less conspicuous.

It will take many years, probably generations, to eradicate such traditional father-to-son practices as a rough kick from a heavy boot to free anything which does not move immediately. This must be accepted when plastics are used on working boats. It is no good saying afterwards that they were not intended for such treatment. That is the treatment they must expect.

Topsides on working boats need ample protection. Fenders other than the occasional old motor tyre are little used in commercial pools and crowded fishing ports. Stout wooden rubbing bands are essential, better are the more expensive Goodyear rubber fenders which in the larger sizes are tough enough to argue with an ocean liner.

An unprotected moulded hull trying to hold its own with a concrete wall or heavy iron-girt fishing-boat is like a lightly armoured destroyer fighting a battleship (or whatever may be the current fashion in the David and Goliath style). Heroics may win a posthumous medal—or a court martial if Fate is kind—but discretion is rewarded with a ripe old age.

VULNERABLE AREAS   Figs. 4.1 and 4.2 and the associated tables show the usual areas where scratches and chafe occur, and summarise methods of protecting them. Detailed descriptions of the methods of dealing with them are covered in the following chapters, where most of the recommended methods of fitting out bear this in mind.

The wooden skeg or keel of a dinghy or launch, if unprotected, will soon lose an inch or so as it is dragged up a concrete hard. The unprotected keel of a small moulded boat has only $\frac{1}{8}$ in., possibly $\frac{1}{4}$ in., to lose, and unlike the wooden boat where the loss is not vital, being only an appendage, it is the hull skin and structural keel—both vital parts of the moulded boat—which are being worn away. Moreover even before being worn through they will have been seriously weakened.

An inch of flesh off a stout company director might even be welcomed but it will expose a fatal spot on a thin, lithe athlete.

Ropes can cause a lot of chafe. Sheets and halyards should lead clear of obstructions, not just when the boat is on an even keel in harbour, but also when she is heeled right over and the hauling ends lead in directions, and bear on parts, which would have seemed quite crazy on an even keel in harbour. Mooring ropes do not always stay in their fairleads—even assuming they are adequate for their job. Wires can be even more destructive and will saw through anything unprotected. Chain is even worse.

Gunwales are obvious places for wear. All good dinghies have fenders, but comparatively few have the kind which covers the top of the gunwale as well as the sides. The top of the gunwale is spared the worst of the sideways bumping, but it still gets quite a lot from the overhanging bow or counter, even the transom, of a parent ship, and also from the underside of piers, stagings and other awkward places which even the best behaved dinghies seem to get into on occasions. In addition the top of the gunwale gets the chafe from oars, ropes, heavy objects or outboard motors momentarily resting on it, fishing gear, the first of the shore grit and all the weight and wear when the boat is turned upside down (which usually happens on a concrete hard, gravel or unpadded non-slip deck), and all will cause bad scratches; so too will carrying it on top of a car unless it is very well padded, lashed down and carefully loaded.

A fender is such an important part of a dinghy to protect both itself and other boats, that it is hard to justify the common practice of fitting it only as an extra.

The stem is seldom given the protection it deserves. Too often it is moulded to a razor-sharp edge, with the idea that it should cut easily through the water. A razor-sharp edge is difficult to mould; moreover it is sure to be resin-rich, and therefore brittle and liable to chip.

Yet the stem has to put up with a lot of abuse. A slight misjudgement when coming alongside may knock an inch off the old country; the old country is not likely to miss that inch, but an inch off a yacht's stem will be serious. The stem has to bear the brunt, too, of someone else's misjudgement, for instance when a sailing dinghy cuts things a bit too fine in a strong tide. With wind against tide a yacht will ride forward over her mooring chain which can then chafe badly on the stem and often jam when being hauled in. A horse-shoe bow fender will protect the stem to a considerable extent from a mooring chain—but it is not an integral part of the boat; it may be forgotten or, more likely, not bought until the damage has shown the need for yet another item to add to the formidable list of essential extras.

Bare feet cause little wear. Soft yachting shoes in theory are easy on decks, but the shore grit they bring with them is like sandpaper. The more non-slip they are, the more grit they will retain, and for a longer time. The days have gone when no one could set a hard-soled shoe on a scrubbed yacht's deck without incurring the loud and colourful wrath of the almighty professional skipper and his teeming crew. Few yard hands now wear the traditional hob-nailed boots (they are clumsy in cars and on motor-bikes), but the stiletto heel with its dainty, lady-like pressure of tons per square inch can do damage undreamed of by the bootmakers of old.

Hard shoes, the unforgivable sin on an Edwardian yacht, must nowadays be an accepted hazard, and they will scratch a polished moulded surface. Thwarts and bottom boards of dinghies, and parts of the decks, cockpit seats, companion-way and adjacent

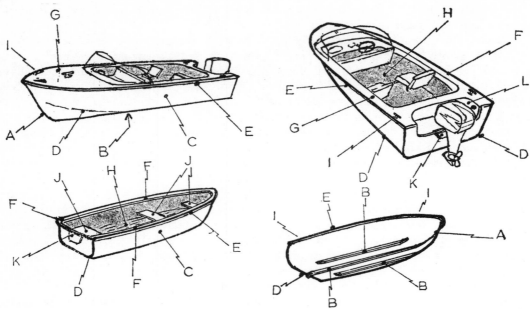

4.1: *Protecting Vulnerable Spots*
Dinghy, launch or runabout.

Place	Cause of Wear	Protection
A. Stem.	From bumping walls and other boats.	Fit brass band or soft bumper.
B. Keel and bilge-keels.	Dragging on hard, beach, trailer, etc.	Use wood keels and protect with brass bands.
C. Topsides.	Bumping.	Fit good fender and moor with care.
D. Corners and lower edge of transom, chine and spray chine.	Contact with harbour walls, etc.	Fit protective pieces.
E. Sides of gunwale.	Bumping and chafe from other boats, pontoons, walls, etc.	Fit a good fender. Wood will absorb more bumping than a moulding. PVC fender also good.
F. Top of gunwale.	Bumping and chafe from oars, ropes, equipment, feet, fishing gear, underside of piers, etc.	Fit overall fender or use wood and touch up as needed. Top corners of transom are particularly vulnerable and aggressive.
G. Deck.	Feet, moorings, dumping heavy objects, etc.	Use a renewable covering, preferably non-slip.
H. Bottom boards.	Feet and equipment.	Make of wood and touch up when needed or leave bare; cover with Trakmark.
I. Tie-down points.	Chafe from trailer lashings.	Fit eyes in the proper places. Use soft padded straps.
J. Thwarts.	Feet, clothes and equipment.	Make of wood and touch up as needed, or cover with embossed PVC.
K. Outboard motor pads.	Marked by clamps and "teeth".	Use special PVC or metal mounting pads.
L. Motor well.	Steering wires, refuelling can, bumping when mounting motor.	Ensure clear leads for steering cables and use fairleads; use plastic refuelling container; mount motor carefully (do not mount a heavy motor single-handed).

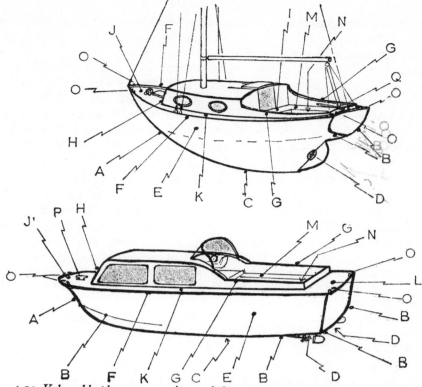

4.2: *Vulnerable places on a cruiser and the ways to protect them and avoid damage.*

Place	Cause of Wear	Protection
A. Stem.	Bumps and anchor chain.	Metal band or rubber bumper.
B. Corners of transom. or counter, chines and spray deflectors.	Bumps and chafe, particularly from dinghies and harbour walls.	Metal bands, wood or rubber. Difficult to protect without making unsightly.
C. Bottom of keel.	Abrasion when slipping or aground.	Stout metal bands.
D. Around propellers.	Abrasion from sand and cavitation. (Only severe on high-powered cruisers.)	Difficult to protect. Extra thickness will compensate.
E. Topsides.	Bumping.	Wood or rubber rubbing band, but no real alternative to fenders and care.
F. Rail or covering board.	Chafe from ropes, boarding ladder, etc.	Use wood and touch up as required.
G. Coaming.	Chafe, particularly from sheets, tiller and general wear. Very vulnerable and conspicuous.	Use wood and touch up as required. A brass or chromium-plated strip may be needed to protect the wood.
H. Corners of cabin top.	Chafe from ropes, kicking, etc.	Wood, metal or soft plastic protective strips. Arrange clear lead for sheets.
I. Companion-way or entrance to deck house.	Concentrated wear from feet.	Wood grating, metal or PVC treads, doormat.
J. Foredeck.	Chafe from mooring chain.	Keep chain off deck with wood slats and a plate round the mooring cleat.
K. Side decks.	Localised wear from feet, particularly around step from cockpit.	Trakmark or renewable coating of non-slip resin or paint.
L. Aft deck.	Localised wear from gang plank and feet (mainly in Mediterranean ports).	Rubber rollers on gang plank. Wood pad on deck and protect deck as for companionway.
M. Cockpit seats.	Wear from feet, worst at step-down points.	Wood, metal or PVC treads, slats or mats. Should be non-slip.
N. Cockpit floor.	Wear from feet.	Wood or wood grating.
O. Around fairleads.	Mooring ropes, wires or chain.	Use good fairleads of adequate size with a lip.
P. Around cleats.	Mooring ropes, wires or chain.	Mount cleat on wood or PVC pad.
Q. Cockpit.	Rubbing tiller, winch handle, etc.	Re-align or protect with wood, metal or PVC strip.

areas of a cruiser must be considered vulnerable to footmarks and to scratching. Fortunately some of the most obvious places are usually made non-slip, which, if sensibly
done, will afford protection against wear and mask the effects.

Any polished surface which is liable to be stepped on will be impossible to keep free
from scratches. This applies also to normally vertical surfaces which may become almost
horizontal when sailing hard. Thus the sides of the cockpit as well as the floor need to be
feet-proof—and preferably non-slip as well; it is unlikely to be smooth sailing when you
have to brace yourself with one foot on the side of the cockpit—and still less likely when
you need both feet there. These conditions are not unusual in British waters.

NORMAL MOTION CAUSES WEAR   A boat is seldom still. Even in harbour
there is usually a gentle motion, sometimes not so gentle, from passing boats, a swell
outside or just the movement of the crew. Outside harbour there is continual movement,
varying from violent in a gale to gentle rocking on a calm summer day, and there is often
vibration, too from an engine. Even on a river or lake there is plenty of movement.
Movement of the boat creates movement of anything loose, and while a rattling tin in a
locker may do little harm except to the sleep of the watch below, a hanging oilskin, a
door-catch or a marlinspike on a handy hook, can make marks in a day or so which will
be difficult ever to remove.

Anything moving means wear, chafe and scratches. The only answer is to make sure
everything is secure. It is not only the boat which will get worn; the object itself may wear
even more. A hanging oilskin will not suffer harm in a weekend, but on a long passage it
can wear right through. So too can smart shore-going clothes, especially ladies'.

Motion at sea is expected, although it may come as an uncomfortable surprise to
some; but many boats are amphibious and travel more on their road trailer than on the
water. Anything loose on a journey by trailer will cause more wear than in a gale at sea,
for the motion on a road is rough going on the average, small wheeled trailer even if it
has springs—and plenty have not. The boat will be marked if the lashings are not tight,
and kept tight by frequent checking and adjustment. The lashings themselves should be
soft and protected where they bear on the boat. Loose lashings will allow the boat to jump
around and get damaged. I know one small sailing cruiser which was trailed down to the
South of France and came back quite a different shape! Continental roads can be straight
and fast but on the average they are a lot more bumpy than most British country lanes.

SOURCES OF WEAR AND ABRASION   Abrasion, scratches and wear are
usually caused by one or more of the following:

1. Rubbing from ropes, wires, sheets, moorings, anchor-chain, etc.
2. Contact with the shore or other boats: e.g. a beach, hard, harbour walls, piers,
   running aground, crowded landing stages, bumping dinghies, etc., as well as while
   launching, hauling out, loading on to a trailer and travelling on a trailer.
3. Rubbing from moving parts of the boat: e.g. tiller, winch, starting handle, oars.
4. Wear from shoes and clothing, or scratches from fastenings, buckles, buttons and also
   fingernails, jewellery, rings, wristwatches, etc.
5. Resting, bumping down, sliding and moving equipment, stores, beer-crates, fishing
   gear, oars, water skis, either in use or while loading and unloading.

6. Motion of loose or hanging objects due to movement of the boat or vibration when under way, at moorings or on a trailer.

Most of these are fairly predictable and can therefore be prevented. Some are a matter of plain common sense, others are only obvious to an experienced sailor.

METHODS OF PROTECTION   The commonly used methods of protection are:

1. Abrasion-resisting gel coat and other coatings or finishes.

Good for minor scratches and abrasion but of limited value once the gel coat or coating is penetrated.

2. Extra thickness.

Compensates for wear but cannot prevent surface scratches.

3. Wooden protective pieces, and use of wood instead of reinforced plastics in vulnerable places.

Good protection in depth and can be renewed. Expendable. Fairly easy to touch up and maintain good appearance.

4. Ditto, using metal.

Good protection, heavy but usually thinner than wood. Often used to protect the wood in severe cases.

Appearance may be unattractive unless plated.

5. PVC, rubber, polythene, etc.

Good resilient, bump-absorbing protection especially for fenders. Some kinds are perishable and degraded by sunlight.

DESIGNING FOR LOW MAINTENANCE   Designing for low maintenance is a subject which has had little attention, probably because so many people are under the rosy impression that no maintenance is needed anyway. But intelligent design is very important if the maintenance is to be kept low or approach the maintenance-free ideal, and the yacht is still to retain the smart appearance which a yachtsman would rightly expect on a wooden boat—at least at the start of the season. At present there is more maintenance-saving protection on most wooden boats, which are painted regularly every year and probably touched up during the season, than on most fibreglass boats which are still believed to need no maintenance—ever.

An experienced owner—and the GRP boat industry has not prospered or become accepted by selling only to the mugs—will want a good finish throughout the life of the boat. He will compare this with a wooden boat and think in terms of decades, not just years. Fibreglass boats are now being accepted seriously by experienced, hard-sailing yachtsmen because of their strength, toughness and lightness. Low maintenance is a bonus point, but no serious and careful owner really thinks seriously of no maintenance at all. There are too many other things on a boat to need attention, engines, mast, rigging, sails, anti-fouling; even if the topsides do not need painting.

Low maintenance will not be achieved just by saying that the boat is GRP and leaving it at that. Certain parts of the moulding must be protected from scratches and wear, the finish must be good in the first place, and a useful life of fifty years must be reckoned on. Only sensible design will ensure that maintenance of a smart appearance is kept low, for fifty years—or even five.

All the following chapters emphasise this point.

INFLUENCE OF COLOUR ON MAINTENANCE The easiest colours to touch up are white and black. These colours are the purest and change least with exposure to sunlight; but do not kid yourself that they do not change at all. It is no use putting on a patch of Persil-white if the surrounding white moulding has darkened to a yellowish tinge. There are four hundred shades known as white, and even more shades of black. This shows the difficulty of matching even these two simple colours.

A clean scratch will show up least on a white moulding; the lighter shade formed by the scratch will be inconspicuous against the white background. However, the rough surface of the scratch will soon attract dirt and show up as a dirty mark against the white background. With black the opposite happens. The lighter shade of the rough scratch will show conspicuously when new but will tone down as it gets dirty. A scratch on a coloured hull stands out whether it is clean or dirty.

Modern pigments for polyester resins are very fast to light. Some are better than others, and your colour or resin supplier should be able to advise you on this, but only certain colours can be used with epoxy resins. All colours will change slightly with exposure to sunlight; the change may not be noticeable by itself—until some new colour of the "same" shade is used for touching up and stands out like a flower catalogue. Black changes least, white goes slightly yellow or grey, dark colours become lighter and bright colours lose their brilliance. This takes some years and with good pigments the changes will not be marked.

Once a moulding has been painted scratches will show much more plainly due to the difference in colour. This may not be very noticeable if the paint and the moulding are exactly the same colour, but will be very obvious if the colours are different; it can be taken for granted that after some time a paint, nominally the same colour as the moulding, will have faded whereas the protected moulding underneath will not.

From the point of view of reducing maintenance this conspicuousness of scratches is an objection to the idea of moulding boats in standard colours for stock during the off-season and painting to the customer's requirements before sale. Moulding boats for stock in the off-season is a sound economic idea, but it is probably better to stick to a good selling colour like white, and mould the coloured boats only to order.

Some moulders are prejudiced against gel coats and finish all their mouldings by filling and painting. This gives a better finish than a bad gel coat and a poor mould, but is not as good as a good gel coat, properly applied, in a first-class mould. Their object is praiseworthy, but to some extent it is an admission that they cannot apply a good gel coat or use moulds with a poor surface finish. (This does not apply, however, to pressed boats.)

When painting, therefore, less maintenance will be required if the underlying moulding is coloured the same colour as the paint, at least to the depth of a moderate scratch. Any other colour will make the scratch very prominent.

INFLUENCE OF SURFACE FINISH ON MAINTENANCE A bright glossy finish, almost a mirror finish, is the sort of finish a fibreglass boat ought to have.

This is a proper "yacht finish." You get only what you pay for and the best finish requires the most maintenance—and a lot of polishing—to keep it so, and inevitably it shows the slightest mark which would never be noticed on anything more mediocre.

I have noticed that a matt finish, particularly if white, can still look smart. It does not look quite as smart as a really well-kept glossy surface, but much better than an indifferent glossy surface. However, it must be kept perfectly clean, and it must be intentionally matt, very fine, even and free from scars and halos.

The moral here seems to be that for a low-maintenance boat a carefully applied matt surface would be easier to maintain in a smart condition than a glossy one. The essential condition is regular washing down to keep it clean. The surface of the mould or pattern must be given a skilful rubbing over with a medium burnishing paste or very fine steel wool. This could also be done to a hull that was already moulded. A matt paint on the pattern would do it if free from brush marks. This is not an easy way out for a lazy mould-maker. A badly finished mould will produce a badly finished boat and probably have glossy patches or streaks to give the show away. This finish must be worked for.

I first noticed this effect at one of the Boat Shows. I was going around looking out particularly for really well finished boats. The best ones stood out by their brilliant polish and bright highlights, but these highlights also showed up every minor defect. The highlights in an exhibition are very harsh because of the many lights all around. However, one boat struck my eye purely because it was a large expanse of brilliant white, and it took a little while to realise that there were no highlights—but there were also no defects visible.

A patterned surface, e.g. a small pinhead pattern, is also effective for interior mouldings, and retains an attractive finish better than a smooth surface. It should be matt.

A glossy surface is like a skin-tight gown: a girl needs a good figure to wear it—but if she can do it the effect is magnificent. Few boats have really got a perfectly smooth line (and one made in a plaster mould is always very wavy), but a mirror finish will show up every defect and the slightest waviness. A very fine matt surface masks well, yet it can, if properly done and maintained, still look very smart.

PROTECTION SAVES MAINTENANCE   There is nothing new about any of the places that I have shown on pages 70, 71, to be liable to get worn, and there is little in all this that is peculiar to moulded boats. Wooden boats have worn and chafed at much the same points for generations. In the most vulnerable parts of a wooden boat the wood is protected by metal; the annual fitting out, or a touch of paint during the season, will cover up traces of the rest and keep the boat looking smart.

But on a moulded boat an important aim is to cut down on maintenance and to eliminate it if possible. Scratches and wear mean maintenance, and it is very much better to avoid a scratch or chafed place than to have to touch it up. Remember, a fibreglass boat is like a car. It is not difficult to touch up a scratch, but very hard to make it blend invisibly with the rest of the coloured surface. The proper course on a car is a complete respray; similarly on a boat a badly scratched or chafed area may mean that the whole boat has to be painted.

There would be far fewer silly, impracticable, unseamanlike mistakes made, and more design aimed at reducing maintenance, if more designers, and particularly moulders, responsible for detailed design actually went to sea and found out what happens—and, unless they are designing a purely river boat, I really mean to *sea*; not a short trip for press photographs on a fine afternoon, or a very well convoyed cross-Channel stunt, but some honest dirty weather work with the nearest land under several fathoms of cold salt water.

Proper protection need not look unsightly. If considered carefully at the design stage it can be made inconspicuous and look what in fact it is—an integral, essential part of the boat. At present, if fitted at all, it is usually an afterthought—and looks it.

WEATHERING The gel coat is the principal protection for the structural GRP beneath, the basic glass and resin wherein lies the strength of the boat. But a gel coat is little more than a thick layer of paint and as with paint it will be attacked by water and weather. No one expects paint to last forever in a hostile environment.

The gel coat finish needs protection and maintenance. Its life is limited although it can be prolonged by care and maintenance. It will last longer if the surface is polished regularly and the boat is laid up under cover. Every GRP boat must be painted one day, not only for appearance but to preserve the gel coat for the life of the boat. The bare gel coat will not last more than 10–20 per cent of the potential life of the boat. For the rest of its life it must be painted.

At first only the surface gets weathered. When jaded this can be burnished away to reveal fresh bright surface beneath. But as weathering develops, especially if neglected, the gel coat becomes etched and eroded like an old temple and can no longer be revived by burnishing. At that stage painting is necessary to preserve the gel coat from further erosion.

IMPORTANCE OF GOOD GEL COAT By far the most conspicuous part of the boat is the gel coat. Indeed little else can be seen of the structure of the boat. If the gel coat is poor the whole appearance will be poor and little can be done to improve it. Moreover a poor gel coat will weather rapidly and seriously. This cannot be hidden. The boat will look terrible and its value will sink. When two years old the boat can look ten.

Bad gel coats are porous. Water will permeate through to destroy the gel coat and attack the structural resin and glass beneath. A sound gel coat is essential not only for appearance but also for structural reliability.

The most practical solution is painting the boat years before it is due, but the porous surface poses a problem and requires a system carefully planned for sealing rather than finish. Even so it may not be successful and require frequent complete renewal. In theory gel coats can be removed and renewed, but this is so difficult and expensive that it can only be a most drastic solution. From the owner's view the best course is to paint and sell—quickly. A boat with a bad gel coat will be a rapidly increasing trouble and expense.

WILL IT LAST? Early boats are not a fair guide. Materials, and even more techniques and experience, were primitive, experimental and not relevant to modern boats. But it was also before cheap mass production and more care was taken.

Theory suggests a life of fifty years or more for a yacht. Practice suggests a GRP boat will last at least as long as a wooden one. Experience shows that only good boats will last. We must not judge GRP by bad boats. Obsolescence, not durability, limits life. GRP boats ought to last, but builders do not build to last because buyers will not buy to last. Our over-numerous children, living in a world stripped by us of all vitally important materials, will curse us and our guzzling society.

CHAPTER FIVE

Odds and Ends

On anything larger than a dinghy there will be far more work in fitting out than in the actual moulding; and a great deal of this is similar to conventional wooden construction.

In the main fitting out falls into four categories:

1. Joining moulded sections together.
2. Major installations such as engines, shafts, keels, tanks, mast step, spars, etc.
3. Attaching woodwork, either wood trim or major structural assemblies, bulkheads and accommodation.
4. Attaching minor fittings such as cleats, ventilators, fairleads, etc.

The methods used have been described in Chapter One. The following chapters show how these methods are put into practice for the various parts of the boat—with examples also of how it should not be done.

All the faults described in later chapters have actually been seen, even the outrageous ones. Many of them have been seen, too, on wooden boats, particularly light plywood ones, for stupidity and ignorance are by no means confined to the shady fringe of fibreglass boatbuilders. Most of these faults are only details, yet apart from the basic hull shape, which is a different matter and unchangeable, it is entirely intelligent attention to detail which makes the difference between a comfortable, safe, seaworthy boat and a wet coffin.

More boats come to grief because of a comparatively minor failure such as a rudder fitting, cleat, shroud-plate or skin fitting, than from shipwreck or collision, although a major disaster is very often the direct outcome of an initial minor failure. Very rarely indeed does the whole boat just fall to pieces.

CO-OPERATION BETWEEN THE MOULDER AND FITTING OUT FIRM

There must be clear agreement between the moulders making the hull and the yard or amateur fitting out the boat if this is done separately (and even if done in different parts of the same organisation), as to the extent of the framing which will be fitted, its exact position and type. Many other points too must be settled beforehand, such as the method of attaching the deck, bulkheads, engine bearers, and their positions.

Co-operation over this will ease the job of fitting out, because a type of frame and position favourable for the moulder, or standard for a moulded part, may raise a lot of problems when that part is made in wood. A moulded frame, so easy to put in, can be the devil to alter, and on "dry" fitting out it may be impossible to replace it neatly.

The time for co-operation on these details is before moulding starts. The fitting out people will avoid a lot of surprises if they can make a careful inspection of one of the standard moulded boats soon after moulding and see exactly what they are going to get. The moulder too needs full co-operation, plans showing the position of every fitting, detailed instructions and nothing left to chance or assumption. Changes may be necessary; a good moulder will have many cost saving suggestions. No design is ever perfect, but all changes must be mutually agreed beforehand. Supervision is necessary to ensure the instructions are adhered to. No hull should be accepted until checked and surveyed. It is important to make this quite clear in advance.

DISTINCTION BETWEEN SEAGOING AND RIVER BOATS In this book the two main categories are dinghies and cruisers. In general "cruiser" can be taken as meaning any cabin boat from the smallest pocket cruiser to the largest luxury gin-palace, and also most commercial boats and fishing-boats. The larger open boats such as launches and lifeboats can also be classed as cruisers because of their size.

There are two clear subdivisions for cruisers; river boats and seagoing boats. (The difference between motor cruisers and sailing cruisers is more social than practical.) River boats obviously have an easier time (discounting the risk of collision), and are not likely to encounter flying spray, breaking wavecrests, green seas and rough conditions which demand the higher strength and very much better water sealing if life on board the seagoing boat is to be tolerable and safe in any but the calmest conditions. Failure on a river boat is undesirable but it is seldom serious; failure offshore may have fatal results.

This distinction is quite clear, but the terms are obviously related to the boat's size. A river boat means one which by reason of its size, purpose and locality is unlikely to encounter waters which are rough for its size. It will usually be confined to canals and narrow slow-running rivers. Everything else must be considered seagoing. I do not say ocean-going, although this is only an extreme development, but any boat using such popular coastal waters as the Solent, Thames Estuary, Clyde or Long Island Sound will frequently encounter rough conditions which demand strong, properly secured fittings and hatches which keep the water out; on the other hand a 30-foot cruiser on the Norfolk Broads or the Thames at Windsor will not normally encounter anything rough.

Large lakes such as those in the British Lake District or the Alps, long wide reaches of a river such as the Thames below London (and for a small boat a lot higher), and any fast-running river (which usually includes any tidal river), can produce rough conditions in a fresh wind which will be very wet and definitely "seagoing." The same conditions will not necessarily be as "seagoing" for a larger boat, and naturally a working boat which has to be out in all weathers, summer and winter, will encounter rough conditions more often than a yacht which is only used on occasional sunny afternoons.

Note that small lightweight cruisers today can be highly mobile because of car trailers. An inland river boat may be on the open sea a thousand miles away a week later. Any cruiser that can be trailed must be considered "seagoing" for its use cannot reasonably be confined, and this means nearly all fibreglass cruisers up to 25 feet or so, because, being inherently light, they are easily trailed and they are built in numbers which cannot usually be absorbed by a local inland market. In this context "seagoing" may seem an odd description for a boat which will travel so far on land! (Note this is an islander's view. A continent could have a large market for strictly river boats—but also larger, rougher lakes and rivers.)

"Dinghies" include all open boats, sailing, motor, rowing, and runabouts and miscellaneous small craft up to about 18 or 20 feet. Few dinghies can really be considered "seagoing," and yet they are too small to be unaffected by river conditions. All dinghies therefore come into the same category with little distinction between where they are used. The remarks on mobility apply even more to dinghies.

WHO SHOULD DECIDE A BOAT'S CATEGORY Obviously it is for the owner to decide whether he wants a boat for the river or to go to sea. One day bureaucracy will invade this last refuge of freedom and decree that boats will be classified for restricted use, with regular seaworthiness tests and proficiency examinations for the owners—and snoopers to enforce the law, fines for offenders and woe betide you if you get stuck on the mud and are not back in barracks by dark.

But until that day it is the builder or designer who should decide whether a boat is a "river" or "seagoing" boat not the owner, for a boat usually has a series of owners each of whom may have quite different ideas from the man for whom it was originally built. The new approval scheme introduced by the Ship and Boatbuilders' National Federation, the trade organisation, is a step in the right direction, as this is a voluntary scheme within the industry.

It is easy enough for the designer or builder to blame the owner who goes to sea in a boat not intended for it—but anyone concerned with trying to popularise a class should be careful of this attitude; it is very much easier for a class of boat to acquire a bad reputation for being weak and wet than to lose it despite extensive and successful improvements. A reputation, either good or bad, has a habit of sticking, and it will stick as much to the designer's or builder's name as to the class of boat. As the aim with all fibreglass boats is to build as many boats from one mould as possible, to amortise the mould cost, it is a wise idea to ensure that any river boat will at least be reasonably safe and seaworthy if it finds its way to other waters.

Few people can swim more than a few hundred yards even to save their lives, and even if supported by life-jackets (which it is more than likely they will not be wearing). It is easy enough to drown in a river and it can be a lot more unpleasant. Given Hobson's choice, I would prefer to swallow clean salt water than industrial effluent mixed with sewage and spiced with detergent.

Some people claim that every man has a right to drown himself, or at least to risk drowning if he wants to—a view which is not usually shared by his wife and family (particularly if on board) or by the local lifeboat crew. Nevertheless many people are new to boats and have more enthusiasm than experience. The risks should be taken with open eyes; drowning should not come as an uncomfortable surprise. Besides a dead man cannot come back as a satisfied customer for another, bigger and more expensive boat. He may even still owe the H.P.!

The buyer comes for a boat not a coffin. It is the builder, or his salesman's responsibility, and a very real responsibility, to make sure that an inexperienced buyer knows the difference.

FINE WEATHER AND FOUL There is no such thing as a "fine weather boat," either cruiser or dinghy—there are only "fine weather sailors," and even that is wishful dreaming. The weather changes quickly, not only in Britain where such a change in our maligned climate can usually be seen coming, but even more in those sunny dreamlands like the Mediterranean where the fierce Mistral and other local winds can strike viciously without warning out of a clear blue sky. Many fine weather places too have regular strong afternoon winds and the romantic Trade Winds would keep most northern pleasure-sailors harbour bound for months.

"We shall never go to sea in Force 5 . . . We shall only sail when the sun is shining . . . We only want a boat for the river . . ." Such remarks are all too common; yet all rivers lead down to the sea, and an estuary can be rough (indeed crossing the bar at a river mouth can be a really frightening experience). Plenty of river dinghies, too, are taken on holiday to the seaside.

Although I refer repeatedly to bad weather do not get the idea that messing about in boats is always a cold, wet, uncomfortable business. It is not and there are many, many days even in our fickle European summer when warm sun shines on a smiling blue sea and sailing is everything one dreams of. Yet many a family dinghy picnic starts out in just such tempting weather but ends up plugging into a Force 4 or 5, with wind against tide, to get home—and in a dinghy that is wet. It is under Force 5 conditions, say one reef down, that ordinary people get into trouble, for only the bold or the very foolish deliberately sail in a real gale. Force 5, even Force 4, is rough and pretty uncomfortable for a small boat, motor boats as well as sailing, and more than enough to show if it is not a safe boat. A "yachtsman's gale" starts at about Force 5—just a working breeze to old Admiral Beaufort!

The question of being "caught out," the ability to withstand really bad weather if necessary, is another matter. But even so any good seagoing boat would have a reasonable chance of riding out the sort of bad weather it is likely to encounter. But a river boat, used under conditions for which it was not designed, will need very skilful handling, and quite a lot of prayer, to come safely through bad weather. It is still true that any boat going more than about eight hours sailing from a good harbour should be capable of riding out moderately bad weather for the time of year. Local conditions might influence the warning time and so would the reliability of an engine.

An ocean racer or deep-sea cruiser, of course, must be able to ride out the worst the sea can do in its uglier moods. But today hundred-mile open sea passages can be undertaken in reasonable safety, even in really small pocket cruisers, by intelligent use of weather forecasts and given adequate time to allow a choice of weather. The greatest danger is not so much the weather itself, but a rigid schedule which demands sailing on a certain day, probably to get home in time, because that may mean taking a risk on the weather.

The distinction between prudence and timidity is very hard to define, and indeed it cannot be defined, for timidity in one case would be prudence in another. The bold and skilful succeed where the faint-hearted and inexperienced perish, and there are all too many who will applaud a man if he succeeds, but if he fails will ridicule him without mercy as a fool for trying.

GRP BOATS AND TRADITIONAL GOOD PRACTICE Just because a boat is made of a new material one should not discard everything learnt about earlier boats. GRP boats must still float, and motor or sail, and they are subject to just the same arduous conditions that boats have had to withstand since time began. A GRP boat may be a pretty piece of moulding—but it is first and foremost a boat, and that must never be forgotten.

Because some GRP boats have acquired a reputation for strength and toughness, other builders of lesser boats think that traditional sound practice and even common sense can be forgotten. This is never so. Yet who is to set the standard? Some famous old-established boatbuilders who have turned to GRP do so in name only. Their boats are moulded by others and often largely fitted out by others, too. When boats are factory made, production convenience, not boatbuilding, often dictates what is done, and planned obsolescence has replaced ideas of durability. Progress is only forward if not to the detriment of the boat.

One may scoff at the supposed ingrained conservatism of the builders of wooden boats, but their practice is based on one criterion—it is known to withstand the actual working conditions. Wooden boats have had to meet these conditions for generations and there is a wealth of experience to draw on. Their builders build what they know will stand up not only to the normal conditions but also to the occasional really rough conditions, and they only change when experience shows it is possible. Moreover they are not nearly so conservative as is generally supposed; synthetic glues, laminated frames and plywood have been accepted readily and have made notable changes.

An enlightened traditional approach is the correct one. Modify established sound practice to suit the new materials—but do not throw it all out of the door. I hold no brief for those who will not change, but when it comes to fitting out a moulded boat sound boatbuilding practice is a better basis than a wealth of experience on cars, caravans, housebuilding, furniture—or none at all. It does at least provide a reliable yardstick in a field where conditions are unpredictable and pure theory inadequate.

This is not to say that these industries cannot teach boatbuilders a lot about modern, efficient mass-production techniques. They can, and many boatbuilders have learnt how to mass produce boats in a way and in quantities that would amaze their grandfathers. But one can mass produce something which works, and equally one can tool up to mass produce something which does not. It is just a question of knowing, or being set upon, the right lines to start with.

USE OF WOOD Opinions differ about the use of wood on a fibreglass boat. The "no maintenance" school say, "Why have wood, it needs maintenance?" Others prefer wood because "It looks nice, more like a proper boat." But the main point in favour of wood is its greater ability to absorb chafe and the ease of touching up or replacement.

To touch up one scratch on a moulded hull is not difficult, but when there are masses of them as is often the case if the boat has been rubbing on something, it becomes tedious and painting is the answer. Yet to get a colour match involves painting the whole boat, just as it does with a car—and that is the end of the "no maintenance" holiday. The alternative is to accept the scratches and a permanently scruffy appearance which no owner of a wooden boat would tolerate. If that is the price of "no maintenance" it is too high for a keen boat owner.

A wooden gunwhale would also get scratched and chafed, but it is easier to touch up bad scratches on wood, and when repainting or revarnishing is needed this is confined just to the comparatively small areas of woodwork.

Some parts like gunwales can, and should, be protected with a durable, soft fender, but it is impracticable to use a soft fender everywhere—and how does one protect without getting the protective pieces themselves chafed, dirty, and in need of maintenance?

The crux of the matter is appearance. "No maintenance" and "yacht finish" are incompatible.

A valuable advantage of wood is its ability to absorb chafe and bumps. A wooden rubbing band can be 2–3 in. thick (50–75 mm.) but the average GRP hull is only $\frac{1}{4}$–$\frac{3}{8}$ in. (6–9 mm.). A deep gouge in the wood will not weaken the boat and is easily patched up. But $\frac{1}{4}$ in. of GRP can soon be worn away even though it is harder than wood, and it will shatter more on impact. This is the boat itself being worn away, not replaceable protection, and it will be seriously weakened long before it is actually worn through.

This depth gives wood a better ability to absorb punishment than the thin moulded shell. Of course the moulding could be made thicker to withstand wear—and often is— but this is expensive if it is to be really effective, e.g. a tough working boat can have a wooden gunwale or rail 6 in. thick; an equivalent thickness if moulded would be very uneconomic. Moreover, it still does not get over the problem of protecting the surface from unsightly scratches and marks.

It may sound as though I am advocating a return to wooden boatbuilding. Far from it, but there is little point in advocating a material, however good it may be in itself for a purpose for which it is not suitable, and for which there is an economic, readily available and better material. For the actual hull moulded fibreglass is unbeatable, but certain vulnerable parts need the additional protection which is conveniently afforded by cheap, thick, expendable wood. There is no single all-purpose material.

So although at first sight it may seem better to have no woodwork at all, and therefore no maintenance, experience shows that a certain amount of woodwork can be kept looking smart with very much less trouble than touching up the scratches on the moulded surface. Scratches in vulnerable positions must be considered inevitable.

All-the-year-round working boats are not the only ones to have hard use. The average yacht's tender or small dinghy, and any boat using a crowded club pontoon or public landing stage certainly does. In fact most small boats are condemned to a life of bumping, grinding and exposure to the elements which makes a dodgem car's life look soft and which would reduce a shining automobile to battered rusty scrap quicker than Eastern roads and native drivers.

Chapter Four points out the parts of a dinghy or cruiser which are most vulnerable to wear and most in need of protection. But these are to maintain a smart appearance. A working boat needs such protection even more because of its rougher life, with ropes and wires, pots and fishing gear, and the fenderless, devil-take-the-weakest conditions of commercial pools and close packed fishing harbours. Here the wood in turn may need the protection of iron or brass bands (complete with projecting screws) to compete on equal terms!

For fitting out a single moulded boat, or one of a short run, wood is the obvious material to use as it avoids the large number of patterns for sub-mouldings which would be needed if everything was moulded. The accommodation, most of the interior work and even the deck and cabin top may well be made of plywood, particularly where the hull is a shell moulded by another firm. Even now many production cruisers consist of little more than a moulded hull, deck and superstructure with all the internal work made of plywood. This is partly because the production runs do not justify extensive sub-mouldings, but also to a very large extent from personal preference. It seems that yachtsmen are quite happy to have a fibreglass boat—provided it looks like a wooden one.

PAINTING The normal finish on a fibreglass boat is the natural smooth, glossy, coloured moulded surface. This is the ideal, but unfortunately it seldom stays that way. There is a trend on better-class boats, where good appearance for many years is of prime importance, to forestall the inevitable and paint right from the start.

Every boat kept afloat in coastal waters needs anti-fouling; other parts like non-slip decks, boot-topping, decoration, cove line and name are often painted on too.

The procedure and preparation for painting are covered under "Maintenance" in Chapter Twenty-three, pages 263–6.

SUB-MOULDINGS When an amateur or conventional yard fits out a moulded boat, most of the work will be a question of making and fitting wooden pieces, furniture and standard fittings to the moulded hull, using glass fibre and resin only for "matting-in" connections. Sometimes no moulding materials will be used at all, and all joints and attachments will be "dry", but this is no longer recommended except as a last resort.

But once he starts to use the materials an intelligent worker will soon find they can be used for more and more parts; not for everything—only a pig-headed fanatic does that—but for many things where wood is more difficult to shape. A crude mould can enable a sound part to be moulded right in position, exactly to shape, and eliminate many hours of skilled shaping and fitting. But if a single moulded part needs a carefully made pattern and mould, ten times as expensive as the part itself, while an acceptable wooden part can be made more quickly and cheaply, then wood is the obvious choice.

Rules are impossible, everything depends on the circumstances, the shape, quantity needed, finish required, strength, durability, conditions to be withstood, access, availability of materials both wood and plastic, the relative ease and cost of making the mould and moulding compared with making the piece in wood, and, of course, personal preference. There are many conflicting factors.

Many parts can be either moulded or made of wood as best suited to the circumstances: e.g. bunks, seats, hatches, engine cases, outboard motor wells, sinks, lockers, drawers, galley units, fish wells, wells for glass bottoms, chain lockers, ventilators, mast-steps, canopies, awnings, shower units, buoys—and many others. It will be easier once some experience has been gained and the steps are obvious. Then the possibilities are endless.

A boatbuilder used to working in wood will probably retain a preference for it. Among other things his reputation is at stake, and a craftsman's reputation is a valuable thing. He knows he can do a good job in wood and will not adopt a completely new material and process unless satisfied that he can turn out as good a job. At the same time few intelligent craftsmen, and a good craftsman is not stupid, are blind to the advantages of a new material or to economic realities—certainly not in small firms, although in large ones they may have to turn a blind eye, and toe the union line.

GEL COAT REMOVAL (*a*) Sanding is dusty, tedious and requires much skill with a power sander. The first layer, if not the whole moulding, is usually the same colour. It is difficult to judge depth and there is grave risk of weakening the boat. (*b*) It can be warmed with a blowtorch and scraped off. This is *not* like burning off paint. It must not get hotter than strictly necessary. The gel coat must soften only and not burn.

Both are drastic, only for use when simpler measures have failed. The smooth moulded finish will be lost for good. Painting is inevitable.

CHAPTER SIX

Decks

HULL TO DECK JOINT The commonest major item to be attached is the deck. Ideally it should form an integral part of the boat and therefore the join must be strong. The methods of making and attaching the deck fall into two clear categories:

1. The deck is moulded, and the problem is to join two finished mouldings. This is the commoner case in production and on small boats.
2. The deck is made of wood, and it is the normal fitting out problem of building a wooden deck on to a hull.

The great majority of GRP boats now have moulded decks whether they are production boats or bare shells, including the largest sizes where mould costs are very high and numbers few. There may even be a choice. Undoubtedly a GRP deck is better where it can be adapted, but the versatility of a wooden deck should not be despised where one-off or a few boats are wanted on a more or less standard hull. Many owners still have their own very definite ideas. In particular commercial requirements vary widely and often call for a very specific design; standard hulls have been fitted out for such diverse purposes as individual yachts, pilot cutter, fishing boat, ferry boat, survey launch, armed patrol boat, ambulance, mission chapel and exotic replicas for film sets or holiday camps.

As the deck is such an integral part of the structure, my recommendation is to buy the moulded shell complete with the moulded deck wherever possible and consistent with the operational requirements.

The join between a moulded deck and moulded hull should be moulded over with an overlapping butt-strap or angle fillet so that it virtually becomes all one piece. Sometimes this is all that needs to be done with a small plywood deck, but a conventional wooden deck must be properly supported with deck beams and shelf. The hull, too, needs the structural bracing given by the deck beams and shelf—in fact the problem is much the same as fitting a deck to any other boat.

The normal loading on a deck tends to close the angle between the deck and the hull, and so to open the outside of the joint (Fig. 6.1). A well-designed joint strengthens the outside as well as the inside with a butt-strap or through-fastenings, which can well be combined with the fastenings for the fender, rubbing band or toe-rail.

Bonding the deck to the hull by filling the joint with resin glass putty is not good enough by itself, although it is commonly done on a small cheap boat—and often too on boats which try to justify a higher price by pretensions to quality. It is a fair method of sealing the join, but it is much more satisfactory if combined with bolts or pop-rivets, or an angle moulded behind, because a resin glass putty is not an adhesive and cannot "weld" the mouldings together. Both deck and hull are likely to be somewhat flexible and give as the putty is packed in. This puts the moulding under permanent stress and distortion. An epoxy putty is a stronger adhesive, but the joint must still be designed properly for bonding. Pressure is usually essential for good bonding with any adhesive.

A moulded angle fillet inside ties the deck to the hull very effectively and also provides physical support for the deck. It can be used with a wooden deck as well as a moulded one; indeed it is easier to join and support a wooden deck, particularly a plywood deck, by moulding than to shape and fit wood. A "wet" angle fillet will secure a moulded deck, but with a wooden deck it should be combined with fastenings and used primarily for support. Many of the methods illustrated are suitable for either plywood, planked or moulded decks.

When a deck with a turnover edge must be fitted to a hull remember that the exact thickness of the "inside" of the deck and the radius of the inside angle cannot be made to close tolerances and may have wide variations, particularly local undulations. A moulded angle does not take the same form as bent metal. Metal bends about its neutral axis, giving an inside radius which is less than the outside (Fig. 6.2). The individual layers of a moulding tend to retain their thickness when they are laid up layer by layer in the mould. Consequently the inside radius will be, in theory, the same as the outside radius. In actual practice it is usually greater, due to bridging and filling. Close tolerances will necessitate grinding or filing the inner face to make it fit.

A shelf or stiffening member around the edge of the hull will help to preserve the shape after release from the mould until the deck can be fitted to hold it all together. When newly moulded, uncured and "green," the hull is flexible and will tend to slump under its own weight and the increasing weight of added equipment and workers. It must be very well supported in the proper shape during cure, which means not only while fitting out but in storage and transport beforehand too. It is equally important to support the deck. The shape in which the moulding cures will become the natural shape regardless of whether it was the moulded shape. Forcing it back to its proper shape will stress it just as surely as deflection under load. Consequently forcing to fit will prestress and permanently weaken it. Stress cracks show how common this is.

Do not bolt up solid. Leave a good clearance and pack with resin putty or use a gasket. It is impossible to mould to tight tolerances. As well as distortion, shrinkage or thermal changes of the moulding, the mould is subject to dimensional changes. Clamp the deck in position before bolting to avoid ripple distortion developing as bolting proceeds.

Deck beams for a wooden deck can be proper wooden deck-beams, fitted before the deck in the conventional way, or they can be "top-hat" sections or angles moulded to the underside of the deck to stiffen it after it has been fitted (Fig. 6.3). The latter is usually possible only on a boat small enough for a sheet of plywood to span the deck, although they can well be used to supplement a few wooden or pre-moulded deck-beams used to provide initial support. They can also be used when the whole deck and cabin top are prefabricated separately.

A moulded deck will usually be moulded complete with all its deck-beams and attached as a single unit. Deck beams are essential even on quite small boats. Most loads on the deck are concentrated loads, such as heavy feet, crates of beer or rigging attachments, unlike the loads on the hull which are well distributed by a cushion of water.

The method of attaching deck-beams to the hull will depend on the facilities available. The "dry" method will be to rebate them into a wooden shelf in the usual way; but moulding fillets over the beam ends and shelf without rebating (Fig. 6.4) is quicker and

86

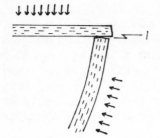

6.1: *The principal forces acting on the hull—deck joint will tend to open it along the outer edge, 1.*

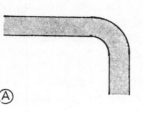

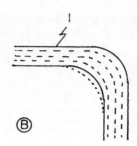

6.2: *Radius of bends.*

When a piece of metal is bent, A, the inner radius is smaller than the outside but when reinforced plastic is moulded into a bend, B, each layer tends to keep its own thickness so that the inside radius is the same as the outside, or even greater as shown dotted. The mould face is on the outside, 1.

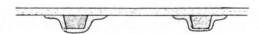

6.3: *Deck beams. Top-hat section deck beams are easily made and can be fitted while the deck is in the mould. They are also an easy way to make deck beams for a plywood deck.*

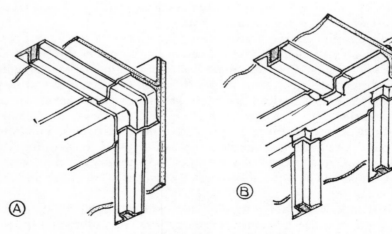

6.4: *Joining the deck beams to the shelf.*

A. *The moulded angle under the deck is formed over the deck beams and the frames to tie them all together.*
B. *The deck beams and frames are butted against the shelf and the moulded angle connects them all together. The beams and frames can be rebated into the shelf as well, but for most purposes the moulded angle, if well thickened, is sufficient.*

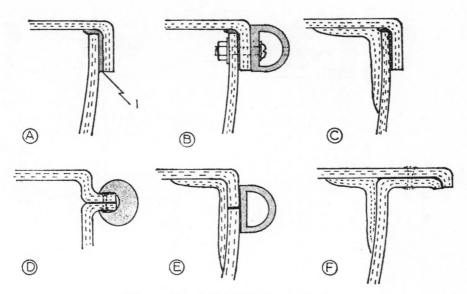

6.5: *Deck—hull join* (i)—*small boats*

A. *Deck bonded to hull with filling of resin-glass putty. Not recommended except for the smallest and cheapest boats.*

B. *Resin-glass putty backed up bolts or rivets. These may be the bolts used to secure the fender.*

C. *A moulded angle will join the two together firmly and make them virtually one moulding.*

D. *Outward turning flanges, bolted or riveted together and covered with a "clip-on" extruded PVC or aluminium strip.*

E. *Butt-joint backed with a butt-strap in the form of a moulded angle. Rubber fender hides the join.*

F. *"Bathtub" flanges, riveted together and backed by a moulded angle. A strong method of construction but very liable to get damaged and hung up on obstructions. Only suitable where ease of handling and a good grip are of overwhelming importance.*

probably stronger. Moreover separate lodging knees are not needed. The fillets can even form the shelf itself, or be combined with the moulded angle joining the hull to the deck.

A conventional wooden shelf should be screwed or bolted to the moulded frames. This is a case where wooden cores for "top-hat" frames provide convenient and secure points to screw into. The shelf could be glued on, but as this could cause delamination of the frames, and it is an important structural member, it is better to screw as well as glue.

When fitting out a shell moulded by another firm, there must be clear agreement, before moulding starts, as to the extent of the framing which will be fitted, the type and exact position. It is advisable also to settle exactly how the deck is to be fitted and to discuss this with the moulder. He can make the job very much easier (and also, inadvertently, much more difficult) without much trouble to himself, and this is particularly the case when the fitting out will be entirely "dry." Early detailed planning and discussion will pay handsomely and are much better than waiting until the moulded shell is delivered. It may then be too late to mould on a shelf, frames or bearers which would have made such simple, secure points of attachments for woodwork, and which the moulder could have done so easily.

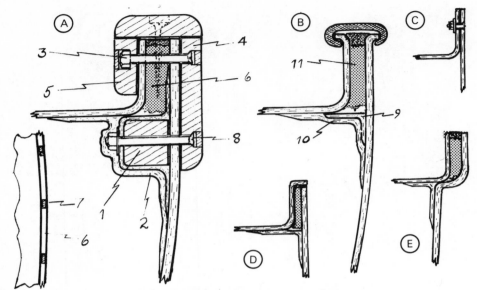

6.6: *Hull-deck join (ii)—upturned flange.*

A. *A typical and generally satisfactory arrangement. The hull itself is stiffened with a shelf moulded over a wooden core,* 1. *This preserves the hull shape until the deck is fitted and provides a firm landing for the deck. The deck is secured by moulding over the join,* 2, *but backed up with through bolts,* 3 *and* 8. *These bolts also secure the rubbing strake,* 4, *and facing piece,* 5. *Note how the bolts do not bear directly on the GRP and the rubbing strake is replaceable. The gap between hull and deck is filled with resin putty, wet mat or sealant, preferably flexible. Wooden spacers,* 7, *are inserted to take the screws for the capping. Dowels cover all fastenings neatly. The gap allows reasonable moulding tolerance, essential on such large mouldings. The spacers also prevent distortion when bolting up.*
B. *Another common method using an extruded PVC capping sprung over moulded lips. The filling,* 11, *should be epoxy as it needs to bond well. Note the moulded angle shelf,* 9.
C. *A weak method, not recommended. Hull and deck are bolted together directly and not backed by GRP moulded beneath. High stress round the bolts. Seepage likely. The countersink is weakening and a nucleus for decay. Distortion almost inevitable.*
D. *A lip moulded to the deck provides seating and location. However without a shelf the hull will probably distort before the deck is fitted and it lacks the stiffness to withstand pressures during sealing, even from just pushing in wet mat or putty. In any case it is difficult to get any sealing in satisfactorily.*
E. *Here a moulded knuckle forms the shelf and location for the deck, and may be combined with a decorative feature or spray deflector. This knuckle is very vulnerable and likely to be damaged.*

Fig. 6.6A shows the method which has given least trouble in service. Note that inside faces are better bonding surfaces than gel coat faces. Good sealing is essential. The moulded angle underneath should prevent water actually coming through but will not stop water lodging in the joint, leading to decay at this important point.

The drawings show various combinations of deck joint, and also toe-rail, fender, etc. Different combinations can be used according to choice and are not associated exclusively with that joint. Toe-rails, capping, scuppers, etc., are covered in the next chapter.

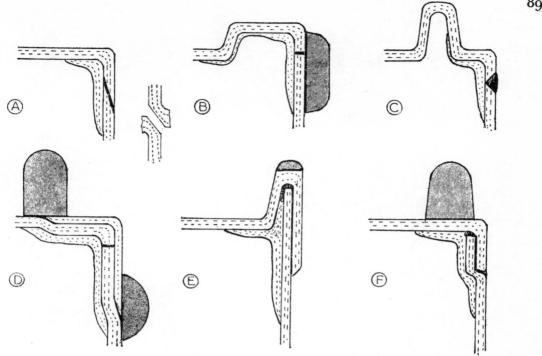

6.7: *Deck–hull join (iii)—downward flange.*

A. *Scarfed joint. Difficult to make neatly and not recommended. On production it is quicker and neater if the angle of the scarf is moulded, not sawn (see inset), and the lip trimmed afterwards.*

B. *Butt-joint backed by moulded butt-strap. Raised moulded toe-rail. Wood rubbing strip hides join.*

C. *V-joint filled with resin-glass putty and backed with moulded butt-strap. Moulded toe-rail. A narrow toe-rail like this is harder to mould than the previous wide one.*

D. *Butt-joint with double butt-strap, outer strap recessed. Outer butt-strap will be rough but it could be a sub-moulding, bonded and bedded on "wet" mat. Wooden toe-rail hides upper joint, aluminium section the lower.*

E. *Lap-joint strengthened with butt-strap. Moulded toe-rail capped with half-round metal strip. Narrow toe-rail will be awkward to mould. Flaws, or a thick, brittle puddle of resin are likely.*

F. *Flush lap-joint strengthened with butt-strap. Wooden toe-rail.*

The basic requirements of a good joint between deck and hull are:

1. A generous amount of overlap. This can comprise butt-straps.
2. A good butt-strap or fillet covering the join, on both sides if possible, to "weld" the two parts into one moulding. Alternatively through-fastenings can be used.
3. An angle, stringer, shelf or flange to give physical support to the deck. This may be formed by the moulded shape or added later, or it may be a conventional shelf.
4. The equivalent of a shelf to maintain the hull shape after release from the mould.
5. A permanently watertight seal which must not permit water to lie in the joint.
6. Adequate tolerances to allow for some dimensional changes of moulding and mould.
7. Provision for toe-rail, capping or bulwarks, and fender or rubbing strip.
8. Provision for scuppers.

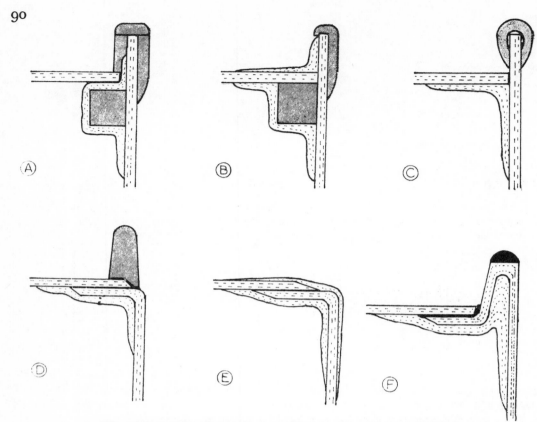

6.8: *Deck–hull join (iv)—Flange suitable for plywood or moulded deck.*
A. *Moulded top-hat section shelf. Wooden rail.*
B. *Wooden shelf, deck secured by moulded angles. Wooden capping.*
C. *Pre-moulded angle. More suitable for smaller boats. Aluminium or PVC capping.*
D. *Inward flange on hull. Joint strengthened later with moulded angle. Wooden toe-rail.*
E. *Inward turning flange. Deck secured by double butt-strap. The butt-strap may be rebated and flush as in Fig. 6.7 D.*
F. *Inward turning flange combined with moulded toe-rail as part of hull. Metal capping on rail. Strengthening butt-strap advisable; note filling needed inside toe-rail.*

NON-SLIP DECKS Moulders tend to underrate the slipperiness of a highly polished deck on small boats such as runabouts, small cruisers and sailing dinghies. A bright, highly polished deck looks very smart in a showroom; it is, after all, the part of the boat which is most visible, but to try to keep a footing on it, even to sit on it, when it is wet, and sometimes moving in all directions as violently and rapidly as a bucking bronco, is quite another matter. Yet these are quite normal conditions when under way and even to crawl along a smooth, wet deck to reach a mooring in harbour, is like walking the greasy pole—with much the same penalty for slipping.

More attention is usually paid to making cruiser decks non-slip, but this is frequently inadequate or based on a false impression of the effectiveness of the methods used under normal wet conditions. Many surfaces give a good grip when dry but are slippery when wet. But remember that a small boat's deck is normally wet from spray except in very calm weather, and even dew can make a deck dangerously slippery.

Three methods are used to make decks non-slip:

1. Mould in a pattern.
2. Cover with a non-slip, stick-on covering.
3. Paint with a non-slip finish.

1. Decks are often given a moulded pattern such as a diamond pattern or "mock" Trakmark because it is easily produced by sticking Trakmark on the mould or original master to give a patterned surface, and it then avoids the cost and trouble of making the deck non-slip during fitting out. Embossed wallpaper also gives a wide range of patterns.

This is certainly very much better than a smooth deck, but disappointing compared with proper Trakmark, because it is hard and rigid with a glossy surface, and it has poor non-slip value when it is wet.

A moulded pattern will get worn, and it will chip as it is likely to be resin-rich. (If it is not resin-rich it is likely to have flaws, which are even more vulnerable.) It cannot be replaced when it does get worn or damaged, and it is almost impossible to remould.

2. It is much better to have a smooth deck and cover it honestly with real Dunlop Trakmark or similar stick-on covering. Trakmark is a patterned PVC sheet with a fabric backing which is stuck down to the deck with adhesive. It is not easy to lay well with the pattern running straight and true, but it bonds firmly and looks very neat if laid carefully. It wears well and does not show marks or scratches. If it does get worn you can rip it off and replace it.

The non-slip properties are excellent, wet or dry. It is soft and flexible, and grips like a motor tyre or yachting shoe. The rigid moulded diamond pattern, the "Mock" Trakmark, cannot give like this; in comparison it is like the difference between a rubber motor tyre and a rigid moulded imitation, which would obviously have little grip and would wear badly.

Trakmark is kind to bare feet, and the soft surface keeps down the noise from footsteps, clattering blocks or a heavy shower, all of which can be very disturbing for the watch below; it is inevitable that a thin, hard, moulded shell will tend to be noisy, although there have been few complaints on this score. A wooden boat also resounds and is noisy under the same conditions.

Another stick-on covering is Safety-Walk, made by the Minnesota Mining and Manufacturing Co. (3M). In appearance and feel it looks like a self-adhesive, coarse, "wet and dry" sandpaper—which in fact it is. Its non-slip properties are really good, but woe to anyone who goes sliding across it in sunbathing rig, because human flesh was not made to withstand such brutal treatment. Consequently it is more suitable for commercial craft where the black or green surface is more in keeping, and the sharp, abrasive surface bites stout seaboots not bare feet. The usual form is in pads, tiles or strips, not rolls, and it can be used for difficult danger spots like companion-way treads as well as floors and decks.

3. The cheapest way to make a deck effectively non-slip is to paint it with a non-slip paint or resin.

Sand the deck to break up the gloss and give a key, prime with one of the special primers for use over glass-fibre/polyester mouldings if recommended by the paint manufacturers, and then paint in the usual way. On production it is possible to mould a rough, keying surface in the first place and so avoid a lot of sanding; it is a waste of effort to make a polished mould, if the moulding is going to be painted.

An ordinary deck paint will need renewing every year. Deck paint soon builds up a substantial thickness, which after five or ten years would have to be removed; removing paint from a moulded boat is a bit of a problem and unskilled attempts will do more harm than good (see Chapter Twenty-three, on Maintenance, page 265).

It is more in keeping to use a modern, highly durable non-slip paint based on poly-urethane or epoxy. There are also tough rubbery paints and plastics coatings including one based on high friction brake lining materials. Industrial flooring finishes are sometimes suitable and very hard wearing.

A very good non-slip finish can be made with polyester resins, the ordinary moulding resins, by mixing in a large proportion of a hard, coarse filler. Powdered quartz—BSH grade is a suitable size, so is 20 mesh granite or flint—makes a very hard-wearing deck and gives a first-class foothold, wet or dry. The proportion is fairly critical, if there is too little filler the surface will be "wet" with resin and glossy, and will not be non-slip enough; too much and the surface may powder and crumble. As a rough guide the proportions of filler to resin should be 6 to 5, but this will depend on the materials being used, the resin and the type of filler.

An easily obtained alternative is fine sand, bird sand is a good size, and some paint suppliers can provide a fine silver sand.

The preparation is important. As well as sanding the surface to provide a key you must also wash it down very well to remove any traces of release agent, dirt and foot-marks, as this coating will usually be done in the final stages of fitting out; a light wipe over with acetone is sometimes recommended to condition and clean the surface. How-ever, opinions differ about the use of acetone, and some authorities condemn it. There is no doubt that it must be used sparingly, and it is probably wise to use it only when the deck has become very dirty during fitting out and the possible harmful effects of using acetone are less than the bad adhesion which would result without it.

Do not forget that other parts of the boat need to be non-slip too, parts where slipping may not mean a man overboard, but could result in injury or loss of control of the boat. The cockpit or wheelhouse floor are obvious places, so, too, are companion-way steps, bridge-deck and cockpit seats where the crew will step to dash forward. Not so obvious, perhaps, is the cabin sole in the galley or heads, and that handy shelf in the wheelhouse or cockpit where a pair of binoculars, Sailing Directions or a drink may be put down. It is sometimes as inconvenient for an object to slide as for the crew to slip; this is more im-portant in moderate weather than in rough, because in really rough weather everything will have to be lashed down anyway—if the boat is not safe in port.

Cabin tops are far too commonly smooth, glossy and very slippery when wet, or at best have patches of non-slip with plenty of slippery gloss between. Non-slip may not look so nice, but cabin tops are for walking on. Some moulders really ought to try reefing— under conditions when reefing is needed in a hurry.

Nor are non-slip surfaces only required on sea-going cruisers and big boats. No dinghy helmsman can steer if he cannot keep his seat, or if he slides to the lee side every time the boat heels, while a trapeze man needs a very secure foothold.

For those less arduous applications a moulded pattern, or moulded ridges, may be sufficient. However, the Trakmark type of pattern should be avoided in places subject to wear, because it is difficult to renew. A more open pattern of ridges is preferable. These should not be continuous or they may hold puddles.

HEAT DISTORTION   In the tropics and the glamorous sub-tropics, too, a yacht's deck can get hot. I have even known a deck get too hot to walk on in British waters—but rarely. It certainly happens in the Mediterranean, and that latitude covers most of the U.S.A.

A deck can get hot enough to affect its strength. The heat distortion point, as I have explained on page 60, of many resins is not high; but in practice the most noticeable effect is likely to be a greater susceptibility to marks, e.g. from stiletto heels or heavy weights. However, it is a thing which should be borne in mind on any boats likely to be used in hot areas or built for the export market, if part of the deck carries a large and important load. An obvious case is a mast stepped on deck; less obvious are cleats and mooring bollards, where heat could possibly cause unexpected failure.

Boats used in the tropics should really have the decks moulded with a resin having a higher heat distortion point, and as a safety factor the deck should be stronger and thicker than is strictly necessary in milder temperatures. Dark colours should be avoided.

Fortunately, as far as yachts are concerned, the most severe strains occur when there is plenty of wind and water around to keep the decks cool, and the deck will only get really hot in harbour or in a calm. It is likely to be more serious on commercial boats, because they may be used in places too hot for pleasure and be busiest in harbour.

The cost may preclude it on a cheap boat, but a strengthened deck to allow for hot sunshine should really be fitted as standard on any luxury or middle-quality yacht. The Mediterranean and Florida sunshine attract such boats like wasps to a jam sandwich, and fibreglass boats are so light that the only limitations to trailing are the sizes permitted on the roads, while anything larger can sail there. Moreover, given time for a three or four weeks' cruise, there are many places which a small cruiser can get to from the shores of Britain without even trailing. Spain, for example, and even Northern Spain can be hot.

Consequently it is almost impossible to say that any particular boat will not go to a warm country at some time in its life even if it is just for a holiday cruise, while the romance of ocean voyages lures many people in all sorts of boats, few of which were ever built for the purpose.

SANDWICH DECKS   In theory the advantages of a sandwich deck—high rigidity, unobstructed headroom and insulation—are attractive. In practice they cause more trouble than any other single feature of GRP construction. Delamination is the problem. Very few moulders can, or even know how to, make them properly. About 90 per cent are defective. Most develop delamination early and probably never bonded properly in the first place. The older the deck the less likelihood of severe new delamination developing rapidly.

It is claimed that it does not matter if a sandwich delaminates, a view which I fear is tempered by the high expense of making good—or, alternatively, having to replace the boat. Yet a delaminated sandwich must be weaker. Moreover there will be severe secondary troubles from water seepage leading to decay within, invisible and unsuspected. In my view, if a deck is meant to be a sandwich it must be properly made. Anything less must be condemned. It should never be tolerated on a new boat and no owner should be required to accept it or a bodged-up repaired sandwich deck.

TESTING FOR DELAMINATION

TESTING FOR DELAMINATION A sandwich nearly always delaminates between the outside skin and the core. Signs that the deck may have delaminated are: creaking, movement, vibration, hollow sound when touched, or almost any unusual behaviour. When tapped or rubbed (non-slip resounds well) delamination will sound hollow but may be difficult to detect if the skin is thick. There is an art in knowing how hard to tap or what weight instrument to use. The bond may have failed yet the skin be close to or touching the core. A heavy tap will push them together and sound solid where a light tap or rub sounds hollow. It is a fair bet that there are other places where the bond is poor, patchy, or in spots not large enough to detect or yet separated but inherently weak.

A sense of proportion is vital. A small patch after years of use on an otherwise sound deck is not much to worry about. Even if the bond is failing it is likely to take years to become serious. But widespread patches on a newish deck show the bond is poor and either never was bonding or is spreading rapidly. This is a major defect.

REPAIRING DELAMINATION

REPAIRING DELAMINATION Repair is difficult but may have to be faced as it is likely to develop with age anyway or from damage such as a sideways bump.

Search by rubbing and pinpoint by tapping. Plot and mark the outline of all hollows. This requires care. Try to find if water has got in. If so God help you. Look for damage, loose fastenings or crushing in way of hollows. If any it is almost certain water will be in already. A sub-surface detecting moisture meter (Aucon) can confirm it. Otherwise drill holes. Note damp can collect away from its entry.

Bonding to a damp core is impossible. So is drying it out. A solution has yet to be found!

If it is not damp, or by ingenuity it can be dried out, drill pairs of holes in every hollow, multiple holes if need be. Inject resin through one of the holes leaving the other as a vent, using a syringe, oil can or cake icer (polystyrene ware is dissolved). Press the deck down to work out air and apply weights. This job requires a first-class adhesive so use epoxy not polyester which is a poor glue.

Instead of holes only in the hollows located, they can be drilled all over on a pattern regardless of delamination. This assumes a bad bond which, if the deck is new, is probably right. Then if, or more likely when, further delamination develops in apparently sound areas it can not spread far before it is held at a bonded patch.

This repair is unlikely to be fully effective and can never be as good as a sandwich properly bonded in the first place. If water has seeped in it will already be too late. At best it is a makeshift, at worst a waste of effort. On a new deck delamination promises trouble for the life of the boat. If it is serious my advice is to sue if you can, sell if you cannot.

CHAPTER SEVEN

Deck Fittings

TOE-RAIL, CAPPING AND BULWARKS A moulded toe-rail, as in Fig. 6.7C, is a neat method and often used, but note the remarks in Chapter Four about chafe and wear. The top of a moulded toe-rail really does need the protection of a wooden capping or rail, or a metal strip. A chrome plated brass strip looks smart, even if not to everyone's taste, and will certainly look neater than the bare, scratched moulding, but the moulding should be designed for this and have a flat moulded along the top (Fig. 6.7E). It will be much harder to fit a strip to a round-topped moulding as an afterthought, when experience proves it necessary.

Similarly a turned-up flange, Fig. 6.6A, should not be left unprotected. Apart from wear and damage, this will rely on any sealing between the two mouldings to keep out water. A capping will shed the water and reduce the chance of leaks.

Figs. 6.5 to 6.8 show various arrangements of toe-rail and capping, as well as deck-joints.

My own preference is for a toe-rail or trim of wood because it is easy to keep smart; it can be touched up easily or replaced if worn or damaged. If maintenance of any kind is taboo then it should be capped with metal, but it should certainly not be left bare.

An outward turning or overhanging flange (Fig. 6.5F) is very easily damaged, and the damage is likely to be serious, as the cracks or torn area will probably extend well across the hull and deck; the flange is unlikely to break off cleanly but will take part of the deck and hull with it. Apart from the trouble of repair there will be the nuisance and damage of a leak. An outward turning flange will hang up on every obstruction and is very difficult to protect with a fender, either fixed or temporary. It seems to be more common on motor cruisers and is often associated with flaring bows.

It does not even need clumsy handling to damage this type of flange; the mild wash of a passing boat when moored is quite sufficient to drop that edge on to a pier—and leave it there.

All toe-rails, capping, etc., must be well bedded down. The fastenings will usually be through-fastenings, and no leak is so annoying and uncomfortable as an occasional drip from above.

There is nothing like stout bulwarks for giving a feeling of security, but they are features more appropriate to big ships than to the modern pocket cruiser where the demand for 6-foot headroom regardless gives a freeboard already high enough to discourage a nervous diver; the addition of bulwarks on top of this would make it look like a prestige office block. However they are still popular among real working seamen and fishermen who believe in keeping the sea where it belongs.

Bulwarks must be strong, otherwise the sense of security will be false and dangerous. The usual practice in wooden construction is to carry a proportion of the frames right up

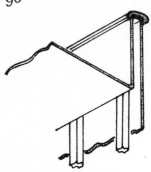

7.1: *Bulwarks. A completely watertight join is obtained if the deck is carried up to the rail on the inside of the frames. The join to the hull skin at the top should be one of the recommended deck–hull joints.*

to the rail. A good method for a moulded boat is to carry the deck up to the rail also (Fig. 7.1), so that the hull and deck form a leakproof sandwich structure with the frames between. This avoids the need for careful fitting around the frames, and potential leaks.

SCUPPERS An eminent designer once told a junior draughtsman, "Throw a bucket of water on your drawing and see what happens." Figuratively speaking this is good advice, because scuppers must be thought out on the drawing-board. Water, cascades of water, will get on to the deck, and it must get away easily, rapidly and with the least discomfort to the crew. This is more important on a sailing yacht than on a motor yacht, but even a motor yacht can take it green over the bows, and working boats like fishing-boats need large unchokable scuppers. Even on river boats and fine weather craft this point must not be overlooked; a moderate summer thunder shower can soon drive home the uncomfortable point that the cabin doorway is lower than the rail. The same applies to cockpits.

Rails should not be continuously solid. It is easy enough to make gaps in a wooden rail, either complete gaps or cut-out slots along the bottom (Fig. 7.2). Easy enough also to provide gaps in a moulded toe-rail—on the drawing-board—but difficult to incorporate them after the mould has been made if experience proves them necessary.

Making scuppers in a turned-up flange would seem quite simple—just a matter of cutting slots in the flange; but it is very important to ensure that they are watertight, and that cutting the slot does not expose the inside of the boat or leave a weak point which may break through later (Fig. 7.2D). Even with a moulded angle underneath there is the risk of water seeping into a long joint to appear through a flaw at the other end of the boat; this sort of leak is easy enough to cure but may take months to trace.

With this deck-join I favour scuppers in the form of a series of small tubular slot sub-mouldings which can be pushed into the cut-out slots and sealed in. They are easily made on wooden plugs or cardboard tubes. A more complicated method for production boats would be to mould them as part of the deck moulding, mating with slots in the hull (Fig. 7.2E). These methods will ensure at least that there are no weak spots and should eliminate potential leaks. Alternatively the scuppers can be sealed by moulding all round the cut-out slots, but this will not be so neat and is not easy to do reliably on a long narrow slot. The sealing must cover the top of the slot as well as the bottom because water can cascade along the deck to quite a depth (even from the humble bucket), and with sufficient force to travel upwards under a fair pressure to hunt out weaknesses.

A moulded deck can have moulded depressions in way of the scuppers. These will collect the water and allow larger scuppers which are less easily choked. As these depres-

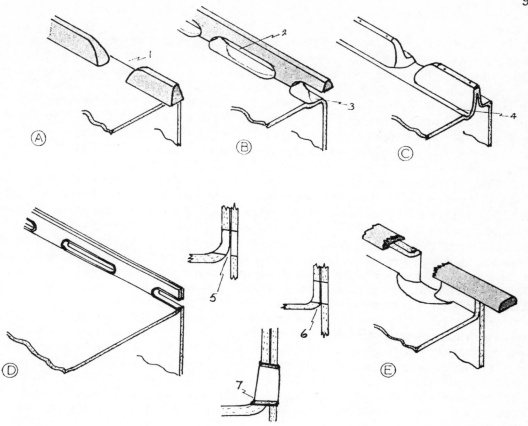

7.2: *Scuppers.*

A. *Simple wooden toe-rail, cut away in places,* 1.

B. *Wooden toe-rail, slotted for scuppers,* 2. *Moulded depressions in the deck,* 3, *collect the water and double the effective area of the scuppers. In some cases the depressions alone under the toe-rail would be sufficient.*

C. *Gap in moulded toe-rail. Note also the moulded "gutter,"* 4.

D. *Slot scuppers in an upward flange joint. If cut carelessly they will expose the inside,* 5; *even if not immediately exposed they can leave a weak point,* 6, *where the moulding is dangerously thin. A well bedded sub-moulding,* 7, *will avoid this trouble.*

E. *Scupper moulded into deck section of upturned flange joint and fitting into slots cut or moulded in the hull. The wooden capping (cut away for clarity) would extend across the opening.*

sions can also form the actual scuppers by passing completely under a separate rail, this method can eliminate the labour of cutting the rail to form the scuppers at deck level. There is a lot to be said, too, for a moulded "gutter" all along the edge of the deck.

All scuppers must be of adequate size to free the water quickly and pass the muck which will choke a simple pipe. The amount of this muck can be surprising, shore grit (often wind-blown off a quay or bank), fluff, the odd rope's end, to say nothing of ice-cream papers and cigarette ends dropped by spectators on the quayside. (This is one of the few cases where a Boat Show is a fair test for real conditions, and is severe under a balcony.)

A common and simple method with an upturned flange is to use drains through the deck discharging via pipes below through holes in the side or into the self-draining cockpit. These drains must be large, unchokeable, unable to leak and in the right places. Hoses below, usually plastic, must be well protected against physical damage. Often they are in the quarter berths and very easily kicked (it is difficult enough to wriggle into the average quarter berth without worrying about hazarding the boat as well). A good way is to embed them. Pipework must be very sound. A drip will be a severe nuisance, especially over a bunk. Fracture or disconnection will cause great discomfort, damage to equipment and belongings below, demoralisation and will endanger the boat.

The deck fittings are often sink drains with easily clogged gratings. They will clog less if the grating is cut away but may block lower down where they are more difficult to clear. Pipes should be straight and easily cleared at sea. Bath-size drains rather than small sink drains should be used, with large-bore pipes below. The deck fittings must be recessed into the deck otherwise they will stand proud and not drain properly. This implies that they are essentially part of the design and not an afterthought. Commonly drains are too far aft and in the wrong place when the boat is ashore and more down by the bows. Puddles then lie on the deck all winter and will be harmful in the long term. Internal drains can be damaged by ice.

All openings in the hull must have seacocks. Drains may open well above the water-line but will be under water when sailing. Draining to the cockpit reduces the number of hull openings but will make the cockpit wetter. Alternatively drains can be shared.

Any opening below can let water in even though intended to let it out. What use is a sound hull if kept afloat only by pieces of polythene pipe secured by clips which are loose, rusty, or even not there. I was brought up on the idea that the fewer hull openings the better, for any one can sink the boat. More boats sink through defective plumbing than through shipwreck or storm.

Many boats collect puddles of water on the lee cockpit seats when well heeled and the spray is flying. Cockpit seats need little drains of their own: no one likes sitting in a puddle. Often the water drains away into lockers, but wet lockers are a nuisance and the water must still go somewhere. Generally it will make its way below where, if the boat has a shallow bilge, there may be no place for it and it becomes an even greater discomfort.

Boats are only still and dry in the Boat Show; unfortunately it is often there, away from their natural element, that they get sold.

WINCH The anchor winch carries a heavier load than any other part of the boat with the exception of the mast-step on a sailing boat.

The method of attachment needs a large factor of safety. It is not just the steady pull of getting up the anchor. There are the overloads of strong hands on a fouled anchor (I once nearly put the bows under by trying to lift a very heavy mooring which I had hooked), and if the winch is used as a mooring cleat, as it often is, it must take the severe shock loads of snubbing in a gale. A hydraulic winch needs very strong reinforcement below.

Obviously it is not a thing to be lightly screwed through an unstiffened deck. It must be firmly bolted through a large block, widely spread to embrace at least two deck-beams.

However, this still leaves the strain carried mainly by the deck and it is a sound plan to put in extra deck-beams and a king plank.

ANCHOR CHOCKS The anchor must have chocks, both to protect the deck and to hold it in position. Eyes must be provided, too, for lashing it down. Without chocks an anchor will slide around and leave nasty scratches on the deck, and it is heavy enough to do damage if anything gets in its way. Even vibration will cause marks, and the anchor will still move enough to cause scratches if lashed down but without chocks.

Shaped wood chocks or well-fitting metal ones will hold the anchor firmly in position and can be secured quite lightly. However the lashing eyes should be well fastened. There will be little strain on them under normal conditions, even when quite rough, but ropes have a habit of catching on an anchor and can rip out anything light. This applies to motor-cruisers as well as sailing boats because a mooring rope can foul an anchor just as effectively as a sheet.

Chocks could be moulded in, but this is not recommended. Choice of anchor is definitely a matter of the owner's personal preference and moulded-in chocks would restrict the boat to that type and size of anchor. Some boats have anchor lockers moulded flush in the foredeck, which stow it neatly out of the way. Again they should be versatile.

SHEET WINCHES The main consideration with a sheet winch is usually to fit it in the best position for quick, convenient working with a clear lead for the sheets. It must be well secured, of course, and bolted into a stout block or metal brackets, which are also well secured. A large pad or extra deck beams should be fitted. Often the winch is mounted on a bulge in the moulded coaming, which needs to be stiffened not only under the winch but at the sides and deck angle too.

The main load is normally in one direction, but sheet winches are sometimes abused and used for mooring, or getting off the mud with the pull in quite a different direction.

A large mounting block on the deck may act as a breakwater when water is cascading along the lee deck. A badly shaped or positioned block will splash water into the cockpit or into the face of the unfortunate crew member detailed off to work the winch. The skeleton type of bracket is drier.

CLEATS There are two important considerations about cleats.

a. The cleat must be in a convenient position for making fast and to give a clear lead to the rope.
b. The cleat must be firmly fastened down.

A battery of cleats around the cockpit or the mast must not interfere one with another, yet each must be readily accessible, and the rope must lead clear from the cleat to the sail, block or fairlead. This may require a clear lead over an arc, as unless the lead is to a fixed fairlead the direction will vary.

It is better to have too many cleats than too few. Ropes may catch and foul on them, yet somehow there always seem to be more ropes than cleats to fasten them to. Moreover designers and builders seldom take into account the odd things like a tiller lashing or mackerel line, which I find often occupy an important sheet cleat. I suppose they disapprove of people like me who lash the tiller and fish (or snooze) instead of sailing in deadly earnest.

Fig. 1.10 (page 26) shows the nasty thing that happens to cleats that are not put on properly. It must be the rule that no matter what strain comes on a cleat, fair or unfair, it is the cleat or its fastenings which fails, *never under any circumstances, the boat.*

Obviously this needs proper design and forethought, but it can be taken as a general rule that no cleat may be attached to a moulding unless that moulding is strengthened first in the vicinity of the cleat. Extra thickness or a block underneath is the minimum requirement. Sometimes it can be combined with stiffening members. Obviously the larger the cleat the greater the strengthening needed by the moulding.

A cleat may be put on with the intention that it should carry only a light load; but as long as it is there it is possible to be misused in moments of stress or plain ignorance.

A typical example of this was a motor-cruiser with a series of cleats around the rail for hitching on fenders (commendable forethought—most builders seem to assume that every owner of such a boat has a bevy of bikini-clad models to dash hither and thither with fenders as needed). A light line and quite a small cleat are all that is needed to hold up a small yacht fender—until it catches under a jetty on a rising tide. After the owner had lost a couple of fenders in this way he did the obvious thing: he replaced the thin string on the yacht's fenders with a length of stout terylene rope. Next time they caught under the jetty there were two ragged holes in the deck where two little cleats had been.

This would not have happened if the deck had been thickened under those cleats but to the builder they were just two silly little fender-cleats, lightly loaded, no need to worry, bolt them straight on.

If the moulding fails, it is sheer bad design and absolutely inexcusable. As long as the cleat is there it can be used. It does not matter whether it is used for the right purpose or the wrong; the cleat *must* fail before the moulding. A cleat is cheap enough to replace; it is very much more expensive to patch up the moulding, and meanwhile a hole may endanger the boat, or at least cause damage and much discomfort below.

SHEET FAIRLEADS The same considerations apply to a sheet fairlead as to a cleat. It must give a clear lead to the sheet and the moulding must be strengthened in its vicinity so that if anything fails it is the fairlead or its fastenings which goes overboard —*never* part of the deck.

Fairleads are unlikely to get the abuse which a cleat can suffer, but nevertheless the strains can be a lot more than predicted. In particular a flogging sail can whip off a fairlead which it could never pull off by a steady pull. The pull on a fairlead is usually upwards. It must therefore be through-bolted, not secured by wood-screws into a block.

The common methods of strengthening a moulding under a sheet fairlead are increased thickness and using a wooden block, embedded or open (Fig. 1.10, page 26), and positioning the fairlead over a stiffening member. These are all covered in Chapter One. Chain and mooring fairleads are covered in Chapter Twelve.

STANCHIONS No yacht stanchions can be expected to withstand the strains liable to be imposed on them. If a jetty is fouled or a heavy man makes a determined—or desperate—grab, it will bend them at least. The best stanchions are now made of rod or tubing which will bend, not break off, when most needed, and can be bent back again (a yard job rather than an on-the-spot repair). Another alternative is to use galvanised piping, which is cheap enough to replace, and which also bends, although sometimes too easily.

On a very small cruiser, stanchions and lifelines must be considered to give limited protection only, more for moral support or steadying purposes than as a stout impenetrable fence. But they should certainly not be despised in this rôle. I fitted simple stanchions and lifelines on my five-tonner years before they became fashionable, and in fact they were considered definitely odd and a bit cissy. Nevertheless they gave good service and such a tremendous sense of security that when I went on board very much larger boats which did not have them, I felt positively unsafe and instinctively crouched for some support. Such was the value of a single wire barely fifteen inches high; it made all the difference between being "on" a boat and "in" one, which counts for a lot when out of sight of land—and that little boat was more often well out of sight of land than my laughing friends' boats were outside the river.

The weak point of every stanchion is the foot and the attachment to the boat. It takes a considerable strain to bend a good stanchion—yet it *must* bend and not pull out or damage the moulding.

The problem is easy enough on a boat with bulwarks, because the bulwarks will give good support; usually, however, the stanchion must be bolted to the deck with no other support.

The stanchion must therefore have a good strong foot, as wide as space will allow, and it must be firmly bolted. Screws will pull out; it *must* be bolted. A foot with a turndown flange, as in Fig. 7.3B bolted through the side is better supported against an inward grab.

The greatest strain on a stanchion is usually inwards, because a man will more often grab at the weather rail than fall against the lee one, and as the stanchion will normally be placed as far outboard as possible the outside bolts have little leverage for holding the stanchion against an inwards pull. A man walking along a heeling deck will usually find it easier to walk along the weather or drier side of the deck, where the lifeline is in a convenient position to hang on to, and the cabin side gives a secure foothold, than along the wet lee side where the lifeline will be far downhill, and, unless there are good bulwarks, there is little except water to walk on.

If suitable standard fittings can be obtained, they are usually most economical, particularly if they are considered at an early stage and the boat is designed to fit the sockets. If they have to be made up specially it may well be easier and more economical to mould them, in particular to mould them in position, rather than to fabricate them in metal. It will be safer to bolt on any moulded sockets rather than rely on pure bonding unless they are formed as part of the main moulding as in Fig. 7.4B and 7.4C.

Stanchions should be readily removable and therefore it is much better to use stanchions fitting into sockets rather than bolting them down direct. They should be a secure but sliding fit and be retained by pins, not rust.

Stanchions are commonly removed when the boat is laid up, but in addition they may have to be removed often during the season. Forward or midships stanchions are removed frequently to launch or stow a dinghy (unless the crew is invariably so strong that it can be manhandled over the top). Others may need to be taken out to avoid damage when the boat is lying alongside a wall or pier, or even to avoid fouling a sail or rope. This is likely to need doing smartly and that means without a spanner or heavy hammer.

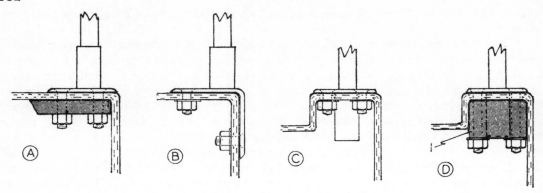

7.3: *Stanchion Mounting (i) Bolting to the deck.*

A. *Common type. Socket is bolted through the deck and a plate or block underneath.*

B. *Stronger type. Flange is turned over and bolted through the side.*

C. *Socket mounted on top of moulded toe-rail with the socket projecting through the deck. A rather weak method.*

D. *A better version of* C. *The through-deck projection of the socket is mounted in a block of wood, resin-glass putty, syntactic foam or solid moulding. In this way the socket is firmly embedded and the bolts are of less importance.*

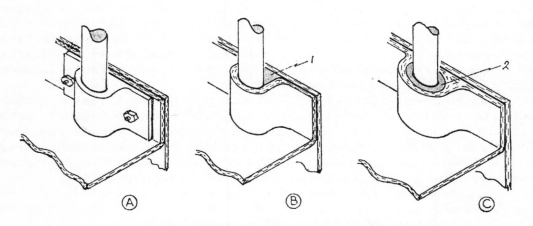

7.4: *Stanchion Mounting (ii) Fitting to upturned deck flange.*

A. *Standard side-mounting socket bolted to flange.*

B. *Socket moulded in the deck flange. This may leave a large gap, 1, which it is difficult to seal.*

C. *Improved method of moulding the socket in the deck flange. A short length of tube, 2, is moulded in to form the socket. Note now the face of the flange is continuous and can be properly sealed.*

The socket in both B *and* C *must be blind or sealed off to prevent leaks.*

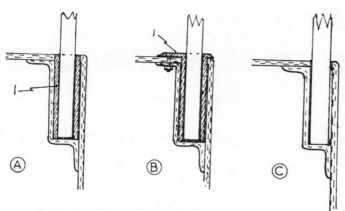

7.5: *Stanchion Mounting (iii) Embedded socket below the deck.*
A. *Metal or Tufnol tube embedded against the side of the hull.*
B. *An improved version. The flange, 1, is bolted and bedded down, makes a more watertight joint with the deck.*
C. *Socket moulded directly around the end of the stanchion projecting through the deck. Stanchion must be treated for release and also given a suitable clearance for ready removal by wrapping with thin polythene, wax, or filing down after moulding the socket.*

Stanchion sockets need to be bedded down well. The large leverage will make them work, and they are sure to leak unless a permanently flexible bedding compound is used. This is another reason for using sockets, as otherwise the stanchion would have to be bedded down every time it was taken off, just one more item of maintenance on what is supposed to be a maintenance-free boat. All sockets which pass through the deck must be blind, i.e. the ends must be sealed, otherwise there will be leaks below. The remarks about through-deck chain-plates in Chapter Eight apply largely to stanchion sockets also.

Obviously the boat must be amply strong where the stanchions are attached. It is another typical case where the fitting must bend or break, but never the boat. The hull must be well thickened, and the stanchion bolted through a block or plate underneath, or better, through a deck beam or the hull-deck angle fillet.

Another method of mounting stanchions is to embed a length of larger pipe against the inside of the hull to form a socket below the deck, with the stanchion fitting through a hole in the deck (Fig. 7.5). This will give a long and very firm mounting. The hull will need to be strengthened, but the extra material for embedding the tube will do much of this in itself. The bottom of the socket must be sealed, and, as embedding it will involve moulding over a hollow space, the bottom should be plugged first with wood, putty or paper. A flaw or pinhole here will produce a very annoying little leak. The chance of any leaks from around the head of the socket can be reduced by fitting a flange at the top and bedding this down. Ordinary plumbing fittings could be used for an economy job but as the tube will not be replaceable, care is needed to avoid corrosion. Under normal conditions it will be full of water, unless there is a simple outboard drain-hole.

A further extension of this idea is to mould the complete socket (Fig. 7.5c). This is quite easily done by placing the stanchion in position through the hole in the deck, and moulding all around the part projecting through the underside of the deck. Obviously the stanchion must be treated with release agent. A piece of polythene around it would not only ensure release but also enough clearance for ready removal. The socket should be given a generous thickness to allow for some wear, the stanchion itself can corrode because the socket will still be full of water for most of the time. However it is now only the removable stanchion which can corrode, and this is replaceable. A better-class yacht would, of course, have non-corroding stanchions of stainless steel or aluminium.

SAMSON POST A samson post must be fitted through a large block under the deck. This block should extend as far as the deck-beams on each side.

A samson post is not there for decoration; it is there to be pulled around, and that pull must be spread over the boat. If the deck is not strong enough to withstand the pull the samson post will soon carve it up. It is important, therefore, that the strain is spread over a large area and ties in with deck-beams and framing.

The heel, too, must be firmly secured. It should fit into a socket in an embedded wooden block, or a metal step, moulded on to the keelson. On a small boat it would be sufficient to make a socket by moulding an angle fillet around the foot of the samson post, while it is held in position.

To prevent leaks where the post passes through the deck it needs a wooden moulding fitted closely around it and well bedded down; alternatively an angle flange could be moulded around the post and bolted and bedded down. If the position is standard, e.g. on a production boat, it would pass through a raised panel formed in the deck, to act as a natural watershed, and even if not standard it is advisable to form a flange as for hatches on pages 129–31.

The usual place for a samson post is on the foredeck to take the mooring, but smaller posts are often fitted aft at the quarters for stern ropes and sometimes for fishing gear. These can be secured to the shelf by moulded straps. If there is no shelf, the angle between the gunwale and deck, or, in an open boat, the gunwale itself, should be well thickened for strength.

VENTILATORS Ventilation is often a neglected feature, particularly in the lower price range, and is something which the owner or yard may well want to fit later. Ventilators carry little load and could be fastened by bolting straight through the moulding. However this is not good practice. A large opening will weaken the moulding in its vicinity and therefore it should be thickened to compensate. A low, flush-mounting ventilator will be subject to little strain, but an upstanding cowl or mushroom type may foul ropes and be subjected to grossly unfair treatment. This type of ventilator therefore should have a fairly generous block underneath it to spread a foul load and prevent the deck being damaged (Fig. 7.6).

I make no apology for describing the "Dorade" type of waterproof ventilator, as this is the sort of thing which can be moulded quite easily. The principle, which is very much older than the famous ocean-racer which it is now named after, is to allow both water and air to enter the cowl together, but to arrange baffles in a box beneath so that only air finds its way below past the baffles, and the water goes out through drains (Fig. 7.7). There have been a number of interesting variations of this, using inaccessible and wasted corners of the boat as the box.

The inlet into the cabin should always be fitted with a shut-off plate or bung because

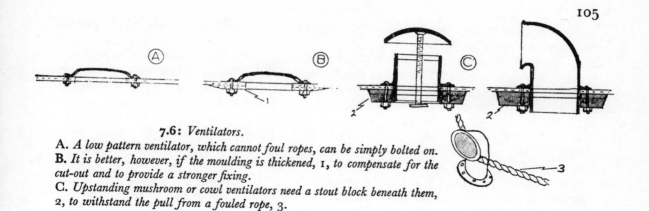

7.6: *Ventilators.*

A. *A low pattern ventilator, which cannot foul ropes, can be simply bolted on.*
B. *It is better, however, if the moulding is thickened, 1, to compensate for the cut-out and to provide a stronger fixing.*
C. *Upstanding mushroom or cowl ventilators need a stout block beneath them, 2, to withstand the pull from a fouled rope, 3.*

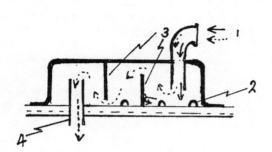

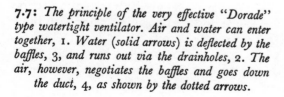

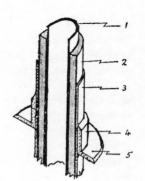

7.7: *The principle of the very effective "Dorade" type watertight ventilator. Air and water can enter together, 1. Water (solid arrows) is deflected by the baffles, 3, and runs out via the drainholes, 2. The air, however, negotiates the baffles and goes down the duct, 4, as shown by the dotted arrows.*

7.8: *Stove-pipe.*
Moderate heat stove-pipe. *A thin metal pipe, 1, is covered with asbestos, 2, and bound with a layer of glass cloth or rovings, 3. This outer layer can be thin for protection only, or thicker and structural. Attachments can be made without using fastenings in contact with the hot pipe, by moulding a thicker ring round the pipe, 4. This can also be formed into a flange, 5, for direct fixing.*

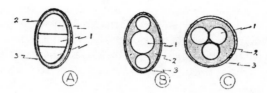

7.9: *Combination mast–exhaust-pipe, etc.*

A. *Cross-section of the mast described on page 107. Ducts, 1, asbestos lagging, 2, moulded skin, 3. A complicated and expensive design.*
B. *Simpler design using standard pipes.*
C. *Ditto with circular section.*

there is a limit to the ventilator's water filtering capacity. When completely submerged it will let in water.

Any space containing a fuel tank needs a separate ventilator. Ventilation is important to prevent rot. Below there is often as much woodwork as inside a wooden boat, and some builders use inferior woodwork where not seen. GRP will not alter the general damp air and mugginess, mildew is common, and there are still cooking and other smells.

STOVE-PIPES, FUNNELS, EXHAUST PIPES, ETC. Stove-pipes, galley chimneys and hot exhaust pipes must not go through a deck or moulding without adequate space around them. If it needs to be watertight this opening must be sealed with a plate or filling which is a poor heat conductor. A deck fitting will usually have a spaced upstanding flange to deflect water and this can well be moulded either as part of the deck or as a sub-moulding.

Hot pipes also should not touch or run close to the moulding. It would be considered very bad practice on a wooden boat, but whereas wood will char and scorch before it burns (and is usually overthick so that it can afford to lose quite a lot), polyester resin will also soften. Structural failure can occur due to softening of a highly stressed part by excessive heat long before the boat is actually on fire.

Fortunately the resin will give ample warning by its smell long before there is any serious danger of fire, but the softening and smelling points are likely to start at the same order of temperature. Softening will not be of serious importance unless the part is highly stressed. It does not melt and lose all its strength suddenly like polythene. It softens gradually and it will still retain a large proportion of its strength, probably about 50 per cent, until it actually catches fire and burns away. It is not possible to give any figure for the softening temperature; it varies widely between different grades of polyester resin from about 120° to 400° F. (50° to 200° C.). The lowest resins are unsuitable. Yet good marine resins are little above the low end of this range and weakness increases with time. Use higher heat resistant resins where heat may be critical.

Fig. 7.8 shows one method of dealing with pipes and chimneys above and below decks. A thin metal or asbestos cement pipe is covered with asbestos and then bound with glass cloth or rovings. As the asbestos will be soft and absorbent it will be necessary to put on a very thin layer of glass cloth, say a single turn, pre-impregnated on a nearby surface, and allow this to set to act as a firm, non-absorbent backing for the subsequent layers.

The outer skin can be thin and act as protection only or it can be thicker and structural. The inner tube could be a very light metal tube, or a flexible tube, relying entirely on the moulded outer skin for all support. Note that fastenings through the asbestos are undesirable—because they will act as heat paths and possibly cause damage to the outer skin. Even loosening will allow water to penetrate with deleterious secondary effects and reduced insulation. It is more satisfactory to thicken the outer skin, preferably in the form of a ring, so that it is strong enough to carry attachments. The most important case is probably where guys have to be fitted. It is quite easy also to form a flange on the outer skin for direct fastening to the deck.

Using a flexible inner tube it is easy to make up rigid insulated pipes in any shape. This could be a considerable time-saver compared with the extensive jointing and fabrication necessary with conventional pipework.

Care will be needed at the end of the pipe, or where the insulation ends, to prevent the moulded outer skin coming into contact with the hot pipe. However, this will usually be at the cold end, which simplifies the problem. It may be possible to arrange an air-gap, or a collar of weatherproof non-conducting material.

Fig. 7.9A shows an interesting example. This is the mast of a luxury motor-cruiser which serves also as the exhaust pipe (twin 200 h.p. diesels), galley and hot-water system chimney, and engine-room ventilator. All these services run as three separate and elaborate ducts up the inside of the metal mast. The metal mast was covered with asbestos lagging and protected by a fibreglass skin moulded over the outside. The most heat-resisting resin available was used, not so much because of the working temperatures, which were fairly low, but for emergencies in case anything went wrong with the sophisticated heat-exchangers below (as in fact happened on trials!).

Unfortunately, as too often happens, I was called in at a late stage in this project when the metal mast had already been made and the builders were scratching their heads, wondering how to insulate it. It would be a lot cheaper to make, and I think more satisfactory, if it was made as three separate tubes of standard section (and therefore inexpensive) embedded in asbestos lagging with a structurally thick moulded mast laid up over the bundle, or even moulded separately in two halves (Fig. 7.9). In this case cost was of little object, but this nowadays is rare. To save costs it is vital that the specialist is called in at an early stage, preferably while the boat is still on the drawing-board and certainly before she is half built.

CHAPTER EIGHT

Shroud-plates and Rigging

THE rigging will be much the same on a fibreglass boat as on any other light-displacement boat. And, if the maintenance on the rigging is also to be low, it should be of stainless steel for standing rigging, and synthetic rope, Terylene (Dacron), nylon or whatever else science produces for running rigging. Galvanised steel and natural fibres will require more frequent renewal and are seldom used now even on the cheapest boats.

Our major concern here is the method of attaching the rigging to the moulded hull. This really does need sensible design and suitable precautions to spread the load. Rigging forms a large and concentrated local load, the type of load which the moulded hull is least suited to bear. It is essential to spread this over a wide area.

This can be illustrated by considering a telegraph pole and a tree. A telegraph pole is held up by sticking it into a hole; a tree is supported by a mass of roots stretching out all round it and tapering away. The telegraph pole will stand as long as the ground is firm and thick and as long as it carries little load. When a top load is applied (represented by a change in direction of the wires) it must have a stay or it will be pulled over. But the tree carries a large top and withstands fierce storms, even when growing in soft ground, held up by its widespread root system. The traditional shroud-plate on a wooden boat is like the telegraph pole; it produces a concentrated loading and only works when the "ground", the boat, is firm and thick. An attachment to a moulded boat needs to be like the tree-roots with the loading well spread out and tapering away.

The usual rule of thumb is that the main rigging must be strong enough to support the weight of the boat. This is pointless unless the other links, the shroud-plates and the attachment to the hull, can carry this load too. Failure of the boat will mean a fairly expensive remoulding job and probably widespread damage.

A safer rule is to ensure that the hull in way of any rigging attachment will withstand a strain greater than the breaking strain of any wire attached to it. It should be substantially greater, because it is a lot easier to replace the wire than to thicken up the hull, and the wire might be replaced with a larger size or by stronger stainless steel in place of ordinary galvanised steel. Too often the size of the wire is increased—perhaps of necessity —without a thought for the attachment to the boat. Indeed the person who fits or orders the wire may, quite understandably and justifiably, be incompetent to judge whether any strengthening is needed. It is as well to allow a generous margin of safety here and allow for a wire of, say, two or three times larger size. It is easy enough to do this during the fitting out and the extra cost will be very small.

The rigging should not be tightened and set up permanently too soon after moulding.

GRP does not always fail predictably or suddenly at a given stress level. It is progressively weakened by overstrain at stress levels only 20 per cent of the theoretical limit. Strength is also reduced severely by fatigue at even lower levels and at cycle times representing a few years' normal sailing. High local stress concentrations at shroud plates are just the conditions for this. The strength may appear adequate initially, but unless there is a large margin, only achieved through good stress distribution, the GRP may fail unexpectedly later. The steady strain of the rigging may also cause distortion through creep, sometimes enough to disqualify under strict class rules, and most likely on a light or newly moulded boat. Rigging should not be left set up tight for at least three months after moulding.

SHROUD-PLATES The conventional shroud-plate with a long straight tang, as is usually used on a wooden boat, bolted through the topsides, should never be bolted through the topsides of a moulded boat without extensive precautions to spread the load (Fig. 8.1). Bolting straight through the moulded skin imposes much too severe a local strain on the moulding and, because of different coefficients of elasticity, E, the strain is likely to come on just one screw.

A long straight tang is not a good shape, and unfortunately it is the only type stocked by most chandlers—doubly unfortunate because the shape is not even ideal for wooden boats. This means that specially made shroud-plates may be needed. However, they are not difficult to make and if you use your ingenuity you can devise very simple ones. It is vastly preferable to make special shroud-plates rather than to use unsuitable ones just because they are readily available.

Plate-shaped shroud-plates (Fig. 8.2) will distribute the stresses over a wider area, and one large plate will serve two or more shrouds better than separate plates. To reduce weight it can be made as a skeleton fabrication, either from welded strip or by cutting away large holes in the plate.

Stainless steel is commonly used. GRP is not suitable, even when the shape is too difficult for simple metalwork, because of weakening from fatigue, overstrain and crushing under high bearing pressure.

It is common to embed blocks of wood or metal fabrications to which the shroud-plates can be bolted either inside or outside. These inserts distribute the load properly and eliminate the high bearing pressure of bolts alone. Pads may also be necessary to space the tangs inboard to clear a toe rail.

The hull should be thickened in way of the shroud-plates because this is a high stress area. Lloyds' Rules call for a general thickening of the topsides here for a length equal to the yacht's beam, and certainly the thickening should extend well beyond the immediate area of the shroud-plates, like the roots of a tree.

If attachment is to the cabin top this too must be thickened and strengthened with frames or bulkheads to transmit the load to the hull, especially as the path is usually a dog-leg. Stress cracks in this area show that the need is commonly underrated. Cabin tops are always weakened by windows, which are often very large, and are usually lighter mouldings anyway. Where possible, fasten through to a bulkhead.

A sound method is to use eye or U bolts through the deck with a plate underneath so that the strain is transferred to the moulding by the upwards pull of the plate under the deck, not by fastenings through the hull. This gives lower bearing pressure and better stress distribution (Fig. 8.4) and is applying GRP theory correctly.

Moreover, with a "U" bolted through the deck the bolts are purely in tension and the moulding in the vicinity is in moderate compression, both conditions they are well suited for. A side-mounted plate inevitably exerts a shearing or bending strain on the

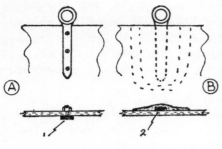

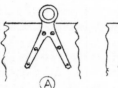

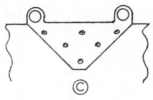

8.1: Shroud-plates—bad design.

A. **Wrong:** *Shroud-plate bolted straight through hull without any thickening or stress distribution. This will probably pull through the hull or pull part of the hull away.*

B. **Not Recommended:** *Shroud-plate embedded. Although the strain is well distributed it will be impossible to replace the shroud-plate if it gets damaged.*

8.2: Shroud-plates. Stress Distributing Shapes.

A, B. *These spread the stress over a wider area than the simple tang.*
A *is neater and lighter, but* B *is simpler to make.*
C. *Two attachment points combined into one large plate.*
D. *A similar type but made as a skeleton to save weight.*

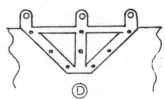

8.3: Shroud-plates. Bolting to thickened hull.

Hull is well thickened, 2, *and attachment made by a metal plate,* 1.

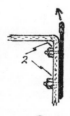

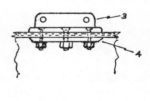

8.4: Shroud-plates.

A. *The ideal case; an eye-bolt fastened through the deck with a plate underneath,* 1, *so that the upwards pull is distributed by the plate.*

B. *The usual case; all the upwards pull is taken by the fastening bolts,* 2. *The bearing area is small and therefore the pressure is much higher, and the bolts can bend or "work" in the holes.*

C. *A practical case; a stout metal angle,* 3, *bolted through a metal plate,* 4, *underneath the deck. The direction of pull is not ideal, but the assembly is easily and cheaply fabricated, the attachment point is well outboard and the pull is taken and distributed by the plate underneath.*

N.B.—*For simplicity, hull or deck thickening has not been shown, but it is assumed that the hull and deck have been adequately thickened in each case. There is often a thick overlap in this vicinity which can be used.*

bolts, and a very much higher bearing pressure on the moulding. Bending of the bolts would crush the moulding and the bolts will then work loose, and also leak.

On a wooden boat it is obviously correct to attach the shroud-plates to the side because the deck is a separate piece and less able to resist the upwards pull than the topsides. But a moulded boat with the deck firmly joined to the hull by moulding so that it is virtually all in one piece is quite different. Moreover the thickening in way of the shroud-plates can extend well down the sides to give the same advantages as a shroud-plate on the side.

A "U" bolt through the deck will usually come at a very strong part of the boat where it is already well thickened by the matted-in angle fillet joining the deck to the hull, and the angular shape of the rail is inherently strong and stiff. There are obvious economic advantages in using extra thickness which is already there instead of adding more.

Eye-plates can be bolted down properly and make a much more watertight fitting than a tang passing through the deck.

For extra strength, and to allow better stress distribution, several shroud attachments can be combined into one fabricated plate with eyes. A cheap and simple method is to use a length of angle as in Fig. 8.4c. This also has the advantage of putting the eyes further outboard than can be done with "U"-bolts. The pull may not be quite in the right place, but the ease of installation and cheapness together with an adequate number of holding-down bolts (for which there is ample room) will compensate for this small disadvantage.

Fitting a tang through the deck and bolting it to the side, as is often done, has the worst points of both systems, i.e. it transfers the strain by bolts, not a pressure plate, and the tang through the deck will be difficult to keep watertight without regular maintenance.

A plate under the deck overcomes the problem of different coefficients of elasticity and the strain can be distributed over the moulding naturally and evenly.

Another method, preferable in cases where the deck is not moulded, and thus part of the hull, e.g. when a wooden deck is fitted, is to embed a large plate in the side of the hull to which a side shroud-plate can be bolted (Fig. 8.5). The large plate will spread the stress, yet still allow cheap, standard shroud-plates. The plate can be extensively perforated to reduce weight and also to allow the moulding to intermesh with the plate. A fabricated skeleton plate could also be used and would be lighter. This method gives the good stress distribution of the plate with the simple attachment of standard, bolted, side mounting shroud-plates. Note that the stress is distributed by the plate, not the bolts.

A small boat can use a wooden block, either embedded or open. A racing dinghy with an ultra-light, thin hull needs as much care in designing the chain plates as with the highly stressed rigging of a large racing yacht, but a small knockabout dinghy with a proportionately thicker, tougher hull and primitive rigging, needs little extra strengthening. On such a boat a simple wood block inside would be ample. However even this sort of boat should have something to distribute the stress.

There is a tendency to use tangs passing through the deck and bolted to the inside under the impression that external shroud-plates look unsightly. However, they have been accepted on wooden boats for generations, and many people prefer a traditional appearance. A moulded boat with outside shroud-plates might even be mistaken for a wooden one occasionally.

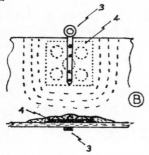

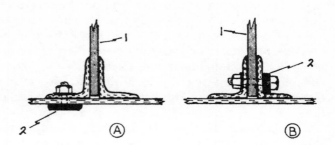

8.5: *Shroud-plates. Bolting to an embedded plate.*

An ordinary shroud-plate, 3, is bolted to an embedded plate, 4, of considerably larger area. Perforations reduce the weight of the plate and give intimate embedding.

8.6: *Fastening a shroud-plate to a bulkhead. There is often a bulkhead, 1, in way of the shroud-plates. It forms naturally firm stress-distributing attachment points for the shroud-plates, 2.*
A. Bolting an outside shroud-plate through the angle fillet of the bulkhead.
B. Bolting a through-deck shroud-plate to the bulkhead.

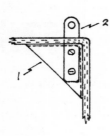

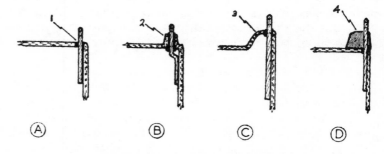

8.7: *Shroud-plate bolted to a web, 1, formed between the deck and the hull. A through deck chain plate is shown, 2, but it can also be used with an outside shroud-plate, if the web has a generous flange.*

8.8: *Shroud-plate passing through deck.*

A. **Not Recommended.** *Sealing at deck level, 1; any water lying or cascading along the deck will cover and possibly lodge in the seal. Consequently if there is the slightest leak here a lot of water will find its way below.*
B. *A moulded collar, 2, around the shroud-plate will keep the seal above the level of water lying on the deck and much of the water cascading along it. Only suitable where the position is known before moulding.*
C. *Passing the shroud-plate through a moulded toe-rail, 3, will also keep the seal clear of the deck.*
D. *With "dry" construction the shroud-plate can pass through a well bedded wooden toe-rail, 4.*

On anything larger than a dinghy there should be a bulkhead or frames in the vicinity of the chain-plates because something is needed to resist the inwards, squeezing pressure as well as the upwards pull. The current trend, too, is for a mast stepped on deck supported by a bulkhead underneath. These bulkheads form natural stress-distributing points for attaching the shroud-plates. The plates can be bolted either to the bulkhead itself, or to the outside of the hull and through the bulkhead flanges (Fig. 8.6).

Another method sometimes used is to form a triangular web between the deck and the hull and bolt to this (Fig. 8.7), which also distributes the stress effectively. The corners, however, must not form hard spots. On a big boat the web should be large, and preferably backed by an embedded plate on the hull.

When shroud-plates have to be bolted through the topsides, the stress can be distributed better by moulding in metal inserts or bushes where the bolts are to come. These can be positioned by pins through the mould; a groove or flange will give a better grip to the insert, which should also have a flat, if it is threaded, to lock it in position. A snag with this method is that although the inserts can be positioned exactly, many yacht fittings have the holes drilled at random by a junior boy. Consequently the fitting may have wide variations in the position of its fixing holes. A nylon insert which accepts a wood screw accommodates a wider tolerance than a metal one. An insert like this is a convenient way to spread the bearing pressure of the bolts which can be severe on a highly stressed fitting secured by a few bolts only, particularly when the moulding is thin.

Shroud-plates do get damaged. An embedded shroud-plate (Fig. 8.1B) will be impossible to repair without hacking away GRP. Consequently it must never be embedded in the main lay-up. A simple straight tang can work loose. Bonding to metal, especially stainless steel, is poor and will be broken by the different elasticities and thermal expansion. The tang must have a mechanical grip, e.g. lugs, or it will pull out.

Through-deck tangs are better left exposed below, and bolted to an embedded plate. Leaking seals are very common. Water will be trapped within the embedding of a shroud-plate, which is almost impossible to mould close and without pockets or seepage paths. Stagnant pockets of water will cause decay from within where the moulding is most vulnerable—and weakness cannot be tolerated here. The decay will be visible only when bad enough to have eaten right through. In fact many boats do show decay here. Also stainless steel will rust when air is excluded. Rust stains are often the first sign.

The most difficult problem is when fitting shroud-plates during "dry" fitting out. Thickening the moulding is then likely to be impracticable, so, if possible, arrangements should be made for the moulder to do it during moulding; but this must be planned at an early stage and certainly before moulding has finished. It is a help if the moulder can mark or paint the limits of the thickened area because it is not so easy as one might think to detect it afterwards.

If arrangements have not been made with the moulder the stress must be spread as well as can be arranged otherwise. A wide metal plate or possibly plywood inside, to which the shroud-plates could be bolted, would be reasonably satisfactory, particularly if the shroud-plates shown in Fig. 8.2 are used. The plate or plywood would be better if glued on or linked up with frames and bulkheads. Shroud-plates should be oversize or of generous section to reduce the stresses and extension under load. On a wooden boat shroud-plates are often bolted through frames, but on a moulded boat this must be done with caution. The material of the core should be investigated first because if this is light the frame might be crushed by the bolts. They would be suitable if it had a solid core of wood or other reasonably incompressible material. This could be arranged with the moulders beforehand. It would be possible to fill a hollow core with resin putty or syntactic foam.

Badly designed shroud-plates, and in particular shroud-plates bolted directly through an unthickened hull, are likely to tear out, together with sizeable chunks of the boat.

They will probably tear out, too, long before the mast and rigging are hard pressed. This is a clear case where the rigging or chain-plates may be allowed to fail, but never the boat; this requires special care and intelligent appreciation of the factors involved. Slavishly following what grandfather did will result in certain failure of a relatively expensive nature. In fairness, however, the best high-class boatbuilders of grandfather's day turned out beautiful light racing yachts and used some sound and advanced practices which would be equally suitable on modern moulded boats. There is nothing new in the principle of distributing the full sail rigging load over a lightly built hull (and grandfather sailed with an enormous gaff mainsail and jackyard topsail). On moulded boats, however, it must be done to a greater or less extent on every boat, whether a racing boat or not; that is the novelty, and that is why it is important to think before attaching shroud-plates in a traditional way.

SEALING THROUGH-DECK SHROUD-PLATES If shroud-plates do pass through the deck they should, if possible, pass through a raised step or tube (Fig. 8.8). This will ease the problem of sealing.

A shroud-plate seal at deck level will be covered by any water lying on the deck from rain or spray, and will be subject to a moderate pressure from water cascading along the deck or when sailing with the lee rail under. Consequently, if there is a small leak due to bad sealing, water will get below every time the deck gets wet, even from a slight shower or dew, and when the deck gets very wet, sailing hard, the amount of water which finds its way below is likely to be considerable.

Raising the point where the shroud-plate emerges from the deck and is sealed, by moulding a raised step or tube, keeps the seal above the level of rain water or spray on the deck and acts as a natural breakwater. It may still be underwater when the lee rail is well under, but this will be much less often. The raised step or tube also provides a longer and better sealing path.

Sometimes a moulded toe-rail can be used, or the raised flange of the hull-deck joint. With "dry" fitting out a well bedded toe-rail or block should be fitted.

The sealing material must be permanently elastic and non-ageing. Ordinary putty will give endless trouble and so too will moulding them in, because neither putty nor resin have enough flexibility. See Bedding Down, page 33. Shroud-plates through the deck require regular inspection and maintenance. Ideally the sealant should be an elastomer, e.g. polysulphide (Thiokol), silicone, polybutadiene or a neoprene sleeve.

The natural extension and inward pull on the shroud-plate when sailing hard (to say nothing of accidental bumps and kicks) will create enough movement to cause any rigid sealing material to break away. Fortunately the greatest strain is always on the weather rigging, the side which is not awash. The lee rigging is always slack, which means there is no movement of the shroud-plate and no strain on it during its wettest conditions. Nevertheless, unless the sealing material is truly elastic, water will soon find any weaknesses caused by strain and movement on the previous tack.

FORESTAY Forestays are simpler than shrouds, as they are attached to a naturally strong part of the boat. A well moulded pointed stem will need little special to stiffen it, and the attachment is usually to a good stem fitting with well spaced fastenings. The stem is often thickened anyway, being a main structural member, more than is necessary just for attaching a forestay.

Sometimes, however, the main forestay, or an inner one, comes up through the deck inboard of the stemhead. This is usually associated with a long overhanging bow, and the forestay must therefore pass through the deck and be attached part way down the stem, as the deck is unlikely to be strong enough to carry this by itself. Sometimes the forestay ends at a fitting on the deck and there is a separate wire or tie-bar from the underside of the deck fitting to the stem. This is a good method which overcomes any problems of sealing where the forestay passes through the deck.

There is a danger of delamination unless an attachment part way down the stem is through-bolted. However this is not likely on a sharp "V" shape if the point of attachment is well spread and embedded well down in the moulding.

BACKSTAYS Standing backstays can be treated like shrouds. They usually come to a point on the counter, or on the transom by way of a bumpkin (or boomkin), or to the quarters if they are split or double. The quarter attachment points can be very strong because of the inherently strong shape, and it is not difficult to thicken them as well. The root of a bumpkin needs proper support. It is stronger to rest it against the transom at deck level, rather than bolt it to the deck, unless a special step can be moulded or fixed to it.

The strain on runners is divided between the shroud-plate and the levers or tackle. The requirements for the shroud-plate are similar to those of the main shroud-plates, provided the resultant direction of the load is appreciated. In the simple case this is not the direction of the stay but the bisector of the angle between the stay itself and the part along the deck, and the strain is twice that on the wire.

The pull on the levers is theoretically along the deck, and for most of the time it is, but it may be substantially upwards while setting up the levers, particularly if the levers are stiff or difficult to set up, e.g. when setting up a lever (from choice or necessity) while the boom is bearing against the stay. The large leverage involved can produce quite a considerable upwards component.

The levers are an important part of the rigging and need to be bolted down securely. The deck should be strengthened and any mounting block should tie in with deck beams. This is best considered at the design stage.

The deck needs to be protected with a small pad against the bump as the levers come down; otherwise it will get marked and possibly slightly chipped. A pad should be fitted at both ends of the levers' travel.

MAST-STEP The current trend is to step the mast on deck, thereby avoiding an obstruction in a small cabin.

The neatest mounting is a depression or step moulded in the deck. Other good methods are a fabricated metal or moulded step bolted to the deck later. In one class this is combined with a ventilator. A separate mast-step has the advantage of being adjustable—an important point on a prototype boat. A moulded-in step is better left until the later, and modified versions, by which time the position should be certain. Alternative rigs may be ruled out with a fixed moulded-in mast-step.

A mast stepped on deck requires good support underneath and is usually supported by a substantial bulkhead or steel pillar.

The traditional method is to step the mast through the deck and on the keel. A wood block or metal step is needed to spread the large and concentrated load. Although the keel of a moulded boat is the strongest and most substantial part of the boat, it is not like the massive, solid hunk of wood in most wooden boats. The downward thrust of a modern bermudian mast is large, and it is important to spread this concentrated loading over a considerable length of keel. The mast-step must be mounted on something solid, preferably the ballast. It must not rest on a hollow box such as the thin lining of the bilges.

Substantial frames or bulkheads are still required to form the lower part of the mast-rigging triangle and resist the "squeezing" effect of the mast and rigging.

The deck can be moulded with a raised flange around the hole for the mast. This will make sealing easier and act as a natural breakwater to keep the opening above the level of water on the deck. It also forms a good base for a skirt and does away with the need for mast wedges, at least for keeping out the water. The edges must also be sealed.

The flange round the mast-hole will give a better bearing surface for the mast wedges, as a moulded deck is thinner than a wooden deck. Also a moulded deck is not so solid as a stout wooden one. Rigid mast-wedges should be avoided if possible, as, if driven home too firmly, they could damage the deck. The area around the hole needs to be well strengthened to resist this, possibly with a stout wooden block as well as thickening. Flexible wedges of rubber would be preferable. A sandwich deck must have an insert.

Alternative rigs or adjustment of the mast position will be difficult if the flange round the mast is moulded in permanently. A preferable alternative is a separately moulded flange or skirt which can be bolted down or moulded on in any position.

PIN RAIL If the mast is stepped on deck a pin rail by the mast presents few difficulties. The upwards pull of the halyards is balanced by the downwards thrust of the mast. At the rail the effect is to add to the upwards pull of the shrouds.

When the mast is stepped on the keel, there is a real tendency for the pin-rail to pull the deck up. Stout deck beams are essential, but better is a tie-bar or wire below from the pin-rail bolts to the mast-step.

RUNNING RIGGING The loads imposed by the running rigging are mainly where it is made fast on a cleat or passes through a fairlead. These have been covered in Chapter Seven, Deck Fittings. The important point is to spread the load under the fitting.

The mainsheet horse obviously requires good fixing, and as the pull is substantially upwards it must be through-bolted and tie in with deck-beams or a bulkhead.

Some sails may be tacked down to the deck. Any special eye for this must be well fastened and the deck reinforced in its vicinity. Headsails are often tacked down in this way and impose a strong upwards pull; good performance demands that they are set up tightly with winches or tackle which imposes a large initial strain even before the wind fills the sail. Slackening of the luff is very undesirable. This means there must be no give in the deck where the sail is attached. A light deck may need a tie-bar or wire underneath down to the stem. However, such a sail is usually set on a stay which will need such a tie anyway. The strain on a jib track can come at *any* point so it must be through-bolted all along with a plate beneath. Screws into inserts or rails commonly give trouble. If fastened to a wooden rail this must also be well bolted down. Rigs are usually altered sometime during the life of the boat. All fastenings should be accessible.

CHAPTER NINE

Cockpit and Coamings

COCKPIT On a production boat the cockpit is often moulded as one piece with the deck, and probably the cabin top, too (Fig. 9.1). This is undoubtedly the best method, as it does away with any joints, together with the labour of fitting, and leaks are impossible, but it is likely to be an unjustifiable complication for an amateur or in small scale work. However, it is well worth considering a separately moulded cockpit in conjunction with a wooden deck, or a simple one-off moulded deck, particularly if the cockpit is to be self-draining.

The advantages of such a "drop-in" cockpit are the complete freedom from leaks, a smooth, easily cleaned, low maintenance surface which can be non-slip, and the greater space below as the minimum of framing and support is required. There is also a saving in weight. In the simplest case the cockpit is simply slung from the deck beams. However, it will have to support a considerable weight of humanity, and possibly greater weight of water (a small cockpit may hold half a ton of water—when swamped). Top-hat stiffeners all round are essential, and wooden or moulded bearers are an economical way to support the weight. The bottom is often plywood backed, or sandwich.

It is cheaper to make the cockpit moderately thin—and support it adequately with top-hat stiffeners and bearers than to make it a strong load-bearing shell. However, it should not be too thin. Unlike the hull, where the loads are well distributed, a cockpit carries concentrated loads from the crew's feet. Under the shock movement of rough seagoing conditions these loads will be at least twice the crew's normal weight, and a lot more if a slipping crew meets the deck coming up.

Builders of river boats should not scorn these conditions. Bumping over the wash of a passing barge or motor-boat can rattle the back teeth too, the faster the boat the bigger the bump—and claims of planing speeds are quite common nowadays for cruisers built for use on the most severely speed-restricted waters, and sometimes even for houseboats. Most lakes can quickly produce waves big enough to give any small cruiser a real tossing.

The relative ease of construction compared with plywood depends on the shape. Plywood may be easier for a plain box shape, but moulding would be easier for anything more complicated. Fig. 9.1 shows a simple "drop-in" cockpit which would be easier to mould than to make in wood even for a one-off cockpit. Apart from any question of ease of construction, plywood has all the disadvantages of fabrication in wood and the inevitable multiple joints to be sealed.

The seats can be moulded as bulges in the cockpit moulding. This does not unduly complicate the moulding or the construction of the mould. It saves the trouble of making separate seats and gives more room below. Lockers can be incorporated as described in Chapter Twenty (pages 225–7).

The seats are sure to suffer a good deal of wear, and will get scratched and marked. It is better to recognise this fact and protect them with plywood panels, slats or permanent

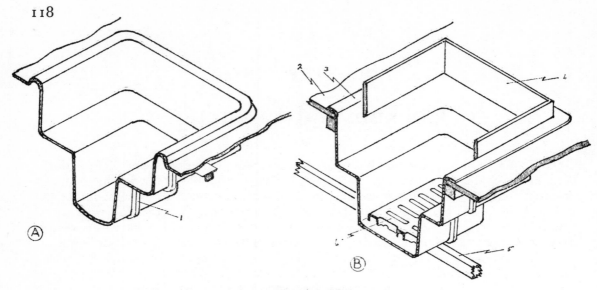

9.1: *Moulded cockpit.*

A. *Cockpit moulded in one piece with the deck and probably cabin top also. Seats and coaming all moulded in. Note how top-hat stiffening rib, 1, goes right round.*

B. *Wooden deck, 2, and moulded "drop-in" cockpit, 3. The coaming, 4, is of wood and the weight of the crew is taken by a stout wooden member, 5. Note the moulded grating, 6.*

upholstery. If the surface is moulded, a raised moulded pattern will make a drier seat than a smooth polished surface, particularly on those wonderful fine nights with a moon shining on the water, nights which are wasted in harbour, where the only drawback is the dew on the seats.

The same considerations regarding non-slip decks in Chapter 5 (pages 90–93) apply to cockpits too, and cockpits get more concentrated wear than decks. A moulded pattern is not so non-slip, and more difficult to repair if worn or damaged, than stick-on Trakmark or a non-slip paint or resin. A grating is the best answer, and it is warmer on the feet because there is often a little water which does not get away even in a good self-draining cockpit. A grating, too, will spread the concentrated load from feet.

When well heeled the cockpit floor may not be the logical place to stand—indeed it may be impracticable. Crazy places like the sides of the cockpit and well must then support the wear and lurching weight of a bracing foot. This weight will be a lot more than the cockpit floor withstands under calm conditions. Coamings, too, will be used for hanging on to or be grabbed at for support in emergencies—and the lee rail may have to carry a dead weight of misery.

In rough weather, therefore, the cockpit must withstand heavy bodies lurching, falling and bracing themselves inside it. Such effects are not confined to vertical static loads on the cockpit floor or seats, but will be shock loads applied to any part of it.

Moulded gutters and gulleys for the drains of a self-draining cockpit will help draining at difficult angles of heel. Drain-pipes should be crossed (Fig. 9.2) otherwise the cockpit will be self-filling as well as self-draining; when heeled drain outlets will be under water.

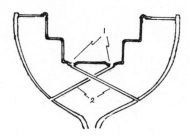

9.2: *Self-draining cockpit.*

*Moulded gutters, 1, will assist drainage. The drainage pipes, 2,
should be crossed for proper draining when heeled.*

Sound plumbing is important. Seacocks must be fitted and *be easily accessible.* Pipes should be short and well protected from damage. Commonly they run through lockers and spaces used for stowage of heavy and bulky objects, e.g. rubber dinghy, oars or outboard, and near engines or hot exhausts.

It is easier to mould a grating than make it in wood, where all joints must be rebated. The mould is simple. Nail smooth strips of wood on to hardboard to form the edges, and small blocks to form the "gaps." If in use the edges of the gaps rest on the cockpit bottom and carry the weight, the grating can be lightly moulded. Wood stiffeners can be moulded in. Cut generous grooves in all flanges to form waterways.

COAMINGS Cockpit coamings are often moulded as part of the deck or cockpit. This makes a neat job and looks smooth and smart, but it is very important to protect the top from chafe (Fig. 9.3). It will be impossible to renew a coaming moulded in one piece with the deck if it gets damaged—yet by its very position it is an area that is prone to damage on any boat. They can be repaired, of course, but this takes time and trouble, and can very seldom be done without it showing. Moreover this approach is not consistent with the need to reduce maintenance to the minimum.

One may wonder why a part well inboard is so liable to damage. Certainly it is well protected from serious impact such as a rubbing-band or even the topsides may have to endure, but it will get a great deal of that continual minor damage otherwise known as fair wear and tear. It is the obvious momentary resting place for heavy objects, a box of stores, a crate of beer or a battery; it will be stepped on, kicked and knocked; ropes will rub on it, even on a motor-cruiser there is need to pull on a mooring rope, and on a sailing-boat there will be a lot of chafe from hauling on sheets. The angle of pull on a sheet may seem quite clear in harbour but it can be very different when heeled. The wear can, and should, be reduced by intelligent design, but it is almost impossible to eliminate it entirely.

Every time this will leave a small scratch, a mark or a chip, so that after a season or two the top of the coaming is a mass of dirty little scratches and scars, not the glossy polish which the rest of the boat should still retain. It shows, too, because the coamings are a very conspicuous part, and will be an annoying eyesore if not kept in good order.

A moulded coaming must therefore be protected with a capping of wood or metal. Wood is cheap, easily touched up and renewed, but it requires a little regular varnishing. Aluminium extrusions look neat; they must be made of a proper corrosion-resisting grade of aluminium or they will soon look horrid even if used only on the river, and they are soft enough to be scratched easily. For high-class work a chromium-plated or stainless steel capping is the obvious choice. An extruded plastic capping would also look smart

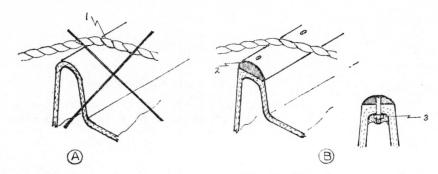

9.3: *Moulded coaming.*

A. **Wrong.** *Unprotected top of coaming will be chafed badly by ropes, 1. Note that this coaming top is integral with the deck and cannot be replaced.*
B. *Wooden capping, 2, is more easily touched up and can be replaced easily if secured by screws into embedded nuts, 3.*

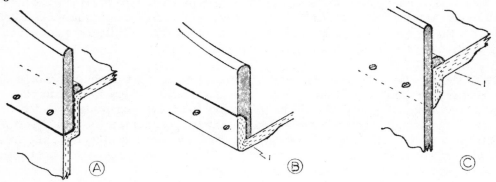

9.4: *Attaching a wooden coaming.*
A. *Stepped joint suitable for use with a moulded cockpit.*
B. *Turn-up flange. Note how the angle is thickened for strength, 1. This method has the advantage of being inherently watertight due to the turn-up flange.*
C. *Turn-down flange. A neat method of joining the deck to a wooden cockpit.*

and could be in a distinctive colour; it must be of an outdoor quality, resistant to sunlight. The capping is there to get worn so it must be readily replaceable, otherwise there is little point in having it.

I prefer a wooden coaming to a moulded one, even if protected. It is more easily touched up with a lick of varnish and a spot of filler than a moulded coaming. The maintenance needed is so little it can be done during a fine weekend cruise—but because of this small amount of regular maintenance it will retain its smart appearance indefinitely. 9.116.1 A wooden coaming looks attractive and provides a prominent touch of the traditional for those who still hanker after wood. For such a small area an expensive wood like teak is not an extravagance. Wooden coamings must be securely attached: Fig. 9.4 shows some methods of attaching a wooden coaming to a moulded deck.

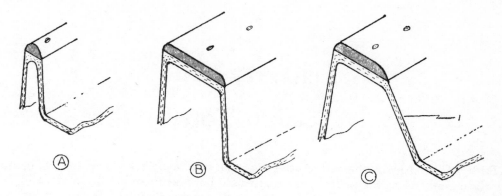

9.5: *Shape of moulded coaming.*

A. Not Recommended. *Deep narrow coaming is difficult to mould and release, and is very prone to flaws.*
B. *Broad coaming is much easier to mould and therefore is likely to be better moulded.*
C. *Sloping face makes for even easier moulding and certainly better release, but note that this shape will tend to make a wet boat as it is a poorer breakwater.*

A wooden coaming simplifies the deck mould, an important point for an amateur. A deep trough—and the mould for a coaming is bound to be a deep narrow trough—is a difficult shape to mould. It is more likely to have flaws, cavities, and brittle resin-rich edges which may be undetected until a knock breaks the brittle shell and exposes them— and in that position frequent knocks are inevitable regardless of whether the boat is a sailing or motor-cruiser.

A moulded coaming—or the moulded base for a wooden coaming or capping— will be much easier to mould if it is wide (Fig. 9.5). And why not make it wide? A narrow coaming is only following blindly the style of a wooden coaming. The tradition is to have a coaming to keep out water, not to make it very narrow. Coamings are often formed into bulges to form the mounting for sheet winches. The inside of the bulge makes a handy cubbyhole.

Moulded coamings should never be considered for a working boat. The hard use would soon wear and damage them. They should be made of substantial sections of wood so that they have a generous depth to absorb wear and chafe, and, of course, they must be readily renewable.

MOTOR CRUISERS Cockpits are usually large and wide, and plywood is more suitable for this than GRP. A good framework is essential for support, usually of wood strutted to the girders or engine bearers.

Hatches or panels are needed for access to engines or tanks beneath. Little-used panels for tanks should be screwed and bedded. Engine hatches must be easily accessible and are difficult to seal well. Some seepage is common, but the cockpit should still be inherently self-draining. A good door sill is most important and often overlooked. Without it the cockpit will drain into the cabin at every heavy shower.

CHAPTER TEN

Cabin Top

CABIN TOP   Ideally the cabin top is moulded in one piece with the deck (Fig. 10.1). There are many advantages: leaks are impossible because there are no joints, and, being all in one piece, the weight, cost and space of joining members and fastenings are saved. Also saved is all the skilled labour of fitting and making the separate cabin top, and the absence of joints eliminates many sources of weakness.

From an amateur's point of view there is little difference between the amount of work involved in knocking up a bulge in the pattern or mould for the deck and making the cabin top properly in wood; but there is no doubt that the integrally moulded cabin top is the better proposition and it is almost as easy to mould the deck with the cabin top as to mould the deck alone.

Deck beams, too, are in one piece, and continue unbroken right round the cabin top, giving a homogeneity unknown in any other construction.

Sometimes the deck is moulded and the cabin top is made of wood, either from expediency or to give the traditional appearance of varnished wood, certainly a very attractive finish if well made, which may be considered worth the substantial drawback of greater maintenance and possible leaks in hot weather. A veneer or even thin plywood glued to the cabin sides or laminated in the moulding would give the same appearance without the structural disadvantages. This idea has so many attractions, combining the traditional appearance of wood with the strength, lightness and jointlessness of moulded construction that I am surprised it is not used more extensively. Printed paper or gauze also gives a most realistic simulation of wood.

A similar problem arises in attaching a moulded cabin top to a wooden deck. A moulded cabin top has considerable advantages even when the deck is made of wood, For a stock boat it is certainly easier to mould it than to build it in wood and some production boatbuilders have done this even on wooden hulls; it is a leakproof, one-piece construction (a boon in hot climates) and may be translucent to give light below. It is lighter than wood, yet stronger. If you are building one-off the work would be much the same as in making it in wood; the cost might be greater, but this is more than matched by its superiority.

A translucent cabin top eliminates the need for skylights, and gives plenty of light below. The non-leaking skylight has yet to be invented; they are always a source of weakness and easily damaged by careless crew or sea. The translucent area should not be overdone. In hot weather the "greenhouse" effect can be overpowering, and at night a large illuminated cabin-top will dazzle the watch on deck. I recommend either small areas of good translucency in an otherwise opaque moulding, or a moulding that is only moderately translucent all over giving a more diffused light and protection from roasting

10.1: *Cabin top moulded in one piece with the deck. Note how the moulded deck-beams continue right round the cabin top.*

and dazzle. Unfortunately a moderately translucent moulding tends to look rather "muddy". An alternative is to tint it, but the effect is an acquired taste and can quite upset the calculated impact of carefully applied cosmetics.

A translucent cabin top gives an amazing sense of spaciousness below and overcomes the claustrophobic effect of a solid deck combined with low headroom; it gives a feeling of being almost in the open air, which is quite uncanny until one is used to it.

The integrally moulded cabin top will usually be opaque like the deck. However, it is not difficult to make patches of translucency. If the deck is already moulded this will have to be done by cutting away the deck to form openings. The cheap way is to bolt down premoulded pieces of translucent moulded sheets, or possibly Perspex (acrylic sheet). They must be very well bedded down and are put in in a similar way to windows. A better and more secure way is to mould them in. The pre-moulded sheets are placed in position and joined to the deck by moulding butt-straps overlapping both sheet and deck. It can also be done by covering the opening with smooth hardboard, and moulding the translucent patch *in situ*. Resin and glass should be translucent grades to avoid muddiness.

It is even easier to incorporate translucent patches in the deck while moulding. Mask the intended area of the light on the mould with a piece of wood, cardboard or a special moulded jig taped down with masking tape. Sometimes masking tape itself is enough. When the rest of the moulding is finished, take out the mask, trim the edges and mould the light in translucent material. To be on the safe side it is usually desirable to touch up the release agent. A thick moulding is often made coloured and opaque only on the gel coat and first layer or two, the rest being uncoloured. The masking is then needed only on these opaque layers and the rest of the lay-up can proceed unhindered.

This may take longer than cutting out a window after moulding and is not so suitable for rapid production. However, it is stronger, as the light is a structural part of the boat, part of the moulding itself, and it is impossible for it to leak. It cannot, of course, be used when you want a window you can see through, but only to give daylight to dark compartments and cabins. An alternative to a mask is to pre-mould the light and place this in the mould first. There is a danger of the effect being spoiled by resin running behind the light during moulding.

Although I keep mentioning deck leaks, do not get the impression that every wooden deck leaks as a matter of course. Many boats are absolutely dry, most are nearly so, but a few can make life absolute hell for the crew. It is very much harder to keep a deck tight than a hull; a deck is alternately wet and dry, hot and cold throughout its life, and has a mass of openings and through fastenings—moreover the slightest drip will be noticed. One drip down the skipper's wife's neck when she is feeling seasick can terminate the

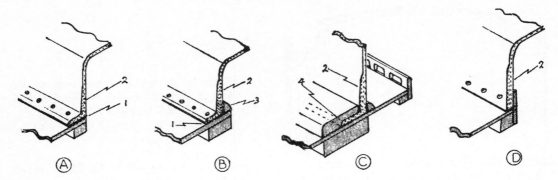

10.2: *Joining a moulded cabin top to a wooden deck.*

A. *Simple flange connection. This is the cheapest case and it must be well bedded down, 1, or it will leak. Note how the angle is thickened for extra strength, 2.*

B. *An improved method, similar to the above. The wooden moulding, 3, acts as a stopwater in case movement of the cabin top loosens the seating, and creates possible leakage paths.*

C. *A better method for larger yachts. The flange is covered after bolting down with a covering batten, 4. The deck is extended into the cabin to form a shelf or grab rail.*

D. *Cabin top has no flange and is bolted to a wooden coaming. This method is suitable for "dry" construction as the cabin top can be cut to fit the deck camber. In the other methods the cabin top must be padded if it does not fit.*

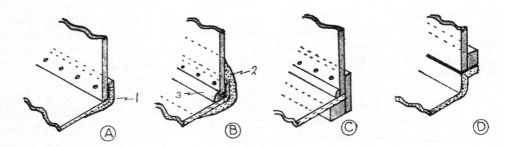

10.3: *Joining a wooden cabin top to a moulded deck.*

A. *Simple joint bolted together. Note how moulded flange, 1, is thickened for strength. This is an adequate cheap joint, and the upstanding flange makes leaks improbable.*

B. *Moulded fillet, 2, moulded on to the plywood cabin sides and also strengthening the flange. Wooden moulding, 3, gives a neater appearance to the outside of the joint.*

C. *A largely wooden joint with no moulded flange. Suitable for "dry" construction or for adding a cabin top in a position not foreseen when the deck was moulded.*

D. *Z-flange more suitable for a prefabricated cabin top.*

voyage as quickly as premature twins, whereas gallons of water can stream into the bilges without undue discomfort to anyone.

It is my experience that every opening in a deck and every joint is a potential leak. Good workmanship and good maintenance can keep them tight, and usually does, but reducing their number reduces the chances of a leak, and thus the need for maintenance.

A cabin top must be securely fixed on. It presents a large area to any sea coming aboard, and it is not only deep-water ocean voyagers who meet malicious waves; there are plenty in strong tidal waters, smaller than ocean monsters, but just as wicked and many times as many, and of course, being nearer home, there is a greater chance of meeting one. A race or river bar, too, can give enough nasty experiences for unlimited moaning around the other bar if the boat gets back.

A damaged cabin top will not be quite so serious as a large hole in the bottom, but if the seas are bad enough to damage it, more water will follow quicker than pumps can push it back. Only an iron morale will be unaffected by the shambles below, and loss of morale wrecks more voyages than tempest or rock.

Fig. 10.2 shows various methods of joining a moulded cabin top to a wooden deck and Fig. 10.3 a wooden cabin top to a moulded deck.

The simplest method of attaching a moulded cabin top to a wooden deck is a simple flange. This must be well bedded down and firmly bolted or the natural working and movement of the cabin top or deck will open up leakage paths. If such paths develop there is nothing to stop them. A wooden moulding inside will act as a stopwater in case of seepage. A moulded fillet will do this even better, as well as strengthening the join.

A difficulty with a flanged cabin top like this is fitting it to the deck. The deck may vary a little from the plans—wood can seldom be repeated exactly—and if the camber is not just right the cabin top will have to be packed to make it fit. As well as being time-wasting this increases the possibility of seepage. The flangeless type (Fig. 10.2D) can easily be trimmed to fit the deck, and for this reason it is to be preferred, despite the extra wood-work involved and the rather weaker method of attachment.

The same considerations about leakproof joints arise when joining a wooden cabin top to a moulded deck. A moulded upturned flange acts as a natural stopwater as well as an easy, sound mounting point. It is worth adding a moulded flange even when the opening for the cabin top is unplanned and cut out later, instead of being formed during moulding. It could be done after the cabin top has been fitted just for sealing. In "dry" construction it can be made of wood. Note that a moulded deck or cabin top should be well thickened and strengthened all along its edge where the fastenings will come. This should be continued well past any flange or angle.

Deck beams can be joined to the cabin top beams by moulding a sleeve to overlap both parts (Fig. 10.4). If the beams do not coincide a moulded carling, formed as a top-hat section, will be needed. Beams must not end abruptly or they will form hard spots. It is pointless to stiffen the top but leave the sides unstiffened, and moreover severely weakened further by large windows. Beams should continue down the sides as in Fig. 10.1. The angle of a cabin top beam can be stiffened with a web (Fig. 10.5). Sometimes a web alone is sufficient without the beams.

FITTING WINDOWS A simple way to fit a window is to cut out the opening with a pad saw and bolt on a piece of Perspex larger all round by about 1 in. (2.5 cms.). The

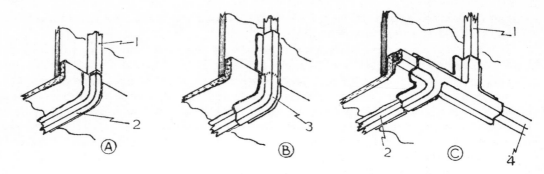

10.4: *Joining beams.*

Where the top-hat deck beams, 2, coincide with the cabin top beams, 1, as in A, they can be joined with a moulded channel, 3, to provide continuity of strength, B.

If they do not coincide, as in C, a top-hat section carling, 4, will be needed, and the beams joined to this by moulding channels. Remember that a beam ending without a logical termination is a source of hard spots and stress concentrations.

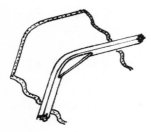

10.5: *Angle of cabin top beam strengthened with a web.*

Perspex must be well bedded down. A sealer strip is a convenient way to do this, but whatever material is used it looks rather crude because the sealer will be visible through the Perspex. A wood or metal surround is needed to hide the sealer and make the window look neat (Fig. 10.6). Being exposed to light through the Perspex the sealer will be more inclined to age and leak than if it was bedding down wood or anything opaque.

If the position of the window is known at the time the mould is made a flange can be moulded in. An outside flange may spoil the smooth draw necessary for release, and introduce the complication of a split mould; an inside flange can be formed using a panel lightly fastened to the mould so that it comes away with the cabin top and is released separately. This is described on page 52. A moulded flange is neater than a plain cut-out window and strengthens the opening. The Perspex is fitted in the same way and as the sealer is still visible through it, a frame is advisable for neatness. It is also a sound plan to compensate for the loss of strength due to the cut-out by increasing the thickness all round, or beading the edge.

Thin Perspex will accommodate some curvature in one direction even when cold; however, by heating it in hot water, just short of boiling point, even thick Perspex can be formed to more complex shapes, and when cool it will retain this shape.

Perspex is the trade name for methyl methacrylate acrylic sheet made by I.C.I., Ltd., although in Britain the word is loosely used for all acrylic sheet, sometimes even for anything transparent that is not obviously glass. There are other trade names such as

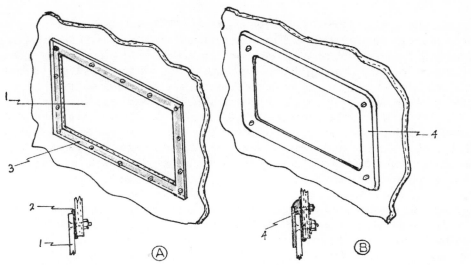

10.6: *Attaching windows.*

A. *The simplest method. Screw Perspex, 1, directly to the moulding, sealing with ordinary bedding compound or sealer strip, 2. This does not look neat because the sealer will show through, 3, and, because of the unprotected edge, there is also the chance of leaks developing if the sealer is not applied evenly, or gets hard with age.*
B. *A wood or metal surround, 4, looks much more professional and will deflect water away from the edge of the sealer, so that leaks are unlikely.*

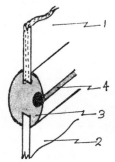

10.7: *Claytonrite sealing-strip.*

The moulding, 1, and Perspex or glass window, 2, fit into slots in the extruded plastic section, 3. A special strip, 4, fits into a third slot afterwards and compresses the other two to make a tight seal. It can be a smart contrasting colour or brightly metallised.

Plexiglas, Lucite and Oroglas in other parts of the world for similar materials, the general technical name for which is acrylic sheet.

A suitable thickness of Perspex would be $\frac{1}{8}$ in. (3 mm.) for a river cruiser; a seagoing cruiser should have at least $\frac{3}{16}$ in. (5 mm.) for a small window, say 9 in. (23 cm.) square, and $\frac{1}{4}$ in. (6 mm.) up to about 18 in. (46 cm.) square. Larger windows will need to be even thicker, but 18 in. is quite large enough for safety. Double these thicknesses would be advisable in a vulnerable position, e.g. forward of the mast or any lights in the topsides, and also for a hard-driven boat like a modern ocean racer.

For a seagoing yacht windows must be strong and preferably fixed, relying more on waterproof ventilators for fresh air. A well bedded fixed light seldom leaks, an opening one or a skylight seldom does not. Large windows in a deck house or cabin are delightful when in harbour giving plenty of light and an interesting view (which is just as good for the quayside loungers looking in as for languid guests looking out). However, they should be strictly river-boat features, for they are very vulnerable at sea. A large broken window in bad weather can be an acute embarrassment, and it is easily done by a heavy wave in the wrong place. The same applies to the modern trend for large windows in doghouses.

Any windows should be capable of withstanding as much punishment as the cabin top itself, and the frames must be equally tough, too. If this is not so they should have stout shutters for use in bad weather, however unpopular this may be. Obviously this is impossible in a wheelhouse where a number of small tough windows are much safer than a few large panoramic ones even if the field of view is not quite as good.

The best combination is small fixed windows for the view, translucent moulded cabin tops and hatches for light and waterproof Dorade ventilators for air.

A very neat window can be made by using Claytonrite self sealing weatherstrip (made by Howard Clayton-Wright, Ltd., Wellesbourne, Warwick). This has a treble slot section (Fig. 10.7). One slot goes over the moulding and one takes the Perspex or glass, which in this case is cut smaller than the opening. A special plastic filler strip is forced into the third slot and compresses the other two, thus making an effective seal. This strip can be in a smart contrasting colour or metallised. The result is neat and looks very professional. For best results the moulding should be the same thickness as the Perspex and smooth. This requires the inside face of the moulding to be filed flat.

It has been found that windows secured by weatherstrip can be stove in by a heavy wave, impact or even a good accidental kick. The present trend, which I recommend, is to use metal framed windows of aluminium or stainless steel wherever the cost will allow, and certainly on any seagoing boat. They also provide some stiffening and are much more tolerant of thickness, even taking the double thickness of an inner lining, which avoids the problem of sealing the inner lining around a window.

There is now a wide range of proprietary window fittings, both fixed and opening; several firms specialising originally in caravan and aircraft windows now make windows for boats in corrosion-resisting materials and fully marinised. There is no need to use the traditional, expensive, heavy brass portlights. Double channel extrusions in aluminium or plastic can also be bought for making one's own sliding windows. These are good for river boats but are not watertight or strong enough for use at sea.

The old aircraft type of astro-dome never seems to have caught on for boats. I am rather surprised at this, because they can be quite tough and are not difficult to make out of Perspex. They do give a very good view of conditions on deck, the sails, wind and weather or possible dangers without one having to don oilskins and brave the elements. This is invaluable for the skipper during his watch below and for anyone who sails alone or short-handed—as one often has to nowadays when all one's friends have boats of their own! Another useful device which serves the same purpose in a simpler but more limited way is a panel of Perspex in the top of the doghouse or coach roof. Doghouse windows usually give a good view of the sea, but not the sails; this Perspex roof panel shows the sails, mast and burgee at a glance from the dry comfort of the cabin.

CHAPTER ELEVEN

Hatches

HATCHES Being in one piece, a moulded hatch cannot leak—at least not through the top—and it can be made translucent, which does away with a separate deadlight.

A weakness in the construction of most hatches is strength around the hinges (Fig. 11.1). Both the hatch and the coaming should be reinforced to double thickness for 3 in. (75 mm.) all round each hinge, preferably with inserts too. The vicinity of the catch or stay also needs reinforcing. To accommodate the extra thickness or inserts the hatch may be formed into a bulge, so maintaining the inside clearance. Hinges must be strong, securely fastened (through-bolted where possible) and replaceable. Flush foredeck hatches often suffer from damage to the hinge by being stood on when too full to close properly.

A hatch must never be allowed to open further than its hinges allow. The ideal is for the hinges to allow the hatch to open right back to deck level. If this cannot be done there must be a stop to limit the opening to a safe amount, otherwise the hinges are sure to be wrecked. This stop must be permanent; it is bad practice to allow the opening to be checked by, say, the mast. When laid up in winter the mast may not be there but the stop is just as necessary. Sloping the hinged side of the hatch allows it to open wider.

A hatch should always open forward, i.e. have the hinge on the forward side, so that a sea coming on board slams it shut, not open and possibly overboard. A forward opening hatch gives shelter, and, with triangular hinged wings at the side (Fig. 11.2), it can often be left open at sea for ventilation even when there is some spray flying or it is raining.

Hatches are often lift-off type with no hinges, retained by elastic or clips below. A loose hatch is very easily lost overboard, which may gravely endanger the boat and certainly make life hell below. Loose hatches must have a retainer, not a detachable elastic to keep it shut but a long undetachable cord, like the string on a hunting hat, so that it can never be lost even if knocked overboard. At least loose hatches should be buoyant. Most are lost in harbour.

Hatch coamings must be strongly reinforced. They are often moulded as deep channel sections (Fig. 11.8) infilled with resin putty, or combined with sub-mouldings or the inner lining. Deep channels, however, are prone to flaws and need care in moulding, which generally means that they need an inordinate time and skill or else are done badly.

A lot of ingenuity has gone into the design of watertight seals and coamings for hatches—yet many small cruiser hatches are still badly designed and leak. It is easy enough to keep the rain out, that is not the problem; it is the rush of water from a wave which hits the coaming and then travels *upwards* with some force, which gushes casually past the usual simple flange on to the bunks below. The pressure of this water will lift the hatch and squirt its way past joints which are quite proof against a heavy downpour. The simple flange of Fig. 11.3A is adequate for river boats, which have to contend with nothing more than a heavy shower, but it would make a seagoing boat very uncomfortable.

A good hatch needs a deep skirt outside to deflect the water and reduce its force, and

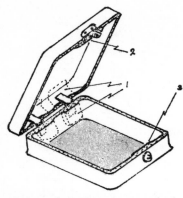

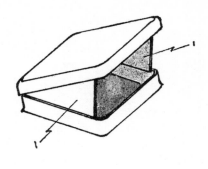

11.1: *Points of attachment are weak places on most hatches. The moulding should be well thickened in way of the hinges, 1, and catch, 2 and 3.*

11.2: *Triangular side-pieces, hinged to the hatch will hold it open to provide sheltered ventilation when it is raining or when under way in moderate weather. The open side must, of course, face aft.*

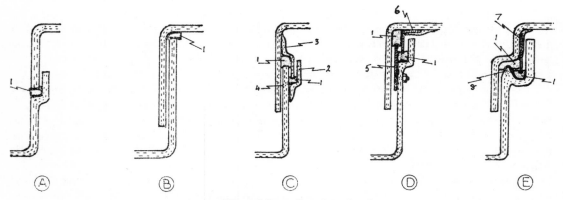

11.3: *Watertight sealing for a hatch.*

A. *Simple gasket, 1. Only suitable for river boats as any wave will spurt through with ease.*

B. *A deep skirt with gasket, 1, will give some improvement. However, this may make difficulty if hinged. It is satisfactory for a lift-off hatch.*

C. *Double seal. Moulded z-sections, 2 and 3, bonded on, hold two separate gaskets and provide a long leakage path. The inner z-flange, 2, must be higher than the outer coaming otherwise water collecting in the trough will overflow inboard. Small drainholes, 4, can be drilled to lead the water outboard.*

D. *Double seal. In this case the double path is formed by a metal or nylon strip fixed to the coaming, 5, and a similar angle section, 6, secured by embedding one edge in the hatch.*

E. *A more sophisticated moulded seal. The coaming has a moulded channel and the hatch a moulded step. A strip of nylon or metal embedded on the hatch, 7, forms one knife-edge, a moulded ridge, 8, provides the other. To avoid the ridge being resin-rich and brittle it should be moulded with lengths of single rovings in the point.*

a double flange inside with a self-draining channel to take away anything which forces its way past the outer seal. The channels can be moulded or the flanges can be of standard metal or plastics extrusions, provided they are joined together at the corners.

A double flange and seal is the only sure way of keeping water out (Fig. 11.3C, 11.3D). It may force its way past one seal, but by then its force will be spent, and it will not be able to penetrate the second. The inner flange must be appreciably higher than the outer, otherwise water collecting in the channel may slop inside. This channel ought to have drain-holes to take the water back outside, but there is always the chance that they may get blocked.

The simple gasket (Fig. 11.3A–B) is very common. To be effective the gasket must be deep, soft, resilient and permanent. Polyurethane or polyester foam are unsuitable and soon age, crumble or deform. They need frequent renewal with the risk that suitable replacements may be difficult to obtain locally. Neoprene or foam PVC are durable and more effective. Bonding must be good and permanent: the gasket *must* stay put. There must be enough pressure to ensure a good seal; catches must be screw-down or toggle, and preferably adjustable. This is easy enough on the opening side, but no adjustment is possible on the hinge side. If not properly pressed down it will leak. If pressure on the gasket is too great the hinge will be strained or loosened and also leak.

A sharp-edged strip or moulded V pressing into a soft gasket will make a better seal than two flat surfaces. It must be adjusted so that it digs in when the hatch is shut, and then it will continue to seal even if the hatch is lifted slightly by a wave. It takes much less pressure to make a knife edge dig in than to keep two flat faces in intimate and continuous contact.

A large proportion of deck leaks come from hatches. On a big yacht this has often been tolerated, and as long as it went straight on to the cabin sole it caused little worry. But on the modern pocket cruiser it is extremely difficult to escape from a leaking hatch. Most of the comfortable parts of the accommodation will be well within range. Remember it only drips on to the cabin sole in harbour. When sailing and heeled, and a small cruiser heels to a breath, a side bunk will be under the hatch—the lee bunk, too, which may be the only place a really miserable crew can wedge himself into.

SLIDING HATCH A sliding hatch, too, is easier to mould than to make in wood; the difficulties lie in arranging the runners and keeping out water. It seems a simple idea to mould a flange on the hatch which will serve as the runner (Fig. 11.4A) but it must be well protected from wear and so must the cabin top. Remember it cannot be renewed without remoulding, and while this could be done with the hatch, it is obviously undesirable as far as the cabin top is concerned.

Runners of wood or metal will last longer and can be renewed when worn. A modern improvement would be to screw on strips of nylon or the almost frictionless but expensive PTFE. Ball-bearing drawer-type runners can also be used, but ease of sliding can be overdone. At sea a hatch which slides freely on its own is a guillotine.

The fixed portions of the slide can be moulded Z-sections or metal strips bonded on. Alternatively they can be formed as bulges in the moulding and the slides attached inside underneath. A flange or coaming around the opening is essential to stop water running in. This is necessary even on a river boat to keep out rain-water. The flange can be moulded or added in wood.

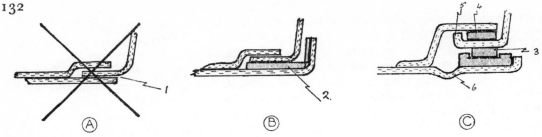

11.4: *Sliding hatch. External slides.*

A. **Wrong.** *Simple wood or plastic runner fastened underneath. The hatch will wear badly and there is nothing to stop water running under the hatch,* 1.

B. *The cabin top has a turn-up flange to keep out water, and slides,* 2, *of wood or nylon to prevent wear. The top flange is purely to retain the hatch.*

C. *A further improvement is to fit a nylon slide to the hatch also,* 3, *giving a nylon to nylon sliding surface. PTFE would be almost frictionless. A soft gasket,* 4, *and outer flange,* 5, *on the edge of the hatch will help to keep grit out of the slides. A moulded gutter,* 6, *leads away any drips.*

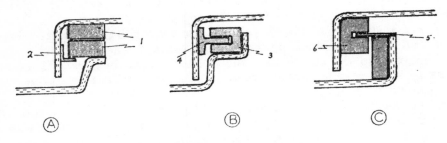

11.5: *Sliding hatch. Internal slides.*

A. *Renewable wood to wood sliding surfaces,* 1, *which could also be made of or faced with metal or nylon. Light retaining bracket,* 2.

B. *Aluminium, brass or nylon T-strip,* 4, *sliding in a nylon channel,* 3.

C. *Brass strip,* 5, *sliding in a grooved wooden strip,* 6.

The slide can be external (Fig. 11.4) or internal (Fig. 11.5) as regards the hatch. Internal slides are preferable because they are less affected by grit. Grit may make a well-fitting slide jam and will always cause excessive wear; it is surprising how much gets on board.

The most difficult part of a sliding hatch to make watertight is the forward end. Again it is easy enough to keep the rain out, but a wave will easily get round the usual S-bend under the hatch and over the coaming (Fig. 11.5A) and cascade below. Most builders of small boats ignore this, either accepting it as inevitable if the owner must go to sea, or remaining blissfully unaware that such a thing can happen.

It is almost impossible to make a sliding hatch watertight and still slide readily, but quite easy to stop the wave getting there. All that is needed is a cover over the forward end of the hatch so that the hatch slides forward under the cover instead of above the deck and exposed (Fig. 11.6B). Such a cover can be moulded separately or it can be a bulge in the moulded deck. It is important to think out how the hatch is to be fitted in position or

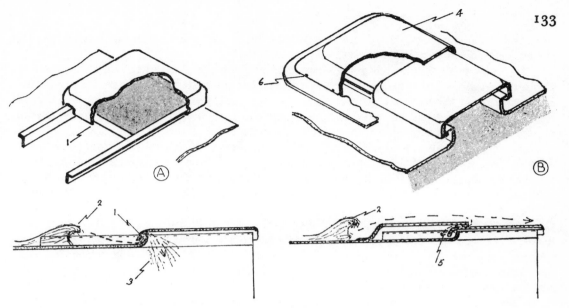

11.6: *Sliding hatch.*

A. *Common type of sliding hatch. Adequate for river boats but it usually leaks badly in rough weather. The inevitable gap at the forward end, 1, is difficult to seal and a wave, 2, coming aboard will easily find its way through, 3.*

B. *Improved seagoing type of sliding hatch, which slides forward under a cover, 4. This may be formed by a bulge in the moulding. Now any sea coming aboard will be deflected over and past the gap at the forward end. Any water which does find its way in, 5, will have spent its force and is unlikely to be able to negotiate the double bend. Drain holes, 6, may be necessary to take away this trickle.*

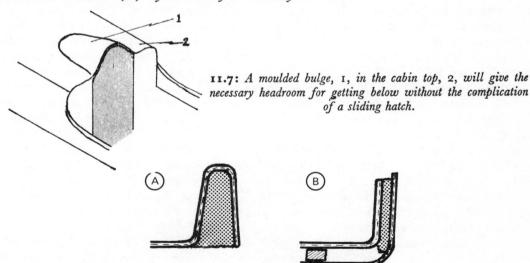

11.7: *A moulded bulge, 1, in the cabin top, 2, will give the necessary headroom for getting below without the complication of a sliding hatch.*

11.8: *Hatch coamings.*

A. *A simple way to mould a hatch coaming. The coaming is moulded and infilled with resin putty or an insert. This is very strong, not easily damaged and has no sharp projections to tear anything.*

B. *A coaming which also forms the join with a deckhead lining. The deck and the lining are both moulded with flanges and the gap sealed with resin putty. This gap is likely to give trouble unless an adhesive putty such as epoxy is used or it is backed up with fastenings.*

removed because this cover will make it impossible to slide the hatch out forwards unless the cover itself is also made detachable.

It is advisable to allow a good clearance between a sliding hatch and the moulded cabin top. A close-fitting hatch may help to keep out the water, but if there is only a small clearance under the forward end as it slides, any grit trapped under it will scar and scratch the cabin top. A soft rubber strip, sometimes fitted in the hope it may keep the water out, is very prone to pick up grit and scratch the surface.

The opening should be well reinforced and stiffened. A lightly built boat may distort when sailing hard, or if the cabin top bears the weight of a man or dinghy, sufficiently to jam the hatch. (Some well built, heavy, wooden boats, too, will open a locker door on one tack and jam it on the other.) All boats distort naturally far more than is generally realised.

COMPANIONWAY Some boats dispense with the sliding hatch and have a fixed moulded bulge instead, to give the necessary headroom. This is a sound idea. What is not there cannot leak, jam or be a source of weakness. It is also cheaper. It can even be fitted as a later modification, perhaps to replace a badly designed hatch, and is suitable for wooden as well as GRP boats (Fig. 11.7).

The aft side of the cabin top often has some rake to it and the companionway slopes to match. Unless the sliding hatch or bulge has a good overhang there will be no protection from the rain, which will drip or fall straight in. The cabin doors must be closed in every shower—no joke on a hot night. A flange of some sort, e.g. a moulded ridge, is also needed to keep out drips which only fall "straight" when on an even keel. When heeled, rain and spray will run and drip sideways relative to the companionway.

A tapered companionway gives more room at shoulder or waist height, where most needed, yet occupies less valuable cabin space lower down. The commonest doors on sailing cruisers are sliding washboards, usually wood but sometimes moulded. The slides too are usually wood and are commonly a weak point. They must be securely fastened into wood pads or inserts behind and well bedded. The edges of the moulding too must be strengthened with a flange, stiffener, or as for hatches. In many cases the doors are strong enough but the slides would be stove in if pooped. Moulded slides will wear and all parts of the slides should be replaceable.

Washboards normally fit in only one way, like a Chinese puzzle. No clues are given to the uninitiated. Simple markings for the order and way round would save much trouble. Washboards are good when in use, but the problem is what to do with them when not in use. Wherever they are put they are in the way of something; few boats have proper stowage, out of the way of everything and reserved for them alone, yet ready to hand, preferably within reach of the cockpit in case a lone helmsman needs to put them in in a hurry.

Motor cruisers usually have hinged doors. There must be secure rattle-proof fastenings to hold them open or shut, and when open they must be protected from damage by someone lurching against them.

It is an unfortunate feature of our time that hatches must be strong and securely locked to resist forcible entry. This applies to all parts—hinges, the hatch itself and the surrounding moulding. Nevertheless locks only deter honest people. If a thief will break in anyway (and many moorings are so deserted that use of force is no problem) there is an argument for minimising any incidental damage.

CHAPTER TWELVE

Stem

SHAPE OF STEM Moulded boats often have a sharp razor-edged stem. This is not recommended. A sharp stem, like any sharp-pointed moulding, is bound to be resin-rich and brittle on the surface; yet a stem has to withstand a lot of bumps—from a tide-borne bottle to a major misjudgement. If it is brittle it will soon get chipped.

A rounded stem is not resin-rich and brittle because it is a more easily moulded shape, and therefore it is much less vulnerable. The basic shape of the boat need not be altered except to put a radius on the sharp razor-edge.

An axe wielded with average vigour will have the same energy as a cruiser going quite gently. No one who respects an axe would use it to chop at a concrete wall, but a boat can easily graze one, even when carefully handled, or it can be bumped by another boat or by tide-borne debris. This shows how important it is that a moulded stem should not be a sharp, brittle, razor-edge.

PROTECTION FOR THE STEM Chips are tedious to patch up, to say nothing of being unsightly. It is therefore much more satisfactory to fit some protection, preferably something which will absorb shocks and is easily renewed. Remember a moulded stem is very much part of the boat; it cannot be taken off and replaced, and it has not got the massive thickness of a wooden boat's stem.

Protection can be the common brass or plated strip or a false wooden stem (Fig. 12.1). Both these will need a flat moulded on the stem to form a firm seating, otherwise their shape will be very tricky. A moulded flat cannot be an afterthought; it must be considered at the design stage. If a stem has to be rounded off or flattened as a modification at a later date it is important that compensating thickness is moulded inside. Otherwise this modification would weaken the stem.

When performance demands a razor-edge stem to "cut through the water" (opinions differ as to its value and necessity), it is better to make one by shaping a false wooden stem (Fig. 12.1D). Then, when putty can no longer restore the edge, it is simple to replace it. Usually it is better to protect the wood in turn with a half-round brass strip.

A false stem must be fastened in such a way that it can be replaced when required. This means that it must be bolted or screwed, not glued and preferably not clenched. The fastenings must obviously be watertight and sealed on the inside. Embedded nuts are satisfactory.

Having suffered a lot of damage, and seen much more, caused by the hard, sharp stem of unskilfully sailed small dinghies (and having, like most other people, even been guilty myself on one or two occasions when everything was not under perfect control), I am all in favour of soft rubber "bumpers." The Alpha dinghy, I believe, was the first to use a moulded rubber false stem and it has always seemed to me to be a thoroughly good idea; the damage done by the stem of a hard-sailed dinghy is devastating, and out of all

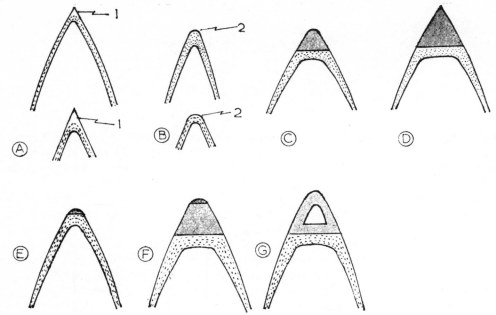

12.1: *Design of the stem.*

A **Not Recommended.** *The sharp-edged stem is bound to be resin-rich and difficult to mould. Insert figure shows how the glass-fibre bridges the sharp stem which is therefore pure resin, 1, and probably has cavities. The sharp edge will be brittle and easily chipped. Little protection is possible.*

B. *A rounded stem has no sharp brittle edge. Note how the glass-fibre layers follow the curve properly, 2. The stem should always be thickened.*

C. *A wooden false stem is more easily touched up and can be replaced readily if mangled. The stem must have a flat mounted on it to mount the false stem which is easily fixed and faired in.*

D. *The wooden false stem can be shaped to a razor edge where the performance demands it. This is acceptable, unlike A, because it can be replaced if damaged.*

E. *A metal strip is often used as protection. This, too, should be mounted on a moulded flat.*

F. *For heavy duty a wooden false stem should be protected in turn by a metal strip.*

G. *A rubber "bumper" is strongly recommended in crowded rivers—by a long-suffering boat-owner!*

proportion to the relative sizes of the two boats. Moreover, although a 20-tonner can be stove in amidships by such an encounter, the dinghy will get away with only the loss of a little more paint from an already bare stem. If I had my way "bumpers" would be compulsory for all boats, particularly small ones.

A soft "bumper" up the stem need not be expensive or unsightly, provided the boat is designed for it. Ordinary "D" shaped dinghy fender will do.

A "bumper" should not be despised on a cruiser either, although this is more for protecting the boat itself. Having plenty of momentum behind it (even a lightly built cruiser will have a displacement reckoned in tons), the stem will soon lose its edge when grated on concrete harbour walls. A soft "bumper" stops this. Of course, well handled boats never hit walls; but I am not talking about a good head-on collision—that is likely to result in serious structural damage, anyway—just the grazes and scrapes of slight misjudgement or momentary inattention. Moreover there are other sources of damage, e.g. the anchor cable will often jam under the stem when getting underway with wind against tide.

All my yachts have had bowsprits—and my present little boat must be the only GRP cruiser to sport one (not my idea—I inherited it). Nowadays bowsprits are derided as terribly old fashioned, except when revived by clever designers to cheat a rating rule. But they do have the advantage of keeping trouble at arm's length. They have their drawbacks of course. I find they tend to sweep grazing cows off the bank when going about in narrow channels, and there was one celebrated occasion when a friend impaled his bowsprited yacht through a cottage window like a knife stuck in a plank.

STEM The stem of a wooden boat is a major structural member and is usually pretty massive. It is a continuation of the keel and backbone of the boat.

On a moulded boat it is basically just part of the shell. However, it is a sound plan to make use of the strong angle shape and thicken it up well to form a girder and have structural value. This is probably more important on a sailing yacht which has to take the strains of the forestay than on a motor-cruiser. In any case the motor-cruiser's stem is often more bulbous and does not lend itself so well to thickening for structural advantage.

As it happens the stem will usually come out thicker than the rest of the shell because it is a logical place for overlaps in the glass reinforcement. These can be planned to come where they have most structural value. If you use a core the stem can easily be made into a "top-hat" frame (in this case perhaps a dunce's cap).

There is little point in protecting the stem from bumps if it is going to fold up at the first minor encounter. Therefore there is good reason for stiffening up the stem and making it into a frame. It is going to be a lot cheaper to stiffen it when moulding than to do a major remoulding operation after it has had a moderate bump.

A further advantage of a protective piece on the stem is to hide the mould line. Any split mould will obviously split down the line of the stem and this usually leaves a mark, sometimes a conspicuous mark, together with small cavities and blemishes. I am surprised how often these are left unfilled on quite good class boats. A protective stem-piece will hide them and save the labour of making them good without showing. This would more than pay for the cost of fitting the stem-piece.

FAIRLEADS Chain and mooring fairleads should be arranged so that the moulding is protected and the chain or rope cannot bear on the boat. This should be so on a wooden boat, too, of course, but often it is not, and at certain angles or, in bad cases all the time, it is the rail which takes the rub, not the metal fairlead. A wooden boat can get away with it, because as a rule it is thicker than necessary along the rail, and it can afford to allow the wood to be worn away until the metal fairlead takes the wear as it should; repeated paint or a scarfed piece will make good the damage to the appearance.

A moulded boat, however, is only a shell, and it is still a thin shell even when reinforced and thickened. Any bad wear and chafe from a badly placed fairlead can be serious.

The wearing effect of an anchor cable or even a mooring rope must not be underestimated. A badly led chain or wire will make quite a mess of a deck edge and can easily wear it right through. Even stout wooden boats have been "sawn" through by an anchor cable jumping its fairlead in bad weather.

Mooring fairleads, both fore and aft, must be positioned so that chain and rope cannot bear on the moulding under any conditions of normal use. Lipped fairleads may be needed. If this cannot be done a separate metal lip must be fitted. This is much easier than repairing a worn moulding and need not be unsightly. Fairleads must have good horns so that chain, and particularly wire, cannot jump out. Only anchor chain leads downwards; mooring ropes may be upwards or backwards.

It is wrong to assume that an anchor cable will always lead clear ahead. Wind against tide will make the boat ride forward over the anchor until the cable grates against the hull. This condition is very common, for a boat lies to the wind rather than to the tide; if they are opposed she will not lie easily but will sheer around continuously and even go round in circles. When you are getting underway in such circumstances the chain will often jam firmly under the stem.

A stemhead fairlead gives a clearer lead than the common bow fairlead (Fig. 12.3). An expensive roller fitting is nice, but not essential. A well designed guide is quite adequate for smaller cruisers and will be much cheaper and simpler. It will save a lot of unnecessary expense, too, if the exact stem-fitting is decided at the design stage, because it will be easier to design the bow then to fit a standard fitting than to make or obtain a special fitting to fit the stem later.

Designing the boat to take a standard fitting applies to other fairleads too. Protective pads or lipped fairleads all add to the expense (which is probably why they are seldom fitted when they are needed), and the need for protection can be largely avoided if the fairlead is sited correctly in the first place—and that means on the drawing-board.

A fairlead must be through-bolted. The strain will normally be downwards, but it will often be sideways and even upwards, e.g. springs always lead aft, and at low tide or against a high wall they will lead upwards at quite an angle. Locks can impose a severe jerking strain on the fairleads, and so can bad weather or river floods.

A good fairlead should offer a smooth rounded bearing surface to the rope in any direction it may lead. Very few do this apart from the large, heavy roller fairleads. Most fairleads are so designed that any rope leading in at an angle, like a spring, is faced with a very sharp turn and an edge sharp enough to cut it. This, of course, is one method of ensuring that the rope will fail before the fairlead is pulled off!

Remember that the deck must be strengthened under a fairlead and that the fairlead must fail before the deck. Ideally the rope or cable should break before the fairlead, and that means the strongest rope it is possible to get into the fairlead. This is a tall order, and it is much more useful to have a fairlead which is large enough to take a good-sized rope, in particular the heaviest hawser likely to be on board (bearing in mind that a later owner may only be able to afford thick sisal, not light nylon), than a fairlead which theoretically cannot be pulled off, but will only accept a small rope.

HAWSE-PIPE AND CHAIN-PIPE Chain or wire, and even rope running through an unprotected hawse-pipe, will cause very severe chafe and will "saw" through the moulding in a short time. A metal liner is essential, and this must have a good lip to it

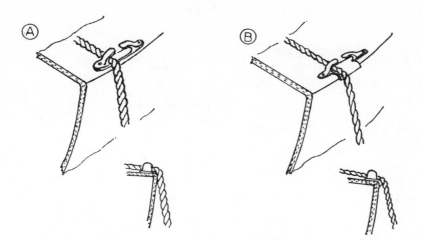

12.2: *Fairleads should have a lip to keep the rope or chain clear of the hull.*
A. *Badly positioned fairlead without lip: note how the rope bears on the hull at certain angles, and will cause wear.*
B. *Fairlead fitted with a lip. Note that the rope now bears on the lip, not on the angle of the hull.*

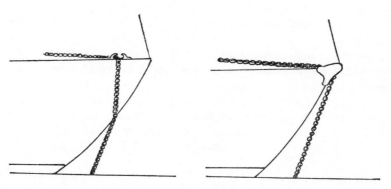

12.3: *Reducing chafe from anchor chain.*
When the boat rides forward over her anchor chain—a common occurrence—the chain will bear on the hull much less if the boat has a stemhead fairlead instead of the standard bow fairleads.

because the chain seldom runs true. (See Fig. 12.3.) A plain metal tube, unless thick and heavy, would wear away and expose the moulding.

The hull needs to be well thickened and reinforced where the hawse-pipe will come, as the strain can be considerable. The weight of a heavy anchor and chain is a lot in itself, but, in addition, snubbing when at anchor, and cable jams when running out, cause shock loads. Proprietary hawse-pipes for GRP do not allow for much, if any, thickening or backing pad, while those for wood need an excessive thickness.

Even the smallest cruiser needs a chain-pipe through the deck. There are many good

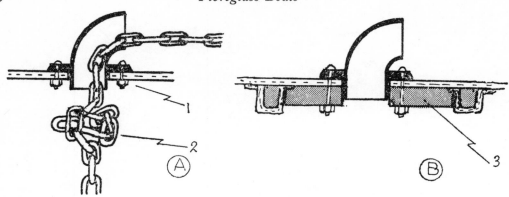

12.4: *Chain pipes.*

A. **Not Recommended.** *Chain pipe simply bolted straight through the deck, 1. If the chain bunches, 2 when running out fast—a common occurrence—the shock will pull out the chainpipe and probably a section of the deck with it.*

B. *The chain pipe should be bolted through a substantial block linking up with deck beams to withstand any shock load.*

proprietary fittings, but a chain-pipe is more than a simple guide, and it requires to be firmly mounted. Chain has a trick of jamming in the pipe. This is more likely on a small boat than on a larger one; the larger boat's anchor winch tends to smooth out the twists in the chain but on a small boat without a winch these twists get fed below, and cause kinks and bunches in the chain. A sudden jam when the anchor and chain are running out fast will impart a shock load to the chain-pipe, and the deck in its vicinity, which will tear out a pipe which is simply bolted through the deck. The chain-pipe needs to be bolted through a substantial block and preferably connected with the deck-beams.

The hawse-pipe, or fairleads, and the chain-pipe are not the only parts subject to wear from the chain. The deck between and any obstructions which bad design may place in the vicinity will also get a lot of wear. Wooden slats or metal plates will avoid this wear. A moulded non-slip pattern is very easily damaged and chipped by this sort of treatment.

The modern trend is to use nylon rope instead of chain. Nevertheless the alternative of chain should always be allowed for with provision for a chain-pipe and locker. Ground tackle is a matter of the owner's preference or needs, not the designer's or builder's whim. Boats going from one marina or dock to another may never anchor. (I have surveyed boats which just did not have anchors.) But boats kept on deserted, wild coasts—which can still be found without going far—need good anchors and, if rock or coral, something which cannot be cut. Nylon must still be stowed below. Some owners motor from an open anchorage while their crews sort out the knitting on the foredeck, but if you take a pride in sailing away, perhaps singlehanded, anchor gear must stow quickly and neatly. Besides, there may be times when you have to.

TOWING EYE The strain on the painter of a dinghy tied up for a picnic by a quiet river bank is quite different from one being towed, half waterlogged and sheering wildly in a following sea. These days any dinghy-builder must consider both conditions.

Small boats must be built with an adequate towing eye on principle. It is a small fitting, and the extra cost is negligible compared with the cost of making good the damage if it does pull out, and the recovery or salvage—if possible!

A towing eye needs to be strong. The Boating Industry Association of America (B.I.A.) recommends that for runabouts it is strong enough to lift twice the weight of the boat and its load; although it sounds very conservative it is a fair guide.

It is easy enough to fit a piece of hardware which meets this requirement, but it is sometimes forgotten that the boat itself must be strong enough, too, and will need reinforcing around the towing eye. The towing eye must be fitted through a stout block to distribute the load, and the moulding must be reinforced to at least double thickness around it (Fig. 12.5). The towing eye must, of course, be a good quality marine fitting and not, like some heavily advertised boats, be brightly plated steel which had rusted away completely when I saw one after less than a season's use. These boats looked very flashy in a showroom or Boat Show, but deteriorated nearly as quickly as a glamour queen taking off her make-up.

An eyebolt should be fitted with a locknut or be prevented, positively, from twisting under load, e.g. with a cotter-pin. Under load a rope will twist and this repeated twisting can loosen an eyebolt. Even if it does not result in the loss of the boat it will cause annoying leaks and enlarge the hole. A bolted eyeplate is better than an eyebolt, because it cannot twist, but it is difficult to find an eyeplate, unless it is specially made, which will fit the shape of the stem.

A double-skinned boat should have the towing eye bolted through both skins, which must either be in contact at that point or have a fitted block between them so that the eyebolt cannot crush them. It is bad practice to fasten a towing eye through one skin only, because it is inaccessible short of cutting away one of the skins if it has to be renewed or tightened, quite a major operation for minor maintenance. Embedding the nut would not be suitable unless adequate means of locking and sealing it can be arranged, possibly a good self-locking nut. Seepage into the space between the skins from a loose fitting is highly undesirable. An eyeplate, however, can well be bolted into embedded nuts as this cannot twist. In these cases a specially made eyeplate to fit the stem might be justified.

It should not be overlooked that a bow buoyancy compartment presents the same problems, and it is just as important that the nut of the towing eye should not be sealed inaccessibly inside the buoyancy tank.

The towing-eye should be in a good position for towing. This is usually well down on the stem so that the bows are lifted. Even if the boat will never go to sea or be towed, an outside eye avoids chafe on the gunwale when moored, and this applies until the boat is large enough to have a deck and proper fairleads.

A larger boat or launch used for open beach work needs a very stout eye, for it will have to be winched up the beach fully loaded, and if it is rough this may not be done gently. Any "snatch" imposes a severe strain on the fore part of the boat, and this must be stoutly reinforced with the area of reinforcement extending well aft to link up with other structural members, particularly the keel. A wooden beach boat has a stout keel, and the towing wire is attached to an eye fixed to the fore part of this keel. The moulded beach boat will be a one-piece shell and if it has a keel at all it will be probably no more than a reinforced channel-section "dent." Therefore it is necessary to spread the strain of the towing-eye over a wide area.

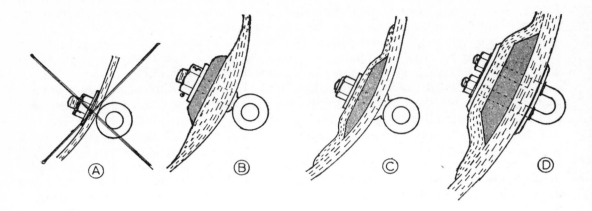

12.5: *Fixing a towing-eye: a. Single-skin moulding.*

A. **Wrong.** *Bolted straight through an unthickened moulding with no block to spread the strain. Also the eye-bolt has no shoulder and the nut is not locked.*
B. *Moulding thickened and block bedded; eye-bolt fastened through block and skin so that the strain is well spread. Nut locked with cotter pin to prevent rotation working it loose.*
C. *Shaped block embedded in moulding and eye-bolt fastened right through block and both parts of the moulding. Self-locking nut.*
D. *Heavy fabricated steel towing-eye suitable for a large beach boat, fastened through a block embedded in an extensively reinforced moulding.*

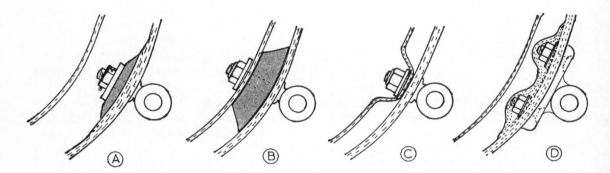

12.6: *Fitting a towing-eye: b. Double moulding.*

A. **Not Recommended.** *Bolting through one skin only. Technically correct and adequately strong but impossible to renew or tighten without cutting away the moulding.*
B. *Interskin space filled with incompressible block, tube, or filling of syntactic foam.*
C. *Inner skin brought into contact with the outer in way of towing-eye which is then bolted through both skins.*
D. *Eye-plate bolted through thickened outer skin and nuts embedded. This can be replaced from outside yet cannot twist loose or leak.*

A towing-eye is a recommended fitting on runabouts and small cruisers, either sail or power, which are meant to travel on trailers. With a stout towing-eye the boat can be winched on to the trailer or even pulled out bodily from firm ground. Without a towing-eye the boat must be manhandled or floated on. Floating on is certainly the easiest method, but it needs a sound hard which will not bog down the loaded trailer or car, and proper axle bearings. Good launching hards are still comparatively few, and, being unremunerative, they are likely to remain that way, certainly as far as the larger trailer boats are concerned. Moreover they are often obstructed or required for their proper purpose—which is unlikely to be launching pleasure boats from inland towns.

A towing-eye makes a strong secure lashing down point when on the trailer in a position which avoids any chafe on the gunwales or deck. Two smaller eyes each side of the transom are also a sound idea for lashing down the aft end. These may be combined with lifting handles, for it is often extremely difficult to get a grip on a smooth, shiny, and probably wet moulded hull.

The B.I.A. recommend a stout towing-eye and lashing down eyes as standard equipment on all runabouts and small cruisers. These would be useful on sailing cruisers too.

SPLIT MOULDING

SPLIT MOULDING It is common to mould the hull of a sailing cruiser in two halves, joined inside with butt straps, because moulding a deep keel or fin raises very difficult problems of access. No one can mould properly while standing on their head in a fume-laden atmosphere working at arms' length deep in a keel, or pushing the glass down with a stick. It is a sound rule that difficult moulding is bad moulding, and conversely good moulding is more likely under good conditions.

Unfortunately the all-important butt straps must still be done under difficult conditions and generally their moulding is not good, especially where only a stick will reach. To compensate they must be really thick and wide, with special attention to the bonding and first few layers. They should be at least as thick as the hull on the centreline. These butt straps hold the boat together under water—no more need be said.

It is most important to seal the join properly outside. This is often skimped, especially under the keel where out of sight and difficult to do, and probably obstructed by the cradle. Water will attack exposed fibres along this trimmed edge. In difficult places inside where the glass has been pushed in with a stick there are generally numerous seepage paths because of the poor moulding. If water can enter through the join it can trace a devious course through the seepage paths and be a troublesome and elusive leak, often trapped within the keel space and therefore not apparent. Water within a moulding leads to decay, enlarging the seepage paths and worsening the leak. If trapped in the keel space decay within will only be apparent when extensive.

As an example of what can happen, I once noticed a very slight weep from the centreline join of a 20 ft. (6 m.) small cruiser, age about two years but which had not been afloat for over a year. A little digging was rewarded by a gush of water from the fin and I measured five gallons. This water had travelled a devious route, mostly in waterways formed by the incompletely filled join and under or through the butt strap, and had then been trapped by a weir effect. The slight weep which attracted my interest was caused by decay just breaking through, originating either at the trimmed edge or the stick-moulded, porous filling behind.

CHAPTER THIRTEEN
Ballast Keels

EXTERNAL A major item on a sailing cruiser is the ballast-keel. Conventional external keels can be used, but there are unconventional internal keels which are often better.

The conventional method is to bolt it to the outside. This is a sound and traditional method. It gives the most concentrated weight at a lower point than any internal keel but for moulded boats there are serious problems which are not met with in wooden construction.

The chief problem is fit. A conventional wooden boat is built actually on the keel; it is bound to fit exactly even if it is the wrong size and shape, because the boat is built round it. Even when not built on the keel, as in some modern methods, there is usually a generous thickness of wood which can be trimmed away to make the boat fit the keel with reasonable ease and without seriously weakening the hull.

GRP hulls are not built on top of their keels. Their shape is dictated by the mould. The keel must be fitted after moulding and so it must be cast to close tolerances. The keel must fit the boat, not the boat the keel as in wooden construction. The hulls must be jigged to prevent distortion, which would upset close tolerances, and the keels should be fitted as soon after moulding as possible.

It is difficult to take anything off a moulded boat, and with only a thin shell, what you do take off is going to be missed badly; trimming a boat to fit a keel that is $\frac{1}{4}$ in. oversize might well weaken the boat to a dangerous extent. It would be a large part of the hull thickness even on a big cruiser, and might well be right through a small one. If done at all it would be essential to compensate for it with extra material moulded inside. The cost and trouble would devastate a slender profit margin.

Forcing the keel to fit will only ruin the moulding, with very little effect on the keel. A lead keel can be trimmed, with the sacrifice of some weight, but altering an iron keel is beyond normal boatyard resources. Therefore a keel, particularly an iron keel, must never be oversize. The lower weight of an external keel gives better performance. Lead is expensive, but is heavier and therefore even lower, so fortunately it is more suitable.

This exact fit is a point which you must establish very clearly with the foundry, making it clear that you will not pay for the keel unless it fits. "Trade" and "normally acceptable" tolerances just will not do.

Accurate location of the bolt-holes seems harder than precision casting. The foundry should position these as accurately as possible, not at random as is often done, because they will probably have to line up with frames, and the boat should be drilled accordingly. Moulded-in holes are likely to involve troublesome fitting.

Casting a keel to these tolerances is a very tricky job and requires exact estimation of the contraction. Every keel must be checked carefully before acceptance.

Tight tolerances can be avoided, and the task of making the keel considerably simpler (and therefore cheaper) if the keel is designed right from the start, as a keel for a moulded boat, and not on the lines of a keel for a wooden boat. Keep the design as simple as possible with no undercuts, lugs or tongues. Make it also an open fit at one end so that it is impossible for it to jam even if oversize (Fig. 13.1). If necessary make the toe of wood, or as a separate sub-moulding put on afterwards, so that it can be trimmed to shape to allow for variations in the keel. Being made of wood or a thin non-structural shell with an open end it will be quite easy to trim. Wood is good enough for British waters, but a sub-moulding or something wormproof would be essential in tropical waters.

Ideally the cast keel would fit close enough for just a thin layer of sealant and no more, say about $\frac{1}{16}$ in. (2 mm.), but this is optimistic. Normally it must be undersize and require packing. Very thick layers of flexible packing will allow the keel to waggle. Therefore the flexible sealant must be kept thin and the rest built up with solid material.

The keel can be built up roughly to near the size required by moulding glass mat onto it. This is allowed to set and smoothed off. It is then bolted on with sealant between. A very large gap might need packing with wood. This should be protected against possible attack by worm.

Some time can be saved by putting the hull and keel together on a layer of "wet" mat, but only to shape the mat to fit. It should not be bolted down but lifted off after setting, trimmed, inspected and built up further if necessary. Note that where faces slide, e.g. at a vertical edge, "wet" mat may bunch and form high spots.

The common practice of bedding on "wet" mat as a sealant is not recommended. Under the high pressure exerted by the keel bolts and the boat's weight, the resin will "wash" out, i.e. it will be squeezed out leaving almost dry, incompressible glass at high spots. In any case "wet" glass has little flow and if the surface is uneven there will be unfilled hollows. Dry, resin washed glass is easily attacked by water, leading to decay and gradual loosening or leaks.

If a resin based bedding is wanted specially, resin putty or a highly thixotropic paste are better. These flow well, unrestrained by glass, with no danger of bunches of hard glass forming. All resin based bedding, whether mat, putty or thixotropic paste, will set hard, rigid and have no give. Some authorities say keels should be solidly fitted but I disagree. The slightest later movement of the keel will crack the join. Apart from dynamic sailing stresses GRP has twice the thermal expansion of iron: in a cold winter climate this alone will crack the joint. There should not be an iron/GRP join with no bedding at all. Under high pressure the gel coat will be crushed, especially at high spots on the iron, or the GRP will be prestressed.

An important practical objection to bedding on "wet" mat, or resin putty or paste, is the time factor. Obviously it has to be bolted up while the resin is still "wet." Yet the minor snags which are highly probable in carefully placing the hull and keel together, aligning, and tightening the keel bolts are likely to lead to delays which exceed the short working time of the resin. If it does set prematurely the keel will *not* bed down and probably will not fit either. Enforced haste in a tricky operation is fatal. Long setting time is essential.

A flexible sealant must be permanently elastic. Age-hardening putties are no use. Very soft sealants will squeeze out too readily. Moderate hardness (say Shore A50) is needed; technically it should be an elastomer which has excellent recovery as well as

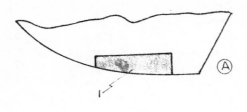
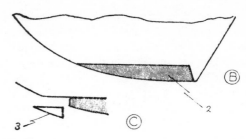

13.1: *Shape of external keel.*

A. *Conventional shape,* 1. *Accurate tolerances in casting are absolutely necessary. Very difficult to fit if at all oversize.*

B. *Preferred shape,* 2. *This cannot be a jamming fit even if oversize. Tolerances can be normal casting tolerances.*

C. *If necessary the toe,* 3, *can be a separate piece made of wood or a sub-moulding, and trimmed to shape. This will accommodate substantial variations in the dimensions of the keel.*

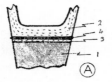
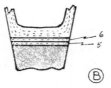
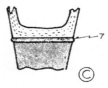
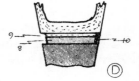

13.2: *Bedding down and padding a keel.*

A. *The keel,* 1, *is bedded down on the hull,* 2, *by building up to shape with mat,* 3, *allowing it to set, filing smooth and then using bedding compound,* 4.

B. *A large gap is filled by building nearly up to shape with mat,* 5, *allowing it to set and then bedding down on a further layer of "wet" mat,* 6.

C. *If the fit is accurate the keel can be bedded down on a thick layer of bedding compound alone,* 7.

D. *When considerable packing is needed, pack roughly to shape with wood,* 8, *and bed down on "wet" mat or bedding compound,* 9. *A ½-in. gap at the edges is recommended so that it can be filled with resin-glass cement,* 10, *to seal in the wood, and keep out worms and rot.*

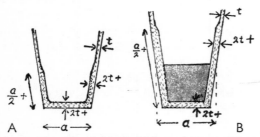
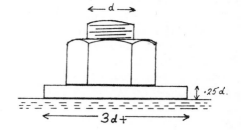

13.3: *Recommended hull thickness in way of keel.* t *is the normal fin thickness, a, the width of the keel.*

These dimensions should be regarded as the minimum.

A, External keel; B, Internal.

13.4: *Minimum dimensions for keel boat washers.*

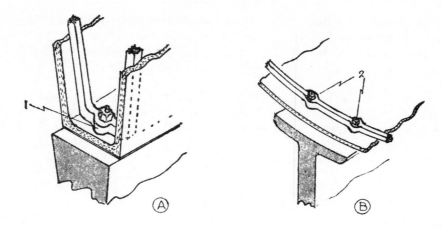

13.5: *Bolting down the keel.*
A. *Keel-bolts should pass through the frames which can easily be formed into a bulge at that point,* 1.
B. *Fin keels should be fastened in a similar way,* 2.

compressibility. Suitable elastomers are polysulphide, silicone and polybutadiene based. (Note not all sealants based on these are suitable and there are others, not mentioned, which can be.) Alternatively a neoprene gasket can be used, but presupposes a gap of fairly uniform thickness. All these are expensive sealants, but quality and the right sealant are essential.

The outside of the join can be faired in with resin putty. This allows more latitude in casting and fitting. On a high performance boat, not only the join but any irregularities in the keel and all fittings will be faired in to give a smooth flow. The ballast keel may be faced up with resin putty all over to eliminate roughness of the casting.

Obviously an iron keel and all ironwork should be galvanised or at least properly treated. Rusting keels, so commonly seen, are not consistent with low maintenance.

Drilling through the GRP keel, which may be an inch or more thick, is tough on drills. Tipped masonry drills can be used. However it is not necessary if the position of the bolts is known accurately and certainly beforehand. Wooden plugs in the mould are easily knocked or drilled out, leaving clean holes.

The hull itself must be strong where the ballast keel is attached. The thickness should be at least twice the fin thickness and must be carried up the sides for a distance equal to at least half the width of the keel before tapering off gradually. Keel bolts must have generous washers. Wide plates are far better. Bolts must be close to frames or pass through bulges formed in the frames. The frame cores at such points must be incompressible.

KEEL BOLTS Keel bolts must be replaceable. Stainless steel or monel are the preferred choice where cost permits, but even stainless steel can corrode and much of it in yacht work is of suspect quality, prone to crevice corrosion. Inner mouldings must not prevent or hamper access for replacement and, equally important, routine inspection or tightening. This is also made unnecessarily expensive if an engine or tanks must be removed, and naturally discourages simple inspection.

Bolts may be lightly moulded over provided the GRP can be cut away readily if need be. This should not be relied upon for essential sealing because it is unlikely to be replaced. Personally I prefer to see keel bolts exposed. Moulding over discourages inspection and keel bolts are too vital to forget. The need to withdraw them for inspection at regular intervals must weigh against claims for no maintenance.

INTERNAL A moulded hull readily lends itself to the simpler approach of using an internal keel. It must be accepted, however, that no internal keel can be so compact or low down as a cast external keel. However the reduction in cost, the simplicity and other advantages are powerful points in its favour; and good design from the start can minimise the disadvantage. It is easily modified in production.

An internal keel is not to be confused with the traditional internal ballast. The old style boat with internal ballast, usually a fishing-boat type, has a wooden keel for lateral resistance and a collection of iron or lead pigs, old fire-bars, stones or cement, according to local custom, stowed in the bilges, usually loose and badly secured. This ballast is high up, but it is used only on heavily built boats with a low ballast ratio, where a high performance is outweighed by other considerations. On fishing-boats the main attraction was cheapness; the only advantage on a yacht is usually easy motion at sea.

The internal keel on a moulded boat is quite a different idea and is basically a hollow fin filled with ballast material. It is much lower down than the old-fashioned ballast in the bilges, roughly in the proper position for a ballast keel, and it gives a similar high ballast ratio; being a fin it also provides the lateral resistance. Moreover it is really firmly secured, an important point, for I know of several boats where lumps of the internal ballast have gone flying through the deckhead when the boat was knocked down by a squall.

Fig. 13.6 shows the general idea. Instead of ending above the ballast keel the moulding is carried right down to the bottom as a hollow fin; its shape will normally be much the same as the shape of an external keel and the space inside is filled with ballast so that the keel is contained within the moulding. This ballast is no expensive, close tolerance casting like an external keel. It may be in one piece but it is much more often loose pieces of scrap metal, punchings, shot, barytes or anything else heavy and compact. Metals cannot be cast in place because the heat would damage the GRP shell. A matrix of loose metal bound with cement or resin is generally used. This may be mixed and poured as a slurry or the binder is poured in alone over the loose ballast. The former is preferable because a viscous binder may not get to the bottom or impregnate the ballast.

When resin is the binder, the high exotherm as it sets may damage the GRP or crack the casting. It should be built up a little at a time. A low reactivity resin is needed, not the usual moulding resins, with the bare minimum of hardeners to reduce exotherm. As cure is unimportant greater risks can be taken than with structural GRP. Water also retards setting and reduces exotherm. Water thinnable resins are obtainable.

Concrete can be used alone, but ordinary mass concrete is deceptively light compared to metal (loose metal is also a lot lighter than solid metal). Preferably it should be made with a dense aggregate such as metal or barytes rather than stones and sand. It should also be a rich waterproof concrete with a high cement content. Cost is of little importance. Tamping and vibration are essential—bubbles are negative ballast.

Loose, unbound pieces are not recommended. Small pieces will fall out if the keel is slightly damaged (a loss of 50 per cent has been found—the owner had not even noticed!). Loose pieces settle and leave voids. Steel will rust if water gets in and although in theory

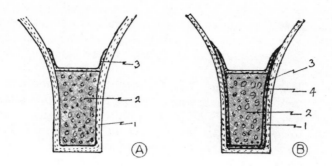

13.6: *Internal keel.*

A. *The moulding, 1, is continued right down to the bottom of the keel so that the keel is contained entirely within the moulding. The space inside is filled with lead or scarp iron, bound together with concrete or pitch, 2. Finally it is sealed in by moulding over the top, 3.*
B. *A refinement is to mould the final layers of the hull in the vicinity of the ballast, 4, with a resin containing a large proportion of heavy filler. Alternatively, it can be plastered on. This blends the keel into the hull.*

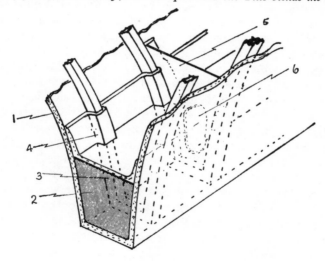

13.7: *Internal keel.*

The hull, 1, should be made strong enough to carry the load of the keel, 2. Frames, 3, are continued right down into the keel and the sealing layer, 4, moulded around them. Extra stiffness and tying is given by web floors, 5, which should have generous cut-outs, 6, to preserve continuity of the keel.

the weight will not change, rusty water will drain away and slowly the ballast with it. Rust swells and may exert considerable pressure, although the extent is at present an unknown factor. I have sometimes wondered if boats with loose ballast rattle: it must bounce about when sailing. Large pieces will hammer and wear the GRP. This is brutal treatment and inviting trouble where, if sealed, it is impossible to see, and difficult even if not. Movement is impossible when bound in a matrix, rust is confined to the surface, and the ballast cannot fall out or drain away.

Cement will cause some corrosion of steel, especially small pieces. But more important, cement attacks glass fibre under damp conditions as are commonly found in a keel if there is seepage or water of casting trapped within. High alumina cement (Cement Fondu) does not attack glass fibre and should be used where possible. The rapid setting might be inconvenient.

Cement contains a high proportion of water. Moulding over the ballast, as is commonly done, will seal in residual moisture, which will be high if sealed soon after casting. As this is alkaline it will be harmful to GRP in the long term. I prefer concrete ballast to be open at the top so that the concrete can dry out over the years. If smoothed and painted over it will be unnoticeable, but may crack at the edges later. These should be sealed with mastic. Just in case ballast works loose it should be made impossible for it to fall out if the boat ever gets rolled over under extreme conditions. A near capsize (and the conditions to cause it) would be bad but not fatal. But a keel through the deck, or chasing the crew round the cabin, would be certain disaster.

Large castings, whether in one piece or shaped blocks, will need packing in place. An accurate fit is not possible or desirable. Great care must be taken not to force them or let them jam under their own weight. Cement or resin can be used here too; where cost allows the stronger bonding epoxy resin rather than polyester should be used.

Internal ballast must bond firmly to the GRP shell. This is important, for then the ballast strengthens the fin and there is no risk of movement, internal chafe or hammering; also there can be no water pockets between fin and ballast. The fin is an obvious place for water to collect. Pockets will lead to hidden decay, and frost damage in cold climates.

An external iron keel is almost indestructible and makes an excellent battering ram. The boat can sit on it, crushing stones as with an anvil. With internal ballast the same impact, crushing and abrasive forces are there but must be borne by the more delicate GRP shell with its easily damaged gel coat. Compared with iron GRP is easily shattered by impact, crushed by stones, or worn away by abrasion, and being the basic boat, albeit the thickest part, it is irreplaceable. GRP under and in front of an internal keel needs to be protected with metal or wooden shoes which, being intended to get worn and damaged, must be readily replaceable. Centreline joins need to be sound too. They are quite inaccessible under the ballast. There have been cases of boats splitting due to faulty joins, generally following some pounding, and satisfactory repair is very difficult.

As well as cheap materials and *in situ* casting instead of precision foundry work, internal keels give other savings. The cost of keel bolts is eliminated, together with complications of fitting and the maintenance and worry throughout the life of the boat—an important point in a low maintenance boat. The extra thickness needed for a strong connection and bearing surface with a heavy external keel is not required, and this offsets the cost of the larger area of moulding to contain the ballast. The weight of the ballast is distributed evenly instead of being concentrated round the keel bolts. However, moulding a deep fin is difficult and may require a split moulding.

The keel is moulded *in situ*, so no separate accurate pattern has to be made with carefully calculated allowances for shrinkage. Scrap metal and cement are cheap and easily handled, and do not require heating. In fact the keel can be home-made very easily and is ideal for amateur construction. Local materials can be used, perhaps some particular waste material is available free—or one might even be paid to take it away and make keels with it!

The handling equipment required is simpler. Lifting and dropping the boat on to the keel, or jacking the keel up to the boat, precisely and gently, is quite a tricky operation calling for careful, accurate handling of heavy objects. When casting *in situ*, no piece need be larger than can be handled conveniently by one person.

However, if the moulding has to be lifted out of the mould or trundled around, it is obviously better to leave the keel until a late stage in fitting out.

Lloyd's Rules call for the thickness of the hull in way of the internal keel to be twice as thick as the rest of the fin, and to continue up the sides for a distance at least half the keel width before tapering off gradually (Fig. 13.3). They also lay down a minimum girth (width plus sides) for this keel thickness of 15 in. for a boat 20 ft. L.O.A. and 33 in. for 80 ft. with intermediate sizes in proportion. On a deep, narrow fin I would prefer to carry the keel thickness higher up the sides than this rule suggests.

The frames should run right down to the bottom of the keel and help to support it (Fig. 13.7). Web floors, which are easily made by moulding against a shuttering, are recommended to tie the sides of the fin together. The webs should have generous cut-outs to allow the keel to be continuous and reduce the amount of lighter plastic material so low down. Solid metal should be used for the frame cores. Why bother about anything lightweight in the area of the keel? It is wasting good ballast space. Lead strips form easily shaped cores, and can be built up to the required thickness.

Any space in the fin keel not occupied by ballast can be used for other heavy stowage such as chain or tanks. Engines, although heavy, are poor utilisation because of the empty space around them for access. Empty spaces are often boxed over to form neat smooth bilges and keep water out of unpumpable pockets. If strong this forms a good box girder, but a light lining gives little strength and often allows bilge water through to collect, hidden, foul and inaccessible in the fin below.

TWIN KEELS The principles are the same whatever the number of keels, but a weakness with many twin keels is the hull strength. The hull must be well stiffened with transverse frames linking the keels. Local stiffening around the keels is not enough: the whole bottom must be stiffened. Most keel movement is caused by the hull flexing, not the keels themselves. Any flexibility here is dangerous and leads to fatigue failure. Small features cause very dangerous hard spots resulting in rapid weakness, cracking and splitting of the hull. Bad failures have been seen within one year.

FIN KEELS A fin keel is easier to fit and overcomes some of the problems of tight tolerances. The keel is easier to drill so that the position of the bolts is less critical. The hull needs to be strengthened and should be at least twice as thick as the rest of the bottom, with ample wide stiffening frames. Usually a large insert or metal plate is embedded as well, matching the keel flange. If the keel is readily detachable for transport the bolts should be blind so that resealing each time is avoided. A sound way is to tap the embedded plate.

Fin keels are fitted late. The hull, meanwhile, must be well supported. Forcing a distorted hull to fit a rigid unyielding keel will prestress and weaken the hull. Similarly, each fin should be checked for shape before fitting.

CHAPTER FOURTEEN

Bilge Keels and Non-ballast Keels

THE NEED Bilge keels are essential to protect the hull from serious wear under the full weight of the boat and its load. The same applies to the keel, and no other parts are subject to wear under such a weight. There is little difference in this respect between a dinghy, a launch and a motor cruiser, or, in fact, any round-bilged boat as opposed to a keel boat. The concentrated weight on a small area can crush the surface of the moulding, particularly if it is in contact with stones or a hard surface, and any movement or dragging will grind away unprotected material with dangerous rapidity.

This is no new problem, nor is it something peculiar to moulded boats. It has existed with wooden boats, but whereas even a dinghy has an inch or two of wooden keel to wear away before any serious part is reached, and this is normally protected with a brass strip anyway, a GRP dinghy has only $\frac{1}{8}$ in. (3 mm.) to be worn away; even on a large boat only $\frac{1}{2}$ in. (12 mm.). Moreover, this is the hull skin itself which is being worn away, and it will be weakened to a dangerous degree long before it is worn right through. Metal protected bilge keels are used as a matter of course on a wooden boat, even a stout one, to protect the hull from wear; it is even more important to protect the moulded boat, because anything worn away is going to be missed badly.

For a dinghy, good bilge keels are essential, and a wooden skeg or keel aft as well; for the usual way to move a dingy is to lift the bow and drag the stern—like Winnie-the-Pooh coming downstairs.

Wood is cheap and offers good protection in depth, but it must be considered expendable, that is, it must be intended to get worn away and must be secured in such a way that it can be renewed when necessary. It is a sound idea to protect the wooden keel and bilge keels themselves with brass strips, as is normally done on wooden boats. Aluminium alloy castings and extruded strip have been used but are soft for hard wear. They must be marine quality. Hard PVC, nylon and other plastics are also suitable.

Often the bilge keels are moulded in as bulges in the hull (Fig. 14.1). There is nothing basically wrong with this provided you fully appreciate that they are going to get worn and make them considerably thicker to allow for a good deal of sacrificial wear, and fit them with brass strips to minimise the wear. An unprotected bulge of normal hull thickness (Fig. 14.2) is quite wrong and very bad practice. It will soon get worn away making large holes right through and seriously weakening the rest. I have seen and repaired many boats with unprotected keels formed as plain bulges in the hull skin without even the elementary precaution of thickening the skin. Such a boat is hardly worth repairing, because even when the skin is not worn through, the fibres will be exposed over a large area so that moisture can penetrate into the moulding. The resultant decay will aggravate the weakness produced by wear.

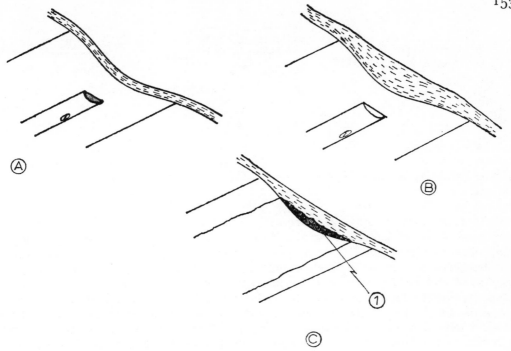

14.1: *Correct design of moulded-in bilge-keel.*

A. *Unthickened bulge protected by brass strip. The absolute bare minimum suitable only for the cheapest boats. dinghies.*

B. *Moulded bilge-keel well thickened and protected with brass strip.*

C. *Hard abrasion-resisting shoe, 1, of resin-glass putty moulded into bulge of bilge-keel, followed by thickened moulding.*

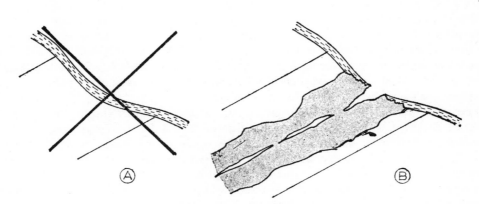

14.2: *Wrong design of bilge-keel.*

A. *Bilge-keel formed by simple bulge in an unthickened hull with no protection against inevitable wear.*

B. *The effect—bilge-keels worn right through in places and severely weakened over their whole length.*

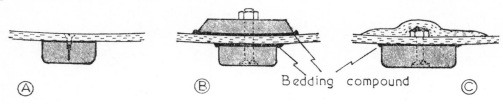

14.3: *Fastening keels and bilge keels.*
A. **Not Recommended:** *bilge keel simply screwed on from inside. A common cause of troublesome leaks.*
B. *Bilge keel bedded down and bolted through a strip on the inside. The strip can be embedded or left open.*
C. *Bilge keels bolted on and nuts embedded on the inside.*

An alternative to using brass strips to protect a thickened bulge is to use a "shoe" of very hard plastic. On some of the launches my company built the bilge keels had a very hard wear-resisting "shoe" made by putting a layer of a special resin-glass putty into the keel bulges in the mould before the gel-coat. This putty was made by adding a large amount of very hard filler such as quartz, slate or carborundum. This produces a surface like a grindstone. In this case, too, the moulded keels were well thickened to make good use of the shape of the bulge for fore-and-aft stiffening. The prototype shows little wear on these keels after six years continuous rough use. One particular advantage of this method is the absence of any problems of electrolysis in conjunction with metal keel bands.

ATTACHING BILGE KEELS The method of attaching bilge keels is extremely important—and one of the commonest causes of troublesome leaks. This is quite unnecessary. Leaks occur because the bilge keels are not bedded down properly, allowing water to seep past the screws as soon as the wooden keels wear and work loose (Fig. 14.3). It is particularly common when the keels are secured by screws or rivets straight through the hull skin. Leaks are not uncommon on a brand-new boat due to bilge keels not being bedded down, even before there is the excuse of the wooden keels getting worn and loose.

The correct method is to bed the keels down on a flexible bedding compound, which is more resilient than "wet" mat. The fastenings must either be sealed over on the inside or be through a strip of metal or wood in the inside which is itself well bedded down or embedded. A screw straight through the hull into the bilge keel (Fig. 14.3A) will not only work loose as the keel wears, and therefore leak, but it will also enlarge the hole in the hull making the leak even worse and the screw looser.

The screw should be through a strip on the inside, or some similar arrangement, to prevent the screw enlarging the hole in the thin moulded shell and even pulling through. Washers are not sufficient as they do not stop the sideways movement which is responsible for enlarging the hole. Ideally these strips should be embedded so that leaks are then impossible.

Another satisfactory and leakproof method is to bolt through a thickened moulding and embed the nuts on the inside. Renewal is then simple. At a pinch the nut or even a strip of wood could be embedded in a cement mixture. This is not recommended where anything else could be used, but it would be useful in "dry" construction where facilities are very limited.

The forces acting on a bilge keel should not be underestimated, as keels are subjected to a lot of abuse. The strain on the fastenings is particularly severe when the bilge keels are made deep to act as grab-rails when the dinghy is carried on deck. A good deep bilge keel with handholes gives a splendid hold on a lively deck, but a heavy man "out of step" with the boat will exert a pull more than twice his weight and the leverage on the fastenings and the moulded skin is formidable, quite enough to tear away anything weakly fastened or to damage a light unthickened hull. With deep bilge keels like this it is essential to consider the strength of the hull, too. This should be strengthened by thickening, but a good batten inside, with the keels through-fastened, will usually suffice.

PROTECTION AGAINST WORMS Wooden keels may not be much use in tropical waters, where the worms will make short work of them as a light snack between proper boats. In these areas moulded keels will last longer, but it is even more important that they are not mere unthickened bulges in the bottom.

Another technique is to sheathe the wooden keels with a layer of glass cloth or mat so that they are protected from worm attack; but if the outer sheathing is once worn away the worms will soon find a way in. It is most useful where wooden bilge keels are fitted already; perhaps because the boat was previously used in temperate climates, or perhaps the exporting builder was not aware of the conditions. A sheathed keel should have metal bands as well to prolong its useful life. This is particularly important on a larger boat as the weight of the boat on the keel as it takes the ground will cause severe wear and probably crushing.

The keels could be moulded as sub-mouldings and bonded or bolted on afterwards. A hollow keel might be crushed, and it would be better to fill them. Wood has been mentioned, but they could also be filled with resin-glass putty, syntactic foam, cement, metal pipe or anything else to hand. Weight will not matter below the waterline on a larger boat and may even be welcome. A light or small boat is less likely to crush a keel.

But if few facilities for moulding or sheathing are available and wood is fitted already, the bilge keels will just have to be renewed at frequent intervals. The method of fastening must receive special attention, be easy to undo and replace, probably frequently, and the fastenings must be sealed on the inside, because they are bound to work loose when the worms get to work. Soaking in creosote and other preservatives will spoil their appetite but this should only be done if the wood is exposed. Anything embedding or intended to be in contact with "wet" resin at any time should not have preservative. (See Chapter Two.)

Some woods are fairly resistant to worm attack. The strips will be small so an expensive wood, if resistant, will be worthwhile. Most of the resistant woods are normally useless for boatbuilding because they are too difficult to work, or do not hold fastenings or are inclined to split. For simple parts like bilge keels and false keels, through-fastened, these objections are of minor importance. However because these woods are not normal boatbuilding timbers it is likely that few people will have heard of them, but they are used for sea defence works—and a protective bilge keel is much more akin to a harbour wall than to boatbuilding. All of these woods are tropical hardwoods, some are not available in Britain but may be available locally.

According to the Timber Research and Development Association, the Forest Products Research Laboratory and others, the woods resistant to marine borers are shown in

Table 14.1. Note, however, that a resistant wood is not necessarily completely resistant. There may be considerable variability between subspecies and even individual trees. It is assumed that the more resistant parts are chosen. Some well-known commercial names, notably teak, are used loosely to cover a wide range of different botanical species of roughly similar appearance and properties. Authorities differ on the degree of resistance (teak is one example), which may be due partly to this variability and loose classification. The best that can be said is that wood sold under the general heading of teak will be more resistant than wood sold under the equally loose headings of mahogany, pine, etc.

Woods resistant to marine borers tend to be resistant also to insect and fungal attack. Those marked * are also resistant to termite attack. (Others may be too. The data has been gathered from various sources.) This is important in tropical countries. Boats have to come ashore sometimes and may be left carelessly resting on damp ground assuming the GRP will come to no harm. In the tropics wooden bilge keels could disappear very quickly and so too could wooden rudders and centreplates. In Britain wood left in contact with damp ground will rot quickly or slowly according to the species.

Exposed bilge keels should be treated with preservative, although resistant hard-woods are mostly too dense for effective penetration. Most preservatives poison or inhibit polyester resins (p. 23) so wood to be sheathed should not be treated.

Table 14.1

Very resistant

Basrolocus or Angelique	*Dicorynia paraensis*
Billian	*Eusideroxylon zwageri*
Brush box	*Tristania conferta*
Ekki*	*Lophira alata*
Greenheart	*Ocotea rodiaei*
Jarrah*	*Eucalyptus marginata*
Kapur	*Dryobalanops* spp
Okan	*Cylicodiscus gabunensis*
Opepe*	*Sarcocephalus diderrichii*
Turpentine	*Syncarpia laurifolia*

Resistant

Afrormosia	*Afrormosia elata*
Gurjun	*Dipterocarpus* spp
Iroko*	*Chlorophora excelsa*
Keruing	*Dipterocarpus* spp
Meranti, dark red	*Shorea pauciflora* and S. spp
Okwen (very variable)	*Brachystegia* spp
Pyinkado	*Xylia dolabriformis*
Teak*	*Tectona grandis*
Totara	*Podocarpus totara*
Yellow cedar	*Chamaecyparis nootkatensis*
Yang	*Dipterocarpus* spp

CHAPTER FIFTEEN

Centreboards, Rudders and Fittings

CENTREBOARD CASE Ideally the centreboard case should be moulded integrally with the hull, but this is not often possible; the deep, narrow, parallel-sided shape does not readily form part of the main mould. It is usually moulded separately and attached afterwards. Remember that the more complicated the mould the more difficult it is to release the boat, and such a shape will be difficult to release; there is also more wear on the mould, more risk of damage, and more touching up between mouldings. Simple moulds are best and virtually essential for amateurs.

Inevitably a centreboard case is a deep, narrow moulding, too narrow for one to get at the inside of it, so a female mould is impracticable, and too deep and straight to be easily removed from a male mould. The simpler way is to make it in two halves.

If the sides are parallel, make up a male former of the required shape, but only half the finished thickness. Chipboard is wide, thick and cheap (Fig. 15.1). Lay this on a flat bench or floor and cover with polythene to ensure release. Lay up the first half section over this, forming a flange on three sides, but not on the side which will be the bottom. Release this half moulding, turn the former over and mould the other half with similar flanges.

The simplest way to join them is to bolt the flanges with sealant between, but the flanges will be prominent and uncomfortable to sit on. A neater way is to trim the flanges to about $\frac{1}{4}$ in. (6 mm.), just enough for a reliable bearing surface, clamp the halves together and mould over the outside edge. A sealing of "wet" mat is not recommended. It will squeeze out, foul the plate and be impossible to trim deep inside, whereas surplus sealant can be trimmed with a stick.

To attach the case to the boat cut the slot in the hull, and trim the edge of the case to the contour of the bottom, fitting over any frames. Paint the trimmed edges of both case and slot with resin because they will be exposed to the water.

Bed the case down on "wet" mat and hold it firmly in position; mould a good angle fillet all round the bottom edge to join it to the boat. This angle must be well moulded and without a flaw, or it will be a continual source of troublesome leaks. It is subject to a considerable strain in use, particularly on a lightly built racing dinghy where the hull may be flexible, and if there is any weakness in the bond to the hull it may come unstuck due to flexing while sailing. This angle fillet should not be stinted and must have a generous area of contact. Be careful to trim any loose glass inside the case.

It is a sound idea to reinforce around the centreboard bolt because this carries a heavy concentrated load and is liable to wear (Fig. 15.2). A metal or Tufnol bush would be an added refinement. Large soft washers will be needed to seal the bolt and prevent leaks; a neater method is to screw a watertight cap, well bedded down, over the bolt head and nut. There would be scope for someone to make this as a proprietary fitting but as far as I know, nothing like it is made for the job. It is important that the bolt should be easy

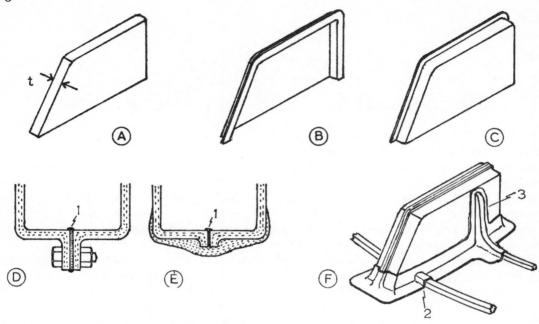

15.1: *Moulding a centreboard case, using a male mould.*

A. *Make a chipboard pattern. The thickness, t, should be half the finished internal width.*
B. *Lay the pattern on a flat surface and mould one half. Note the position of the flanges.*
C. *Turn the pattern over and mould the other half.*
D. *Join the two halves together by bolting with "wet" mat between, 1.*
E. *Alternative join using a butt-strap of glass tape laid up over the join. Note how the tape is continued over the sides to "grip."*
F. *Trim the lower edge to the contour of the hull and join to the hull with a moulded flange. Note how the flange fits closely over the frames, 2; the frames can be continued up the sides of the case as top-hat section stiffening knees, 3.*

to withdraw for regular inspection. "No maintenance" can be carried too far, and should not exclude inspection of the bolt. The plate and tackle must also be easily removed.

A centreboard case normally needs the support of a thwart as well, because it is subjected to a considerable strain. The sideways push of the water against the plate must be balanced somehow, and the best way is by using a thwart or bulkhead to support the top of the case. If this is not possible, mould substantial "top-hat" knees to give support to the sides. These should link up with any transverse frames and are the logical continuation. The hull will be damaged if the knees are attached only to the skin. On cruisers the case must tie in with bulkheads, deck or substantial parts of the accommodation.

The lifting pulley will be a proprietary fitting let into the top. The top should be made detachable, or at least have an access panel, so that the plate can be cleared if it gets jammed with stones or mud. The larger the boat, the more important it is to be able to clear a jammed plate afloat. A slight taper to the sides of the case will make it largely self-clearing, particularly with a tapered, streamlined plate as well (Fig. 15.3).

The top of the case needs to be well above water level if the top is to be removed for access while afloat. This also makes one less place to leak. Some boats are difficult to salvage when swamped or right when capsized because they fill through the top of the case as quickly as they can be bailed out. This seldom applies to racing dinghies for they are designed to capsize, and a capsize is all part of the fun on a freezing winter day.

A centreplate case seriously obstructs the accommodation of a cruiser. One approach is to use a narrow plate and keep the case below the cabin sole, or combine it with a bunk front. Inevitably the top will be below water and, as the price, the top must be completely sealed and watertight: clearing a jam will be difficult if not impossible afloat and not easy ashore. The case should be tapered and preferably moulded integrally with the hull. The lifting tackle should pass up a sealed tube to deck level, certainly well above any possible water level (allowing for pitching, surge and dangerous swamping), or work on a spindle through glands.

CENTREBOARDS There are two theories about the centreboard. One says it must be heavy to keep the boat the right way up; the other claims it should not, because its sole purpose is to stop the boat going sideways. The design of the boat is an important factor and each theory may be correct, but on different boats.

The heavy centreboard cannot easily be moulded, it is much simpler to make it of heavy metal plate, although it could be made on the lines of the internal ballast keels described in Chapter Thirteen.

However, a heavy centreboard has an important influence on the design and construction of the boat. The bolt on which it pivots, the lifting tackle and its attachments, the fastenings and support of the case and all parts of the moulded hull in their vicinity must be made much stronger than when using a light plate.

A heavy metal plate does not fail to safety. If the wire or the bolt breaks it will hang straight down; a well designed system will have a stop to prevent this, but few builders appreciate the danger, and a stop is rare. A dangling plate is out of control and badly supported. If the boat grounds the plate is likely to get bent or the case damaged—or worse. Both the case and the hull ought to be strong enough to withstand this considerable extra strain in the event of the plate getting out of control, otherwise the single minor failure may lead to a series of major ones. All this increases the cost and weight of the boat.

Electrolytic action is responsible for most trouble with metal centreplates. It is important that the bolt or pivot is of the same material as the plate. Similarly if the bolt is inserted through a bush embedded in the centreboard case the bush should be of the same metal, or be non-metallic such as Tufnol or nylon. Other metal under water must also be considered, e.g. brass keel bands, rudder fittings, stern tubes, skin fittings, etc. Fortunately it is the massive iron plate which corrodes in favour of the brass fitting so that apart from surface corrosion the safety of the boat will not be affected; but this is not the case with light alloy fittings as these will be eaten away in favour of the iron.

The second kind of centreplate, based on the theory that it is solely to provide lateral resistance, is mouldable. It is also light and much easier to handle, which in turn means that the tackle, its attachments and the moulded hull can all be lighter, and therefore cheaper. It can be buoyant, or at least of neutral buoyancy, so that, if anything fails, it fails to

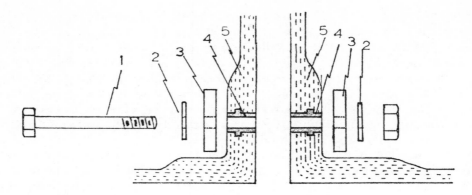

15.2: *Centreplate bolt and mounting.*

1. *Bolt, normally gunmetal except with a steel plate when it* **must** *be galvanised steel.* 2. *Plain metal washer.* 3. *Thick rubber or leather washer.* 4. *Tufnol or metal bush moulded into the centreplate case. The flange locks it securely in position but is not essential. If of metal it must be of the same metal as the bolt.* 5. *Thickened moulding in way of the bush.*

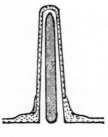

15.3: *Some taper on the sides of the case makes the plate self-clearing and almost eliminates jamming from stones and mud.*

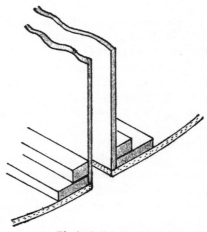

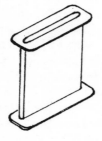

15.4: *Simple dagger-board case made over a "knock-out" male former. Bottom flange is moulded on to the hull; top flange supports and is braced by a thwart.*

15.5: *Typical "dry" construction for a centreboard case using glued plywood.*

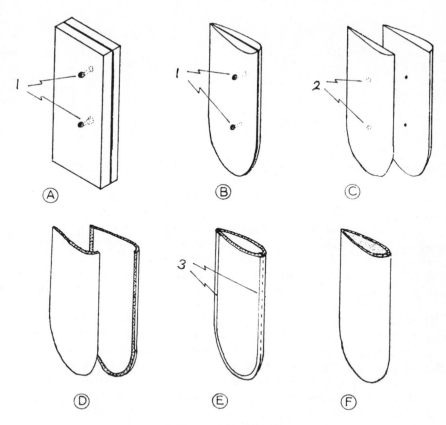

15.6: *Making a centreplate.*
A. *Fasten two pieces of wood together with temporary fastenings, 1, to form the pattern.*
B. *Shape the pattern as one piece.*
C. *Separate the two halves of the pattern for use separately. Fill the bolt-holes, 2.*
D. *From the patterns, mould two half-shells.*
E. *Join the two half-shells by clamping together with "wet" mat between, and cover the joins with several layers of glass tape, 3.*
F. *Alternative one-piece construction by moulding over a shaped core. In this case the pattern or core is not divided.*

safety, and the plate floats back up into the boat instead of hanging down and causing embarrassment. A good boat will still sail after a fashion with the centreplate raised. A light centreplate seems more appropriate to a GRP boat, which is essentially a light boat.

The plate can be made in halves joined by bonding, fastenings or moulding over the edge. A modern technique is to clamp them and fill with *in-situ* foam. This helps to bond them, keeps out water and gives the strength of a sandwich, but is better in theory than practice. It should not be the sole bond. The stresses are high. Use fastenings as well, or better, mould over the edges. Poorly bonded or sealed edges crack, let water in, and decay follows. Bedding on "wet" mat is too weak.

It is easier to shape these patterns if they are made as one. The pattern can be sawn

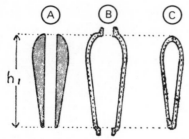

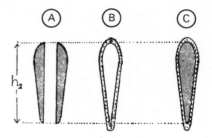

15.7: *Moulding a centreplate—female mould.*

15.8: *Moulding a centreplate—male mould.*

A. *Pattern.*
B. *Pair of female moulds.*
C. *Centreplate moulded from these moulds.*
Note that the pattern is the same size h₁ *as the finished centreplate.*

A. *Pattern or core.*
B. *Moulded centreplate.*
C. *Centreplate moulded over a core.*
Note that the size of the pattern or core h₂ *is smaller than the finished plate by the thickness of the moulding.*

down the middle but it is simpler to make the pattern of two pieces of wood, temporarily screwed together so that they can be easily separated afterwards. If you shape them as one they will match exactly.

The full pattern—mould—moulding sequence can be used, in which case the pattern must be full size (Fig. 15.7), or they can be used direct as male moulds which means that the patterns must be smaller than full size by the thickness of the moulding (Fig. 15.8). Making the pattern full size and using female moulds taken from them gives a perfect outside finish with accurate, checked dimensions. The male mould is a lot cheaper but has the "rough" side of the moulding outside and therefore needs extra work to make it smooth. Also the thickness can seldom be moulded precisely enough for accuracy, particularly on the gently sloping trailing edge.

For close tolerances, high-class work such as a racing dinghy, or for production, the proper pattern—female mould—moulding sequence will be the right approach and worthwhile; for amateur or short run production the direct male mould will be more suitable.

For an amateur making a one-off plate, an easier solution is to make the male pattern and then mould over it, forming the centreplate in one piece and using the pattern as a core (Fig. 15.8). Again the core must be smaller than the finished centreplate by the thickness of the moulding and considerable smoothing will be necessary for that racing finish. Nevertheless, this method has been used successfully by some top-flight racing dinghy people. One advantage is that the core can be structural; it can be of plywood which will itself contribute to the strength, so that the thickness and cost of the moulding can be reduced. A thin moulded skin will give a lot of additional strength to the plywood in just the position where it can be used to the greatest effect.

A core of foamed plastic is lighter and more easily shaped, but imparts less structural strength, so that the moulding needs to be thicker. In fact the entire strength must be in the moulding, but it can still be considered as a sandwich moulding with one skin supporting the other. However foam polystyrene is not strong enough to be considered in this way and the foam should be rigid PVC or polyurethane of about 6 lbs./cu.ft. density.

It is seldom worthwhile to mould a small dinghy centreplate. It is so much easier to make it in plywood. The high strength and racing finish of a good moulded plate are worthwhile on a racing dinghy, and the strength and lightness are a great asset on a cruiser, but it is hard to justify one on a small knock-about dinghy.

The part of the moulding where the bolt will come must be well thickened. This is easy enough on a hollow shell; with a wooden core some of the core should be chiselled away to make a depression each side, deep enough to double the thickness of the moulded skin. On a small boat, however, the core will probably provide enough support in itself.

On a hollow plate it is advisable for the bolt or pivot to pass through a tube bonded to the plate. This will provide a good bearing surface, otherwise there would be excessive wear on the edges of the thin moulding. The method of doing this is described in Chapter One, page 38, and Fig. 1.21.

A wooden core should be well sealed, so that it is not exposed to the water. A hollow plate, however, can be made free flooding to reduce its buoyancy, as is done with lock gates. The inside moulding and finish must be sound enough for continuous immersion.

RUDDERS A rudder is not easy to mould, but its shape is not difficult to make in wood. It is therefore more often made on conventional lines of wood or metal. Wood can be sheathed either for protection or additional strength or a combination of the two. Note that for this purpose glass cloth or woven rovings is the correct material, not mat.

Where the rudder is to be moulded it can be done in a similar way to the centreboard.

Conventional metal rudder gear, fitted on sound conventional lines, is still hard to beat for strength and reliability. Tufnol or nylon bushes and bearings are an improvement, but the weight of a wooden or moulded rudder will always be much less when the boat is afloat.

Some means must be incorporated for turning the rudder. This is not so simple as it sounds because considerable forces are involved in use and the attachment is to one edge only; moreover certain unfair conditions, particularly sternway in a sailing boat hove-to in bad weather, or when a boat is aground, impose very severe strains not only on the rudder but on the mountings, tiller, steering gear and the hull itself. Power boats more often have balanced rudders but they are even more liable to be abused.

It is no use saying the rudder is not designed for such treatment; it has got to be. The mast and the rudder are the things which, according to the late Claud Worth, must not fail under any circumstances on any sailing boat capable of going offshore. Fifty years later one might say that the engine is an alternative to the mast on power boats, but the rudder must always be well-nigh invulnerable.

Embedding the rudder stock in the moulded rudder (Fig. 15.9), as I have seen suggested, is not good enough even if it is squared. The square will eventually begin to turn in the moulded hole, started perhaps by some extra strain; once there is any movement the hole will soon wear until it is round, and then all control is lost. This can happen quickly enough to enlarge some backlash into disastrous loss of control within a few hours, and certainly during a single rough passage.

Bending the stock or forming a tongue will give reliable positive control, but it will be difficult to repair and require very accurate positioning during moulding. It would be satisfactory if applied to a rudder that was moulded in two halves.

The best method is to fit substantial side arms which are welded or forged on to the rudder stock. Alternatively they can be attached with some positive connection like a square shaft in a square metal socket, a keyed shaft or flanged coupling.

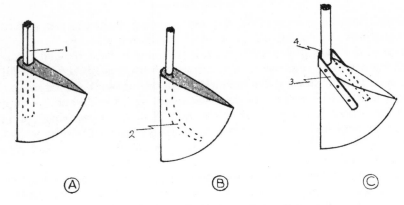

15.9: *Joining rudder to rudder stock.*

A. **Not Recommended.** *Squared shank embedded in the rudder. Strain may enlarge the hole which will soon become quite round and all control will be lost.*
B. *The stock is bent or formed into a tongue, 2. This gives firm control, but is it difficult to repair unless the rudder is made in two separate halves, and it demands precise positioning during moulding.*
C. *The recommended method. Side arms, 3, are welded or brazed to the stock, 4. Alternatively, the connection can be by a squared socket, or a bolted flange.*

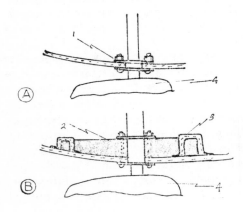

15.10: *Rudder mounting—motor-cruiser.*

A. **Not Recommended.** *The rudder tube is bolted straight through the hull, 1. Just adequate under normal conditions but even if the hull is thickened this can be pushed in by grounding on the rudder, 4.*
B. *The rudder tube should be bolted through a substantial block, 2, and the hull strengthened with frames, 3.*

Where a thick rudder stock can be used, such as on a transom stern, it can be moulded with the blade, either over a core or in two halves and joined together. There will be considerable torsion in the rudder stock which is therefore better moulded in woven rovings or cloth. Particular attention must be paid to the weak part where the rudder stock flares out into the blade. The rudder should be well thickened also in way of the pintles.

Ease of replacement of the rudder fittings must be considered carefully at an early stage. Rudder mountings will wear during the life of the boat and it must be reasonably easy to replace them. It must be possible also to remove the rudder for repair. The simpler it all is the better. An elaborate special casting will be difficult to replace ten years later even in the same country, let alone in some distant part, but a simple fabrication which does not have to fit with high accuracy could be replaced locally anywhere in the world

—an important point for export. The same considerations regarding a casting for a rudder fitting apply as for keels. The casting must be done accurately and must fit the boat because the boat cannot be trimmed to fit the casting.

Standard proprietary fittings are to be preferred wherever possible. Unfortunately there are remarkably few standard rudder fittings for cruisers, consequently repair, even due to normal fair wear, is expensive. Few garage mechanics ever make a part; they take a standard spare off the shelf or at least ring up their local factor. But except for cleats and shackles nearly every replacement part for a boat has to be made or repaired by the yard—all expensive, skilled hand work. Designers and builders add continually to the confusion, because in the absence of satisfactory standard fittings, each class or design has to have yet another set of specially made ones.

A peculiar problem can arise due to the flexibility of a moulded boat if the boat has a counter and a moulded cockpit, and the rudder stock works in the conventional tube. On a stout wooden boat a three-bearing support, if properly lined up, causes little trouble, but on a moulded hull when sailing hard there could be enough flexibility to cause one bearing to jam. This would probably be the upper one at the deck or cockpit, for this part of the boat would normally be the thinner, and also it will be subjected to the concentrated and varying local loads of the crew and rigging.

The answer is to arrange extra frames to reduce possible relative movement as is done on engine installations to prevent momentary shaft misalignment. A simpler and lighter method is to allow the movement but to put one bearing on a flexible mounting. The movement will only be small, it may never be enough to cause anything to jam or even rub, although only a very small movement would be needed to do this with a three bearing shaft, and it would be well within the range of a light flexible mount. It would probably be sufficient to bolt the flange at one end on to a rubber ring.

On a motor-cruiser it is common for the rudder to be mounted through the bottom with no lower bearing (Fig. 15.10). It is important to strengthen the hull in the vicinity of this rudder mounting, not only with a block and extra thickness to give a good bearing surface, but also with extra stiffening frames.

Under normal conditions these extra frames are not necessarily needed but this type of rudder is usually quite unprotected and can be damaged. I have seen a rudder fastened through a hull in a normal and usually satisfactory manner, pushed through the bottom by the boat grounding—together with a substantial piece of the hull. The rudder assembly itself was quite undamaged and was replaced—but not until after the boat had been salvaged, and a lot of consequential damage had been repaired. It should be the rule that if the boat takes the ground on its rudder, even if it pounds, the rudder may get bent but it does not push its way through the hull. A bent rudder may disable the boat, but as long as the boat stays afloat she can at least be towed away, or get home with anything an ingenious skipper can lash up; but if she sinks it is a salvage job and everything on board is damaged or lost, engine, equipment, furnishings, personal possessions—perhaps even lives.

Therefore, it is wise to ensure that the rudder mounting is not just a simple hole through the hull, but strong enough to carry the whole weight of the boat with a generous margin to take care of a bump.

RUDDER FITTINGS Even on a small dinghy the rudder can be subjected to a large strain, particularly when running aground and suffering similar abuse, and it is

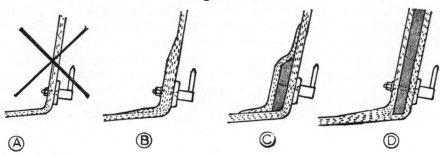

15.11: *Fastening rudder pintles.*

A. **Wrong.** *Pintle fastened straight through unthickened and unreinforced moulding.*
B. *Moulding thickened in way of rudder pintle.*
C. *Pintle screwed into wooden block which may be embedded or open.*
D. *Pintle bolted or screwed into wood core of sandwich transom.*

important that the rudder fittings are firmly secured. The continual movement and pressure will loosen screws that are not firm. It is also very important that they should be readily replaceable, for rudder fittings break more often than any other item of marine hardware, and even if they do not break they can get worn. It is always advisable to use standard proprietary rudder fittings. Trying to replace a non-standard rudder fitting, on a boat which is designed so that it will take only that particular fitting, is an absolute curse and to make a special replacement is inordinately expensive—as well as probably producing an inferior fitting.

The hull must be well thickened, or a block fitted, behind each fitting. If possible, it should be through-bolted rather than screwed (Fig. 15.11). Similarly the fittings on the rudder itself must be soundly attached.

There is no substitute for good quality marine fittings. A rudder pintle is a small item, but a very important one, for failure will disable the boat. The lower fitting will be below the waterline as a rule, and needs to be resistant to corrosion. Light alloy dinghy fittings must be fastened with screws of stainless steel, but sometimes they are made for wooden boats and are supplied with wood screws not bolts. Whatever the temptation, brass bolts must not be used. The electrolytic action will destroy the fitting in a matter of days. I have seen one still fizzing a week after it came out of the water!

SPLIT MOULDINGS When centreboards and rudders are moulded in halves, cracks and seepage round the edge are common. The moulding is highly stressed, tending to open the joint, and it is difficult anyway to seal round the fittings. Inside faces must be well moulded to prevent decay from within.

Edges need to be sealed and secured by moulding over them thickly enough to be non-porous. Alternatively, bolt together with flexible sealant between. Foam filling alone will not seal or bond them together securely enough. They must be clamped while foaming as foam pressure is considerable.

For this application, plywood or sheathed plywood is more logical.

CHAPTER SIXTEEN

Small Boats, Dinghies and Launches

THIS chapter deals with the particular problems of dinghies, canoes, launches, etc. up to about 20 ft. (6 m.), and to some extent runabouts and boats of other plastics materials.

GUNWALES A lot of plastic dinghies, perhaps the majority, have moulded gunwales. The commendable idea is that there should be nothing which needs maintenance, but unfortunately in practice this does not work; unless it is covered completely by a fender, a fender which protects the top as well as the sides, the gunwale will get so many scratches and bumps that some maintenance will be needed.

A fender on a plastic boat, particularly a small boat, should not be considered as an extra. It is an essential part of the boat. Manufacturers would do well to realise that a scruffy and scratched boat does them no credit, in fact it does positive harm to their reputation and it is worthwhile to ensure that their products have a reasonable chance of looking as good as, or better, than rival products throughout their life.

A wooden gunwale, it is true, needs some maintenance, a coat of paint or varnish once a year and some occasional touching up, but the area is small and it does not involve much work; it does at least cover up the previous year's crop of scars—and let no one try to delude you that there will not be scars. It is a lot easier to touch up neatly a scratch on a wooden gunwale with a little filler and varnish, than to touch up a moulded gunwale *without it showing*. Consequently the moulded gunwale is apt to show all its scars, or the efforts to hide them, which are often even more conspicuous. These are not just the current year's crop of scars as on a wooden gunwale, but every scratch right back to the moment it came out of the mould, and possibly original moulding flaws also if the moulder was not conscientious and skilful.

The idea that a plastic boat never needs any maintenance at all is slowly, very slowly, being recognised as over-optimistic. Nevertheless the small amount of maintenance that is needed is not so much to restore the pristine freshness to the finish, as a coat of paint does, but to cover up the inevitable scratches and dirty marks.

Protect the boat from scratches, and the need for maintenance will approach this maintenance-free ideal.

The hundred per cent moulded dinghy is rather like a motor-car; every scratch means a repaint if the repair is to be an exact colour match—and what cries of anguish greet the slightest blemish on man's most treasured status symbol.

Therefore, when deciding between a moulded or wooden gunwale, consider carefully the use the boat will get. If it is completely covered with a good fender, or if it is quite certain that the gunwale will never get bumped, scratched or worn (by other people's children as well as the saintly owner), or if no one cares a damn what it looks like anyway, then a moulded gunwale will do very well. In any other case, a wooden gunwale will be a lot more satisfactory, particularly where a smart appearance is expected throughout its life—not just in a showroom. This is regardless of whether it leads a particularly arduous life or just an average one.

The gunwale can be moulded integrally with the boat (Fig. 16.1). This sounds a simple method but in fact it is not, because it complicates the mould; moreover the inner edge of the gunwale may have to be moulded blind, i.e. in a position which you cannot see while you are moulding it. As a general rule, a place that is difficult to mould is likely to have flaws; this is most undesirable for the gunwale, because no part of the boat is more conspicuous and vulnerable to knocks and pressure, which will certainly expose any flaws there may be.

It is easier to mould the gunwales integrally with the boat if the mould can be rotated so that they can be done with the mould upside down or at least on its side. Otherwise the gunwales must be moulded upwards or "on the ceiling", and this adds considerably to the difficulties and risk of flaws. The design of the gunwales should be as simple as possible with no fancy bits which would make it harder to mould.

The integrally moulded gunwale overcomes the problem of joining the gunwale to the hull very satisfactorily, and there is no conspicuous join line to disguise. However, it may still need some extra finishing work to fill and smooth a mould parting line, as it is likely that a multiple part mould will be needed.

The gunwale needs to be well thickened; the channel section increases the effectiveness of extra thickness. On larger boats it can be built up into a box section (Fig. 16.2).

The usual practice is to mould the gunwale separately in its own mould and join it to the hull later (Fig. 16.3). A common way—not a good way, but just adequate for a cheap dinghy—is to place it in position and fill the gap with resin-glass putty (page 84). A sounder method is to use fastenings as well as putty, using the putty just as a filler. The fastenings can be disguised neatly by combining them with the fastenings used to secure the fender.

Some other methods are shown under "Decks" in Chapter Six.

A gunwale moulded in a contrasting colour to the hull looks attractive and also has the great advantage that if you ever have to paint it to cover up its scars, you only have to paint the gunwale; if it was the same colour as the hull you might have to paint the whole boat to preserve the colour match.

A wooden gunwale may need renewing when badly worn; that is part of its purpose. Therefore, it must not be glued. It will not need to be renewed so often that rivets cannot be used, but screws or bolts are better.

It should always be double with an inner and an outer piece to avoid having the fastenings in direct contact with the hull (Fig. 16.4), which would cause crushing and stress concentration, and it is probable that the gunwale would work loose. Screws should be from the inside towards the outside, because the outside will get most wear; the heads of screws put in from the outside will soon project and do damage if the gunwale gets worn. Moreover the gunwale will work loose. Of course a screw put in from the inside will have a projecting point when the gunwale gets worn. At first sight this may seem even more undesirable, but more wear is needed before the point breaks surface and having less metal, the point is soon blunted, whereas a projecting head will remain jagged and vicious for much longer.

Perpetua, 48 ft. (15 m.) twin diesel motor cruiser, the first large fibreglass cruiser in the world; built in 1954 and still going strong.
Designed by Commander Peter Thorneycroft and moulded and built by Halmatic Ltd. to test whether GRP would withstand the vibration of diesel engines—it seems it does. This boat was a tremendous act of faith at a time when others were only building dinghies, and even they were bold enthusiasts.
Scott Bader

27 ft. (8·2 m.) research vessel for United Nations FAO by David Cheverton Ltd., Cowes. Note the substantial wooden fendering aft.
Roger M. Smith

Fisher 30 ft. (9 m.) MFV type yacht
by Fairways Marine, Hamble. A
yacht of traditional fishing boat style
with large, conspicuous areas of teak
to enhance the effect and mask the

high moulded bulwarks. The inner
face of the bulwarks is integral with
the deck moulding.
Eileen Ramsay

Fitting out 40 ft. (12 m.) workboats at David Cheverton Ltd., Cowes. A 45-passenger launch is in the foreground. Note how little GRP is in evidence. All tools and materials are woodworkers', fitters', etc. This is the fitting-out shop; moulding is done elsewhere.

Roger M. Smith

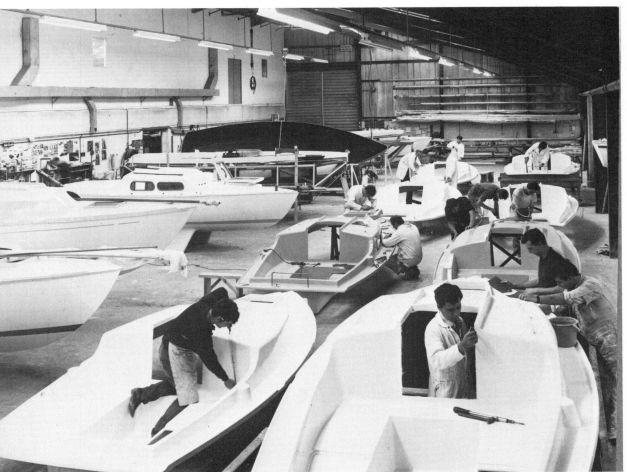

Production line at Hurley Marine Ltd., Plymouth. Note how the decks are being completely fitted out before being joined to the hulls. The hulls themselves are being fitted out in another part of the works, before being joined to the decks.

John Etches

Hand lay-up moulding at Westerly Marine Construction Ltd., Waterlooville, Hampshire. The port side has been partly moulded and the moulder is laying down a thin gauze on the gel coat as the first stage of the starboard side. He is using a mohair roller, the bucket of wet resin is at his feet, and pre-cut pieces of glass for the next layers lie ready to hand. This photograph shows well the inside-out form of the female mould.

J. A. Hewes

Press-moulding a 17 ft. (5 m.) runabout. Here the fin pressed shell is being removed from the die. Note how two moulds are used.

Moulded Fibreglass Boat Co., Pennsylvania, U.S.A.

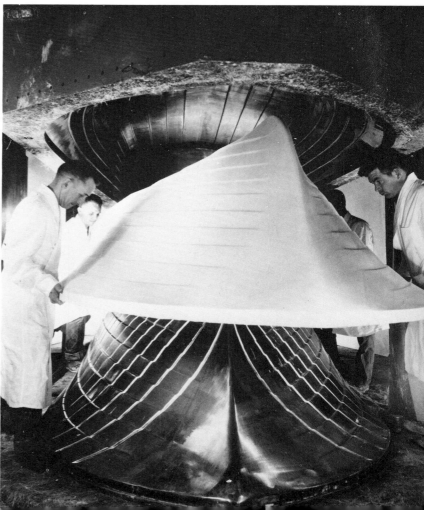

An interesting form of composite construction. (top) The keel, stem and transom, the heaviest and most difficult parts to build, are moulded in one piece. The rest of the boat, with the exception of the cabin top which is also GRP, are of conventional wooden construction. But as production built up this construction was abandoned in favour of full GRP.

J. Stimpson

Cabin of a Westerly Centaur by Westerly Marine. The entire accommodation is formed from a single interior moulding which includes the bunks, galley and cabin sole. Note how the veneer-faced plywood bulkhead and table, and the upholstery and carpeting, disguises this. The deckhead seems to have a foam-backed vinyl lining.

J. A. Hewes

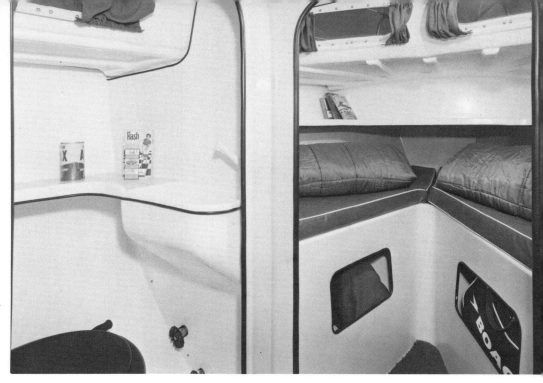

Interior of a Kingfisher Class, Westfield Engineering Ltd., Poole, Dorset, one of the leading exponents of the "mould the lot" school. There are at least ten separate mouldings in this photograph alone, which gives some indication of the carefully designed jigsaw puzzle. There is no woodwork visible at all. The doorways form part of a central telephone kiosk-shaped moulding with four openings, and a sliding door on a moulded trackway capable of closing any two. Note how the sawn edges of all mouldings are covered with extruded plastics channel; also the easy access to the seacocks—would that more builders designed such an excellent feature.

John Etches

A very complicated starboard inner shell for a 41 ft. (12·5 m.) Sortilège by Michel Dufour S.A., La Rochelle, France. The moulded frames provide the stiffening for the outer shell. The flats are attachment points for the accommodation, toilet compartment in the foreground, dinette beyond, galley (in this case not moulded in) and owner's cabin aft.

Carl Ziegler Yacht Agency

The mould (left) for the inner shell (starboard side) of the 41 ft. (12·5 m.) Sortilège by Michel Dufour.

Carl Ziegler Yacht Agency

Moulding (middle left) a sandwich deck, end-grain balsa core. Note the easy curve and the sandbags used to apply pressure—a most important point.

Hugo du Plessis

Filling egg (middle right) crate framing (GRP over polyurethane foam cores) with *in-situ* polyurethane foam prior to laying up the deck on top. The boat is Rotork Marine Ltd.'s Sea Truck.

Channel section fibreglass bumpkin moulded for the wooden cruising yacht *Valfreya* which later sailed halfway round the world.

Hugo du Plessis

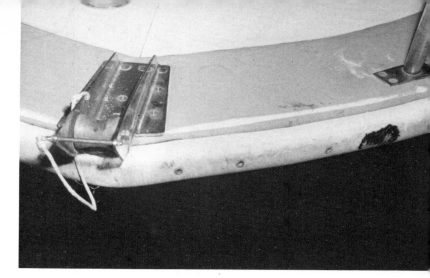

Unfair wear (top) due to careless mooring. The thin white line above the fender reveals where the angle of the deck has been worn away by mooring ropes, with a deeper scar where the rope or wire has been held against the pulpit leg. In time this could cut deeply.

Hugo du Plessis

Angle of cockpit coaming grooved by a rope. The black spots show where it has worn through the gel coat, which is usually thick at such an angle. The lead was meant to go to a winch, but the sheet has been hauled directly to the cleat.

Hugo du Plessis

Scratches on the bottom of a dinghy.
These must be considered fair wear
and tear although they could have
been reduced by better protection and
more careful handling.

Myles Cooper

Damage to the toe of a keel is quite
easily repaired as far as the hole is
concerned. But the shock probably
caused debonding from the ballast
and water could be trapped inside to
cause decay later. Tap for hollows and
drain them.

Myles Cooper

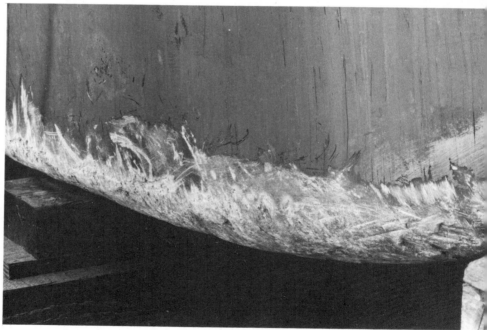

Storm damage: this yacht went adrift and has chafed badly. A good deal of this is dirt but there are also many scratches, some deep, and possibly some minor structural damage. All this is easily repaired but it is goodbye to the non-painting days. It is pretty certain that the topsides will have to be painted to hide the scars unless the repair is done with exceptional skill.

Badly abraded keel from pounding on a reef. The moulding is very thick here but even so one of the problems is to establish how much has been worn away. There may also be crushing or hidden damage to a substantial depth, and hulls moulded in two halves may split along the joint line. Mould on extra thickness, and be generous with it, to be on the safe side. Much of this damage might have been avoided if the yacht had been fitted with a metal shoe to take this sort of wear.

Scott Bader Ltd.

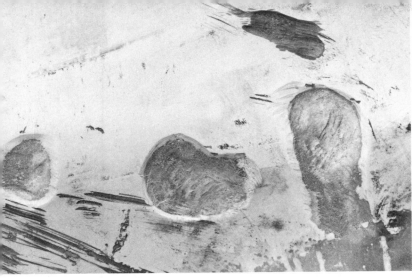

Deep damage from chafe; the moulding has been worn away well into the glass. The areas have been cut back to sound material, ready for repair by moulding more glass and then filling.

Scott Bader Ltd.

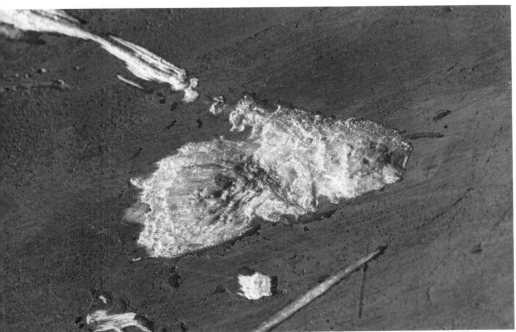

This yacht (above) took on the Île du Sein off the west coast of France, a well-known ships' graveyard where the tides run fast and sharp rocks are everywhere, but survived to sail back to Lymington with half a rudder. The damage is mostly severe abrasion, deep into the glass (left), but there may be hidden damage and crushing to a greater depth than is obvious to the eye.

Myles Cooper

Badly burned yacht. This fire started on the outside due to intense heat from a nearby burning building. Note how the rate of burning was reduced in way of the internal ballast keel, which acted as a cooling heat-sink.

Hugo du Plessis

Close-up of the same yacht (opposite top) showing the glass reinforcement hanging in folds.

Hugo du Plessis

Inside view of the same yacht (opposite middle). Except for a small patch at the gunwale where the flames probably outflanked the shell, the inside is not even scorched and apparently undamaged. The black marks are dirt from firefighting. Despite the apparent structural integrity there is very extensive delamination.

Hugo du Plessis

Motor cruiser (opposite bottom) destroyed by an internal fire. Although very badly burned inside the hull still retains considerable structural integrity and has only burned through in the black patches. The cabin top confirms the fire barrier effect of the layers of GRP. It is now, however, almost entirely resinless glass-fibres.

Hugo du Plessis

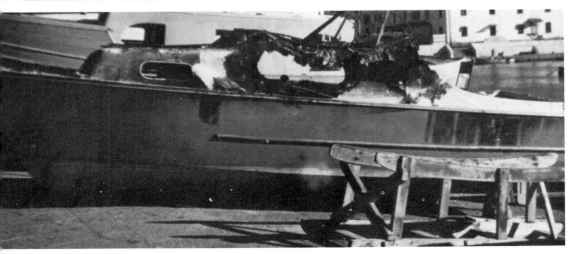

Ashes to ashes. All that is left is a slightly boat-shaped heap of glass-fibres.

Hugo du Plessis

A detail of the previous photo, showing charred woodwork and silvery black glass-fibres. The resin has all burned away.

Hugo du Plessis

This shows the delaminating effect of fire. This boat was badly burned on the outside, but see how the wooden bulkheads inside caught alight at their upper corners and outflanked the fire barrier of the GRP shell.

Hugo du Plessis

Sequence of events, with the fire spreading from right to left. On the extreme left (left) is un-affected gel coat. Ahead of the flames the gel coat softens and crazes and the edges curl up as shown in greater detail (below). Next it catches alight, burns and chars, the gel burns away completely exposing the glass. Thereafter the resin burns away slowly, layer by layer, the glass itself, especially layers of high glass ratio woven rovings, tending to act as fire barriers.

Hugo du Plessis

Decay in GRP. This yacht had an outward-turning hull/deck flange covered by a PVC channel fender. Water got behind the fender and lodged there, as it obviously would. The water probably entered via poorly sealed gaps between the faces of the moulding and attacked the inner faces where they were shattered by trimming and likely to be poorly moulded edge moulding anyway.

Seven or eight years after building the flange on both sides was badly decayed and had disintegrated entirely in places.

GRP can and does decay, and is vulnerable where water can bypass the protection of the gel coat to attack from behind or at an edge. It is particularly vulnerable where water can lodge and stand in pockets.

Hugo du Plessis

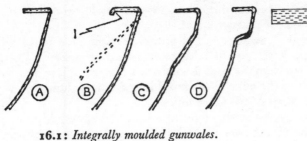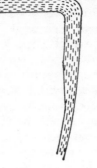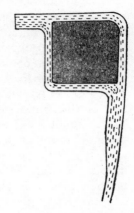

16.1: *Integrally moulded gunwales.*

A. *A simple turn-over flange.*

B. *More complicated turn-over gunwale with lip. This is not easy to mould and is prone to have flaws along the inside edge, 1, which must be moulded in a nearly blind position. With pronounced flare, as shown dotted, this becomes very difficult.*

C. *and* D. *Gunwales formed by a moulded bulge. Type* C *will free itself readily in use, but* D *will hang up on obstructions.*

16.2: *Stiffening an integrally moulded gunwale. Thicken the gunwale to gain maximum effect from the strong shape. Larger boats can use a core to form a box section.*

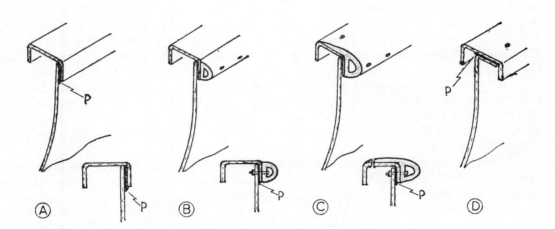

16.3: *Separately moulded gunwale.*

A. *Gunwale stuck on with resin-glass putty, p. 81. Not recommended, but can be used for small, cheap boats.*

B. *Bolts securing "D" fender also join gunwale to hull.*

C. *Ditto. Recommended type of overall fender covers top of gunwale as well as sides.*

D. **Not recommended.** *Outward turning flange is prone to catch on obstructions. Only suitable where a good grip for handling is of paramount importance. p, resin-glass putty.*

Light timber will bend enough without steaming if the difficult stem and corner pieces are cut from solid or laminated from thinner pieces. A saw-cut down the middle is a simple way of making a strip of wood take a sharper bend.

Extruded aluminium has been used in America as a gunwale capping. Rigid PVC channel section could also be used. Both these are available as standard extrusions. There would be scope for an extruded combined capping and fender as in Fig. 16.6, but none of the PVC sections will give much support to the edge of the moulding and this should therefore be thickened, or reinforced with a strip of wood or metal.

A small PVC extruded channel is useful to slip over the inner trimmed edge of a moulded gunwale. This edge often looks a little ragged and untidy, and as it is thin anyway, it will be an uncomfortable and "cutting" grip if the boat has to be carried any distance. On larger boats like sailing dinghies and runabouts, away from the fiercest competition of the dinghy jungle, an aluminium or plastic extrusion slipped over exposed trimmed edges gives a neat and professional touch to the boat. No visible trimmed edge should be tolerated on any boat aspiring to the abused description, "luxury."

The best fenders have a metal strip running through them (Fig. 16.5), to limit the amount they can bend or slide up and down between the fastenings. Fenders will stand a tremendous amount of pure bumping; what soon tears them off is the up and down shearing action of one fender caught over another at a crowded pontoon or over an obstruction. Without the brass strip the fender bends sharply between the fastenings; these quickly pull through; and then lengths of fender hang loose. The brass strip spreads the strain over more fastenings and resists the up-and-down bending.

ROWLOCK SOCKETS Rowlock sockets take a surprising strain, for they are the link between a thirsty rower trying to beat closing time and wind and tide doing their best to stop him. A common, short socket simply screwed through the gunwale will soon pull out or tear away the moulding. The entire strain is taken by the one after screw, which has to withstand a pull about ten times as great as the pull on the oar (Fig. 16.7). Long sockets reduce the bending strain on the rowlocks but do not reduce the strain on this one screw.

Generous blocks of wood will spread the load, preferably with a long socket to take the wear in a good-sized block to spread the load. Where the gunwale forms a deep channel section a filling of resin-glass putty or syntactic foam can be used instead of the block. Alternatively, a long socket or metal tube can be embedded in the moulding (Figs. 16.8 and 16.9).

Fitting a rowlock socket to a wooden gunwale will be much the same as fitting one to a wooden boat. If the gunwale is thin it will need a pad to thicken it and the wooden block must be deep enough to give a good bearing surface.

Rowlock sockets must be positioned carefully so that the oar will not rub on the moulding, particularly on a moulded gunwale. If it does the gunwale will be marked and worn, and need frequent touching up. This is one of the little details which should be thought of at the design stage; later on it may be found impossible to position the rowlock where it does not rub.

Rowlock sockets which are moulded in or mounted in blocks may be blind holes. Blind holes get filled with water and produce a most uncomfortable squirt up one's sleeve when inserting the rowlock. They need a drain hole to the inside or the outside of the

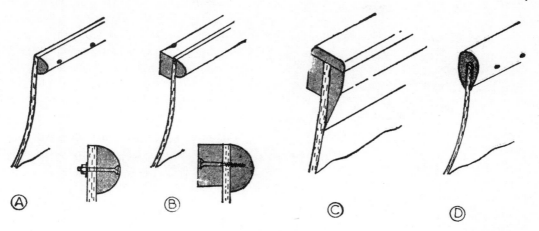

16.4: *Wooden gunwale.*

A. Not recommended. *Half-round moulding screwed directly to hull. Stress concentrations around fastenings.*
B. *Inner wooden gunwale distributes stress and provides firmer anchorage for wooden moulding or fender.*
C. *Heavier wooden gunwale suitable for fishing-boat or working launch.*
D. *Gunwale formed of extended aluminium section.*

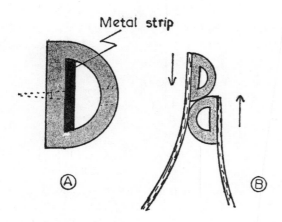

Metal strip

16.5: *Rubber fender with internal metal strip reinforcement.*

A. *Cross-section of fender.*
B. *Up and down shearing action when one fender is caught over another.*

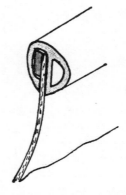

16.6: *Ideal shape of extruded PVC fender and gunwale combined.*

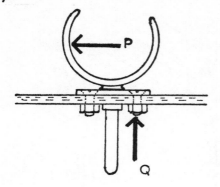

16.7: *With a simple bolted rowlock socket the whole thrust of the oar, P, is taken by the single bolt and surrounding moulding at Q.*

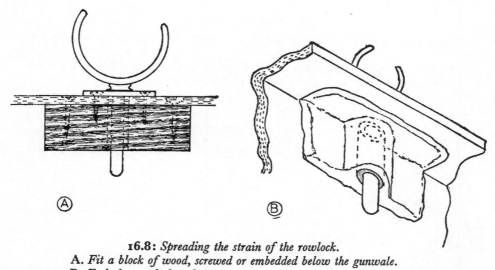

Ⓐ Ⓑ

16.8: *Spreading the strain of the rowlock.*
A. *Fit a block of wood, screwed or embedded below the gunwale.*
B. *Embed a rowlock socket.*

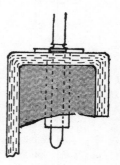

16.9: *With a deep, narrow gunwale, a long socket can be embedded in resin-glass putty or syntactic foam.*

boat to avoid this. It is a small detail but very noticeable; such annoying little faults often evoke more criticism and complaints than major ones.

On double moulding dinghies rowlock sockets must have no connection at all into the space between the skins, otherwise there will be trouble from seepage. Blind holes may be unavoidable, and the fitting must be well bedded down to avoid seepage past the screws. Well embedded long sockets or metal tubes are absolutely essential, as it is impracticable to get between the skins to repair any part that gets worn.

The makers of outboard motors would have us believe that rowing is criminal, but strange to say some queer folk like the peace and the exercise—just as there are still a few cranks who have not succumbed to the belief that feet are only for pushing down accelerator pedals. Outboard motors have a reputation for being temperamental and sulky when thirsty. True one may lose an oar—but at least it floats.

SCULLING SLOTS Few boatbuilders nowadays fit sculling slots. Admittedly sculling (not the energetic Henley stuff but that casual waggle with a single stern oar) is a form of black magic to newcomers and a dying art among yachtsmen who will use their outboard motors rather than row or paddle a yard—and often use more energy in starting them. But sculling is still the preferred method among many real boatmen. It is much more convenient to scull a short distance than to sit down and row, and if the seat is wet one can scull standing up.

In many parts of the world sculling, not rowing, is normal even among yachtsmen. Brittany is one, and it is nearer to England than many popular yachting centres are to London. Boatbuilders thinking seriously of export should fit sculling sockets as standard. In France regulations require boats, including small cruisers, to have sculling slots.

A sculling slot can be moulded in and therefore adds little to the cost. It is true that it reduces the freeboard but this is not critical unless the dinghy has low freeboard and is dangerously overloaded already. The sculling slot needs to be well protected with metal, PVC or leather lining or it will get worn; the moulding needs to be thickened. It can also be formed by cutting out part of the block for the outboard motor and in this case the wood block gives protection against wear (Fig. 16.10).

A sculling slot wants to be the right shape if it is to be effective. A shallow slot is very difficult to use; it should be the full depth of the oar, not half-depth as is common, and slightly horseshoe-shaped. The oar slopes downwards and so can the slot.

A socket for a sculling rowlock can be fitted easily and cheaply on a sailing dinghy or small cruiser, either sail or power, and is a boon if there is no wind, the engine breaks down, or one wants to move a short distance without bothering to hoist the sails. On a modern small sailing cruiser in particular, with its generous beam and high freeboard, it is much easier to scull than to row, and there is only a single long oar to stow away.

Sculling sockets to take a rowlock must be firmly fixed. Sculling may look an easy, unhurried motion, but an energetic youngster swinging on the end of an oar can apply more force than when rowing.

THOLE PINS In most parts of the world thole pins are commoner than rowlocks which are mainly found in yachting circles. Thole pins are cheaper and do not get lost.

Thole pins can be single or double according to local custom. There are many ways

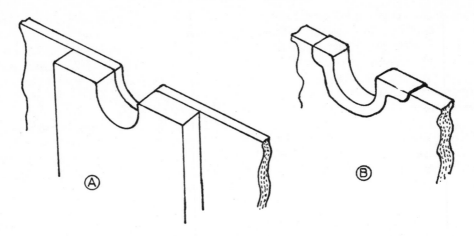

16.10: *Sculling notch in a transom.*
A. *Sculling notch cut out of outboard motor pad. Motor can still clamp each side of the notch.*
B. *Notch cut into moulded transom and protected against wear by a metal or PVC lining.*
N.B.—*The transom needs to be thickened.*

of rowing, and on the whole it is only yachtsmen who can lose their oars, because they are not fixed on, and their rowlocks because they come out.

Any working boat built with an eye to export should have double rowlock sockets so that thole pins can be fitted and perhaps also some arrangement so that a thole pin thicker than the stem of a normal steel rowlock can be pushed in. An advantage of a thick wooden gunwale is that it can easily be drilled for the hole according to local custom.

A thole pin needs just as good a socket as a rowlock, but it is normally a tight fit so there is less wear. Being usually of wood it may need a bigger hole. A permanent pin of brass or steel moulded in would be stronger than wood but might not be acceptable locally.

THWARTS The simplest way to fit a thwart is to mould on a bracket to take the weight and secure the thwart with screws. The bracket can be a simple block of embedded wood, a pre-moulded angle-bracket or a stringer (Fig. 16.11). Sometimes the hull has a moulded step, but this does not look nice and spoils the lines of the boat.

Whatever method is used the positioning must be accurate; the bracket needs to be firmly clamped or taped in position while being embedded or attached. For production, jigs are advisable. Fig. 1.20 shows a simple type of clamp very suitable for a shape like a dinghy.

A bracket of some kind is important because a thwart has to carry quite a weight. Hanging a thwart from the gunwales is seldom satisfactory; screws pull out and it cannot give the support to the hull. Metal brackets and bolts are better (Fig. 16.11).

If moulding facilities are not available the bracket or stringer can be glued on or screwed, or the thwart can be supported by struts. A good alternative is to support the thwart on a built-up box which forms one of the buoyancy compartments.

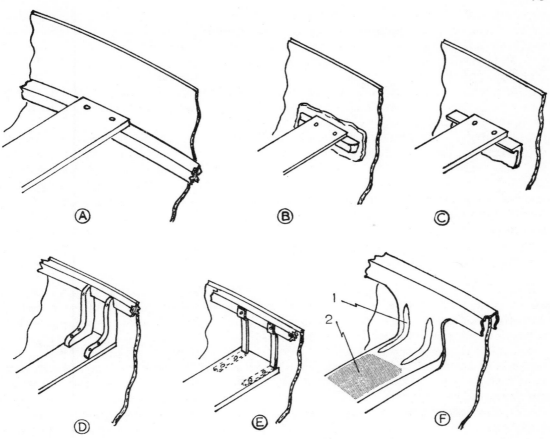

16.11: *Mounting thwarts.*

A. *Thwart screwed to stringers screwed, embedded or glued to the hull.*
B. *Screwed to an embedded or glued block.*
C. *Bolted to a moulded bracket. A metal bracket could also be used.*
D. *Supported by hanging knees from the gunwale. Not recommended unless bolted as the screws are prone to pull out.*
E. *If hanging from the gunwale is essential it is better to use underslung metal or moulded brackets.*
F. *Moulded thwart integral with the gunwale. May be moulded complete with raised or depressed stiffening knees, 1, and patterned seat, 2.*

A light wooden thwart needs a centre strut. Side seats running fore and aft can be supported by moulded webs or metal angle-brackets.

All brackets, stringers, struts, etc., should have a generous area of contact with the hull skin to spread the weight. On the whole stringers are preferable as they avoid hard spots.

A method often used, and a neat one, is to mould the thwart as part of the gunwale moulding, but this requires an elaborate mould, and is only suitable for a production run.

The forward and after thwarts are often combined with the moulded buoyancy compartments. In the double skin dinghies, the maligned "soap dishes," the thwarts, or more correctly the seats, are all moulded as part of the inner skin. This, too, is an elaborate mould, too complicated to be worthwhile for an amateur.

Thwarts can be moulded separately as sub-mouldings, or they can be made of wood. The moulded thwart looks clean and smart, matching the moulded hull, and the mould can be simple enough for one-off moulding. Wood, however, can be touched up more easily and gives a more traditional appearance. The method of attachment is much the same in both cases.

Nothing is so damp as a smooth surface. Smooth town pavements are wetter than a rough country lane. A light evening dew on smooth moulded or varnished thwarts calls for oilskin trousers. A rough surface gives projections to sit on and channels for the dew. It is quite easy to make moulded thwarts with a patterned surface, the rough country lane instead of the smooth city pavement, by sticking an embossed surface on the pattern or mould. This may be Trakmark or embossed PVC upholstery which can give a realistic imitation leather pattern and various other luxurious patterns. Some kinds of wallpaper have an embossed pattern. On large dinghies or launches where it is safe to stand on the seats, a pattern has non-slip value, and is desirable.

BUILDER'S NAME-PLATE AND SERIAL NUMBER In most branches of engineering it is routine to stamp every product with a serial and model number. I do not think I have ever seen a small boat with a maker's serial number, and quite often it has not even got a builder's name on it.

Old-fashioned boatbuilders knew every boat by name and watched over them throughout their life like a shepherd with his flock. Those days have largely gone, and most boats today are built in factories, even if they are still boatyards, in substantial numbers, and are scattered far and wide.

It may be important to be able to identify a moulded boat. Only the builder can easily supply a replacement section if it is badly damaged. But few good designs are static; they are improved continually, and if the builder is to supply the right part he must know when the boat was moulded and what modifications had been incorporated at that time.

One obvious way is to use the usual builder's name-plate, screwed to the hull with self-tapping screws. Traditional brass and modern plastic serve equally well. Both the moulder and the fitting-out yard should leave their name and number on the boat.

It is quite easy to emboss the builder's name permanently on the mould or pattern with letter punches. A light mark is sufficient, and it is better done on the pattern as this will not be a moulded surface. A neater way is to use a paper-embossing press, the sort of thing used for embossing an address on notepaper. A neatly embossed label stuck on the pattern will be formed in the mould and will put the name on every moulding. Another method is to print or write the information on cloth and mould this in, using a patch of clear gel-coat in front of it. It can also be laminated on the back with clear resin after moulding. It is not generally known that if lettering is printed on glass cloth, the cloth will become invisible when it wets out leaving only the lettering showing. The inks used must not run in resin, paint is surer.

LIFTING HANDLES It is often very difficult to get a good grip on the smooth

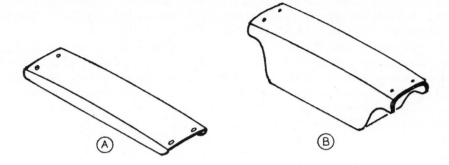

16.12: *Sub-moulding thwarts.*
Thwarts may be formed as sub-mouldings. A. Simple thwart; B. Combined thwart and buoyancy box.

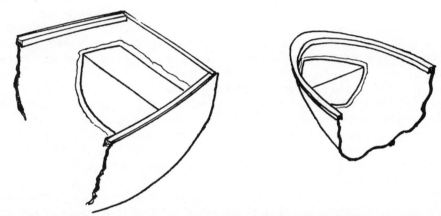

16.13: *Forward and after thwarts are often combined with buoyancy compartments.*

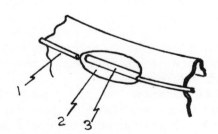

16.14: *Recessed lifting handle.*

1. Gunwale. 2. Moulded recess. 3. Lifting handle.
Sometimes the fender or wooden rubbing band is continued across the recess to form the lifting handle.

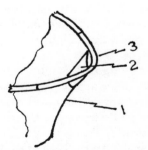

16.15: *Combined bow fender and lifting handle.*

1. Stem. 2. Moulded recess. 3. Stiff fender forming "bumper" and lifting handle.

surface of a moulded boat, particularly a runabout, when it has to be manhandled. The chine is much too slippery for safe handling, the fender, if fitted, is too likely to pull away. The moulded deck gives little grip, and the edge of the cockpit is often not strong enough, or too sharp, and anyway in an inconvenient position for lifting. As well as being naturally smooth, moulded boats are likely to be wet, and possibly slimy too.

Lifting handles fore and aft give a convenient firm grip and reduce the risk of damage from the boat being dropped. Some proprietary fittings are even combined with cleats or fairleads, or tie-down eyes; they can be brightly plated and decorative as well as being useful. Whether one likes their style or not, there is a much wider and better choice of American "hardware" for runabouts than there is of British.

Needless to say lifting handles must be well fastened and strong enough. It is very important, too, that the deck is reinforced in their vicinity with stout blocks and increased thickness, and they must be through-bolted, not screwed. It is worth checking up, too, that the deck is adequately fastened to the hull—this cannot be taken for granted; I know of cases where the deck has been lifted clean off the hull. A deck secured only by a filling of resin glass putty would not be good enough.

Any two lifting handles should be able to lift the whole weight of the boat and its contents. It is worth remembering that the contents may include a lot of water. If by any chance a handle gives way the bump is likely to damage the hull; it may not be serious, moulded boats are pretty tough, but they can be damaged if they are dropped on anything sharp.

As well as giving a reliable grip for handling, lifting handles provide slinging points. In many parts of the world boats are lifted in and out of the water by cranes instead of running down a launching ramp as is the usual custom in Britain, and stout built-in slinging points are much more convenient than passing a strop under the hull, as well as being safer. A runabout or sailing dinghy is too heavy to haul on deck easily like a small dinghy. They must be winched on board or lifted by davits and frequently have to remain suspended from the davits at sea.

Lifting handles can also be moulded into the deck. Fig. 16.14 shows one method, a moulded depression in the deck with a straight bar across it; the wooden rubbing band, if designed to be strong enough, could be used instead. This method is particularly suitable for sailing boats, because it is difficult for ropes and sheets to foul it.

A bow handle can be combined with a bow "bumper," and made of stout rubber, PVC or nylon, or rubber- or plastic-covered metal (Fig. 16.15).

The gunwale will usually serve for lifting a small dinghy, but the turned down edge on the inside of a moulded gunwale, although a secure handhold, is very uncomfortable and "cutting." An extruded PVC or aluminium channel section covers an exposed edge neatly and makes a much more comfortable handgrip.

A dinghy may have to be carried for an appreciable distance. A yacht's tender will often have to be carried a hundred yards or more, and I know of at least one hard that is a quarter of a mile long. Plenty of beaches, too, go out a long way, and these days it is getting difficult to park a car or trailer within sight of the sea. Dragging a dinghy a long distance will do it no good even if it is adequately protected.

Handgrip bilge keels are well worth while for any dinghy carried on deck. More moulders might offer these as a standard alternative among the long list of essential extras. However, it is essential that they are properly fastened and into a hull strong

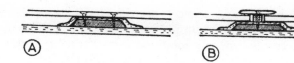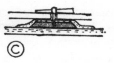

16.16: *Securing bottom-boards.*
A. *Screwed into an embedded or glued wood block.*
B. *Secured by a wood or brass turnbuckle.*
C. *Secured by a toggle through a screw-eye.*

enough to take the strain (see Chapter Fourteen). Otherwise they will be untrustworthy and at sea that spells danger.

Racing dinghies spend most of their life ashore, and trolleys are universal. Nevertheless, they must often be lifted. A racing dinghy too must offer a good grip either way up. A capsized hull that is too smooth and slippery to get a grip on may have fatal consequences.

Most double-skinned dinghies are very difficult to get hold of and they need lifting points. When the inner skin is not continuous, e.g. gunwales and thwarts only, it can have hand holes cut in it, but these should be rounded off and the edges covered, for a comfortable grip.

BOTTOM BOARDS All dinghies need bottom boards; otherwise there is nowhere dry to put anything down. A moulded dinghy is supposed not to leak, but it will still collect rainwater and spray. Without bottom boards it will also be difficult to keep the boat looking clean and smart. Moreover, there is always the risk of a heavy sharp-cornered load, or something dropped, piercing the hull. (It has happened often enough with wooden boats, even hefty ones.) The clean-looking integrally moulded "floor" of the double-skinned dinghy is one of its weak points. It is unprotected from damage and holds water like its rude nickname.

Wood is still the best material for bottom boards. They will need some maintenance, some varnish or paint once a year, but bottom boards are bound to get scratched and worn, and need maintenance in any case; scratched wood can be touched up more easily than a scratched moulding, and it will usually be possible to take them out and do them in comfort. Plywood bottom boards are cheap to make and reasonably durable.

Moulded bottom boards must have a pattern or they will be dangerously slippery —and slipping in a dinghy is likely to make the rude description "bathtub" only too true. Some double-skinned dinghies have a "mock" Trakmark diamond pattern, but a non-slip resin paint gives a much better grip and can be touched up easily. Little can be done about a chipped and worn diamond pattern. The remarks about non-slip decks, in Chapter Six, apply to bottom boards as well.

Real Trakmark adds to the expense, but it is much more efficient as a non-slip surface than its moulded imitation. It is also a good way to cut down the maintenance on plywood bottom boards and protect moulded bottom boards from wear. Trakmark is often used on runabouts for appearance's sake as well as for its functional value. It is more practical than the fitted carpets or leopard-skin of the millionaire class.

An apparently simple way to get a rough surface on moulded bottom boards is to mould them "inside out" so that the rough side is uppermost. On a single-skinned dinghy this blends with the inside finish, but if properly moulded it will still be a glossy resin surface and therefore slippery. The particular firm which used to do this, and claimed its virtues as an irresistible sales point, made very "hairy" resin-starved mouldings which certainly gave a fair grip when new, but they held dirt like a doormat and disintegrated rapidly from wear and weakness of the naked, unsupported fibres. This method is not recommended. It is also uncomfortable for bare feet and dangerous, too, for the upstanding rigid, needle-like fibres break off in the foot.

Bottom boards need to be detachable so that patches of dirt can be cleaned up and lost treasures recovered. To hold them down there is still little to beat a simple toggle or the common turnbuckle, screwed to a block moulded or glued to the bottom of the boat (Fig. 16.16). Wood screws form a more permanent attachment where the boards do not need to be removed more often than at the annual fitting-out time. Bottom boards should always be secured, never loose, or they will be lost every time the boat is capsized or swamped, and it is a curse to have to scour the foreshore on the forlorn chance of finding one's lost bottom board before someone else does. Also they will fall out every time the boat is turned over, and are quite likely to get left behind on the bank.

RACING DINGHIES My personal view is that a lightweight racing dinghy is the wrong application for GRP and it should be plywood, but this is unfashionable and there are many good ones to disprove me. To cut weight, thickness must be reduced to the minimum. GRP is twice as heavy as wood, therefore for the same weight it must be half as thick. The moduli of elasticity are much the same for both moulded ply and GRP so, as stiffness is proportional to the cube of the thickness, half the thickness means only one-eighth the stiffness. This imposes severe design problems because stiffness rather than strength is the major requirement. In most cases this problem is ignored rather than overcome.

Minimum thickness demands a low resin/glass ratio, e.g. 1:1 instead of the usual 2·5:1 or 3:1. This is achieved by using woven rovings or cloth rather than mat but chiefly by very thorough consolidation, much hard rolling and careful control of resin used. This is not a job for the ordinary slapdash moulders churning out cheap mat-based mouldings with a staff of builders' labourers working to a tight, bonus-linked schedule. It is skilled, specialised, expert moulding. It is utterly wrong to think that craftsmanship died with GRP.

Gel coats are a large proportion of a thin moulding, contribute little to strength, and on thin flexible mouldings are prone to crack. If used they must be thin and carefully controlled. One way out is to dispense with a gel coat and paint instead. Paint is thin and light, and less troublesome on flexible surfaces. Water resistance for a boat kept ashore is a low priority and durability is an early sacrifice to ultimate performance.

With a thin, flexible moulding attachments need great care and generous load spreading. The avoidance of stress concentrations and hard spots is absolutely vital. Stiffening attached to the skin should be reduced to the minimum to reduce potential hard spots and save weight. The ideal is a hull which can flex unrestrained. A thin moulding is easily damaged and must be handled with care.

CHAPTER SEVENTEEN

Buoyancy

GRP boats are heavier than water, and so they will sink. Our opponents hail this as a major disadvantage—but that is nothing new; they also said it stood to reason that iron ships could not possibly float. The plain truth is that any wooden boat larger than a dinghy will sink if it is swamped, because the buoyancy of the wood is not nearly enough to support the ballast keel or engines, and even a "buoyant" wooden dinghy will hardly support one drowning man, let alone an overload of overloaded revellers.

All dinghies need reserve buoyancy if they are to support their occupants in an emergency. The better moulded dinghies have built-in buoyancy, although to charge extra for an important safety feature, as is often done, is unjustifiable, regardless of whether the boat is built of wood, metal or fibreglass. However, the dinghy market is fiercely competitive with the rock-bottom prices, against which all others are judged regardless of quality, set by ruthless builders of the barest thin plywood shells, which, although they may be "buoyant," barely contain enough wood to support a bottle of beer.

Runabouts, launches and canoes, too, can have built-in buoyancy, but it is usually impracticable on cruisers, as the buoyancy needed to keep up the keel or engine occupies too much boat—and the demand is always for the most boat in the least space.

Inadequate buoyancy is a complete waste. There is no point in devoting precious boat space to buoyancy if it is not going to keep the boat and crew afloat in an emergency. Moreover it gives a false and dangerous idea of security. Buoyancy as a sales gimmick should be viewed with suspicion.

BUOYANCY TANKS Hollow buoyancy tanks are the cheapest, but also the most unreliable. I do not recommend them. A filling of plastic foam will cost more, but is absolutely reliable and for practical purposes it requires no more space. In the event of a really serious accident, such as a dinghy being run down, hollow tanks could be holed so severely that much of the air would escape, particularly if capsized—and under such circumstances a capsize is more than probable (Fig. 17.1). The double-skinned dinghy is particularly vulnerable to this, as all the buoyancy is in the single space between the skins—all in one compartment—one good hole and all the buoyancy can be lost, whereas it is unlikely that three or more separate tanks will be holed simultaneously.

However, a certain amount of air will usually be trapped inside a damaged hollow compartment, particularly on a double-skinned dinghy, and continue to provide some buoyancy, but for obvious reasons this should not be depended on (Fig. 17.2). Hollow tanks must allow a reasonable margin of safety, and allow for at least one tank to be flooded. Remember the magnificent *Titanic* was called "unsinkable."

In contrast, buoyancy spaces filled with plastic foam will always float—even if cut into little pieces (Fig. 17.3). My advice is to insist on foam-filled buoyancy spaces, partic-

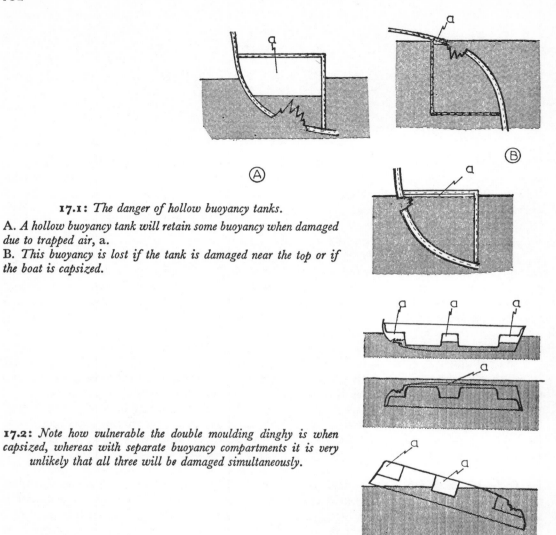

17.1: *The danger of hollow buoyancy tanks.*
A. *A hollow buoyancy tank will retain some buoyancy when damaged due to trapped air, a.*
B. *This buoyancy is lost if the tank is damaged near the top or if the boat is capsized.*

17.2: *Note how vulnerable the double moulding dinghy is when capsized, whereas with separate buoyancy compartments it is very unlikely that all three will be damaged simultaneously.*

17.3: *Foam buoyancy can always be relied upon, either way up, and if cut in half the two halves will float.*

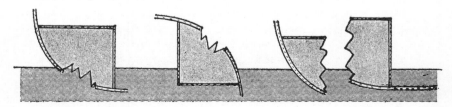

ularly on double-skinned boats; hollow tanks may let you down—just when you need them most. Where there is a large theoretical buoyancy, a partial filling of foam would suffice. It is now unnecessary to allow for one compartment to be flooded and therefore foam filled buoyancy needs less space than hollow, despite being somewhat heavier. This alone will offset the extra cost.

A cheap alternative, and the only case where air-filled buoyancy can be trusted, is to use PVC or rubber buoyancy bags. Many sizes and shapes are made for racing dinghies, and they are so flexible that they can fit into, and fill up almost any reasonable shape. Their cost is low, their buoyancy terrific, and they are the cheapest flotation by far. They can be secured quite simply under the thwarts with straps. They can be trusted, because their condition is visible and easily inspected. If "flat" it is clear they must be blown up. They are surprisingly resistant to damage, because, being very flexible, they give where a rigid tank would be cracked. Again they are essentially separate tanks, so that even if one does get punctured, which is quite difficult, it is almost impossible to puncture two or three at once.

An old motor inner tube is not be to despised either, and quite long voyages have been made on an inflated beach mattress (usually inadvertently although I did once use one to sail to a desert island).

Upholstery and cushions can count as buoyancy. Runabouts with their more luxurious equipment offer most scope for this. However, they must be well secured if intended to support the boat, and attached, yet readily detachable if for personal flotation. Cushions lose their life-saving value if they have already floated out of reach of a non-swimmer—as they probably will do, if they are loose.

Seepage is a common trouble on buoyancy tanks, and on a hollow tank may steal quite a lot of buoyancy; this is another advantage of foam filling. The intake from seepage is unlikely to be serious while the boat was actually swamped, as it would be slow; it is usually built up over a prolonged period from bilge and rainwater, but a flaw near the top of the tank, and this means whichever part is uppermost at the time, will allow air to escape, and this will result in a much quicker and possibly serious loss of buoyancy, if combined with damage or another flaw to let the water in as the air is driven out.

Often the fault is not at the bottom, perhaps half way up the side, so that there is a weir effect, and once the water has got in, it does not run out again. Indeed once in, it is often surprisingly difficult to get it out. Buoyancy tanks, and also the space between the skins of double-skinned dinghies, need drain screws or plugs in a position which will drain completely; it is sometimes more convenient to turn them upside down for this. Well-made dinghies as well as poorly made ones need this feature, for seepage can occur from minor damage as well as flaws.

The major faults are flaws in the fillets joining a hollow tank to the hull, or breakaway of these fillets from the hull, often due to flexing of a light hull in use. The fillets must be well moulded and of generous area; good bonding is essential and the common cause of bond failure is bad surface preparation (see Chapters One and Two). Reject a moulded fillet which looks dry and hairy. It may have a multitude of tiny leakage paths which are impossible to find and stop individually, and not easy to cure *en masse*.

Foam filling will not prevent seepage unless it fills the space completely and has no sponge effect. The commoner slab or block filling leaves a considerable air space all round the edges and between the slabs, but nevertheless it provides good, reliable buoyancy (Fig. 17.4), and the foam still fills a large part, so that even if there is seepage or damage, there is not really very much room for the water. It will not affect the buoyancy of the foam, and none of the common foams are seriously or quickly affected by water.

Plastic foams have either open, interconnecting cells, like a sponge, or closed, non-interconnecting cells like a soap lather (Fig. 17.5). In practice the open cell foam usually used is rigid, not flexible like a sponge and therefore it does not soak up water in the same way. Water can eventually fill it, but so much air will be trapped in the interstices that it will take a long time to get filled up completely and it will retain a substantial proportion of buoyancy. This might not be the case with a flexible foam if of the sponge type. No foam is purely one or the other. There are always a few open cells among the closed and vice versa. Foam polystyrene is made by expanding individual pellets (like the breakfast foods) and has a high proportion of closed cells, but the others are made by "blowing" (a meringue or froth effect) and are unlikely to exceed 90 per cent closed or open cells. This proportion, and even lower proportions, are quite satisfactory because the majority of the open cells will, in fact, be surrounded by closed cells. Plastic foams used for buoyancy are in two main forms: *a*. slabs or blocks; *b*. "foam-in-place." Except with polystyrene it is possible for all foam to be either open or closed as required, but one should inquire first as to which it is.

The slabs or blocks of foam plastic are cut to size and packed into the space. They can never fill it completely, but they are usually cheaper and more convenient despite the high wastage. The foams used are polystyrene, the common, white, very light insulation, polyurethane, the flexible upholstery foam but also available in rigid sheets, foam PVC, either rigid or flexible, and Onazote (actually an expanded rubber but very similar to the plastic foams). Cork and balsa wood can also be used.

The "foam-in-place" foams are two-part mixtures which are mixed and then poured or sprayed as liquids, but they foam up immediately to fill the space completely, usually bonding firmly to the sides as well. Some are simple mix-and-pour types, but others require expensive spraying or injection machinery. The commonest are rigid polyurethane foams of 2–10 lb./cu. ft. density (30–160 kg./m.³). They exert considerable pressure while foaming, enough to lift a man. Precautions must be taken to avoid distortion, especially when the hull is involved.

Buoyancy tanks can often be made quite simply by moulding over blocks of plastic foam, shaped to fit the space. On a one-off job this avoids the complication of a separate mould. The rough finish is little disadvantage, because it will be the same as the inside of the boat, anyway. Indeed, a smooth polished finish to a moulded buoyancy tank only contrasts with the normal rough inside finish surrounding it.

It is not possible to mould directly over polystyrene foam, because polyester resin quickly dissolves it. It must be protected somehow, one satisfactory method is to wrap it in polythene sheet; bitumen paint is also used. The advantage of polystyrene is its cheapness and ready availability; it can be obtained from many builders' merchants.

Other plastic foams are affected to a much smaller extent and are normally satisfactory if the resin sets fairly quickly. However any porosity will drain away a lot of resin so that some covering is an advantage unless moulded with at least two layers, allowing the first to set hard and form a firm backing for the subsequent non-porous layers. Porosity is most likely on sawn edges but I have had trouble in this way when using cork; the large cavities drained away so much resin, and also prevented sound impregnation, that the tank was found to be distinctly porous.

A similar method is to make up a light plywood or hardboard tank as a former and mould over this completely (Fig. 17.6). The plywood need have little strength, as it is only to provide the minimum support while the moulded tank is being laid up over it. It is expendable, as it will be left inside, so needs to be cheap, and there is no need to make anything elaborate, well fitting and firmly secured to the hull. Tacking together with sticky tape is quite sufficient as it will end up stuck to the moulding. The moulding is best done in two stages, allowing the first layer to set before starting the second. This will avoid possible trouble due to the flexibility of a rough flimsy former. This method gives a tank with the strength in the moulding but if preferred the plywood can be made strong and covered with a thin moulding just for durability.

Where no moulding facilities are available, the buoyancy tank can be made entirely of plywood (Fig. 17.7). A foam plastic filling is still recommended; fortunately foam poly-styrene slabs are readily available from local builders' merchants. In out of the way places other materials could be used such as cork, kapok, vermiculite, or local products. Provided it is not too heavy or absorbent, any filling is better than none.

It is not essential even to encase the polystyrene; it need only be fastened quite openly under the thwarts. Most other plastic foams, Onazote and cork can be used in the same way, although the cheaper flexible foams are likely to be degraded by sunlight. Minor damage and wear and tear will not reduce their buoyancy as they are "solid bubbles"—unlike a hollow box which is useless as soon as it has one small hole.

All buoyancy materials must be fixed in securely, and buoyancy compartments must be strong enough to withstand the strain of the buoyancy trying to get out., e.g. a compartment 2 ft. × 2 ft. × 2 ft. has a volume of 8 cu. ft. (0·23 m.^{3}), which means a buoyancy of around 500 lb. (228 kg.). If the boat sinks, that compartment, which is of quite a normal volume for a buoyancy compartment, can exert a lifting force of nearly a quarter of a ton! This force must be prevented from breaking loose or even breaking up the boat if the boat is to stay afloat. Light lashings and screws will tear away. This force, of course, is the extreme case, and only exerted if the boat is held down with the tank completely submerged. Normally the force is no more than necessary to keep the boat up, i.e. equal to the immersed weight of the boat, and the tank floats high in the water.

Racing dinghies need a lot of buoyancy because they must be easy to right after a routine capsize without wetting the crew's feet. An ordinary rowing dinghy which has buoyancy for emergencies only, is considered to have sufficient if there is something really reliable for the crew to hang on to until someone can come along and haul them out of the water or they can swim to the shore. But many waters have hazards like sharks, crocodiles, or bilharzia which call for a very generous margin of buoyancy, more even than a racing dinghy, to make sure the crew's toes are well out of the water!

CALCULATIONS OF BUOYANCY
One cubic foot of hollow buoyancy tank provides 62·5 lb. of positive buoyancy in fresh water, and about 65 lb. in sea water. The metric equivalents are 1,000 and 1,040 kg. per cu. metre. The fresh water buoyancy, being smaller, is the one which should be used in calculations.

Polystyrene foam gives about 60–62 lb. of buoyancy per cu. ft. in fresh water, a negligible difference compared with the hollow tank.

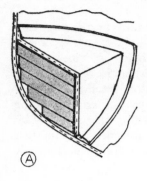
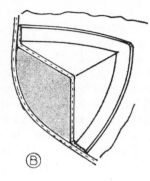

17.4: *Foam-filled buoyancy compartments.*

A. *Slabs of polystyrene foam or Onazote are adequate but cannot fill all the space.*

B. *"Foam-in-place" swells up to fill the entire space.*

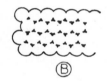

17.5: *Types of foam.*

A. *Non-interconnecting cell structure, i.e. like a lather.*

B. *Interconnecting cell structure, i.e. like a sponge.*

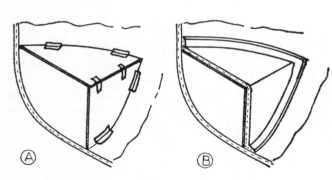

17.6: *A one-off moulded buoyancy tank.*

A. *Shape thin panels of plywood or hardboard and "tack" in position with sticky tape.*

B. *Mould over the panels to form the buoyancy tank. Note the generous overlaps on to the hull.*

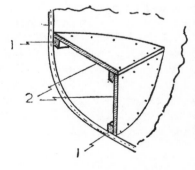

17.7: *A "dry" construction buoyancy tank.*

1. *Battens glued to the hull.* 2. *Plywood panels glued and screwed to the battens.*

The buoyancy of the common foam materials in fresh water is shown in Table 17.1.

Table 17.1
Buoyancy of foam materials in fresh water

Material	Buoyancy	
	lb./cu. ft.	kg./m.³
Foam polystyrene	60–62	960–990
Foam PVC	50–58	800–930
Foam polyurethane	52–62	830–970
Foam isocyanate	50–56	800–900
Onazote	50–58	800–930
Cork	46–49	730–790
Balsa wood	40–60	640–960
Air in fresh water	62·5	1,000
Air in sea water	65	1,040

The positive buoyancy considered necessary to support a man in water seems to vary. The 1960 International Convention on Safety of Life at Sea specified 14½ lb. (6·5 kg.), the Ministry of Transport 17½ lb. (8 kg.), the Air Registration Board 20 lb. (9 kg.), British Standard 3595 35 lb. (16 kg.) carefully arranged to float, not drown the wearer—a proviso lacking in the others.

However, a good guide is to allow one-tenth of the man's weight; this gives a figure of 20 lb. or about one-third of a cubic foot for a 14 stone (200 lb.) man. This will support the man in water where is he nearly buoyant anyway; but if he is to sit on or in the boat with dry feet he will require enough buoyancy to support his whole weight, ten times as much.

These figures are only the buoyancy necessary to support the crew. The boat itself, the equipment, stores, engine, etc., will need support also, although some materials, of course, like wood, will float in themselves and will contribute to buoyancy. Their contribution, however, must not be over-estimated; cold calculation is safer. Fortunately this is one of the few cases in dealing with a boat where the calculations are easy and the forces involved are definite and predictable.

Reinforced plastic is heavier than water, and so it will sink, but it is not very much heavier, much less than steel for example, and does not need much to support it. The specific gravity is about 1·5 (note that the composite material is lighter than glass), so that its immersed weight is only one-third of its weight in air—and all fibreglass boats are light weight boats anyway—so that buoyancy for a moulded boat is not a serious problem. For example, a small moulded dinghy weighing, say 50 lb., in air needs only 16·7 lb. of buoyancy to support it, about ¼ cu. ft., little more than an empty one-gallon oil can tucked under a thwart. A substantial amount of wood trim will reduce this.

In contrast, an engine and its equipment, or a ballast keel, heavy items in themselves, need buoyancy of 90 per cent of their dead weight for support. That same ¼ cu. ft.

which supports 50 lb. of dinghy, will support only 18·5 lb. of engine, about half the weight of a small outboard motor.

All materials weigh less in water, which is why the buoyancy required for support is always less than the dead weight in air. (We have all heard of Archimedes jumping out of his overflowing bath and running naked through the streets of Thessaloniki crying "Eureka!"). Many materials weigh so much less that they float and contribute to the buoyancy.

A sandwich construction normally has a lightweight core and inherent buoyancy, the amount depending on the thickness and material of the core; it can be relied upon to support at least the bare hull, and may be reckoned unsinkable.

Table 17.2 gives figures to illustrate these points.

To appreciate the figure properly, remember that 100 lb. of lead is a small lump, but 100 lbs. of reinforced plastic is a lot of boat. (The old trick question of which is heavier, a ton of lead or a ton of feathers?) Lead needs ten times its own volume of buoyancy for support, but reinforced plastic needs only half, and man one-tenth.

Table 17.2

Material	S.G.	B_b	V_b	V_b/V_x
Reinforced plastic	1·5	0·33	0·53 cu ft.	0·5
Man	1·1	0·1	0·16	0·1
Aluminium	2·6	0·63	1·0	1·6
Steel	7·9	0·88	1·4	7·0
Lead	11·4	0·92	1·5	10·4
Oak	0·85	— 0·39	— 0·62	—
Mahogany	0·6	— 0·9	— 1·44	—
Foam polystyrene	0·01	— 61·5	— 98·0	—

S.G., specific gravity.

B_b, Buoyancy factor $= \dfrac{\textit{Submerged weight}}{\textit{Deadweight in air.}}$

V_b, Volume of air buoyancy in cu. ft. to support a block weighing 100 lb. in air when immersed in water.

Negative sign indicates buoyancy contributed.

$$V_b/V_x = \frac{\text{Volume of air buoyancy to support 100 lb. as above}}{\text{Volume of 100 lb. of material}}$$

The volume of other buoyancy materials to give similar buoyancy can be obtained from Table 17.1 and proportional calculation.

The following examples show how to apply these figures to get the buoyancy required for any particular boat.

1. *Eight-foot Dinghy*

	Material	*Weight lb. W*	*Buoyancy factor B*	*Buoyancy needed lb. = W × B*
Moulded hull complete	Reinforced plastic	60	0·33	20
Outboard motor	Steel	40	0·88	35
Equipment and load	Mixed	40	0·5 (average)	20
Crew of four at 200 lb.	Man	800	0·1	80
				155 lb.

155 lb. at 60 lb./cu. ft. = 2·58 cu. ft., say 3 cu. ft.
Equivalent to 3 slabs of polystyrene foam 3 ft. × 6 in. × 8 in.
Buoyancy contributed by woodwork, if fitted, would be about 15–20 lbs.

2. *Twelve-foot Runabout*

	Material	*Weight lb. W*	*Buoyancy factor B*	*Buoyancy needed lb. = W × B*
Moulded hull, deck, seats, etc.	Reinforced plastic	300	0·33	100
Outboard motor and equipment	Steel	240	0·88	210
Equipment	Mixed	100	0·5 (average)	50
Crew of 6 at 200 lb.	Man	1,200	0·1	120
				480
Woodwork	Wood	50	− 0·9	− 45
				435

435 lb. at 60 lb./cu. ft. = 7·25 cu. ft., say 7·5 cu. ft.
Equivalent to a shaped forward compartment 3·5 ft. × 2 ft. × 2 ft., and an aft compartment 4 ft. × 1 ft. × 1 ft.

3. *Fourteen-foot Sailing Dinghy*

	Material	Weight lb. W	Buoyancy factor B	Buoyancy needed lb. = W × B
Moulded hull, deck and sub-mouldings	Reinforced plastic	200	0·33	67
Rigging and equipment	Steel	30	0·88	26
Centreboard	Steel	40	0·88	35
Outboard motor, 4 h.p.	Steel	40	0·88	35
Sails	Terylene	20	0·09	2
Crew 4 at 200 lb.	Man	800	0·1	80
				245 lb.
Mast and Woodwork	Wood	50	− 1·0	− 50
				195 lb.

195 lb. at 60 lb./cu. ft. — 3·25 cu. ft., say 3·5 cu. ft.

N.B. This is the buoyancy needed to keep it afloat, but if it is the sort of dinghy which capsizes easily, and must be righted readily, very much more will be needed, perhaps ten times as much, say 25–30 cu. ft.

4.   *Twenty-foot Sailing Cruiser*

	Material	Weight lb. W.	Buoyancy factor B	Buoyancy needed lb. = W × B
Moulded hull, deck, etc.	Reinforced plastic	1,200	0·33	400
Keel	Lead	1,000	0·92	920
Engine	Steel	200	0·88	176
Equipment	Mixed	400	0·5, average	200
Crew 4 at 200 lb.	Man	800	0·1	80
Stores, water, etc.	Mixed	100	0·5, average	50
				1,826 lb.

1,826 lb. at 60 lb./cu. ft. = 30·5 cu. ft.

This takes up a lot of a small boat, one whole berth space, but note how small a proportion is now needed to support the crew, less than 5 per cent.

These figures are only approximate, although fairly typical. It is important to work out each case according to the actual weights.

The worst conditions and most overloaded state must always be assumed, for it is then that an accident is most likely. It is wise to consider the answer as the bare minimum and allow a generous margin. This is particularly important when relying on hollow buoyancy tanks where buoyancy can easily be stolen by seepage or damage. It should be assumed in the calculation that at least one hollow buoyancy tank is out of action. This is not necessary with foam-filled tanks.

Some thought should also be given to the question of trim. The crew will find it easier to cling to a boat the right way up, rather than to a smooth slippery bottom, and the boat may have to be towed while still partially waterlogged.

When I learnt to sail I was taught that to capsize was a highly unseamanlike and dangerous practice; and so it was, for those dinghies could not be righted. The modern dinghy is capsized for fun because it can be righted. But unfortunately this fashion for easy capsize, easy righting, has spread even to family, picnic dinghies, with no pretensions to out-and-out racing machines. I have often been asked by fond, and admirable mothers, to recommend "a dinghy for little Johnnie to learn to sail on, something easily righted because it is so important for him to learn how to right after a capsize." This is a very dangerous approach; it is very much better to learn how to sail and how *not* to capsize. Also the constant fear of a capsize has handicapped many timid children from learning how to sail at all, and discouraged many able, but not so active grown ups from teaching them.

A capsize can be all part of the fun in a race, with rescue boats all around in case of trouble, but sometimes if by oneself a mile from the shore it can be very serious. If little Johnnie is anything like me, and I was not exceptional, his main idea will be to sail as far out to sea as possible. I soon discovered that if I did not look round until I was well out to sea I could not see a frantic mother waving on the shore. If Johnnie's boat is unlikely to capsize mother can sit back and worry herself to sleep, but if he is in a modern easily capsized dinghy, even if it is easily righted—under normal conditions—she has some justification in sending for the lifeboat.

The boats I learnt to sail on had their faults in plenty, but they were, and the survivors still are, a popular local racing class. As racing dinghies they are now dismissed scornfully as Old Men's Boats or Kid's Stuff—yet a lot of our top dinghy helmsmen learnt on these particular boats, and three of them at least are now in the world championship and Olympic class. Which all goes to show that it is more important to learn to sail than to capsize!

There is a grave shortage of good, modern, safe family boats, stable enough to forget about capsizing, and large enough, say 14 to 16 ft., for estuary and open sea sailing. Father may hanker after speed, few people like to be overtaken, on the water or on the road, but mother will think more of the children's safety. Only a stable boat is safe with children around, yet a stable boat need not be a slow one—compared with others of its type. It will not have the speed and performance of a racing dinghy, it cannot have, just as a family saloon car cannot expect to beat a dashing young man's high-powered sports car—and certainly should not try to with the family inside.

Racing dinghies are for the agile and skilful. A boat for the family, for beginners—and old men too—should be virtually uncapsizable, stable, and a boat to sit in, not out.

They can still be fun to sail, not quite so exhilarating perhaps, but they will be much more fun for a young family, yet they can still give good sport racing. In fact they can be truly dual-purpose boats which cannot be claimed for a fashionable racing dinghy. If we must have monster national classes, is there not room for some safe family class boats? Perhaps they exist already if one could search diligently through the hundreds of classes and could distil the truth from the sales talk.

SMALL CRUISER BUOYANCY It is not unusual to see small cruisers fitted with buoyancy compartments. The merits of this are questionable. They occupy a large part of the useful accommodation and the smaller the cruiser the more valuable every scrap of living and stowage space. The boat may sleep four, but it is difficult at the best of times to *live* four in a small boat *and* stow their belongings *and* stow the ship's gear. This is so even on boats a good deal larger. It is difficult to escape the conclusion that if a small cruiser needs buoyancy she is not seaworthy enough to be a cruiser at all.

On the other hand this may be the beginning of a trend, and one day all yachts may have buoyancy, perhaps even be compelled to have it. Ships are made as unsinkable as possible with watertight bulkheads so why not yachts? However the approach should be towards watertight compartments of usable space as on a ship instead of substantial waste of usable space in the already severely limited accommodation.

Developing this idea further it would be quite possible to have watertight lockers. At present small cruiser buoyancy commonly consists of sealing the underbunk space—the most useful (and often only) storage area. If instead of sealing this space it was fitted with watertight hatches, proprietary fittings similar but larger than those now used on dinghies, this invaluable space could still serve as storage. Of course in theory the contents would detract from the buoyancy. In practice the locker would never be filled with more than about 50 per cent of the total air space and much of this would be clothes, ropes and other things of fairly neutral buoyancy. Even heavier items like stores are mostly things which would have to be on board anyway, and therefore require buoyancy to support them. It is so much easier to arrange a very generous surplus of usable buoyancy space to allow for contents than to sacrifice much-needed storage space for permanently sealed and un-usable buoyancy which would, of necessity, be kept to the minimum.

Of course these lockers would lose the advantages of being foam filled, but to compensate they could consist of a lot of separate spaces, thereby at least giving the benefit of spreading any risks. This too would allow for the obvious hazard of lids not being fastened properly, or being lost. Foam filling can still be used for inaccessible places.

OCEAN CRUISER There has been a sudden, alarming rise in attacks by killer whales in mid-ocean with sensational survivals and, presumably, non-survivals. They now seem a hazard to be reckoned with on ocean voyages. Very few yachts could survive such onslaught. There is a case for large, sealable, watertight subdivisions, e.g. fo'c'sle and aft, so that the boat would stay afloat at least long enough for emergency repair, help to arrive or the crew to take to a life-raft in a well-organised manner.

Why ocean cruisers only? There are more rocks around the coasts than whales.

CHAPTER EIGHTEEN

Outboard Motors and Runabouts

In this chapter I refer repeatedly to the Boating Industry Association (formerly the Outboard Boating Club) of America's *Engineering Manual of Recommended Practice*, abbreviated to B.I.A. Recommendations, and I am grateful to the B.I.A. for their permission to do so.

The B.I.A. have managed to get agreement on many common dimensions for outboard motors, boats and fittings, so that any motor in the right power range will fit an outboard boat, because both are built to the same standard transom dimensions. This is a wonderful example of intelligent co-operation throughout an industry, and I have the utmost respect for the B.I.A.; without such co-operation it would have been quite impossible for runabouts and outboard cruisers to have become so popular or for the modern high-powered outboard motor to have been developed to such efficiency. It is the key to the present mass production of both motors and boats.

From this the B.I.A. have gone further and produced a code of practice covering safety, minimum standards of fittings and many other important points including trailers. Similar co-operation is sadly needed in the British and European yachting industry, where every manufacturer still has his own ideas about dimensions and mounting holes, not only for engines but for every little fitting.

The fast outboard cruiser and runabout, like the high-powered outboard motor, is essentially an American development. The American motors are available in most parts of the world and are often locally made, as it has become an international industry. Also there are now several European and Japanese manufacturers of similar powered motors, but as all of them have an eye on the enormous American market, and even more on the market for American-style motors in their own and other countries, they are obviously built to the same standard dimensions.

It seems plain common sense to design a boat with these same standard transom dimensions, so that any of these millions of motors will fit, but there are still a few people who know better.

Note that B.I.A. standard dimensions are all quoted in inches. Equivalent metric dimensions have been rounded off to the nearest mm., generally on the important side. In a few cases this may be critical. In others tolerances are wide and such accuracy is pedantic.

STANDARD TRANSOM DIMENSIONS Figs. 18.1 to 18.4 show the standard transom dimensions recommended by the B.I.A. Any boat built to these dimensions will be able to carry any outboard motor of appropriate power which is also built to B.I.A. dimensions. Motor makes will differ in detail and performance (probably less than their advertisements claim) but all will fit these transoms. This applies to nearly every large

194

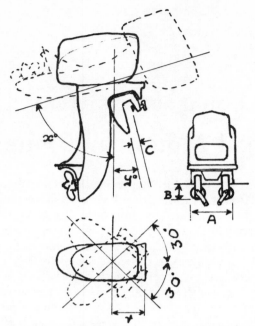

18.1: *B.I.A. Recommended Practice. Outboard motor dimensions (normal use).*

Standard transom heights:	*short shaft* 14½–15 in. (368–381 mm)
Standard transom heights:	*long shaft* 19½–20 in. (495–508 mm)
r *Normal radius for remote steering attachment.*	10 in. (254 mm)
Remote steering range.	30° *minimum each side.*
x° *Tilt angle.*	*To hold at 75° when motor on 14° transom.*
y° *Transom angle.*	7° *to* 24°.

Motor		h.p. kW	Under 5½ Under 4·1	5½ to 12 4·1 to 9·0	12 to 55 9·0 to 41	Over 55 Over 41
Motor clamping area	A	in. mm	7¼ 184	8¼ 209	10¼ 260	15½ 393
	B	in. mm	2½ 64	3½ 89	3⅞ 99	3⅞ 99
Clamping range	C	in. mm	1–2 25–51	1¼–2⅜ 32–60	1¼–2¾ 32–70	1½–2¾ 38–70

	Motor	h.p. kW	Under 5·5 Under 4·1	5·5–12 4·1–9·0	12–61 9·0–46	61–91 46–68	91 and over 68 and over
E	Cut-out length	in. mm	21½ 547	21½ 547	21½ 547	24 610	30 762

"N.B. *As a safety measure, when the inboard section of the motor cut-out is formed by the back of a seat, creating the possibility that a passenger's arm may be caught between the seat and the motor in the event of a sudden tilt-up of the motor, add 3 in. (76 mm) to dimension E.*"

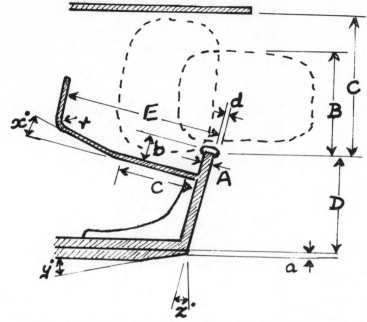

18.2: *B.I.A. Recommended Practice. Motor well dimensions.*

"Motor wells should:

1. Raise the static float-line above the transom cut-out.

2. Reverse water striking the forward well coaming rather than directing it forward and upward.

3. Have steering and motor accessory parts located as high as possible with an aggregate open area not exceeding 16 sq. in. (100 cm²).

Dimensions not dependent on motor size:

a. $\frac{1}{2}$ *in.* (12 mm) Maximum   r. 3 *in. radius* (76 mm) *Maximum.*

b. 6 *in.* (150 mm) *Minimum*   x° 18° *Maximum*

c. 9 *in.* (228 mm) *Minimum*   y° 10°

d. $\frac{1}{16}$ *in.* (1·5 mm). *See Note* 1.   z° 12°–16°

"Note 1. *If transom cap strip extends more than* $\frac{1}{16}$ *in.* (1·5 mm) *aft of the transom, the aft surface of the transom should be built up to bring the extension of the strip into tolerance." Alternatively, cut it back.*

(iii) *Dimensions dependent on motor size:*

		h.p. kW	Under 5·5 Under 4·1	5·5–12 4·1–9·0	12–61 9·0–46	61–91 46–68	91 *and over* 68 *and over*
A	Transom thickness	in. mm	$1\frac{1}{4}$–$1\frac{3}{4}$ 32–44	$1\frac{3}{8}$–$1\frac{3}{4}$ 35–44	$1\frac{3}{8}$–2 35–50	$1\frac{5}{8}$–$2\frac{1}{4}$ 41–57	$1\frac{5}{8}$–$2\frac{1}{4}$ 41–57
B	Motor clearance	in. mm	14 356	17 432	21 534	28 712	28 712
C	Cover height	in. mm	18 458	$22\frac{1}{2}$ 572	29 737	$32\frac{1}{2}$ 826	$32\frac{1}{2}$ 826
D	Transom height (vertical)	in. mm	$14\frac{1}{2}$–15 or $19\frac{1}{2}$–20 368–381 or 496–508	$14\frac{1}{2}$–15 or $19\frac{1}{2}$–20 368–381 or 496–508	$14\frac{1}{2}$–15 or $19\frac{1}{2}$–20 368–381 or 496–508	$19\frac{1}{2}$–20 496–508	$19\frac{1}{2}$–20 496–508

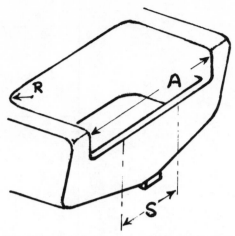

18.3: *B.I.A. Recommended Practice. Motor well dimensions.*

	Motor	h.p. kW		Under 61 Under 46	61 and over 46 and over
A	Minimum motor well width	Single motor	in. mm	33 838	33 838
		Twin motor	in. mm	54 1372	60 1524
S	Twin motor centreline spacing		in. mm	22 559	26 660
R	Maximum radius		in. mm	15 381	20 508

"Motor well dimensions are those required to clear current outboard motors (1971) under normal conditions of turn and tilt with remote controls attached. Where it is impractical to maintain these recommended dimensions at the front of the motor well, alternate provisions may be employed to maintain the desired height, such as upholstery or foam blocks which give when motors tilt without damage to motors or motor well.

"Motor well widths given are minimum widths inside of any edge radii.

"Where high deadrise (deep vee) boats are designed to accommodate either single or twin motors, a standard transom height should be available at all motor centreline locations. A straight transom often can be maintained by accommodating either a long-shaft single motor or short-shaft single motor or short-shaft twin motors."

outboard motor in the world, and most dinghy-sized motors with the notable exception of British Seagull.

The dimensions may be modified. No good rule cannot be improved and the B.I.A. should be consulted for the latest information. Sudden or drastic change is unlikely; too many boats and motors are involved now—some 10 million boats and 15 million motors.

SMALL OUTBOARD MOTORS Under about 5·5 h.p. (4·2 kW.) an outboard motor needs little to mount it on. Its push and weight are small and almost any transom

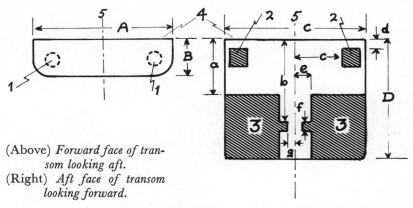

(Above) *Forward face of transom looking aft.*

(Right) *Aft face of transom looking forward.*

18.4: *B.I.A. Recommended Practice. Motor mounting area.*

1. *Motor clamp area.*
2. *Bolting area. 2 in. square (51 mm). Necessary only for motors over 50 h.p. (37 kW).*
3. *Bolting area. Necessary only for motors 40 h.p. (30 kW) and over.*
4. *Top edge of transom.*
5. *Centreline of motor.*

"Bolting areas must be clear on the forward face of transom, flat on aft face of transom and should have no obstruction through transom. For twin motor installation . . . the two areas may be made continuous."
Note maximum transom thickness dimensions on **18.2.**

(i) *Dimensions not dependent on motor size:*
a. $6\frac{1}{2}$ *in.* (165 *mm*). b. $8\frac{3}{8}$ *in.* (212 *mm*).
c. $5\frac{7}{16}$ *in.* (138 *mm*). d. 1 *in.* (25 *mm*).
e. $1\frac{7}{8}$ *in.* (47 *mm*). f. 1 *in.* (26 *mm*).
g. $\frac{3}{4}$ *in.* (19 *mm*).

(ii) *Dimensions dependent on motor size:*

Motor	h.p. kW	Under 5·5 Under 4.1	5·5–12 4·1–9	12–55 9–41	55 and over 41 and over
A	in.	$7\frac{1}{2}$	$8\frac{1}{2}$	$10\frac{3}{4}$	$15\frac{3}{4}$
	mm	190	215	273	400
B	in.	3	$4\frac{3}{4}$	$4\frac{3}{4}$	$4\frac{1}{8}$
	mm	76	120	120	105
C	in.	$9\frac{1}{2}$	13	13	$15\frac{3}{4}$
	mm	241	330	330	400
D	in.	$7\frac{1}{4}$	$7\frac{1}{4}$	$10\frac{1}{2}$	14
	mm	184	184	266	356

will carry it. The common limitations are clamping thickness and stiffness. A GRP dinghy needs wooden clamping blocks inside and out, to make the transom thick enough for the motor clamps to grip and to protect the GRP from being crushed under the pressure of the clamps.

Larger motors, up to about 12 h.p. (9 kW.) will need a stiffened transom with a moulded or wooden gunwale, and knees to transfer the thrust to the hull, as in Fig. 18.6.

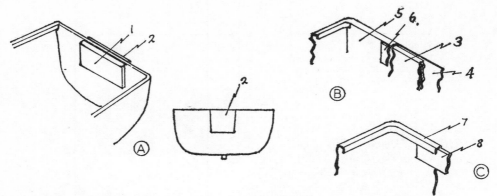

18.5: *Stiffening a transom to take an outboard motor:—a. low-powered motors.*

A. *Wooden pads inside, 1, and outside, 2. These are as much to protect the surface of the moulding, and build up the thickness, as for strength.*
B. *Wood core, 3, embedded between the outer skin, 4, and inner skin, 5. Wooden pads, 6, are still needed for protection.*
C. *Moulded channel section gunwale, 7, with infilling wooden block, 8.*

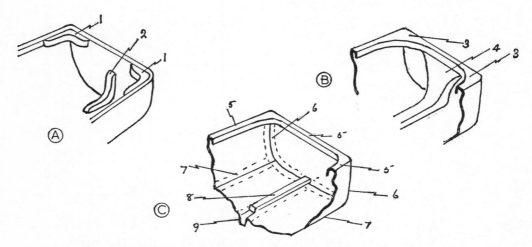

18.6: *Stiffening a transom to take an outboard motor: b. large motors.*

A. *Substantial knees at the corner of the transom, 1, and large knee at the bottom of the transom, 2.*
B. *A moulded gunwale can be widened to form knees, 3, and the keelson extended upwards, 4.*
C. *Thickening naturally stiff parts to form strengthening members. Moulded gunwale, 5; corners of the transom, 6; chine, 7; keelson, 8; keel or skeg, 9.*

LARGE OUTBOARD MOTORS A large motor has a powerful thrust. This is not surprising as its power is comparable to an average European family car (so is the cost!). A boat cut in half by its own motor is an old joke—but it has actually happened. Motors over 12 h.p. need mounting as carefully as inboard engines of comparable power despite their light weight and portability. Racing boats need very strong transoms and mountings because as well as the thrust there is violent movement with high dynamic stresses. Their motors may be of a power unknown when the boat was built.

The requirements are:

1. A transom strong enough to take both the weight and thrust of the motor.
2. Means of transferring that thrust to the hull.
3. A safe hull for the size of motor.

Transoms are often of sandwich construction with a thick wooden core forming the whole transom or just the upper part carrying the motor. Clamping areas, and preferably load-bearing areas too, must have solid inserts. Sandwich construction is notoriously unreliable, especially under conditions of vibration. The core should be solid wood for structural strength and thickening rather than the conventional light non-structural core, and should extend over the full width. Transoms are often wide for planing or to carry multiple motors, and these need to be very strong. The thrust needs to be transferred to the hull by knees or thickened transom angles. A moulded keelson with large knees up the transom is better. The naturally strong shape of the hull/deck join, chines, spray rails, etc., can be emphasised by thickening. Curvature will strengthen a transom simply and economically.

Transoms should be built to take the largest motor allowable under the B.I.A. formula below. There is then no doubt. With a wide range of standard mountings it is virtually impossible to prevent a larger motor being fitted. Whether people should be restrained forcibly from their own follies is a moot point.

Large outboard motors are generally associated with fast boats and are considered playthings rather than serious working motors. But they are effective at slow speeds too, and for various commercial craft where power is needed at low cost and weight. Such use may not be truly economic, but the saving in installation costs will pay for many years' running as well as allowing the use of a lighter, cheaper or existing boat.

BOAT POWER CAPACITY The B.I.A. recommended maximum power for a boat is obtained from the following formulae and reference to Table 18.1.

Overall length (in feet) × stern width (in feet) = Factor K

or

Overall length (in metres) × stern width (in metres) = Factor M

Round off Factor K to the nearest whole number or Factor M to the nearest tenth. Over K = 57, or M = 5·3, h.p. may be raised to the nearest 5 h.p. or equivalent. Reduce power by 50 per cent for flat-bottomed, hard-chine boats. Overall length need not include outboard brackets, covers and similar appendages. Stern width is the widest part of the transom excluding fins and sheer, but may include spray rails if they act as chines or part of the planing surface.

"While the majority of boats can be adequately and safely powered using this

Table 18.1

Factor K		under 35	36–39	40–42	43–45	46–49	50–53	54–57
Factor M		under 3·3	3·4–3·6	3·7–3·9	4·0–4·2	4·3–4·6	4·7–4·9	5·0–5·3
Boat capacity	h.p.	3	5	7·5	10	15	20	25
	kW.	2·2	3·7	5·6	7·5	11·2	14·8	18·6

Factor K Factor M		over 57 over 5·3	Remote steering and 20 in. (500 mm.) ,transom height or equivalent	No remote steering or transom less than 20 in. (500 mm.) or equivalent
Boat capacity	h.p. h.p.		2 K – 90 21·5 M – 90	0·75 K – 20 8 M – 20
	kW.		16 M – 67	6 M – 15

method . . . minor changes in hull form may result in the ability of the boat to carry more or less power. Before finalising recommended power capacities boat manufacturers should confirm the boat's ability to handle the recommended power by running the appropriate test courses." These test courses are of cocked hat shape and vary according to speed. Space does not allow their description here but up-to-date details may be obtained from the B.I.A.

A more powerful motor will make a planing boat go faster but can make it uncontrollable and dangerous. It is also very dangerous on a small non-planing boat such as a dinghy. Every displacement boat, i.e. one not designed to plane, has a natural top speed which is a function of hull form and the load it is carrying, not engine power. It is sheer waste to exceed this, as a small increase in speed will require a massive increase in power. There will be more spray, noise and fuss, which will give an impression of speed, but the boat can actually go slower. A planing hull too overloaded or dirty to get up and plane will behave in the same way.

PROTECTING THE BOAT Some large outboard motors have "teeth" on the outboard side of the mounting bracket. These are intended to give a better grip on a wooden transom, although at the expense of the paintwork. A moulded hull will be crushed and damaged by such teeth and therefore any boat designed to carry a large outboard motor needs a permanent protective pad on the outside of the hull. This can be of wood, but there are also some neat metal or PVC pads.

The clamping screws, too, should not be in direct contact with the moulding because the intense localised compression, aggravated by vibration, will also crush the surface of the moulding. Wood, metal or PVC pads are needed to spread this clamping force.

The thickness of any outer or inner protective pads must be considered when deciding on the transom thickness; otherwise the eventual total thickness will be too great for the motor and the protection may have to be abandoned.

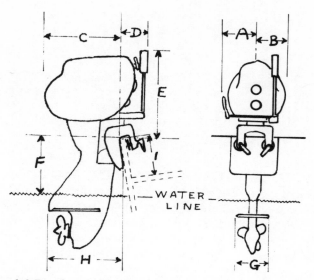

18.7: *B.I.A. Recommended Practice. Outboard motor dimensions for Sailing Boats, Single Motor, Non-tilting, Non-turning.*

"*. . . These dimensions provide the minimum space including clearance required for installation in inboard wells where the engine neither turns nor tilts, and where steering is provided by the boat's rudder. The transom or mounting bracket should comply with the Motor Mounting Area Recommendation (18.4).*

"*Inboard wells of these dimensions should be self-bailing and only be installed where the outboard motor is protected from striking underwater objects by the keel or other boat structure. Dimension F minimum values represent the maximum water level for standard long-shaft motor operation. Ventilation should be adequate to dissipate exhaust gases which may rise in the well.*"

Motor	h.p. kW	Under $5\frac{1}{2}$ Under 4·1	$5\frac{1}{2}$–12 4·1–9·0
A	in.	8	10
	mm	203	254
B	in.	7	8
	mm	177	202
C	in.	14	17
	mm	355	431
D	in.	9	9
	mm	228	228
E	in.	19	19
	mm	482	482
F	in.	15–$18\frac{1}{2}$	15–$18\frac{1}{2}$
	mm	381–469	381–469
G	in.	8	9
	mm	203	228
H	in.	15	15
	mm	381	381
I	in.	6	6
	mm	152	152

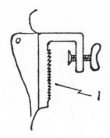

18.8: *Powerful outboard motors often have "teeth", 1, on the face of the bracket to give a good grip into wood. These will crush a moulded transom unless it is protected.*

PRECAUTIONS TO AVOID LOSING THE MOTOR If a big outboard motor works loose it can get quite lively. Having to paddle home adds insult to the injury of losing an expensive motor. There are some neat metal and plastic clamping plates which have a lip to prevent the motor jumping overboard if it does work a bit loose. To get past the lip the screws have to be purposely slackened off a considerable amount.

It is well worth having a good eyebolt in the transom or a stern cleat so that the motor can be tied on with a safety lanyard or chain in case it does drop overboard—but secure the lanyard before lifting the motor into position. It may be too late afterwards, because the greatest danger of dropping it is when fitting or taking off the motor.

Thieves now appreciate the value of an outboard motor and many have been stolen (at considerably less risk to the thief than stealing cars or housebreaking). A chain and padlock is an alternative to a lanyard. On some motors the clamping screws can be padlocked together to prevent anyone undoing them but do not leave the key at home because a motor can work loose without the clamps being moved. Clamping screws need to be checked regularly. Unfortunately many outboard powered boats are left in places which are deserted for long periods, such as a mooring, club park or beach, and a determined thief will have plenty of time to force a lock undisturbed. Probably the best that can be hoped for is to encourage the thief to steal an easier one nearby which is not locked on. "Locks only deter honest people."

SELF-DRAINING WELL A low transom will take the cheaper short shaft motors but is too low for proper seaworthiness. A well allows a high false transom inboard to maintain freeboard. The well must drain outboard and not allow water to slop or drain inboard. Openings for controls should be sealed or be above the transom level.

Clearance must be allowed for likely obstructions. In particular, where the rear seat is near the well there is danger of an arm being trapped when the motor tilts violently on hitting an obstruction. Allow 3 in. (75 mm.) extra clearance for this.

A sailing cruiser's inboard well should extend to deck or self-draining cockpit level, and never be open to the inside of the boat. There will be surge as the boat pitches or heels and it would fill through the well if swamped.

STEERING GEAR Boats designed to take motors of 30 h.p. (22·5 kW.) and over should have provision for remote steering. Where steering is not factory installed the builder should provide mountings for pulleys, fairleads and end fittings, allowing for both pulley and mechanical steering.

Steering gear must be well secured. Steering will be light under normal conditions but it uses considerable leverage. If anything jams, e.g. if the motor is stuck in mud, there

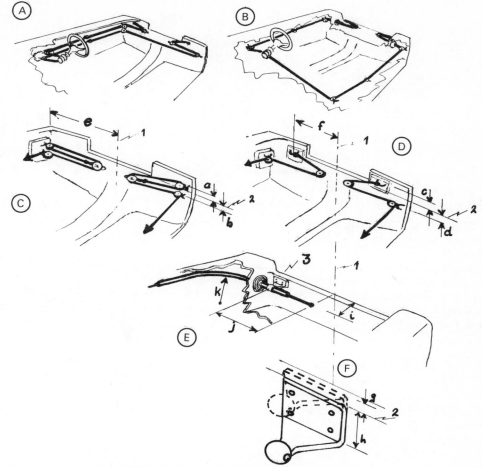

18.9: *B.I.A. Recommended Practice. Steering installation.*

1, *Centreline of motor or motors;* 2, *top of transom;* 3, *steerer cable attachment bracket.*
A. *Pulley and cable steering, single side.*
B. *Pulley and cable steering, both sides.*
C. *Three-part becket giving 45 in. (1,140 mm) cable travel for motors over 50 h.p. (37 kW), combined or single.*
D. *Two-part tackle giving 30 in. (760 mm) cable travel for motors under 50 h.p. (38 kW) combined or single.*
E. *Mechanical steering. Nominal cable travel length 8½ in. (216 mm).*
F. *Alternative standard positions for steerer cable attachment bracket.*

a. *1 in. (25 mm) Maximum.*   b. *1 in. (25 mm) Maximum.*
c. *1½ in. (38 mm) Maximum.*   d. *1½ in. (38 mm) Maximum.*
e. *24 in. (610 mm) Minimum.*   f. *22 in. (559 mm) Minimum.*
g. *½ in. (13 mm).*   h. *2¾ in. (70 mm).*
i. *6⅜ in. (162 mm).*   j. *17¼ in. (438 mm).*
k. *8 in. (203 mm) Minimum radius.*

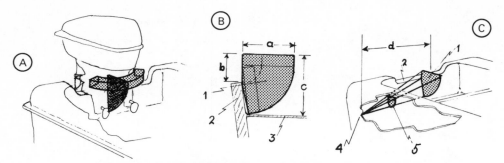

18.10: B.I.A. *Recommended Practice. Steering cable clearance.*

a. $9\frac{1}{2}$ *in.* (241 *mm*).   b. $5\frac{1}{2}$ *in.* (140 *mm*).
c. 11 *in.* (279 *mm*).   d. 16 *in.* (406 *mm*) *Minimum.*

A. *Shaded area shows the locus of movement of the steering attachment as the motor turns and tilts.*
B. *Dimensions of "target", 1, and relation to transom, 2, and bottom of motor well, 3, at closest permissible distance.*
C. *Showing the use of the "target" to determine the size of opening, 5, necessary in the side of the motor well or other obstruction which the steering cable passes through.*
    "*The space requirement is generated by a line out of the pulley or cable anchor point, 4, which passes around the 'target' located at the centreline of the motor transom bracket. The total volume thus generated should be kept clear for steering rigging.*"

will be a strain on the steering gear. Also it must withstand the shock loads caused by the motor striking an obstruction. The B.I.A. require pulleys, cables and attachments to withstand a pull of 750 lb. (340 kg.). This requires strong mountings and good load spreading. Through-fastening will entail external screw heads. They can often be hidden behind a rubbing band, flash or crest, but if well plated they need not look unattractive even if not hidden. The alternative is to fasten into embedded wood blocks or metal anchorages. These must be arranged so that the load is in shear, or be embedded widely enough to withstand the substantial delaminating pull. Attachment to stringers or frames is preferable. Similarly wood screws should not be used unless in shear. Bolt through the block before embedding. Pulley sheaves should have a minimum score diameter of 2 in. (50 mm.) to reduce wear, and should not have a swivel attachment at the motor if the cable angle is more than 135°.

    Pulley and cable steering should be arranged as in Fig. 18.9 with a three-part becket allowing 45 in. (1,140 mm.) cable travel for over 50 h.p. (38 kW.) combined motor capacity and a two-part tackle allowing 30 in. (760 mm.) travel under 50 h.p. These apply to single or multiple motors. Pulley and cable ends should be as far outboard as possible and located within the dimensions shown, to prevent undue tension as the motor turns and tilts.

    Cables must not bear against bulkheads, seats, well side or any obstruction under any conditions of turn or tilt. This would strain the wires and can also saw through the GRP and cause the steering to jam. Fig. 18.10 shows the locus of movement of the motor attachment. This "target" gives the clearance at any intermediate point. Cable clips, joints, turnbuckles, etc., should not pass through openings.

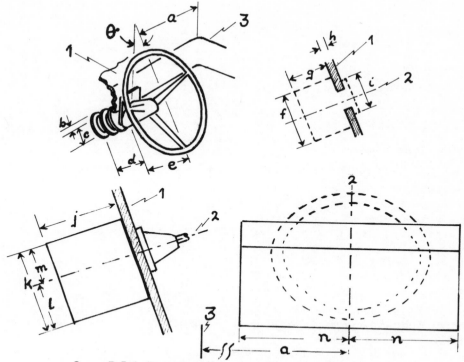

18.11: *B.I.A. Recommended Practice. Steering wheel installation.*

1. Front of dashboard   2. Centreline of wheel   3. Cockpit coaming

Steering wheel :

a. *Distance to cockpit coaming (pulley steering)*   17 in. (430 mm) Minimum.
b. *Distance to cockpit coaming (mechanical steering)*   22 in. (558 mm).
c. *Wheel to dash distance along axis.* $7\frac{1}{2}$ in. (190 mm).
θ. *Mounting angle,*   parallel to dash or inclined 20°.

Pulley size limits :

b. $\frac{5}{8}$ *in. (16 mm) Minimum.*   d. *7 in. (177 mm) Maximum.*
c. $2\frac{1}{2}$ *in. (63·5 mm) Maximum to* $3\frac{3}{4}$ *in. (95·3 mm) Maximum.*

Space envelope for cable and pulley steering :

f. *8 in. (203 mm).*   g. *7 in. (177 mm).*
h. *1 in. (25 mm) Maximum.*   i. *5 in. (127 mm).*

Space envelope for mechanical steering :

j. *8 in. (203 mm).*   k. $8\frac{3}{4}$ *in. (222 mm).*
l. *5 in. (127 mm).*   m. $3\frac{3}{4}$ *in. (95 mm).*
n. *11 in. (280 mm).*

"*Mounting brackets should position the steering wheel face parallel to the dash or inclined at 20° to it, and* $7\frac{1}{2}$ *in. (190 mm) from the dash measured along the axis of the column.*

"*Steering cable drums as shown will establish possible steering ratios of* $5\frac{3}{4}$ *turns maximum of the wheel to move the motor 45° one side of centre to 45° on the other side. This steering ratio is achieved when the motor's remote steering radius and cable installation are in accordance with the Recommended Practice* **18.1** *and* **18.2**.

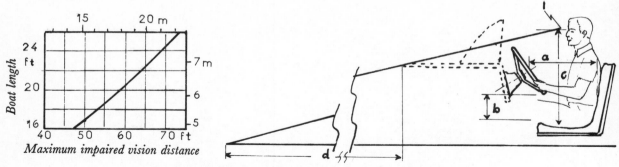

18.12: *B.I.A. Recommended Practice. Seat and wheel relation.*

a. Centre of wheel-rim to seat back:
    23 in. (584 mm) Minimum to 25 in. (635 mm) Maximum.
b. Bottom of wheel-rim to top of seat cushions:
    7 in. (177 mm) Minimum to 11 in. (280 mm) Maximum.
N.B. *These dimensions are to uncompressed seating.*
c. Average adult eye-level, 1, above the compressed seat:
    30 in. (762 mm) Minimum to 34 in. (863 mm) Maximum.
d. Maximum allowable impaired vision obtained from the graph.

   "On boats on which steering wheels are not factory installed equipment, seats and dash panels should be so located by the builder that a steering wheel (as in **18.11**) *may be fitted to the dash in order to provide a comfortable craft.*

   "The average eye-levels of men and women fall between 30 and 34 in. (760–860 mm) above the compressed seat. Vision should not be obstructed by wheel rim, windshield framing or other structure. Construction should not restrict the driver's vision at minimum eye-level beyond the . . . minimum forward impaired vision distance at all normal running trims."

   A motor always tilts in the fore-and-aft line. If it hits something when on full lock it rises on the line of the keel (parallel to it with multiple motors), *not* in the direction of the screw, as might be supposed.

   Tension springs help to keep wires tight but may cause backlash or shimmy if too light. They should have an extension of 2 in. (50 mm.) and a spring rate of 50 lb./in. (0·9 kg./mm.) to prevent shimmy. Twin motors should be connected by a rigid tie bar.

   Steering wheels are mounted with the drum or mechanism behind the dashboard. Standard mountings are either parallel to or inclined at 20° to the dashboard. Fig. 18.11 shows the space envelopes needed. Pulleys must be positioned to give a lead at right angles to the steering drum, so the two pulleys will not be in line. The space behind must be unobstructed and the cable drums must handle the length of cable required.

   Push-pull mechanical steering mechanisms, e.g. Morse, Teleflex, etc., are popular and simpler to install. It is essential to follow the directions carefully, especially regarding the minimum radius for bends. It should be possible to mount the standard steering cable attachment bracket either way up to give two normal alternative positions. Mounting positions should be marked or templates supplied. The bracket must be to starboard.

OUTBOARD MOTOR CONTROLS
Provision for remote steering must include appropriate remote controls. Small motors are controlled at the motor. Large ones

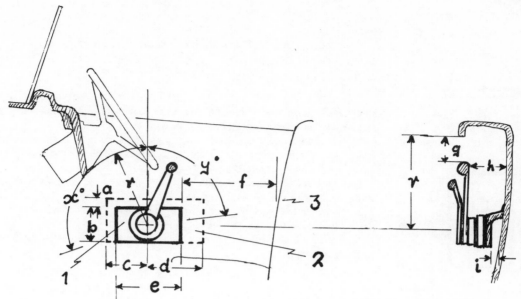

18.13: *B.I.A. Recommended Practice. Remote-control mounting.*

a. $1\frac{7}{8}$ *in.* (48 mm).   b. *6 in.* (152 mm).
c. $6\frac{1}{8}$ *in.* (155 mm).   d. *8 in.* (203 mm).
e. *10 in.* (254 mm).
f. *16 in.* (406 mm) desirable to seat back, 3.
g. $2\frac{1}{2}$ *in.* (64 mm) Minimum.   h. $2\frac{1}{2}$ *in.* (64 mm) Minimum.
i. *1 in.* (26 mm) clearance.
r. $14\frac{1}{2}$ *in.* (368 mm) radius minimum clearance.
x° 110°   y 85°

"All boats fitted for the installation of remote-control steering and motors with remote controls shall be fitted with a remote-control mounting pad.

"The mounting pad, 1, should be 6 in. × 10 in. (152 × 254 mm) in size and should be mounted so that the pad face is substantially vertical and parallel to the keel centreline. The clearance specified guarantees minimum knuckle clearance of 2½ in. (64 mm) under any overhanging structure using standard control levers. Similar clearance is required around and behind the levers. The pad location should permit full range of control without interference with dash or coaming structure and without arm or elbow interference with seats or other structure.

"The location of the remote-control pad mounting should be such that the control leads therefrom have unobstructed access to the motor."

are intended for remote control which commonly includes starting, instrumentation and electrical services. For special applications or in an emergency they can usually be manipulated at the motor also.

The B.I.A. standard dimensions (Fig. 18.13) allow for clearance: at least $2\frac{1}{2}$ in. (64 mm.) knuckle clearance is needed above and behind the levers. Not every control unit will use the full arc, but the combined single-lever control does have a wide arc.

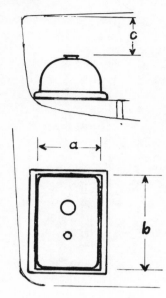

18.14: *B.I.A. Recommended Practice. Portable fuel tank.*

a. $12\frac{3}{4}$ in. (324 mm). b. $19\frac{1}{2}$ in. (495 mm).
c. $11\frac{1}{2}$ in. (292 mm).

The dimensions show the minimum clear area required for stowing a single tank. The tank should be prevented from moving by cleats, I, preferably combined with lashings or holdfasts.

The minimum vertical clearance above the tank bottom to any structure above shall be not less than $11\frac{1}{2}$ in. (292 mm) to facilitate removal of the tank from the boat for refilling.

Any tank with a capacity of over 7 U.S. gallons (5·8 Imperial gallons, 26·6 litres) shall not be considered portable.

All portable tanks shall carry a label "Caution. Remove tank from boat when filling to reduce fire hazard".

Tanks should be located on the opposite side from the helmsman's position to balance weight.

LEFT- OR RIGHT-HAND DRIVE

In Britain cars have steering-wheels on the right-hand side and boats have them on the left. In the rest of the world it is the other way round, left-hand drive for cars and right-hand for boats.

The Rule of the Road at Sea states categorically that all vessels must give way to other vessels approaching on their starboard hand. It is obvious therefore that a wheel on the starboard side, or "right-hand drive" is essential to cover this danger sector. The B.I.A., too, are emphatic on this point (and if any country should have a "car complex" it is the U.S.A.).

This left-hand drive complex seems to spring from an obsession with rivers and canals (yet British rivers are mostly too small for navigation and the canals derelict) and ignores the open seas around our island shores; it is a peculiar obsession for a people who pride themselves on being a seafaring race and whose adventurous ancestors were among the first to use the oceans as highways.

Certainly the rule in narrow waters is for traffic to keep to the starboard hand, and so by analogy with driving on the roads the boat is given a left-hand drive; but there is absolutely no comparison between two lines of close-packed cars, hurtling towards each other at high speeds on comparatively narrow roads, and leisurely river traffic passing at little more than walking pace in a channel which, as far as a small boat is concerned, is relatively much wider than any road.

Moreover there are very few rivers which do not have speed limits which are as severe a restriction to a fast boat as a ten-mile holiday traffic jam to a racing car.

Anyone from Britain who has driven on the Continent, or for that matter anyone from a drive-on-the-right country who has visited drive-on-the-left Britain, will know that the only drawback is when trying to overtake. On steep and narrow mountain passes it is a definite advantage to drive on the side nearest the edge, as this gives a very much better idea of how close one can get to the rough rock face or precipitous drop when a large lorry insists that might is right. In Italy, a drive-on-the-right country, heavy lorries all have right-hand drive.

Overtaking on a river is not a problem. Visibility is good and speeds are low. But if the river or canal really is narrow then a good view of the bank and in particular of underwater obstructions is essential. This can only be obtained with a right-hand drive because with left-hand drive both the underwater obstructions and the bank itself will be hidden by the bow for some way ahead. Moreover in the extreme case when caution is the better part of valour it is easier to reach out and hang on to the bank from the side nearest to it or even to abandon ship and jump ashore when disaster seems inevitable.

At sea, on lakes and reservoirs, in most estuaries, sheltered waters and even wide rivers and canals, there is so much space relative to the boat that the Rules for Avoiding Collision at Sea will apply, not river (or road) rules; boats travel freely in all directions, not in the constricted, parallel rat-runs of roads. Such free movement demands right or starboard-hand drive.

I cannot see that it would be prudent or considerate to use the speed of a fast motor boat under any conditions so restricted that they resemble roads, and I do not know of any harbour or river authority which thinks so either. No boat has the precise control of a car: it is too much affected by waves, currents and other factors. A crowd of fast boats in a restricted waterway will kick up dangerously rough conditions. The racing at Paris on the Seine, a broad, placid river wider than a motorway, makes it so rough that serious damage to boats is usual. For the crews it is a tough, dangerous race and casualties are common.

Left-hand drive cannot be justified for a motor boat except by analogy with fast cars on narrow roads. Such an analogy is obviously ridiculous. Our rivers are not yet like our roads—thank God. We would be foolish indeed if we ever made such a mistake again.

FUEL TANKS Small motors usually have the tank on the motor. Larger motors either plug into a proper built-in tank or have a portable tank. The builder must allow space to house a portable tank and also leave enough clearance above and around it so that it can be removed easily for refilling (Fig. 18.14). Replacement when full and heavy will be far more awkward.

Convenience of getting it aboard without damage to the boat should also be considered. A wide gunwale or side-deck, for example, will mean either that it will be an inconvenient lift to get the tank aboard in one movement, or that the tank will be rested momentarily on the side deck with risk of persistent scratching at that point. A moulded gunwale or rail, too, is likely to get accidently knocked and chipped in the process.

A standard large portable tank when full will weigh around 70 lb. (36 kg.). Most men can lift this quite easily if it is a straight lift, or at least like to think they can, but it is quite a different matter to lift this out of a dinghy and lean across, all with one hand of course because the other will be holding on to the boat. A lady or youngster will have real difficulty.

Portable tanks must not rattle around. The minimum requirement is fitting chocks to hold it in position. Even then a tank can jump out in rough going and should have lashings. In contrast with proper tanks, the regulations for which are very strict, spare cans are commonly any old thing, thin, weak, rusty and generally leaky if upset. It is even more important therefore that they are firmly secured in a proper position provided for them. Spare cans are essential equipment. No motor boat should put to sea without one—and it should be full. The lifeboat statistics prove this.

RUNABOUT SEATS Runabout seats must be strong as well as luxurious. The motion will often be violent. Fireside armchairs will show the strain after a guest's children (never one's own, of course) have been jumping on them—yet that is exactly the treatment a runabout seat must put up with in bumpy conditions, except that it is not only children but hefty grown-ups bouncing, or being bounced on them.

Reinforced plastic is the best material for the frame of the seat. The shape is simple, so the pattern is easily made up from wood or plaster, and it is worthwhile even for a one-off job. It will be well upholstered and the standard of finish will not be seen so the mould may be primitive.

It is equally important that the attachments and support are strong, too, and, of course, the boat itself in way of the attachments—a point sometimes overlooked. The seat should be screwed or bolted to stout bearers or brackets moulded to the hull, and the hull should be well thickened in way of the brackets. On a double skin boat, or where the bottom is a double moulding, the seat supports can be formed in the inner moulding. Detachable and fold-flat seats must be fastened just as securely.

Where moulding facilities are not available the seats can be made of plywood. They should be fastened to frames or stringers and not attached directly to the hull skin unless the load can be well spread with a large pad.

WINDSCREENS A fast boat like a runabout or speedboat needs a windscreen. The windscreen is to keep off spray rather than wind, because the speeds are not really high, compared with those of a car or motor-cycle, little more than a downhill run on a push-bike, but there is nothing like a foaming bow-wave to give a wonderful impression of speed.

A light breeze on the beam can blow a continuous fine but damping spray from the bow-wave back into the cockpit even on a fine day; and on a roughish day only a really hardened old salt will appreciate the solid green water constantly flung into his face.

A "wrap-around" windscreen gives better protection than a straight one. A lot of spray is windblown and does not come straight over the bow.

Few windscreens are adequately supported; a windscreen must expect, and be able to withstand, localised knocks and bumps from hard objects as well as a cushioned wallop of water. Many are of light gauge Perspex or acrylic sheet which is easily cracked by a careless kick when going forward to moor or disembark, or when handling the boat ashore —$\frac{1}{4}$ in. thickness should be the minimum. Perspex can be self-supporting or be fitted in a frame, and it is easily formed into a curve. Obviously the frame is stronger but also more expensive. A glass screen should always have a frame and be made of safety glass.

Many people have used standard car windscreens. This is a good and cheap way to get a curved screen. The standard frame, however, is unlikely to stand up to marine conditions and it is probably advisable to have this specially plated or else make one of non-corroding material. It could easily be moulded. The screen should be settled at the design stage, so that the deck can be designed to fit the screen. A popular model of car should be chosen to ensure that it can be replaced.

A stout frame can be used as a handgrip in rough conditions, or as a support for a

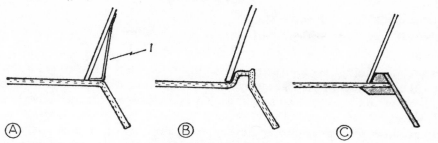

18.15: Windscreen mounting.

A. *Not recommended. Supported by brackets, 1, but windscreen must be well sealed at the bottom to prevent water trickling through.*
B. *Mount windscreen in front of a moulded breakwater or coaming. This provides good anchorage and probably does away with a bracket, if it is well curved. Moulded breakwater can also form a handy shelf.*
C. *"Dry" construction; windscreen mounted against a wooden coaming.*

hard-top or cover. It is often an advantage to stand up to steer or con, as this gives a better view when negotiating narrow channels and obstacles, particularly submerged ones, or with the sun shining on the water. The B.I.A. specify the acceptable limits within which visibility ahead may be impaired by the foredeck, etc., for a driver at minimum average eye level. In the past "aircraft carrier bows" and other whims of fashion, and also bad planing attitudes, have obscured the view dangerously far ahead.

The windscreen should be well sealed at the lower edge, otherwise water will seep or flood under it to the discomfort of the crew. Better still is to mount it in front of a moulded coaming so that seepage is impossible. A good breakwater or coaming will also serve as a firm mounting point. No further support may be needed if the screen is curved, but it is better to have two or three brackets for emergencies (Fig. 18.15).

A wide moulded coaming can often be designed also as a useful shelf for odds and ends. All that is needed is a simple flange, but it should not form a water trap, and should drain outboard, not on to the crew's lap.

Frameless Perspex screens are best secured with soft washers, not bolted down hard. Otherwise a knock or shock, even thermal expansion, may crack the Perspex. If a crack does develop, drill a small hole at the end of it. This will prevent the crack from spreading further. This was standard practice in the old wartime days of subsonic aircraft.

OTHER FITTINGS Other fittings particulary applicable to runabouts are described in Chapters Sixteen and Twenty. These cover such items as lockers, hand grips and lifting handles, towing and lashing eyes, floorboards, gunwales, etc.

FIRE EXTINGUISHERS One cannot send for the fire brigade at sea. Fires must be put out by the crew and put out quickly. Help even if available is unlikely to arrive in time or be any better equipped. Fire is the greatest hazard of all, worse than storm or shipwreck.

Every boat with an engine, especially a petrol engine, should carry fire extinguishers of appropriate size and suitable for Class B (fuel) fires. Small open boats may carry one, craft over 16 ft. (5 m.) and all cabin boats should carry two, and over 26 ft. (8 m.) three or more. Fire extinguishers approved for boats are:

Carbon dioxide	4 lb. (2 kg.)
Dry powder	2 lb. (1 kg.)
Foam	1 gal. Imp. (4·2 l., 1¼ U.S. gal.)

Toxic vapourising liquid extinguishers are not permitted, e.g. CBM or chlorobromethane, CTC or carbon tetrachloride. These are now considered dangerous. But BCF, bromochlorodifluoromethane, is non-toxic and is commonly used in Europe. The approved size is 3 lb. (1·5 kg.).

Extinguishers should be checked every year. Pressurised ones should have pressure indicators. Check the mechanism as well as the contents. When needed they will be needed in a hurry and must work.

A small repetitive-use extinguisher is handy for small fires such as minor galley incidents. This saves the main—and expensive—extinguishers for more serious situations. Many bigger extinguishers cannot be turned off, and anyway must always be kept full. After the fire is extinguished—very quickly for a small fire—they will continue to spray vigorously until thrown overboard in desperation. The mess can be appalling. While this is not important in a serious and damaging fire it is great nuisance just for a galley flare-up, whereas a short burst from a small extinguisher may not even spoil the dinner.

Fire extinguishers should be distributed in various positions and handy to, but outside, the danger areas (e.g. engine and galley). One should always be in the cockpit. Automatic extinguishers should not be installed where the crew may be trapped. A hand extinguisher is needed as well.

The best, and cheapest, extinguisher on a boat is a bucket on rope. Water can even put out a small petrol fire, but chiefly it can prevent the boat itself catching alight until the petrol burns out. Disaster will come from the boat itself burning, not the petrol inside it. Boat materials are Class A fires and are put out with water. Water is plentiful, very near, inexhaustible and cheap. It is clean and comparatively easy to clean up afterwards. Valuable though they are, extinguishers tend to be overrated. Because of neglect—inexcusable, but such things happen—they may not work in an emergency, and what happens when the last one has been used? Others may disagree with this paragraph.

These requirements apply to all boats regardless of construction. GRP is no more hazardous than wood, and with self-extinguishing resins and fireproof coatings can be much safer (page 238).

Early horror stories told of boats being dissolved by extinguisher fluids. "Burn or sink" it was said. This is nonsense. No approved extinguisher will harm GRP even in large quantities, and not even the unapproved ones—unapproved, note, for boats of *any* kind—will do more than soften the surface fairly slowly. The *only* fluid which will harm GRP appreciably is CBM, chlorobromethane, if it lingers in a puddle. Even then it will be absorbed by the GRP or evaporate before it has softened more than about $\frac{1}{16}$ in. (2 mm.) of a sound moulding. This should not prevent a boat reaching port.

The danger, again mainly with the unapproved fluids, lies with bad, porous moulding which allows the fluid to penetrate and attack from within, where also evaporation will be inhibited. The fault lies not with the fluid but with bad moulding—the usual source of troubles—and this, improved by a good spell at the club bar, probably provided the very few instances which started the horror stories.

CHAPTER NINETEEN

Spars

This chapter is based on an article which I wrote for *Yachting Monthly*, January 1969, and is reproduced by kind permission of the editor.

MOULDING spars in GRP is not easy. It requires different techniques from sloshing out a dinghy, and some of these can get to the level of computer sophistication. But with the right approach an amateur can produce a workable spar that will be strong, light, and have any shape, taper, graded thickness or bendability that he may like, although a lot of trial and error, especially error, is likely before the more scientific features have been perfected.

The ideas suggested are not exhaustive by any means. They have been culled from many sources over many years, and I have now forgotten where most of them came from, including my own. A lot have never been tried out and are only ideas, crazy or brilliant to the point of genius as you like. Some have been tried and did not work, but might be made to with greater ingenuity, skill, persistence, cash and the later and better materials.

The problems of making a spar increase dramatically with size. A mast is far more difficult than a boom, which is a lot harder than a boathook, while little is lost if a swizzle stick does not work out as it should. It will be clear which ideas are more suitable for masts and which for boathooks in your particular circumstances, with your circumstances being the over-riding factor. Start with something easy, small and cheap; a boom for the boat in your bath, not a big, difficult mast for an expensive yacht where performance is critical.

MATERIALS The simplest way (cheating almost) is to buy a standard tube. This means finding one of the right size, thickness and cost, and the odds are against this. For small spars stout fishing rod blanks or radio aerial rods could be used. Hollow ones can be obtained. (Ogdens, Smiths & Hussey, a subsidiary of Fothergil & Harvey Ltd.)

The materials used for moulding a spar are very important. Boats are generally made of glass mat but this is not strong enough for a spar and comes to pieces too readily. Something that can be pulled tight is needed, and this means a woven material such as cloth or woven rovings. For really critical applications and highest strength use epoxy resins, not polyester.

The main loads on a spar are usually up and down its axis, certainly for a mast. Unidirectional cloth (a cloth with more strength in the warp than the weft, or vice versa) is often used to give strength in the plane of the spar without wasting weight or material in providing unnecessary hoop strength. It may be ruled out by the practical difficulty of obtaining anything suitable in a small quantity. Note that unidirectional fabric (sometimes called directional fabric) is only stronger if laid with the fibres running more or less straight up and down the spar. If the fabric is laid as a spiral, which is often essential to handle it, the advantages decrease and an ordinary square weave becomes as strong.

Great strides have been made with filament winding, i.e. a single strand wound on, something like a whipping on a rope's end. Very complicated winding patterns have been worked out on computers to give the right winding pattern for optimum strength or flexibility where needed. For those traditionalists whose fingers are their computers the winding should be in a very fast, open spiral, not like the side by side turns of a whipping, so that the strands lie predominantly in the line of the spar, an angle of perhaps 10–20°. One layer or so should be a tight whipping to hold it all together and provide hoop strength, but it will generally be easier to combine it with cloth for this. Single rovings laid along the spar will give better unidirectional properties when using ordinary cloth.

Cloth can be laid on as convenient. Sometimes it is rolled on in long lengths along the spar, like rolling a cigarette, sometimes wound spirally. Easiest moulding is best moulding.

USING A CORE

As with all GRP, a mould or former of some kind is essential. The two main methods are to form it over a core or to mould it in sections and join them together. It is obviously impossible to hand-mould it in one piece in a female mould on the lines of boat moulding.

The core can either stay inside forever or it can be extractable. The core left inside is by far the simplest, but as it is expendable it must be light and cheap. Yet it must be sufficiently rigid to maintain its shape until the resin has set, although outside support will almost certainly be needed also.

Suitable core materials are polyurethane or PVC foam, which are very light but not strong. Balsa wood is stronger but heavier, and cork has large holes which swallow resin like a chief stoker knocking back beer. Polystyrene foam must be well sealed as polyester resin dissolves it quickly. It is safer with epoxy. Wrap it in polythene or seal it with epoxy, paint or bitumen. Test it first by actual trial.

The lightest core is air. A thin tube of paper or cardboard does well, and short lengths can be joined together. Do not use Polycell to form rolled newspaper tubes as polyester resin attacks it. Gummed paper forms a fair tube and there is a good choice of plastic tubes or hose which are generally light although not rigid. Garden hose and yacht plumbing can be used for small spars or boathooks. Drain pipes, sewer pipes and land drains are suitable mast sizes. Simple composite spars have been made by moulding over bamboo.

Ideally the core would be removed afterwards, but the moulding contracts on curing, thereby gripping the core. Pulling out a core with the whole length gripped in a bear hug is quite a different release problem from lifting a boat out of the easy clutches of a female mould. (Seems some moral there. It is generally hardest to escape from female clutches.) Collapsible mandrels are elaborate and expensive—especially if something goes wrong. At amateur level cores which can be deflated or emptied of water or sand are more practicable. Inflated "lay-flat" polythene or rubber tube should be easy to get out and little is lost in materials or weight if it has to stay in. Even low pressure makes quite a firm tube as is shown by the inflatable dinghy. A high pressure reinforced tube would be even stiffer. An inflated tube is light and easily supported. Filling the tube with water or sand, both easily got out, would make it stiffer but harder to handle.

Cores which can be melted or dissolved out are used in engineering. The low heat

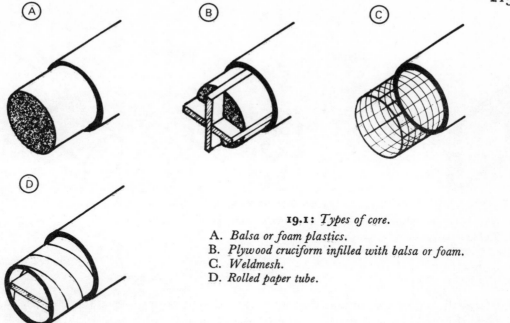

19.1: *Types of core.*
A. *Balsa or foam plastics.*
B. *Plywood cruciform infilled with balsa or foam.*
C. *Weldmesh.*
D. *Rolled paper tube.*

resistance of the resin rules out most meltable substances; even boiling water is above the threshold of damage for most resins. Wax could be used but is expensive for a whole core. Thin sheet wax over a solid core could be melted out without having to apply enough heat to cause serious damage to the GRP, leaving the core loose enough for easy withdrawal. PTFE or even polythene might provide a sufficiently low-friction coating for a mandrel to be withdrawn bodily, but this is likely to need considerable force and some means of gripping the mast firmly enough to counter that force, without damage to the mast. This seems beyond normal amateur scope and is better in theory than practice. Failure will be expensive.

Polystyrene foam can be dissolved out by solvents, but the GRP will be attacked by most suitable solvents except petroleum compounds, which would be rather slow. Polystyrene and some other foams shrivel up very quickly when heated. It is possible that this could be done before the GRP had time to be harmed. All foams are soft enough to be hacked out. In general, however, foams are so light and harmless that it is better to leave them in than resort to elaborate methods to get them out.

In theory paper can be dissolved out, but in practice it has to be scraped away. Something like soap is needed. Mud might be tried in some places. There is much scope for ingenuity, local knowledge and scrounging.

Composite cores give better rigidity and strength for handling, e.g. a thin plywood stiffener of cruciform section padded out with plastics foam to form the shape, or supporting a shell such as gummed paper loosely wound over it. The foam can be easily worked, rigid foam, or the more easily formed and obtainable flexible foam rigidised with resin. Expanded metal and Weldmesh form stiff light cores but would be difficult to extract. Weldmesh in particular is very stiff for its weight (as the name implies all crossing wires

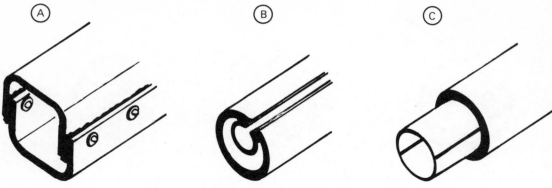

19.2: *Spar made up from sections.*

A. *Two-channel sections can be bonded or riveted to form a hollow box section.*
B. *The sections need not be identical. Here a big one forms the main part of the spar and a little one the track. Both can be moulded on flexible or split moulds, male or female.*
C. *Joins are a source of weakness and difficulty. Here the two sections are moulded as light as practicable, put together and moulded over for the main strength. This main moulding is jointless.*

are welded) and can be obtained in light grades. It is rather intractable stuff to handle, but once formed to shape and the seams welded, bolted or stitched it would be largely self-supporting. Wire netting is more suitable for infilling.

SECTIONAL MOULDING The simplest method of moulding might seem to be to mould the spar in two or more longitudinal sections and join them together. In some ways it is simple, but the method of joining must be worked out carefully. One way is a long overlap glued or riveted (e.g. with pop rivets), preferably both. Bonding along a butt joint is unreliable owing to the small area of contact and the difficulty of getting a proper mating fit. It is better to form an outward flange, which can be moulded to an accurate line, and either cut this back or use it as a feature to add strength in one direction or to form a sail track.

A simple and strong way is to make the two moulded parts form the core, stick them together lightly, and mould over both parts with cloth or rovings, binding it all together. The moulded core should be lightly moulded, the bare minimum for rigidity. This method can also be used with a core built up of other materials such as light plywood, hardboard or paper. Joints can be taped. I have seen a method where two halves of the mould were hinged. The spar was laid up with them open and while still "wet" the mould was closed. Loss of resin, and therefore weakness, seems inevitable along the line of the hinge, and the sharp movement must disturb the "wet" glass. A better way is to lay-up on a flexible metal or plastics sheet which is then bent, moulding and all, into a round or oval shape. When set the plate is removed and the two edges of the moulding bonded or riveted together. This gives a smooth outside finish, too.

ROLLED SPARS Spars can be rolled like a Swiss roll. The lay-up is done on flat sheets of metal or glass and the "wet" cloth simply rolled up. It is rather messy, and dimensional control is difficult unless done on a former. The cloth needs to be kept as tight as

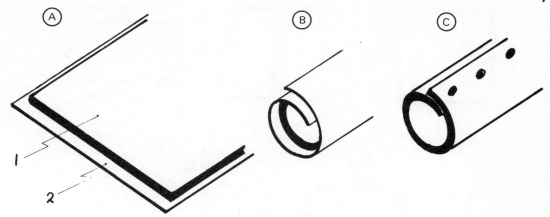

19.3: Rolled mast.
A. *The spar is laid up flat, 1, on a flexible sheet of metal or plastic, 2.*
B. *While still wet the sheet is rolled approximately to shape and allowed to set.*
C. *When set, but still "green" and flexible, the sheet is extracted and the edges riveted or bonded together.*

possible during rolling. The idea is not new. Early hollow wooden spars were similar and were highly regarded.

It would be less messy using the modern Pre-pregs or pre-impregnated glass, but they need heat to cure them properly. Using hardener between the layers like jam in a Swiss roll might work with some glues but I do not yet know of a resin/hardener combination that would be satisfactory, although it is claimed to be possible with a catalysed resin and separate accelerator.

Enquiry to the catalyst manufacturers can unearth interesting and little-known catalysts which set in the usual way to a rubbery state but remain rubbery for an extended period until cured by the application of heat, ultraviolet light, sunlight or age. This allows a real sandwich roll. Spars can be rolled up while rubbery and easily handled, and hardened by external means or allowed to age afterwards. The lengthy time involved may be a disadvantage and it is important to make sure the spar really has hardened properly before being used. Note that the rubbery state of an ordinary catalyst/resin combination does not allow enough time, and the spar will harden while being rolled, with disastrous results. (Fig. 19.3)

Spars can also be made as sandwiches. Thin PVC foam, notably "Airex," is just flexible enough to be rolled and may be made more flexible by heating. GRP is laid up on the foam and while still wet it is rolled to shape, foam and all. More GRP is added outside to complete the sandwich.

DEVELOPED SECTIONS Spars can be built up like conventional box-section hollow wooden spars from flat sections cut from sheet or purposely moulded. But a lot more ingenious ideas are possible where the imagination is not tied to conventional flat sections. The spar can be built up from curved pieces or even quite elaborate mouldings. Mast tracks can be worked in this way. (Fig. 19.4)

While the moulding is "green" and still fairly flexible, which it is for a few hours after

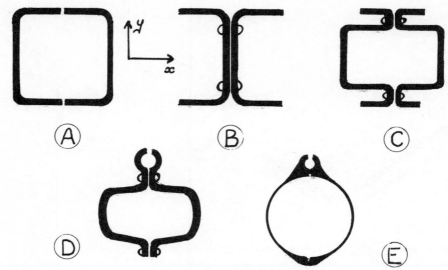

19.4: *Development of a simple box section.*

A. *Two half channels form a box but are difficult to bond or fasten together. However it is strong in both.* x *and* y *directions.*

B. *The same sections are easily joined back to back. This is just as strong on* y *axis but weak on* x *axis. In some cases, e.g. a boom, this is no disadvantage.*

C. *Pulling out the centre and reducing the flanges a little restores the strength in all directions although somewhat less than A.*

D. *One flange must obviously grow into a sail track, the awkward "wineglass" shape of the other withers away. Now it lacks strength on the* x *axis.*

E. *Reduce thickness where it is not wanted, saving weight and cost, and add thickness where it does most work. This gives a spar strong on the* y *axis and adequate on the* x, *so the simple box acquires the sophistication and complexity beloved in this age. Note how the joins are now made with butt straps, not fastenings. Of course this could have been done in the first place.*

setting, it can be bent quite considerably and if held will harden permanently into the bent shape. This can be enough to form a shape which by rights should be considered un-mouldable, or to release from a theoretical undercut. Within limits this does not strain the moulding: it would be strained if forced back into its original shape later.

The conventional shape for a spar is a hollow tube, but the hardest shape to mould is a hollow section. All our moulding techniques and ideas have been built on the simpler case of the open box, typically the boat hull. But a spar need not be hollow. It is, admittedly, a strong shape in all directions, and by judicious distortion of a circular section into an oval or pear shape it can be made even stronger in certain planes. But there are plenty of other sections used in engineering: the simple RSJ or I beam, for instance. This is more suitable where the load is in one direction, but this is often the case in a boat, e.g. a boom or oar. Two channel sections can equally well form a box or an I beam, and the I beam is a lot simpler to join together. The flanges too can be built up to any width or thickness to give the strength that calculation, instinct or trial and error suggest. So can the shape, and unlike buying an RSJ of constant section, the depth of the flange can be tapered very easily according to requirements. Fig. 19.4 shows how this simple idea can be developed until it quickly acquires that degree of complication that seems inseparable from this day and age.

RIGGING AND ATTACHMENTS On all hollow spars, concentrated loads from fittings must not come where they are hollow and thin. Put in solid inserts to take the strain, easily done with a permanent core, or thicken the mouldings. By rabbetting a solid core the extra thickness can be built up without increasing the external dimensions. Both these must be planned in advance. A useful feature is the way the spar can be strengthened externally if more convenient or if the fittings are afterthoughts, as is so often the case with an amateur's experiments. It can be thickened up as much as and wherever needed by moulding more outside. Rigging attachments must be through-fastened, with a compression tube if necessary. Through-fastenings and tubes must be well sealed to prevent leaks into the mast. GRP tubes will bond and stay bonded better than metal. Tracks can be pop-riveted, but a pop-rivet is inclined to pull through or crush GRP, especially if light, unless backed by a wide washer. Obviously this is impracticable: a light metal strip should be embedded within the mast to take the inside face of the pop-rivet. More sophisticated (and more difficult to locate) would be a tapped strip or embedded nuts.

SUPPORT DURING MOULDING Spars are extremely susceptible to distortion during moulding, because they have to be supported while still flexible and "wet." Conventional spar makers start with long lengths of comparatively rigid wood, not something as formless as a wet blanket. Any slight kink will become permanent. The sheer weight of the spar lying on a bench, light as it is, can distort it and cause dents or bulges or lopsided taper. This is less likely if the spar can be hung vertically to set and cure rather than supported horizontally. In the average workshop 10 to 12 ft. (say 3–4 m.) is the best that can be expected. It will probably have to be hung outside to get height, e.g. from a tree or tall building (but even a dinghy mast may look down on an average chimney pot). Yet reasonable temperature control is essential. One way would be to put it in a loose polythene tube and leave an electric fire at the bottom (good entertainment at firework time if it catches fire!). Sensible choice of weather and season is most essential. Working vertically poses problems of access. One method is to hoist the spar a little at a time like knitting a very long sock.

It may well be better to make a long spar in short sections which can be joined together later using a generous moulded bandage or butt strap. A well thought out design would take this into account and have a rabbet for it so that the surface was flush, with the extra thickness coming where needed for attachments.

Another method of keeping it straight and avoiding dents or distortion is to run a very tight wire through the middle; something like piano wire or high tensile fencing wire that can be set up really tight with strainers to immovable objects. This supports the spar evenly from both ends but it may still sag under the weight. If intermediate support is unavoidable when using a core, mould the spar in sections, supporting it on an unmoulded part or where it is already hard. It will mark and probably dent where the moulding is "wet," and if the core is soft these dents and distortions will be deep. Mould one or two layers at a time and move the supports frequently so that the construction remains balanced.

Conventional thinking is to start at one end. One might copy bridge builders and start at the middle, working outwards with two cantilevers. The greatest weight and sag will be in the middle. There is an obvious advantage in being able to support this as soon as it is hard. The supports can be moved outwards from the centre to support each section as soon as it hardens.

Except where the spar is moulded in sections, it must all be done at once. Slow-setting resins are essential so that it all sets together. If the first layers start setting before the outer ones have been finished any movement or bad support (which may be unavoidable at that stage) will cause the early layers to set in a distorted position and this will be irremediable. Once started, work must continue until the spar, or that portion of it, is finished and *supported properly in exactly the right shape* to set and harden. No knocking off, tea breaks, dates or other distractions until it is finished. An alternative would be to do several layers at a time and allow them to set, but each layer must be supported exactly right when setting. This can be a delicate operation.

CARBON FIBRES Ignoring deliberate flexibility, basic mast theory demands a strut, and this must be stiff or it will buckle and fail. GRP is flexible compared with aluminium; about five to ten times more flexible. This flexibility must be overcome by more rigging or increased section, both of which create windage, although the weight may be much the same.

Carbon fibres are stiffer than glass. A millionaire might afford a mast made entirely of carbon fibres, but on a lower plane they have been used to stiffen a GRP mast. Being very expensive they must be put where they will work hardest, i.e. on the outside or in areas of highest stress. Beyond even enthusiastic millionaires, in the government ordered, tax-financed, aerospace class would be sapphire whisker reinforced masts. These at present are super-strength materials for the future and are not yet out of the laboratories.

I do not guarantee that all these ideas will work by any means. They are ideas thrown into the discussion rather than practical details. You must try them for yourself, bearing in mind that what may work for one man may be disaster to another—which applies to anything. But they do open up all sorts of exciting possibilities for novel or very sophisticated spars which give that vital edge when racing, and many men will go to untold expense and trouble to get just that.

Carbon fibres have been hailed as the wonder material but actually their strength (page 45) is comparable to good GRP and less than high-strength GRP, e.g. fishing rods. Their principal advantage is higher stiffness, 20–40 times GRP, comparable to steel. Their major disadvantage is very high cost, £20–£100/kg. A millionaire might have a carbon fibre mast (in left-wing circles yachting and millionaires go together) but for ordinary hard-up yachtsmen (from right-wing circles) it is fantasy.

When used, carbon fibres must work hard. A few hardened old soldiers can stiffen a batch of raw recruits, so a little carbon fibre put where it will have most effect will stiffen a moulding far more than its small proportion would suggest. The reason is simple. When bending, only the outer surface has highest stress, the inside comparatively little. Therefore the place to put a small amount of expensive carbon fibre is right on the outside where its virtue of high stiffness will have maximum effect and its use can be economically justified. It must be high modulus carbon fibre. Some grades are no better than glass.

CHAPTER TWENTY

Accommodation

GRP OR WOOD In general it does not pay to mould the accommodation until the numbers are large. The patterns and moulds will be very complicated, far more complicated than the hull and consequently very expensive. Hull and deck moulds are essential but not interior moulds. For early boats, particularly for a firm starting production, plywood accommodation is satisfactory. Indeed it will need substantial production before GRP competes with template cut, jig-assembled plywood, which will itself become more efficient and economic with increased production.

All interior woodwork must be of good quality. Poor wood will rot as quickly as on any wooden boat. This includes parts that are out of sight (fancy mahogany often hides rubbish) including stiffeners and supports for GRP, a point frequently skimped.

GRP interiors can be gradually introduced when justified by production. By this time the class and the company will be well established, the best compromise for the interior will have been found, and there will be sufficient confidence and capital to invest in expensive interior moulds. Moreover the need to increase production, commonly combined with shortage of good staff, may make the change essential. At what point this occurs depends on the circumstances.

The ultimate case is to have no woodwork below at all. The boat is assembled entirely from a few large, complex, highly detailed mouldings. All fittings that cannot be part of the mouldings are attached on a planned production line basis before assembly so that actually "building" the boat takes a few hours only. This is the future trend. However, one company which did this to a high degree reduced their labour costs to such an extent and cut their selling price so dramatically that buyers assumed the boat must be no good and the company went bankrupt. In many respects they went too far to keep below a psychological price level and in only optimistic anticipation of sufficient orders.

Special circumstances justifying an early introduction of GRP accommodation would be a lack of woodworking facilities and workers, and difficulty in obtaining suitable wood. This can be an important consideration for a firm new to boats and in an area without a tradition of boatbuilding. There is then a good case for moulding as much as possible.

However, there is a lot more to building good boats than sound moulding. It needs engineering and woodworking sections (even if only for making patterns) and their skilled staff. These will need extra capital and a lot more space. Limited resources are better concentrated on moulding, leaving fitting out to yards. The larger, more luxurious the boat the greater the difficulty. Sound moulding is obviously the essential basic foundation, yet is so often overlooked even on expensive boats (indeed especially on expensive boats), but it demands real boatbuilding knowledge and skill to turn that moulding into a sound boat. Hence the development of specialist moulders working closely with conventional builders, both working at production levels which give efficient, long runs.

Below decks the advantages of GRP are much less. Strength and weather resistance are not of much importance. There will be a saving in weight, but on weight-conscious Spartan accommodation this will be marginal and on luxury accommodation it will be of secondary importance. Maintenance will be a consideration; there will be a lot of scuffing, wear and tear, and dirty marks, but this will favour painted or varnished plywood, or a tougher surface such as Formica, rather than GRP. Intangible factors may be overwhelming. Many people who are quite willing to accept a GRP boat are not yet willing to live with it. They are used to wood. Local customs and preferences vary from one country to another. This needs careful study for exports. For amateur fitting out, or a production boat with different accommodation, wood is the only material.

Complicated shapes will obviously be the first items to be moulded, because they are the hardest and most uneconomical to make in wood, or perhaps wood is unsuitable, e.g. a built-in sink unit. Such parts might be moulded right from the start. The engine case, centreboard trunk, tanks, lockers, etc., may have to be moulded anyway and can be combined with parts of the accommodation. The cabin sole is often combined with the bunks and lining to form one large moulding from side to side. Toilet compartments can be moulded complete with wash basin, and galley unit complete with sink, ice-box and crockery stowage, etc. Note however that the more complicated the moulding the more likely it is to have flaws. These are very noticeable, annoying, and damaging to a good reputation.

A very important point to bear in mind when considering moulded accommodation is to make sure that it is absolutely right, that it is convenient and comfortable and has no annoying little snags. Once the moulds are made, alterations will be expensive and improvements will not be made. This is another reason for leaving such an idea until the Mark 3. Several years' use, and rearrangement, will have ironed out the snags, and it will be nearly perfect. Moreover owners' and, more important perhaps, potential owners' reactions to the layout will be known, and one can go ahead confident that it is the best compromise that will satisfy enough buyers to make the mouldings economic. Given the numbers to pay off the mould costs GRP interiors are cheaper and are now essential for mass production. Unlike woodwork it takes little longer to mould an intricate moulding than a simple one. It is common for interior mouldings to include very considerable detail —and the owner must more and more "like it or lump it."

But unless good racing performance is the criterion, cruisers sell on the accommodation, not the hull. Cynics say it is the curtains; in practice it is the layout, finish and suitability. Once the switch has been made to all-GRP interiors every new design introduced afterwards must be designed for GRP too because production will be geared to this and there will no longer be a staff of woodworkers. However, with successful boats already in production, their name made and capital behind them, a firm can plan more confidently. Indeed it must do so because every boat must be planned right from the start for large scale production. If it does not meet this target it is a failure. Therefore the design must be right first time. There is no second chance.

There are plenty of other plastic materials which could be used for the accommodation, but which would be unsuitable for structural parts of the boat. Sheet thermoplastic which is quite easily vacuum formed would be suitable for lockers, sink units and covers.

They can be semi-flexible, which is an attractive possibility for every year brings its crop of injuries and bruises due to people being thrown against hard unyielding wood in rough weather. A padded cell has unfortunate associations, but it really would be the most comfortable thing to go to sea in.

LINING Linings generally take the following forms, applicable to either hulls or deckhands.

1. A stick-on lining applied directly to the inner surface.
2. An inner moulding, thin and non-structural, often incorporating a large part of the accommodation.
3. A structural inner moulding firmly attached to the outer and forming a sandwich.
4. Panels of plywood, melamine surfaced sheet, or GRP attached to battens.
5. Stretched fabric.

For years high-class wooden yachts have been lined and there is an increasing tendency to line GRP yachts, even cheapish ones. The purpose of lining is to hide the inside appearance of the moulding and provide insulation to keep heat out or in, cut down condensation and reduce noise. In the tropics only the deck needs insulating but for winter warmth the hull needs it too. All boats are noisy resounding boxes regardless of construction. External noise can be reduced by sound-damping insulation, but the insides of lockers and the bilges need it as well. Sandwich mouldings are common for decks but usually have a rough underside similar to the normal inside finish of the moulding (see Chapter One).

The commonest stick-on lining is flexible, patterned vinyl or PVC, often foam-backed or quilted. Others are decorative fabrics, leather cloth, veneer or melamine sheet. Attention must be paid to the following:

(a) It must be an attractive, good quality material, durable in a marine atmosphere. It must endure tropical and fashionable sub-tropical temperature without degrading or smelling, including the severe greenhouse effect of sunshine through large glass windows.

(b) The lining must be well fitted without wrinkles, and if patterned the pattern must run in straight lines and not wander. The shape is bound to be irregular so a prominent regular pattern is best avoided. Instead use a random pattern.

(c) Edges need to be well stuck down and fitted properly. A separate contrasting edge strip hides difficulties in fitting as well as holding the edges.

(d) Use a good quality, recommended adhesive. It must be a material unaffected by heat and damp, and which does not attack the lining. Obviously it must adhere to both the lining and the moulding. Run a sander over the surface first to take off the high spots and make the surface reasonably smooth. The lining will stick much better for it because most plastics sheet materials will tend to lift out of hollows. A fabric backed material will be less likely to creep.

(e) It must have no offensive smell. Many stomachs turn at the mere thought of boats and the sea. Any unusual smell may have unfortunate reactions even in harbour, and some plastics sheet and upholstery do have a strong odour. A suggestion is to keep stronger, more nautical smells aboard like tarry rope or fish.

(f) Both lining and adhesive must be resistant to fungi and mildew, not only in the tropics but in temperate climates too.

An inner lining is moulded with the good, smooth face inwards. It m ay be entirely self-supporting, secured at the edges or fastened to battens. Hull linings are usually part of the complex mouldings forming the accommodation. Linings are large and bonded in before the hull/deck assembly, being too large to pass below. They can never be replaced or fitted later, and alterations are impractical. Fixed linings must not cover fastenings or anything that might have to be tightened or replaced. Likely or not, if the fastening is there at all there is a need for access.

Panels, usually plywood or melamine sheet, or GRP for awkward shapes, are fastened to battens bonded or moulded onto the hull or deck. They need wood or plastics covering strips for all joins and edges. If detachable it is permissible to allow the panels to cover fastenings or fittings, but this should be avoided if possible, as it will still be a nuisance and possibly cause damage. Commonly some afterthought gets added which makes it difficult or destructive to remove the panel when actually needed. I consider stretched fabrics or PVC, similar to car head linings, unsuitable for boats. They are too liable to be damaged or stretched by a hand reaching out for support in a hurry.

In hot climates the deckhead needs insulation for comfort. Aluminium foil stuck behind the lining is cheap and effective. Note, however, that as in a car the hottest temperatures come from sunlight through the windows, the greenhouse effect. Sun blinds may be needed, not insulation. Some domestic quality vinyl smells when hot. This applies particularly to upholstery, but car upholstery is made to withstand sunshine. Hot vinyl upholstery can feel burning when lightly clad. Fabrics are kinder.

For the ordinary class of boat there is really nothing wrong with leaving the inside bare or painting it to match the decor. The glossy rippled surface of a well moulded inside is not unattractive, particularly compared to the cluttered and often weeping inside of a wooden cruiser, but if not soundly moulded it will hold dirt and certainly be unattractive. A "speckle" paint has great masking power and the useful ability of making an uneven surface look flat. It upgrades the inside appearance at little cost.

CONDENSATION   Although condensation is not as severe a problem as on a metal boat, it can be a nuisance and is more noticeable because there are fewer leaks. Also, owing to the modern necessity of squeezing quarts into pint pots, by no means confined to GRP boats, more people must live in a confined space. Consequently there is more fug, cooking, tobacco smoke, and damp bodies, clothes and sails. The criterion is not how many a boat can sleep but how many it can live.

GRP will not support mildew. Yet mildew is common on deckheads. This can only grow on a deposit of fug and cooking fumes in the presence of moisture from condensation. Hull ventilation will reduce but not eliminate it. Lockers too should have ventilation, even dry lockers. Sodden ropes lead to rotten wood. Mildew grows even on Terylene sails if left wet. Condensation is reduced by lining or painting with absorbent or insulating paint, e.g. "Korkon." Emulsion paint is often used but sometimes crazes and its compatability with GRP is questionable.

The inside of both main moulding and lining must be soundly moulded even though no one will see them. Stagnant water is destructive to GRP, and badly moulded GRP is particularly vulnerable. This is where decay starts. In cold climates condensation col-

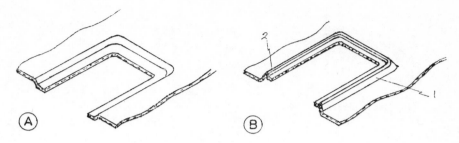

20.1: *Moulding the opening for a locker.*

When the position of the locker is planned beforehand the flange may be moulded in, either recessed, A, or raised, B. The raised coaming, 1, will deflect water, but on a horizontal hatch the lip, 2, should not be high or it will hold a puddle.

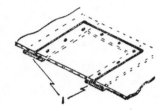

20.2: *"Dry" construction locker.*
Make the flange with plywood, glued to the moulding.

lecting in pockets will freeze and cause severe damage, e.g. under deckheads, behind linings or inside keels. Therefore closed pockets must be avoided. Likely places need discrete drain holes where they will cause little inconvenience. Condensation runs: the pockets will be not where it forms but where it collects.

CABIN SOLE The cabin sole must have strong support whether made of plywood or moulded integrally. It has to bear not just the dead weight of heavy men but, at sea, their dynamic weight, which is several times greater. Wooden bearers or moulded floors right across are a sound method provided they do not end in hard spots. Good access to all parts of the bilges is essential for inspection (especially of keel fastenings), in case of damage, or simply to recover lost objects. Moreover inaccessible bilges are a waste of good storage space. Floorboards and traps should be fastened, yet readily lifted.

LOCKERS Lockers in moulded parts, planned in advance, should have flanges formed while moulding (Fig. 20.1). They can be recessed or raised. A raised flange is better in wet parts, anywhere above decks, in fact, because it will deflect water away from the lid. Water will lie on a flush hatch and it is therefore more inclined to leak. However, a high lip round a horizontal hatch could hold a puddle.

Where the depression or bump formed by the flanges of the locker would cause the moulding to jam in the mould they can be made as detachable panels on the mould, located and secured temporarily by pins or screws but arranged to come away with the moulding and be released afterwards.

It is seldom possible for the inside of the locker or pockets to be formed on the main mould but these too can often be made with "come-away" projections in the mould.

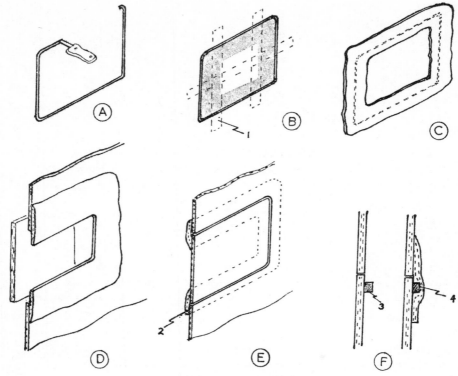

20.3: *Making a locker and lid.*

A. *Cut out the locker with a padsaw as neatly as possible. The cut-out portion will form the lid of the locker.*

B. *Place the lid in position and hold it with adhesive tape, 1. Treat the shaded portion with release agent to prevent the flange bonding.*

C. *Mould the flange all round, overlapping both lid and moulding.*

D. *Remove the sticky tape. The lid will come away because it has been treated with release agent leaving the flange bonded to the moulding. Trim up the edge of the flange to give the size of opening required.*

E. *Where the back is inaccessible the flange must be moulded from the front. In this case treat the moulding with release agent, 2, so that the flange bonds to the lid not the moulding.*

F. *If a watertight seal is needed, lightly stick a strip of rubber or wood around the edge of the lid before moulding the flange. This will form a groove in the flange to take a sealing strip.*

N.B.—*The sealing strip must be larger than the groove to allow for compression, and cannot be used itself to form the groove.*

Alternatively, they can be formed as sub-mouldings or made of plywood. The lids will look smart if made as sub-mouldings, possibly in a contrasting colour.

A common requirement, however, is to make a locker where none was planned. The opening is easily cut with a pad saw. It needs to be done neatly because it will be conspicuous, and the cut-out portion may be needed as a lid or door.

If the locker is to be closed it will need a flange to support the lid. This can be made of wooden strips glued or screwed to the inside of the opening (Fig. 20.2), well bedded down but it is neater to mould the flange and it can be done as follows:

Place the lid back in position and hold it in place with adhesive tape (Fig. 20.3). Apply release agent to the lid but not to the moulding, or wrap the lid in polythene, so that the flange will bond only to the moulding and not to the lid. Lay up the flange overlapping both, working from inside. Remove the lid and trim the opening.

By using the cut-out portion as the lid in this way the opening can easily be arranged on a complex shaped part of the moulding, and the lid moreover is sure to fit properly, in a way that would be quite impossible with plywood (Fig. 20.4).

Access behind to mould the flange is often difficult or impossible, particularly when making an opening on a boat after it has been fitted out and everything is built in. In this case the flange may have to be made on the outside, and precautions taken to ensure that it bonds to the locker lid and not to the moulding, i.e. the reverse of the previous case. However this may look a bit untidy as the "rough" side of the flange will show and contrast unfavourably with the "smooth" lid and moulding. It will be neater to use plywood, provided the shape is suitable, or to mould the lid by taking a mould off that part of the boat before cutting the opening.

In wet situations it is advisable to build up a raised coaming (Fig. 20.5), particularly for a simple opening without a lid or a frequently used hatch which will not be bedded down. Otherwise every drip will find its way in.

The method of closure will depend on the purpose of the locker. An inspection hatch, seldom required can be screwed down. If the nuts are embedded it will be simple to unscrew it from one side at any time (Fig. 20.6). Turnbuttons can be similarly attached for hatches requiring more frequent access. Hinges are simply bolted on, but both moulding and lid should be thickened. Frequently used hatches are often secured by a strip of elastic fastened inside so that the lid is pulled shut tightly. This also prevents the lid being lost.

ICE-BOXES Ice-boxes are scorned on British yachts but are essential amenities in America and the Mediterranean. Any cruiser designed with half an eye on export, which should include every stock boat, should have provision for an ice-box, at least in the plans. It requires a closeable locker which can be well insulated and a smooth easy-clean lining with a small drain. With a fully moulded interior it is often incorporated as part of the galley complex. The lid can be similar to locker lids but well insulated like a food freezer. Slabs of polystyrene foam are commonly used for insulation. Flexible polyurethane is easier to handle in a confined space and complex shapes.

An ice-box can be built later. Plastics foam insulation is built up to shape first and the inner lining moulded against it. Polystyrene foam is unsuitable as it is dissolved by "wet" polyester. Use rigid polyurethane, PVC or, if the shape is complex, flexible polyurethane rigidised with a few coats of resin. With this method no separate mould is needed. It can be formed right against the boat's side or a bulkhead, thus making maximum use of the space available. Solid, glossy moulding is essential.

If the shape permits, or as a standard alternative fitting, the inner lining can be made as a separate moulding on a male mould, bonded in position and insulated with *in-situ* foam. This gives a smooth moulded finish instead of the "inside" finish obtained when moulding in position.

A built-in refrigerator can be made in the same way, on larger yachts it would be a cold store. Being built-in it can make use of any odd corners which might otherwise be

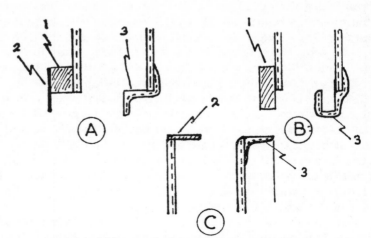

20.5: *Adding a raised coaming to a cut-out opening.*

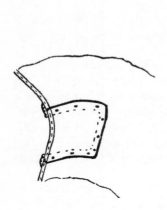

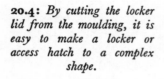

20.4: *By cutting the locker lid from the moulding, it is easy to make a locker or access hatch to a complex shape.*

On decks, cockpits and other wet situations it is advisable to have a flange to any cut-out locker to reduce the chance of leaks. This is easily done with strips of wood, 1, and plywood or metal, 2, to act as shuttering.
A. *This shows the arrangement of the shuttering and the finished flange, 3, for a z-flange.*
B. *Ditto for a U-flange.*
C. *The lid will be more watertight if it, too, has a flange.*

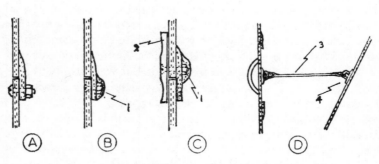

20.6: *Methods of securing a locker lid.*

A. *Infrequent access and both sides accessible. Secured with ordinary screws and nuts, and well bedded down.*
B. *Infrequent access and only one side accessible. Secure with screws and embedded nuts, 1.*
C. *Frequent access: turnbutton, 2, secured with a screw into an embedded nut. This will prevent the nut turning.*
D. *Very frequent access; lid held down by elastic, 3, fixed to an eye, 4, inside the locker.*

wasted. Moreover, any shape is possible, even if highly complex, e.g. over and between ribs and frames, so that the ice-box or refrigerator can make the utmost use of whatever space is available. There is no limit as to the size and it is a simple way to make a well insulated, easy-clean, cold store, hold or fish well.

There should be provision for drainage as the ice will melt. The wrong way is to drill a few holes in the bottom (Fig. 20.7); water will drip down on to the plastic foam which is likely to soak up a certain amount, perhaps a lot if it is a spongy kind. A good foam should not be affected by moisture but it will destroy the insulation value of the foam. The right way is to put in a small tube and lead it down clear to drip harmlessly into the bilges. A metal tube would conduct heat too well; a polythene tube is an insulator. It is not easy to bond to polythene; ideally proper pipe connections should be used but it will not be easy to insert these after the lining has been made. They would have to be put in first and embedded. A moulded glass-fibre tube which will also be an insulator, could be moulded in satisfactorily and one suggestion is to bind a polythene tube with "wet" glass tape, or thin mat if no woven material is available. The resin will not bond satisfactorily to the polythene but will grip it well enough by friction, and the outer sleeve of glass-fibre will bond firmly into the ice-box lining.

A refinement to prevent transference of heat via the tube is to have a thick porous plug on the end of the tube, e.g. a chunk of soft flexible plastic foam, or a filter plug, but it must be the spongy kind with interconnecting cells, not separate cells, because the water from the ice must percolate through it.

HOOKS AND EYES My own wooden boats have always acquired a collection of brass hooks and eyes for hanging, lashing or securing a variety of items from dish cloths to sea anchors. A place for everything and everything in its place means that there must be means of keeping it there despite any antics the boat may perform. Otherwise there is only one place for everything and that is the cabin sole—for that is where everything will be. The smaller and cheaper the boat the more acute the problem, for a large luxury yacht should have plenty of lockers.

Screwing in hooks at random is impossible on a moulded boat. They must be confined to whatever woodwork there is, but if timber cores have been used for the top-hat frames there will be many more points for hooks and eyes. A self-tapping screw will also hold a tag or clip well enough in a light cored top-hat frame (Fig. 20.8). Anything attached to a top-hat section should be bedded down otherwise there is a chance of moisture penetrating and causing trouble. This is probably more important with a timber core and a lot depends on its situation. Needless to say, when any such attachment is no longer required and removed the hole should be plugged as soon as possible. Attachments should not be made to top-hat frames if it is known that these have been moulded with a uni-directional material.

However, it is also quite easy on a moulded boat to "tack" a clip or tag with "wet" mat on to the thin hull skin. It is rather wasteful to mix up some resin just for one small tag but if a number of such lashing points can be done at one time it is quite economical.

For a single fixture use glue to attach a tag or loop of tape. Two-tube epoxy glue is strong but rather slow setting. It laminates well with glass tape or even rag. Impact or rubber adhesives are quick but tend to creep. Laminating is possible with ordinary glues but a drying or solvent-evaporating glue may be soft for a long time if used thickly.

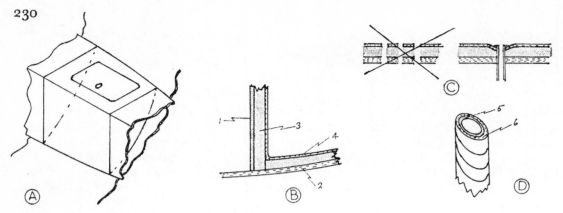

20.7: *Ice-box.*

A. *By moulding the ice-box in position it can be fitted into awkward and otherwise useless spaces. Moreover, it makes the utmost use of such space.*

B. *Typical cross-section: Plywood bulkhead or partition, 1; hull skin, 2; plastic foam insulation, 3; moulded lining, 4; laid up directly over the foam.*

C. *The right and wrong way to make drainholes. Plain drilled holes may damp the insulation and reduce its effectiveness even if they do not damage it. An embedded tube will lead water clear away. A small depression, made by reducing the thickness of the insulation over a small area, will aid drainage and bring the embedded tube flush with the general bottom level.*

D. *Method of making drain-tubes. Bind a small polythene pipe, 5, with "wet" glass tape, 6.*

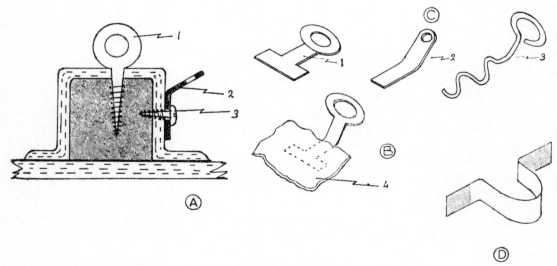

20.8: *Small attachment points.*

A. *With a wooden core, a screw-eye, 1, can be used. With other core materials, use a small bracket held by a self-tapping screw.*

B. *Large soldering tag "tacked" in position with "wet" mat.*

C. *Suggested forms of tags for use as (B): heavy duty soldering tag with lugs bent flat, 1; aluminium strip, 2; bent wire, 3.*

D. *Loop of tape glued on.*

Double-sided tapes or pads are quick and convenient. Rolls of sticky tape such as cellulose or PVC are useful for light stowage. PVC is fairly water- and weatherproof, and suitable above deck. There are many other industrial tapes.

Large soldering tags make handy fixing points. A wide, long heavy duty tag with side lugs which can be bent down (Fig. 20.8) gives a better bonding surface and is a good shape for embedding. Other tags can be made from aluminium strip or bent wire.

For a heavier attachment embed a block of wood and fasten the eye into that.

Stranded elastic with a braided covering can now be bought readily, often in made up lengths with hook-ends, the sort of thing used to secure luggage to cars. A cheap alternative is plastic coated spring clothes line. It is strong enough for securing light things and easy to fit by screwing small hooks into the ends. It will eventually rust of course because it is steel but this will take some time below deck. The small end hooks are the parts which rust most but these could be replaced by brass hooks. The ends of both kinds can hook into small holes drilled in the interior mouldings.

There are various other devices such as suction backed and self-adhesive plastic hooks sold for domestic use which can be used on boats as well; no doubt plenty of other ingenious devices will be thought up and adapted for GRP boats too.

Designers and builders should not ignore such mundane requirements as a place to hang a dish-cloth, coat-hooks and that handy nail beside the hatch for a watch or marline spike; those little things, different for every individual, which turn a moulding into an efficient and comfortable boat. This is where plenty of woodwork has an advantage over 100 per cent GRP.

DAMP IN LOCKERS　The lining of the accommodation seldom extends to lockers, which are commonly formed by moulded bulges in that lining. Condensation is a problem particularly in cold weather. Lockers need linings or at least battens to keep the contents clear of the cold hull.

Modern bilgeless designs, especially twin keel, have nowhere to put the inevitable bilge water when heeled except in the lockers with everything else. Commonly the bunks and cabin sole are one large submoulding. Lockers and bilges share the space behind. Lockers should be sealed off by a moulded angle. But access for moulding is awkward and awkward moulding is generally bad especially as this is often considered unskilled boy's work. So annoying seepages are extremely common.

ROT POCKETS　The average GRP boat breaks every rule about pockets of stale air, breeding-grounds for rot, which we were brought up to avoid on wooden boats. Yet there is often a lot of wood below. Some is good wood, preservative treated or marine ply, but much is rubbishy, hidden behind mouldings or expensive-looking veneer. Experience confirms that there is trouble in store for GRP boats with poor wood tucked away out of sight. Ventilation behind linings, lockers, bilges and hidden or closed spaces is as important as on a wooden boat.

This rot will not infect the hull or deck as on a wooden boat, although rotten wood will produce the conditions which cause local decay in GRP (page 280), and the by-products too can be harmful. But accommodation will come adrift or disintegrate.

CHAPTER TWENTY-ONE
Inboard Engine Installation

ENGINE installation is the realm of the marine engineer and is a specialised job. In this chapter we are concerned more with the effect an engine installation may have on the design and construction of a GRP boat or ways in which the GRP construction may make a difference to the engine installation.

ENGINE-BEARERS All inboard engines require engine-bearers, but the recommended method of attaching them to the hull is quite different from the methods used on a wooden boat. They must still be strong and massive, for it is these bearers which transfer the push of the screw to the boat and carry the weight of the engine, the heaviest single item on a power boat. Massive bearers spread the weight of the engine and damp out vibration.

The engine-bearers may be no more than large top-hat section frames, using a wooden core or a light core with solid inserts where the bolts will come. They may also be open wooden bearers, or fabricated in steel, secured to the hull with substantial matted-in angles. Bolting the bearers through the hull, even if it is well thickened, is bad practice as it imposes a severe local stress around the bolts instead of spreading the load over a wide area. When fitting out "dry" it is really essential for the moulder to put in the engine-bearers while moulding, or at least to mould in substantial fore and aft members to which the actual engine-bearers can be bolted. It is not easy to mould a top-hat section to the precision necessary for an engine-bearer even using a specially shaped core; it is better if the top-hat sections are lower or wider apart than the proper engine-bearers and act solely as firm rigid girders to carry the actual wood or steel engine-bearers (Fig. 21.1). This allows some degree of adjustment and a firmer mounting because the engine-bearers can be bolted through the moulded girders; if the engine was bolted direct to the moulded engine-bearers it would need coach-bolts into the cores, which might have indifferent holding power, with a limit to the number of times such a bolt could be inserted or withdrawn (Fig. 21.2). Alternatively, metal inserts could be used, but they would require very accurate positioning.

On a production boat the bearers can be sub-mouldings, made to shape and bonded on. However, this presupposes a standard engine, and it will be difficult for the owner ever to change it for a better one. GRP girders and fabricated engine-bearers are a more flexible arrangement and will allow an alternative engine installation, either during building or at any time during the life of the boat.

Most wooden boats outlive their engines, and may have several changes during their lives. It is to be expected that a moulded boat will last considerably longer, and if those conservative claims of lasting for ever are to be of any value, it must be possible to replace the more mortal parts such as the engine without too much difficulty. How easy it would

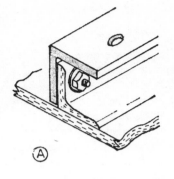 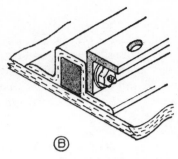 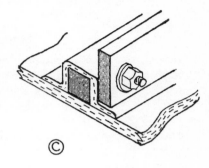

21.1: *Engine-bearers.*

A. *Steel angle bolted to moulded flange.*
B. *Steel angle bolted through top-hat section.*
C. *Wooden bearer bolted through moulded top-hat section.*

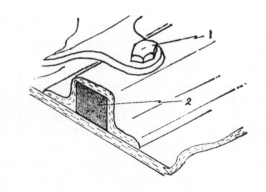

21.2: *Engine-bearers.*

Not recommended. Coach-bolt into top-hat section. This relies on the holding power of the core which is likely to be indifferent. Also adjustment is more difficult and the bearer must be moulded with precision.

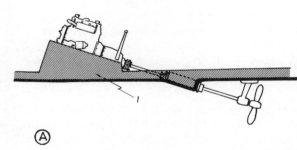 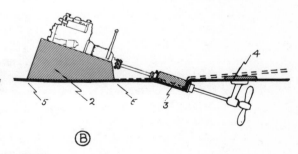

21.3: *Engine bearers.*

A. *Bearers, 1, should extend to link up with stern tube and A-bracket.*
B. *Short engine bearers, 2, and separate stern tube block, 3, and A-bracket pad, 4, can allow the hull to flex as shown dotted (exaggerated) resulting in momentary misalignment. Note also how the short engine bearers form hard spots 5.*

be if all engine mountings within a given range could be standardised, as those for outboard motors are standardised.

The moulded "girders" should be put in while the hull is still "green" and uncured, so that a better bond can be obtained than if they were put in some time later. The best time to put them in is while the hull is still in the mould, even during the actual moulding, so that they are sandwiched between layers of the moulding. Also if they are put in while the boat is in the mould, the hull is bound to be the right shape, and there is no question of the stiff bearers maintaining permanently a shape distorted by bad support.

With long rigid engine-bearers it is very important to avoid hard spots. Hard spots and stress concentrations are described in Chapter Two. Such massive members introduce quite a different flexing pattern; if not done properly this may produce severe local stress concentrations as well as the extra stresses both static and dynamic due to the weight of the engine and thrust of the screws. The engine-bearers or the moulded girder mountings must not end abruptly but must taper off gradually to blend into the hull or end at a cross-member. It is particularly important to watch this point when making any alterations or extensions to the bearers. (See Chapter Two.)

A moulded hull is lighter and more flexible than most wooden boats, so it is a sound idea to extend the bearers to the area of the stern tube and "A" bracket also (Fig. 21.3). Otherwise there could be sufficient movement due to natural flexing of the hull to upset the shaft alignment. As this will happen under way and be only a momentary misalignment it will be impossible to correct. If the engine is flexibly mounted it is essential to fit a flexible coupling. Otherwise the stern tube will be torn out.

The metal engine mounting feet or steel engine-bearers should not be bolted in direct contact with any moulded surface. Considerable pressure will inevitably come on to the moulded surface from the heavy engine and tightly screwed down bolts. The face of the moulding, if it is the normal inside finish, will be uneven so that all the pressure falls on the high spots (Fig. 21.4). Similarly the smooth moulded surface given by the gel coat of a sub-moulding will be resin-rich and therefore somewhat brittle.

A hard, metal surface exerting heavy pressure in direct contact with the moulding will tend to crush the surface. Vibration will aggravate it, and the more the moulding is crushed the looser the fastenings become and the worse the vibration. Remember that resin is not ductile like metal and wood; it does not yield under severe surface pressure, and instead of denting it is crushed like stone or concrete.

Crushing can be avoided by using a thin, soft gasket between the metal face and the moulded face, so that the surface resin is protected from the harsh metal surface and possible "nut-cracker" effect. Thin neoprene, about $\frac{1}{16}$ in. or $\frac{1}{8}$ in. is effective, but rubber, fabric and other materials can be used also. With a small engine a coat of rubbery paint is quite effective. Alternatively use a wooden spacer.

A surface with a normal "inside" finish which is to come under a heavy bolted-down metal surface should be filed reasonably smooth to take off the high spots as well as having a soft gasket to protect it. Extra thickness should be allowed for this. Alternatively build up with resin putty. There must be sufficient access to work properly.

STERN TUBE Most stern tubes are long because it is assumed that they will pass through a considerable thickness of wood. But in a moulded boat they will be short, under one inch except in a large one, and will have to be ordered separately. To get

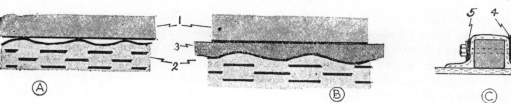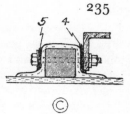

21.4: Protecting the moulding from crushing.

A. *Enlarged diagram of metal to moulding face. The hard, heavy metal engine-bearer or mounting foot, 1, will rest directly on the high spots of the "rough" side of the moulding, 2. These are resin-rich and will be crushed by pressure.*

B. *A thin gasket of neoprene or similar material, 3, will spread the weight more evenly and protect the moulding from being crushed.*

C. *Neoprene gasket, 4, between the metal engine-bearer and top-hat moulded bearer. Another gasket or soft washer is needed under the head of the bolt, 5.*

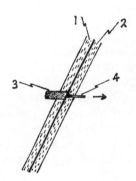

21.5: There is no need to drill the hull to take a stern tube; the hole can easily be moulded in. A wooden plug, 3, is secured to the mould, 2, with a pin or screw, 4. The moulding, 1, is laid up around the plug. Before release, the pin, 4, is withdrawn allowing the plug, 3, to come away with the moulding; it can be driven or chiselled out afterwards.

adequate length to allow a more standard bearing it is not unusual to mould in a block of wood to give sufficient thickness and also to increase the rigidity.

A motor-cruiser hull can be moulded into a streamlined bulge to provide a flat mounting surface and the inside filled with a shaped block. If the shaft position is not known at the time of moulding, or if there is no moulded bulge, a shaped block will be needed outside too.

The screw of a sailing cruiser needs an aperture moulded into the stern, and this must be considered at a very early stage. It will be very difficult to change it later. It will probably need a block inside to provide sufficient thickness for the stern tube, but a narrow moulding could be filled with resin-glass putty or resin/sawdust filler.

It is as well to consider how the size of the aperture on a production boat could be increased during moulding to accommodate a larger screw if wanted for a larger than standard engine. Two or more cavity sizes might be standardised using special filling pieces in the mould to form a large opening.

Enlarging the cavity at a later date will require a major operation; anything cut away must be made good by moulding more on the inside to replace it. Cutting away is likely to penetrate the moulding so that part of the stern will need to be remoulded. It is worth bearing in mind that the power of auxiliary engines fitted to sailing yachts has tended to increase in recent years, and is now double the pre-war figure. As it is difficult to increase the propeller size, because of the problems of enlarging the cavity, there is a case for standardising on a largish engine rather than on a small one, to over-power rather than under-power. A high performance racing boat often has a token size engine; but when the boat becomes obsolete, and most racing boats are outclassed quite quickly unless it is a strictly one design class, the engine is replaced by one of conventional power. It would be possible to have a wood or moulded filling piece to restrict the opening during its racing life but easily removable for conversion when the boat is outclassed.

A quarter installation presents few special problems, and the installation would be similar to a motor-cruiser. It is comparatively easy to change the propeller size.

The vicinity of the stern tube must always be well reinforced and thickened to provide a firm seating. The inside face must be filed smooth and parallel to the outer face or built up flush.

Drilling through a thick moulding will be hard on large bits, and large bits are expensive. If the position is known beforehand a wooden plug attached to the mould as a come-away projection will save a lot of trouble (Fig. 21.5). It can be located temporarily with a pin or screws. Release is no problem, because once the pin is withdrawn or the screws undone it will come away with the moulding to be driven or chiselled out later. On the centre line it will come away automatically as the mould splits.

Another trouble-saving idea is to make the plug well oversize so that there is some latitude in adjustment. The gap around the stern tube can be filled in by moulding later when its exact position and alignment are certain, but note that proper fastenings and bedding down will be needed as well. The filling in around the stern tube is just to locate it. In any case it should not be embedded irrevocably because it may have to be renewed or replaced at a later date.

Vibration of the shaft will tend to enlarge the hole in the hull. The hammering effect of vibration will wear away and shatter the resin around the tube. Good, proper fastenings and extra reinforcement and thickness are important. It is not only normal conditions that must be considered, but also the abnormal such as a bent blade. The stern tube must not come adrift—at least not until you are safely home. I favour a stout embedded wooden block for the stern tube to pass through. If there is any severe vibration the greater thickness and resilience of the wood will absorb and contain the vibration.

"A" BRACKETS "A" brackets form part of the engine alignment and must be firmly mounted. They should be through-bolted into substantial blocks and well thickened moulding.

Flexing of the hull could upset the alignment; the engine-bearers and suitable stiffening members should be extended aft to the region of the "A" brackets as well as the stern tube.

If the boat grounds, it is possible for the "A" brackets to carry a lot of the weight of the boat, and possibly bumping too. The vicinity of their mounting must be well stiffened to withstand this possibility. Of course if this is a serious mishap the shaft and the screw are likely to be damaged, too, and become unusable, but that is not so important as keeping the hull intact. A boat with a bent shaft can be towed home if she is still afloat, but if the "A" bracket has been forced through the bottom, as I have seen happen, it would be a case for a salvage crew, and a minor accident would become a major insurance claim.

STERN DRIVE Stern drive, Z-drive, inboard/outboard, etc., in which the drive comes through the transom instead of the bottom, is a very suitable installation because of its light weight, and the relative simplicity speeds production. Also, mounting the engine aft gives more space for the accommodation. The method of installation varies. Diesels generally require conventional engine bearers as well; lighter petrol engines hang directly on the transom.

The transom-hung method is simpler because no lining up is needed. The engine is bolted directly to the transom at the shaft end. This puts a very heavy strain on the transom especially under lively conditions—an important consideration for racing boats. It needs very large knees connecting with bottom girders giving in effect cranked engine bearers appropriate for an engine of that size. These knees must also absorb the thrust of the engine which is generally of relatively high power. The transom normally has a wood core and the rules for sandwich mouldings apply. The core must be incompressible in way of the engine mounting and the cut-out must be sealed around the edge.

Stern drives are usually made of aluminium alloy. Copper based antifouling causes electrolytic action: tin-based ones should be used. Similarly copper skin fittings should be avoided near the stern drive.

ABRASION AND CAVITATION In shallow water there may be abrasion from sand and debris churned up by the screws. It will usually be slow but should not be ignored. Abrasion of the gel coat will expose glass fibres and lead to decay. Regular touching up of the antifouling may be all that is needed. In worse cases a coating of abrasion-resisting gel coat will give renewable protection. If severe fit external protection pieces.

A more difficult problem is caused by cavitation from a high speed screw. Extra thickness of resin will aggravate the trouble because a thick layer of resin is brittle and liable to chip and crack under the hammering of cavitation. Cavitation is a delaminating effect, a severe plucking or sucking which the laminar construction of GRP is not well suited to resist. In particular layers of woven rovings near the surface make it vulnerable. The first approach should be proper screw design to reduce or eliminate the cavitation. Cavitation can also occur on the bottom of a high speed hull. This is a more difficult problem as it is a function of hull shape and alters according to conditions, speed and trim.

EXHAUST PIPE Hot exhaust pipes must be kept away from GRP just as they should be kept away from wood (see Chapter Seven). An exhaust pipe is usually water cooled and normally fairly cool, but the possibility must always be considered that the cooling may fail—it is not uncommon. There must be no possibility whatever of the moulding being damaged even under the worst conditions of overheating.

It is also vitally important that the exhaust pipe cannot damage anything else under normal or overheating conditions. It must have a clear run and not pass through lockers or spaces where equipment, wiring, insulation, etc., can lie against or near it. It should not run near plastics water pipes as they can melt, and obviously not near fuel pipes of any kind. Cockpit drains, nearly always plastics, generally run through the engine compartment and are underwater of course.

Gel coats sometimes craze around the exhaust outlet. This is not usually the fault of the gel coat, but means the water is too hot. Standard marine gel coats have a low heat resistance, well below boiling water. The solution is to reduce the water temperature, commonly by removing the thermostat, or rearrange the outlet to throw the water clear.

FIRE PRECAUTIONS GRP is not dangerously inflammable but it will burn much as wood does. Precautions can be taken to reduce the fire risk as follows:

1. Normal sound installation and workmanship, and compliance with the appropriate codes of practice. Most fires occur through bad installations.
2. Fitting approved fire extinguishers and ensuring they are in working order (page 211).
3. Moulding with fire-retardant resins.
4. Painting with intumescent resins or paints.
5. Reducing other inflammable materials.

Self-extinguishing resins have been available for years but have not been accepted because generally they have inferior weathering properties, are harder to use or are more expensive. A suitable compromise is to use ordinary gel coats outside to give good weathering (the risk of a boat catching fire from outside is small) and self-extinguishing resins for the body of the mouldings and especially for interior gel coats. Self-extinguishing resins stop burning when the source disappears. First extinguish the fire. If this cannot be done even self-extinguishing resins will burn, albeit reluctantly. They must not be confused with non-inflammable materials. High glass content also reduces inflammability. Intumescent paint or coatings froth up when exposed to heat, forming an insulating non-inflammable layer which protects the surface beneath. These ought to be standard in engine spaces and galleys although their appearance is against the latter.

Both materials ensure that if there is a fire the moulding is far less likely to blaze up, and the crew have a better chance of getting fire under control. It must be emphasised that sound installation and common sense are the only things which will reduce the risk of a fire starting. *Nothing done to the resin can do this.* Fire-retardant materials are the last line of defence (before taking to the lifeboats) and before these come into play severe damage will already have been done to the boat, engine and equipment, and the crews' lives will be in danger. Moreover it will not prevent structural damage from explosion of gas or petrol. It is not the steel of a ship which burns but the paint, furnishings and cargo: the same moral applies to GRP. Most cruisers contain a considerable amount of wood and upholstery.

Self-extinguishing resins produce a lot of smoke, as does ordinary GRP, and this itself will be a hazard although they are not thought to produce toxic fumes. Of course a lot of smoke helps to summon aid!

GRP can delaminate when exposed to heat, especially with woven rovings. This can also be caused by an external fire, e.g. a near-by boat, building or bonfire, even when there is little or no visible harm. It can be extensive and irreparable. A boat should be surveyed after any fire.

CHAPTER TWENTY-TWO

Tanks, Plumbing and Electrics

TANKS Tanks can be installed in the usual way, either made of metal or moulded, but they can also be built in like the tanks on a steel boat. Built-in tanks give the greatest capacity in the space, or conversely the same capacity tanks take up less of the useful space in the boat, leaving more room for the gin and whisky to drink with the water. The saving in space can be 50 per cent. Much weight is saved too, and the double bottom adds strength. Rubber tanks also bulge to fill the space available. (They are thought to be a new idea but I had one made twenty-five years ago.)

A moulded tank will last indefinitely, in fact as long as the boat. Steel tanks must be galvanised, and last on the average only about ten years. Steel tanks, too, are no job for the amateur to tackle, whereas sound moulded tanks are quite easy to make at home or on board.

Ordinary marine moulding resins are slightly affected by petrol (gasoline), especially high octane, and diesel oil and paraffin (kerosene). This is disputed, but we are considering a prolonged period of many years, the life of a boat, not the weeks or months of a laboratory test. Resistance can be improved by moulding the tank, or at least finishing the inside, with the more expensive polyester resins formulated for the best chemical resistance.

Tanks can be moulded translucent or semi-translucent so that the level can be seen without a fuel gauge, a useful point for simple boats. Translucent fuel tanks must not be exposed continually to light or the contents may oxidise, especially during lay-up. GRP is not a magnetic screen. Magnetic gauges can be used direct, thereby avoiding holes.

TOXICITY Despite various reports over the past years, GRP tanks are not toxic and do not taint water. However they must be well cured. If built-in they should have cured by the time the boat is finished. Tanks added later should be left before use for three weeks at room temperature, longer in cold weather. Moulding must be good and all normal precautions taken to ensure a good cure. In case of doubt paint with water tank paint, but the GRP will need keying and priming despite difficult access.

Before use the tank should be well rinsed out and given several changes of water allowing each to stand for a day or more. Sensible people would do this on any tank. Most reported contamination has been traced to other causes such as corroded fittings, sealing compound, builders' muck or foul water. Do not at once assume it must be the GRP.

BUILT-IN TANKS Obviously these must be moulded in position so the mould must be rigged up in the boat. The boat itself will form one side of the tank, perhaps two sides, or one side can be combined with a bulkhead or web floor. To form the other sides make up "shuttering" of wood or hardboard, nailed or screwed together lightly so that it can be dismantled easily. Note that the screws must be accessible from the outside, i.e. they must not be covered by the moulding. To economise in moulding materials the shuttering can be of marine ply and moulded over on both sides so that it becomes a core, or even only on the inside as a sheathing. In this case the strength of the tank will lie in the plywood surround which must be well made and framed. This method is of particular appeal to a cost-conscious amateur.

Mould the sides of the tank against the shuttering and allow generous fillets where the sides join on to the side or bottom of the moulded hull. The hull itself may need thickening and extra frames, too. Frames simply run straight through and the sides are formed around them with glass angles. Frames must be soundly moulded. If porous (as so many are) the contents will seep into the core, perhaps to emerge far away—and certainly somewhere unwanted. Diesel fuel emerging in the cabin via a saturated core would leave indelible memories. On deep tanks the cores must be solid or they may be crushed by the pressure of the contents.

Baffle plates are made in the same way by rigging up a simple shuttering and laying up the baffle plate against it. Baffle plates must be secured to the tank with good moulded fillets. The thickness of the baffle plates should be equal to the side thickness. Baffle plates will stiffen the tank, as well as preventing dangerous surges, and will tie the sides together. They are essential in any tank over 5 gallons capacity (25 l.).

The lid is made separately by laying it up on a flat surface. Cut out the hand holes, one for each space between the baffles, or one larger one over each baffle-plate to give access into two partitioned spaces, and make the hand hole covers as for the locker lids in Chapter Twenty, before fitting the lid. By using proprietary tank hatches (Henderson) or racing dinghy inspection hatches the bother of making them is saved. Well sealed hatches are more important to prevent contamination by keeping foul water and oil out than to keep fresh water in, particularly in bilge tanks. If hatches are raised muck and water are less likely to get in as the hatch is opened.

The lid can be secured by moulding over the join all round the edges (Fig. 22.1). This join carries the full pressure of the tank and the moulded covering-strip should be as thick or thicker than the sides and lid. The trimmed edges will be inside this moulded strip and therefore exposed to the water inside the tank. They should be sealed with resin or at least paint before assembly.

Mould an angle inside to join the centre of the lid to the baffles if the hand holes allow sufficient access. This will have to be done by feel. The lid is subject to much the same pressure as the sides but spans a longer unsupported length. Stiffen the side angles too, where within reach.

Another method of fastening the centre of the lid is to tap into inserts moulded into the baffle plates. A cheap way out is to embed a piece of wood and use a wood screw.

When making tanks I have found it a lot easier to make the whole lid detachable for access (Fig. 22.1). This avoids the rather fiddling job of making hand holes and covers. It requires a flange all round, but this can quite easily be made while moulding. If the space around the tank will allow it an outward turning flange is much easier because then ordinary nuts and bolts can be used. If the flange turns inwards there is all the bother of embedding strips of metal or Tufnol and tapping holes, or of embedding nuts or screws when this is practicable. It is possible to get the best of both worlds with a recessed flange. A built-in tank, however, must usually have to have at least one side with an inwards turning flange, but it might be possible to use a vertical flange particularly if the

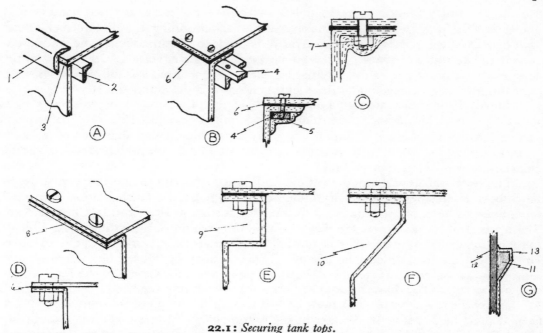

22.1: *Securing tank tops.*

A. *A lid which does not have to be removed can be permanently secured with a moulded angle,* 1. *If the hand-holes allow sufficient access it will be stronger with an inner moulded angle,* 2, *also. Unless protected by this inner angle the edges,* 3, *must be protected by resin or paint as they will be in contact with the contents.*
B. *A removable lid, supported on an inside flange, can be secured by screwing into a tapped strip,* 4, *of metal or Tufnol which is itself embedded,* 5, *under the flange. The lid must be well bedded down,* 6.
C. *A simpler method is to embed nuts,* 7, *instead of a tapped strip.*
D. *An outside flange,* 8, *makes it simpler to secure the lid. As the nuts are accessible there is no need to embed them.*
E. *To save the space required for an outside flange as in* D, *the flange can be recessed,* 9.
F. *A square recess,* 9, *will be tricky to mould as it must be moulded blind. A sloping recess,* 10, *will avoid this.*
G. *A recess will require an undercut in the mould, and prevent release. This can be avoided by lightly tacking or sticking a strip,* 11, *to the mould,* 12, *so that it will come away with the moulding,* 13, *and be released separately.*

difficult few inches of lid along the hull are made a permanent fixture. This will also bring it clear of any frames and make the construction and fitting of the lid a lot easier and probably less liable to leak too. An amateur might embed a wood batten along this edge and secure the lid with wood screws. It will not be opened very often. Again the centre of the lid must be secured to the baffle plates. Obviously a moulded attachment is impossible so it must be some form of tapped fastening.

The lid must be well bedded down with a non-tainting bedding compound as, of course, it would be on a tank made of any other material.

The upward pressure from an overfull deck filler pipe, or just from surges, is quite enough to make the tank bulge, and bulge quite ominously. This happens with steel tanks, too; and I spent many uncomfortable nights on one boat because my bunk was over a tank which bulged up when full. Lloyd's rules call for a designed head of 6 ft. above the filler pipe or tank top, whichever is the higher. Filling at tank top level instead of at deck level will reduce the pressure the tank needs to withstand and hence the cost of the tank. The water contained in the filler pipe is negligible, yet it greatly increases the pressure, typically it trebles the pressure for the very short time it is full, and on a small boat the convenience of filling at deck level is not worth the doubled cost.

Lloyd's Rules recommended a minimum thickness of 7 oz./sq. ft. of glass, say $5 \times 1\frac{1}{2}$ oz. (2·0 kg./m.²). This is heavy for a small boat and might be reduced for a well baffled tank of 5 gallons (25 l.), the sort of tank fitted singly or in pairs in a small cruiser of say 25 to 30 ft. (8–10 m.). It would be a wise precaution to make sure that the hull was of greater thickness in way of any built-in tanks.

The ends, baffles and any part of the tank in contact with the hull may give rise to hard spots. If they have double-angle fillets they will not cause much trouble on a small tank, but on a large one they may need spreading further as described in Chapter Two. The upper and lower corners are likely to have the greatest effect, as it will be difficult to round these off, but it will often be possible to terminate them at a right-angle member. For instance, the flange along the side of the boat to carry the lid can be extended along until it meets a vertical frame or bulkhead, or taper away to blend into the hull. Lower corners can be carried down to become floors or to blend into the keel.

The inside of any water-tank must be well moulded, with plenty of resin on the inner face. It must be as resistant to water as the outside of the hull, although it is often the "inside" or rough finish. Exposed fibres ("donkey's breakfast"), pinholes, cavities and resin starvation must be avoided. It is a sound idea to finish with several coats of a good resin, preferably a chemically resistant one. A layer of surfacing gauze will hold a thick layer of resin and ensure that the surface is resin-rich. Filled resins should be avoided.

Proper pipe fittings are essential. All the remarks on skin fittings (pages 246–248) apply to tank fittings, too. It is not good enough to bond in the fittings or pipes; they must be properly screwed or bolted on and well bedded down (Fig. 22.2).

Quite often it will be impossible to put in the fitting after the tank is moulded because of its position. In that case it will have to be put in position before the tank is moulded and the tank moulded around it. Nevertheless, it must be bolted in afterwards. Fill the threads with putty or soap so that they can be cleared after moulding. A bolted flange will be easier to fit than a screwed one.

Built-in water and fuel tanks should not be in direct contact, separated only by a single panel. Any seepage, flaw or pinhole will mix fuel and water. Always separate them by a double partition so that mixing can only occur in the less likely event of seepage through both partitions simultaneously (Fig. 22.3). Note that a frame should not link tanks. Most have waterways and may be porous enough to form an interconnection.

SEPARATE TANKS　The mould for a separate moulded tank is easily knocked up from hardboard or plywood and can be a male or female one Fig. 22.4. Female moulds are easier to make and release, male moulds give a better inside surface. The lid is made separately in the same way as for the built-in tank and it is attached in the same way.

It is impracticable to knock up a mould for a tank that is anything more than a rough approximation to the shape required, just as a steel tank is only an approximation of the shape and would be prohibitively costly if it was anything else. But with a moulded

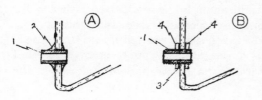

22.2: *Pipe fittings.*

A. **Not recommended.** *An embedded pipe, 1, secured by moulding into the tank, 2, is very difficult to keep water-tight, and impossible if it is a polythene pipe.*
B. *Proprietary screwed pipe fittings, secured by nuts, 4, and well bedded down, 3, can be made really leakproof and reliable, and can be of metal or polythene.*

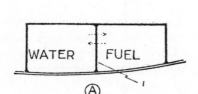
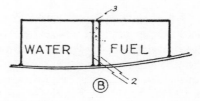

22.3: *Separating built-in water and fuel tanks.*

A. **Not recommended.** *Single partition between water and fuel tanks. Any seepage or flaw will allow fuel and water to mix.*
B. *Double partition, 2, reduces the risk of mixing. If draining to the bilges, 3, it is very unlikely that a sufficient head will ever build up in the space to seep back into either tank.*

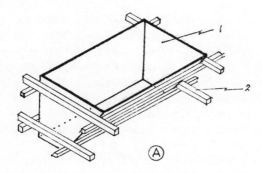
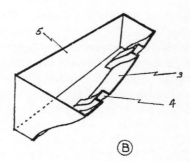

22.4: *Simple mould for a tank.*

A. *Cut-out panels of hardboard, 1, to give the approximate shape and secure in a simple knock-apart frame, 2.*
B. *Close-fitting tank. Mould side, 3, against the side of the boat so that it conforms exactly to shape including recesses for frames, 4.*
Make up the mould for the other simple side panels, 5, as in (A), using the shaped side to close the mould.

tank it is quite possible to mould any difficult side actually on the boat so that it fits exactly not only to the curve of the hull but around and over all frames and stringers too. Obviously the side of the boat must be prepared for release. After moulding, this side is taken out of the boat and joined to the other sides of the tank, or used to form one side of the mould. This allows the tank to make as good use of space as a built-in tank and at the same time to be removable like a separate tank.

On a very small cruiser it is possible to use this method to make close fitting portable containers rather than tanks, which are taken out for filling (or for use), but which stow away securely and in the minimum space.

Most of these tanks are equally suitable for tanks in wooden boats, provided an air-gap is left between the tank and the wooden hull; in fact many of the ideas spring from replacement tanks which I have made or designed for wooden boats.

FUEL TANKS　GRP fuel tanks are approved by Lloyds subject to reasonable safeguards and construction. In the U.S.A., N.F.P.A. standards do not specifically exclude non-metallic tanks but lay down conditions which GRP cannot meet. Integral tanks are also not approved. American regulations are very strict and comprehensive. Boatbuilders looking to the American market, or indeed to the international market, should study them.

Fuel tanks should be heavier than water tanks (Lloyd's minimum 10 oz. glass per sq. ft., say $7 \times 1\frac{1}{2}$ oz. ($3 \cdot 0$ kg./m.^{2})), and greater precautions are needed against leakage. The detachable lid is not recommended, so the lid must be attached permanently by moulding over the join. Inspection plates should be reduced to the minimum; American practice does not allow any inspection plates at all. This is more practicable on a moulded tank than on a steel tank because if access is ever required the tank can be cut away and remoulded without great difficulty.

The design and installation should not allow fuel and muck to lodge on top or around the tank or to saturate adjoining materials and timber. (Diesel fuel in particular can creep along and through wood to a remarkable extent.) The top should be domed, or, if flat, have no upturned flange or projection to trap fuel. The recommended practice in America is for all pipes and gauges to enter from the top of the tank with no pipes or openings of any kind on the bottom or sides. This rules out a simple gravity feed but it will reduce fuel drips and leaks from a bad connection or damaged pipe and is a sound safety precaution.

Fire-resisting paints are suggested for the outside of fuel tanks, particularly built-in tanks. Some of these foam up when heated to form an insulating barrier. Where possible fuel tanks should be moulded with self-extinguishing resins, and there is a lot to be said for having all parts of the boat in the vicinity moulded with self-extinguishing resins also. Good use, however, can be made of these fire-resisting paints.

Tanks must have vent pipes discharging outboard and fitted with flame traps. Spaces containing fuel tanks must be properly ventilated.

The insides of all fuel tanks must be very well moulded, with ample resin on the inner face and a well covered layer of surfacing gauze to give a resin-rich finish. This resin should be a high quality, chemically resistant resin, not ordinary marine quality.

A well moulded tank of adequate thickness will not be vapour permeable, i.e. fuel will not evaporate as it does in a polythene fuel can. Moreover, apart from the lid, it is essentially a one-piece construction with no joins which might be potential trouble spots. The tank can, in fact, be made entirely one-piece by moulding it with a separate body and lid, but to only half the final thickness, less if practicable. The lid is attached by moulding over the join and then the tank is built up to the full thickness by moulding over the entire tank, lid and all. Apart from the initial lid-to-body join, which should be reinforced with a moulded angle of thickness at least equal to the rest of the tank, this will make a seamless tank of uniform strength all over. The baffles, of course, must be put in before the lid is sealed on, and will help to provide the stiffness for handling.

Tanks must be very firmly secured, preferably with straps. Trouble has been experienced with moulded lugs or inserts breaking adrift under rough or racing conditions, and causing fires. This must be made impossible.

EARTHING AND BONDING All metal parts connected with the engine, but particularly all parts of the fuel system, must be electrically bonded together and earthed. Bonding means connecting the parts with wire or conductive pipe so that they are maintained at the same potential. When insulated by plastics pipe and GRP hull or tank, static charges can build up and cause sparks.

Metal and metal braided pipes bond fittings automatically. So does conductive plastics pipe, but it is essential to check the markings on this to be sure. Plain plastic pipe does not do this. However, it is possible for the braiding to get chafed. The filler pipe on the fuel tank, and the deck filler plate, can easily be overlooked because they are separate from the main run of piping, but it is most important that these are properly earthed. Every year boats with petrol engines are burnt out because of fires started by a spark between the filling nozzle or can to the filler pipe when refuelling. The correct procedure when refuelling is to touch the filling nozzle or lip of the can against the metal filler pipe to neutralise static charges before starting to fill, and to keep it in contact while filling. Note that a conductive plastics pipe will not earth currents due to electrical faults.

The damper British atmosphere does not often allow appreciable static charges to accumulate but all the same there are enough dry days to warrant precautions, and the procedure described above when filling should always be adopted. In other parts of the world, particularly on inland lakes and reservoirs in very dry climates, or during a rainless season, the risk of sparks from static electricity must be taken seriously.

The whole system should be earthed by connecting it to a metal plate fixed to the outside of the hull, well below the water-line. For normal purposes this should be a plate or strip with an area of about 36 sq. in.; if there is a lot of radio equipment on board it should be about 12 sq. ft. It is much more satisfactory to earth to a proper plate and not to skin fittings, propeller shaft or keel bolts, as this can lead to rapid corrosion of those parts due to stray electric currents causing electrolysis. However, a non-essential piece of metal, such as a keel band, could well be used.

It is common practice to connect the bonding system to one side of the battery. The British trend is to earth the positive, the American to earth the negative. On a car with a largely steel body it is claimed that earthing the positive reduces the destructive effects of corrosion. Which is correct on a boat should depend on what vital materials are being used under water, but in practice is dictated by the electrical equipment available.

Earthing one side of the supply is usually necessary because most dynamos and starters follow car practice and use the metal frame for the return path. There is much less risk of trouble from corrosion due to stray currents if the electrical supply can be kept floating,

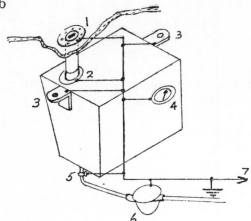

22.5: *Bonding the fuel supply.*

All metal work associated with the fuel supply must be electrically bonded. With non-metallic tank and pipes bonding must be done independently. Parts which need to be bonded are: 1, deck filler (the most important single item); 2, filler pipe; 3, fixing lugs or straps; 4, fuel gauge; 5, cock; 6, filter; 7, engine.

i.e. with neither side earthed at all. Electronic equipment may demand that the supply is earthed, but even so this can often be done through a condenser.

Bonding wires must not be used for carrying current and must be separate from any current-carrying earth return wire.

SKIN FITTINGS It sounds simple to mould skin fittings into the hull so that there are no bolts to worry about, or to mould in simple pipes and avoid the cost of expensive skin fittings altogether. Unfortunately it does not work out like that. It is difficult to get a good bond to brass and almost impossible to polythene. The bond may seem good initially but breaks away later due to vibration or twisting of the pipe during installation.

If brass fittings *must* be bonded-in coat the brass first with epoxy to insulate the polyester from poisoning by the brass. Epoxy also bonds better. There are special polyester resins for bonding to PVC, but trial first is essential. They only work with certain kinds of PVC, usually well plasticised. Short lengths of GRP tube can be embedded safely and are simply made. Do not try to embed polythene, polypropylene, nylon or stainless steel. Wherever possible tubes and fittings should have lugs or be shaped to prevent twisting.

It is very much better to stick to conventional screwed or bolted skin fittings (Fig. 22.6). If well bedded down these will not leak and the joint can be inspected at any time. They can also be replaced if anything goes wrong or if a larger or improved pattern is wanted. Fibreglass boats will last indefinitely, provided they can be kept up to date and worn or obsolete parts renewed. This will include a change of engine. Some moulders claim their boats are immortal and turn out good mouldings which have every chance of success—but make no provision for the renewal of parts which are obviously expendable or obsolescent. It is no good being only half immortal.

The kind of skin fitting with a threaded stem secured with one large nut is more secure than the more common kind with a flange which is bolted on. Bolts can corrode—and usually do—but a threaded fitting will need to be in a very bad way before it is liable to come adrift.

The hull must be thickened in way of any skin fitting. A large hole weakens the hull, of course, but in addition skin fittings and pipes can get kicked and trodden on, particularly when the boat is laid up with the floorboards lifted as is usual practice. Any sized

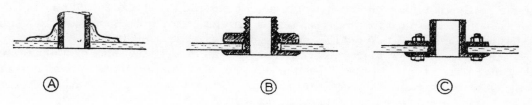

22.6: *Skin fittings.*

A. **Not Recommended.** *An embedded pipe will often leak and relies only on the bonding to the metal or plastic pipe. It cannot be removed or replaced.*
B. *A proprietary fitting secured with a large nut has a generous and well-distributed area of contact. It can be well bedded down and removed as often as required.*
C. *Another method, similar to* (B), *using through-bolted flange.*

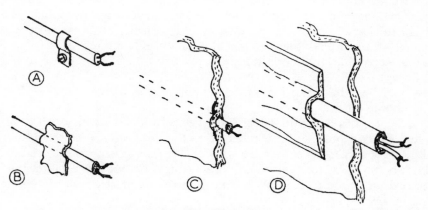

22.7: *Securing electric cables.*

A. *Cables can be secured with clips and self-tapping screws to any part of the moulding which does not form the outer skin, e.g. bulkheads, top-hat frames, etc.*
B. *Tacking with a small piece of "wet" mat will hold a cable anywhere, even on a thin outer skin.*
C. *On a production boat where the wiring requirements are well known, a cable harness can be moulded in when laying up the hull. However, this makes repair impossible.*
D. *On better-class boats, conduit can be embedded. With ingenuity the conduit can form the core for top-hat stiffeners.*

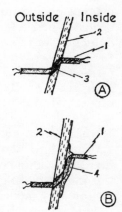

22.8: *Passing a wire through a coaming.*

A. *Drill a hole through the coaming, 2, so that the wire, 1, runs uphill from outside to inside. Seal with a flexible weather-resistant stealing compound, 3.*
B. *A better method which is almost completely watertight is to run the wire, 1, uphill for a short distance inside the coaming, 2, and embed this part, 4.*

fitting may receive the B.F.I. technique (politely described as Brute Force and Ignorance), and a good hammering; the fitting will usually withstand this if it is a good one, but the hull will not unless such treatment is foreseen. For this reason it is a sound idea to mount skin fittings on a block to spread the strain.

All openings below water must have sea cocks no matter how small or unimportant they may seem. This is a very important objection to moulding pipes straight into the hull. Pipes can be easily damaged, especially modern plastics piping. So much is installed in an extremely casual, indeed dangerous, manner. Note that an opening normally above water may actually be under water for prolonged periods, e.g. when heeled or due to the wave pattern at speed, and also, which can be important, once a considerable amount of water has got below. All fittings must be installed with just as much regard to electrolytic action as with other boats. In this modern plastics fittings have the advantage, but everything must be of good quality and suitable for sea water (even river craft may get to the coast). Some domestic plumbing fittings are neither strong nor durable enough for boats.

Skin fittings are often embedded with the nuts moulded over under the mistaken impression that this will prevent leaks. It does not. It only makes it harder to do anything about it if there is one. The embedding GRP is often light and porous (especially where it is done under uncomfortable conditions) and the bond to brass is seldom good or permanent enough to prevent seepage. Sea cocks should be mounted in the open on well bedded wooden pads, or thickened moulding. All nuts should be accessible for inspection, tightening or replacement. Embedding hides trouble: it does not prevent it.

Sea cocks should be accessible, the more accessible the better. They are there to be used—and used in a hurry! Needless to say every sea cock must be in working order and maintained so. There may be little time to look for a hammer or spanner—or like the proverbial plumber, go home for one.

On high performance yachts skin fittings can be recessed and faired in so that the bottom is as smooth and flush as possible. This means that the positions are planned and known before moulding. It is easy to place wooden discs on the mould to form recesses, so that the layout need not be the same for every boat. Skin fittings can be recessed later but this means cutting into the moulding, perhaps to full depth, and must be amply compensated by moulding inside.

More good boats sink through defective plumbing than through shipwreck and storm. They do not hit the headlines because they commonly sink on their moorings and are salvaged. The boat may not be a spectacular total loss, but much equipment will be ruined and insurance will never cover the lot.

PLUMBING More boats sink through defective plumbing than through shipwreck or storm. They may not be a headline-hitting spectacular total loss if they sink or nearly sink at moorings and are salvaged, but nevertheless much equipment and personal possessions will be ruined.

In the highest quality work plumbing will be in good copper or stainless steel throughout, with proper fittings. This, however, is rare even below the waterline and nearly all plumbing is in plastics pipe secured with clips. Pipes must be of good quality, preferably heavy-gauge PVC or fabric reinforced hose. Avoid cheap garden hose and thin-gauge polythene pipe. It is vital that the normal push-on joints are secured by rustless stainless steel, screw tightened clips. Far too many pipes are secured by very rusty ordinary steel clips—or no clips at all. Often as not these are under water, unprotected from damage and attached to sea cocks which cannot be shut! The remarkable thing is that more boats do not sink.

Pipes should be protected from physical damage. They should not run through lockers or spaces where this can happen. In particular there should be no risk of them being pulled off fittings, as can happen only too easily. Long runs should be secured with clips. There must be no risk of damage from heat. Avoid exhaust pipes, engines, galley stoves, etc., bearing in mind the probability of overheating some day and the risk of engine or galley fires.

Plastics pipes soften under heat. A pipe that is firm and seems adequately supported can become flexible and sag when the engine compartment is at working temperature, especially in hot climates. In extreme cases the pipe could touch moving parts or hot metal and rupture under water. Repeated heating will cause creep. In cold weather plastics pipes can become hard and brittle, and prone to damage from vibration and flexing. While unlikely to be a problem on yachts this can be serious on working or fishing boats.

W.C. Opinions on this item of equipment vary enormously. For some it is more important even than the engine or sails, for others, it is unwanted at any price. However, these days only the most Spartan owners seem bold enough to sail without one.

Installation presents few special problems. A firm mounting is important as the effort of working the pump, particularly when it is stiff or blocked, will exert a large strain on the closely spaced fixing screws. Also it is often installed in parts of the boat where weight-lessness, otherwise described as a need to hang on like grim death, may be experienced in rough seas.

It should be mounted on a stout block, embedded or well secured by matted in angle fillets in the same way as engine bearers. A frame of metal or moulded angles to which it could be bolted would be a superior way of mounting.

The plumbing is little different from that in any other boat. There is the same need for sound workmanship and common sense. All pipes must be fitted with sea cocks, and, as wise skippers like them closed when not in use, they must be readily accessible, preferably in the open and not boxed in or hidden under tight floorboards. Note that the "Ballhead" which mounts and discharges straight through the side cannot be shut off. Plastics soil pipes seem universal. Lead is not consistent with the light weight of GRP.

The position of the device needs to be chosen with care and is probably harder to fit in than any other item on the boat. Space is needed, not only to sit but to stand—in so far as it is possible to stand at all in a small boat. Yet privacy requires it to be tucked away in a corner. Moreover mere privacy from view is not enough. Good ventilation is very important and a thin bulkhead or curtain is a poor acoustic screen.

Headroom is usually obtained either by placing it in the main accommodation amidships, or under the forehatch in the fo'c'sle. Amidships is satisfactory on a large boat but difficult to screen on a small one without interfering seriously with pleasanter parts of the accommodation; under the forehatch is likely to be very cramped and "sick making" when the hatch is closed at sea, while in harbour it is perfectly clear to every passer-by why a head with a rapt expression is sticking out of the forehatch.

My own opinion is that a W.C. is far too often fitted in a small cruiser as a matter of course, as a sales gimmick or status symbol, without ever thinking whether the boat would be better without it. There is an impression that such a fitting is absolutely vital. It is not, and it is one piece of equipment which would be much better as an optional extra on any boat under 30 ft. (10 m.), at least.

An owner, whether a bachelor or not, who sails alone or normally with a male crew will find that a bucket which can be used anywhere from the fo'c'sle to cockpit, even on deck (when out of sight of land or spectators), and stowed away in a locker when not in use is a much pleasanter shipmate. Some keep a special bucket for the purpose, others use the one bucket for everything. It may be some embarrassment in very crowded or fashionable harbours. When the owner marries there will be a firm demand for improved mod. cons.—and firmer demands for prams, houses and other things incompatible with treasured boats. Unfortunately the absence of a W.C. is reflected in the second hand price. The problem becomes really acute in the small family cruiser, and if the W.C. is of such overwhelming importance, as so often it is, the family would do better to stay at a seaside boarding house. Many small boats are floating W.C.s equipped with sails or engine—a well-known outspoken yachtsman's description not mine.

Inland waterways mostly require a chemical toilet, holding tank or chlorinator according to local byelaws. Simple chemical toilets are cheap. They must be firmly secured and have a lid which seals (with a place to stow it), keeping not only the contents in but the smell too. Inland waters can be quite lively. Expensive recirculating types have now become available.

Recent byelaws in Britain, spurred by local authorities' concern at the growth of urban yachting and crowded yacht basins, demand holding tanks which can be emptied only at sea or pumped into shore sewers (which usually go straight into the sea anyway). Typical regulations require all yachts entering a British yacht basin to seal their W.C.s or discharges. Ready means for doing this should be provided on all boats.

Holding tanks are one more domestic necessity to be squeezed into an ever smaller space. They need not be close to the W.C. and can be moulded in like water tanks. Unless a pump is used they must be lower than the W.C. This limits the position in a small cruiser. Chlorinator tanks should not be of polyester GRP although they could be epoxy. It would be unwise to use the hull. Polyester resins will be attacked by the chemicals used in a lot shorter time than the life of the boat. The same applies to holding tanks if chemicals are used.

Design a space for a W.C. but do not fit one as standard on a small cruiser just for the sake of having one; only if the boat is of appropriate size for it to be done properly and unobtrusively. Preferably design more than one alternative place. There is no one solution that will satisfy more than a proportion of owners and their families. The best position will depend far more on what the boat is used for than on the boat itself. In the cramped surroundings of a small cruiser many people will prefer its room to its company.

ELECTRICAL INSTALLATION   The electrical installation on a moulded boat is basically similar to that on any other boat, and good practice is just as important.

Securing wires may be a difficulty because clips cannot be nailed at random into the hull. Wires should be run along woodwork or frames using wood screws and conventional clips, but, where the moulding is thick enough, or hollow, self-tapping screws can be used to secure the clips, e.g. along the thick overlapping angles of a frame or bulkhead, or into a top-hat section stiffener (Fig. 22.7). Self-tapping screws into the hull skin are not recommended even if thick enough because the pilot hole is likely to go right through even if the screw does not. (This applies, of course, to any thin-skinned boat.)

Wires can be glued on, fixed by double coated pads or held temporarily by PVC adhesive tape. They can be "tacked" on with small pieces of "wet" mat. Extending this, the whole wiring can be embedded during moulding or later. GRP is a good insulator.

Replacement would be a problem as the wires are fixed there for ever. In case of failure the only solution would be to embed a further run of wiring. However, if stranded wire is used of adequate capacity and the installation is properly protected, renewal should never be necessary as far as the electrical side is concerned. However, physical damage to the moulding cannot be ruled out. It is important that the circuits are properly fused and of adequate rating. Overheating would cause a fire.

On a larger boat, conduit, either metal or plastic, could be embedded and the wires inserted later while fitting out. The position of the fittings, however, needs to be known beforehand. Conduit could be used to form the core of top-hat sections where the run is suitable.

Wiring should not be run through the bilges, even where it is the only clear place to run it, because of the danger of fire from gas or petrol, or damage to the wire or connections from damp. With the unpredictable growth of electronics and electrics, boats should be built with service ducts to simplify initial fitting and future additions. Detailed planning is all very well, but owners are individuals. Each owner will have his own ideas and fresh gadgets to chose from. Designers, like bureaucrats, like to force owners into a standard mould for production convenience.

Ropes and chains can chafe wires on deck; wires to pulpit lights are particularly vulnerable.

The choice of wiring is limited. Yacht wiring requires thickish wire to reduce voltage drop yet it needs little insulation because voltage is low. This is the opposite of mains wiring. Car wiring is single core because an earth return is universal. Table 22.1 shows maximum length of run (go and return) for common domestic wiring and shows the superiority of a 12-volt system. The higher temperature ratings should be respected. Engine compartments and deckheads under tropical sun can easily exceed the lower temperature and even the higher.

It is generally easier to mount fittings on woodwork or bulkheads. Where they must be attached to the inside of the GRP glue or embed blocks and screw to these. On inside mouldings they can be through-bolted. Self-tapping screws are permissible too. Few neat, marine quality, surface mounting switches are available. The usual practice is to make up switch panels.

Wires passing through the moulding or bulkheads should be sealed in with "wet" mat or sealing compound. Ideally all cable outlets through the deck or hull should be done with watertight plugs and sockets, e.g. for navigation lights or searchlight. Proper watertight sockets are expensive. On a small boat a satisfactory lead out can be made by drilling a hole through the cabin sides so that the hole runs downwards and outwards, i.e. incoming water must run uphill (Fig. 22.8).

Dry batteries can be used on a very small boat where the lights are not used for prolonged periods; two 6-volt "Powerlite" batteries connected in series can last a season, and it should be possible to stow these away on the smallest of pocket cruisers.

Motor cycle batteries are light enough to take ashore easily for recharging and are

Table 22.1

Length of Run for 5 per cent Voltage Drop

Type of wire	Current rating (Note 1)	Car side light 6v., 1A. 6 watt ft.	m.	Car side light 12v., 0·5A. 6 watt ft.	m.	Radio or cycle lamp 6v., 0·3A. 1·8 watt ft.	m.	Radio or cycle lamp 12v., 0·15A. 1·8 watt ft.	m.	Torch bulb 3·5v., 0·3A. 1 watt ft.	m.
3A. twin flex 16/·20 mm. (domestic lighting flex)	3	6	1·8	24	7	20	6	80	24	12	3·5
6A. flex 24/·20 mm. (small power, TV, etc.)	6	9	2·7	36	11	29	9	116	36	17	5·2
15A. flex 30/·25 mm. (domestic power, fires)	15	16	4·9	64	19	53	16	215	64	30	9·4
flat twin 1·0 mm. (house lighting)	12	12	3·5	48	14	40	13	160	48	24	7·0
flat twin 2·5 mm. (house power, ring main)	21	31	9·3	124	37	104	31	408	124	60	18·0

Note 1. Temperature factors:

Ambient temperature	°F.	95	104	113	122	131
Ambient temperature	°C.	35	40	45	50	55
% current rating	%	96	92	87	71	50

Note 2: Length of run is "go and return".

another good idea for a small boat, especially an engineless one, where the space and weight of a car battery would be an embarrassment. It is surprising, however, how long a car battery will last when only used for lights, especially if the main cabin lighting is by oil. A "dud" car battery will supply a light load for years after it is no longer able to turn a self-starter.

BATTERY STOWAGE GRP is unaffected by battery acid and will not become saturated by it. However, it is always as well to keep accumulator acid under control because other materials, woodwork, clothes, etc., can be damaged by it.

The best stowage for a battery is in a moulded watertight box so that any spillage is kept within the box. There should be a reasonable space around the battery or it will be difficult to get it in and out. A lid is not essential but it does prevent anything metallic falling across the terminals, which could cause a fire as well as running down the battery.

The box can be moulded in as part of the boat or made like built-in tanks. It needs to be fastened to the boat securely, as a heavy battery can soon tear itself adrift. The battery itself must always be firmly clamped down.

STARTING Separate supplies for lighting and engine are thoroughly recommended even on small boats. This allows the lighting, radio and electrical auxiliaries to be used to the limit in harbour without worrying about running down the starting batteries. If the engine has no hand-starting, separate supplies are virtually essential. Most yacht petrol engines up to moderate size can be turned by hand, if it is really essential, and if there is provision for it and room to swing the handle, but only the very smallest diesel engine can be turned over by an average man working in the average cramped position, even if hand-starting is provided at all.

Various forms of impulse-starting are available but are rather too expensive just for stand-by use. A friend with a heavy old auxiliary yacht used to wrap the end of the main sheet round the starting pulley and gybe all standing. It was all right as long as he had plenty of sea room but required rather tricky seamanship when leaving his mooring.

ACCESS There must be ready access for inspection or repair to the engine and everything connected with it, including the tanks, the whole run of the fuel pipes, exhaust system and cooling. The whole run of the LP-gas line must also be accessible, and all pipes ending under water. Every sea cock must be within quick and easy reach bearing in mind that some folk have arms that are short, fat or both, and they do not like being burnt or mangled in the process.

Every piece of equipment may have to be repaired, removed or replaced and it must be possible to do this without cutting the boat to pieces. Production convenience increasingly tends to install equipment before the major assemblies are brought together, making replacement impossible. This may make sense for production, but which is the more important, production convenience or the needs of the owners in the years ahead? New boats should not go wrong but most of them do—some very wrong—and the troubles are mostly with equipment and fittings.

GAS Bottled LP-gas must be installed strictly in accordance with the codes of practice. National codes vary in strictness. For export the highest standards are essential. Piping must be in approved copper with as few joints as possible, secured at frequent intervals to prevent any movement or pulling and protected by sleeves through bulkheads and partitions. It must be readily accessible throughout its length and nowhere boxed in, or hidden behind panels or mouldings. It must not run through the bilges. Butyl, neoprene and nylon are not approved except for short flexible connections to the regulator or appliance and these *must* be proper gas hose.

The best modern practice puts the cylinder in a separate locker draining outboard above the waterline and with no opening into the boat. If it has to be pierced for the pipe this must be high up, well above the drain. Gas lockers are usually in the cockpit well away from the galley. Closing the tap after use is a nuisance and probably forgotten or funked if wet and cold outside. A tap inboard at the end of the copper pipe is an alternative which is not so safe, but is more likely to be used. The gas locker should not be used for any other stowage, especially ropes, etc., which could catch the pipe.

Gas cylinders must be well secured to prevent all movement. This is seldom done firmly enough if at all. The best method is close-fitting chocks to hold the base and a clamp or tiedown to hold the cylinder firmly in position and prevent wobbling or vibration which may damage the regulator or fatigue the pipe. Cylinders can get thrown out of chocks when the going gets rough, and chocks alone do not prevent wobbling. Equally good stowage is essential for spare cylinders, full or empty, and the locker should accommodate at least two cylinders of the largest size likely to be used. To allow the cylinder to rattle around the locker is asking for disaster. There should be versatility to allow different sizes of cylinder according to local availability; e.g. Gaz is available in most European countries but Calor cylinders are not.

Designers should remember too that some prudent owners will not have LP-gas aboard at any price. Alternative cooking arrangements are essential, e.g. paraffin or alcohol but never petrol. Versatility is more important than a very ingenious, complex, detailed galley moulding which will only take one stove—a gas stove. Neither should designers dictate that owners shall *not* have gas. Owners may demand gimbals too.

LIGHTNING　　Lightning strike on a boat is rare but if it does happen it is dangerous. When a thunderstorm is overhead statistics do little to allay fears. Opinions differ on whether a lightning protector works by deflecting a strike elsewhere or conducting it harmlessly away. There is probably truth in both, but there is a difference between the situation of a boat's mast which is always low and near the ground, and a tall structure projecting into or near the thundercloud. Theory tends to be based on the latter. Lightning is highly capricious: it strikes largely where it will, jumps anywhere, takes short cuts of feet or miles, and is very nasty stuff to have around. Controlling it, if it does come, is a chancy business especially as it will be at very close quarters. Information is still scanty as to why lightning will strike one low object in preference to another. It will strike a low tree as well as a high one, and down into a valley as well as high ground.

The B.I.A. recommend that an earthed mast or earthed metal antenna (but not GRP) will give a high degree of immunity within a cone 60° each side of the vertical. Metal masts, rigging, tracks and fittings should be permanently bonded and earthed during a storm. Shackles on the earthing wire should be bridged. Wood is sufficiently conductive to provide electrostatic earthing for deflection but not to act as a conductor. The shroud plates on wooden boats are usually external and end near the water so the leakage path is short. But GRP is a good insulator (its original purpose: boats came much later) and shroud plates are commonly well inboard. The leakage path and even a wet path is much longer. Earthing therefore is more important. It can be a permanent heavy gauge metal strip or a wire thrown overboard in a storm. A strip from the forestay can be unobtrusive and is comfortably clear of the cockpit. Remember that lightning also strikes in winter when the boat may be laid up ashore, and when it may be aground.

In my view earthing should always be external, not, as is often recommended, through the cabin to a keel bolt or earthing plate. Inside the cabin is the very last place anyone should want lightning. Also this bypasses the safety of the Faraday cage effect of a wet hull. There seems little evidence that unearthed metal masts are less likely to be struck. Once the rain starts they will be earthed effectively anyway, but will not be safe conductors unless properly bonded.

The prevention theory is more comforting, but make sure of a conductor as well. Even a conductor may not prevent damage. The terrific current surge produces powerful mechanical forces and the induced current can burn out internal wiring and electronics even with no direct connection. Anyone touching or near a wire is in danger, and no theorist has yet explained how to keep away from wires in a small sailing boat.

CHAPTER TWENTY-THREE

Maintenance of GRP Boats

THE NEED FOR MAINTENANCE Traditionally yachts are smart. GRP yachts are very smart when new and it is assumed that owners want them to remain so. Whatever the demerits of annual painting, it keeps a wooden yacht smart for fifty years. A GRP yacht should last as long and at any stage look as well. In practice this is not so. The poor thing gets progressively more scratched and more weathered until, at a very early age compared with a wooden boat, it looks scruffy and decrepit despite being still perfectly good structurally. A smart yacht is a painted yacht. Except for the very few years initial no-painting holiday, this applies to GRP too.

A GRP boat is a low maintenance boat, but there is no such thing as a "no maintenance" boat, and never has been or will be. Lives depend on properly maintained engines, sails, rigging and ancillaries as well as on a sound hull. Boats in coastal waters need regular antifouling. GRP itself amply repays a little maintenance with a better finish retained longer and higher resale value. Appearance is less important with working boats but they still need prompt repair and protection against the weather. GRP will not rot if neglected like wood, but it can decay.

TIME SCALE The initial gloss should last with no maintenance for two or three years. This may be considered the initial "no maintenance" holiday, although what is done—or not done—will have an important effect in later years. After five years the boat will have a dull finish and the colour will have faded, although probably only noticeably beside a new boat. After about seven years without maintenance the appearance will no longer be acceptable to the average owner and at ten the boat will look dingy and old, and cry out for paint to hide its shame.

These age figures are vague: the spread can be very wide. A good boat might go ten years or more. A poor gel coat will be badly faded and dull after only two years. Generally wear and tear will predominate, the cumulative annual crop of scratches will have a greater influence than the weather. Even the best boat, if carelessly handled, can look very poor after a year or two.

It is common for boats to be sold after two or three years. For first owners who sell so soon, GRP may indeed appear to be a "no maintenance" material. But future owners pay for it because maintenance should start from the beginning.

To be ever buying new is the philosophy of our profligate age. We greedily grab the Earth's very limited supply of materials for ourselves with no thought for those who come after. *They* too will need a share for their very existence. All *we* do for them is ensure that they will be too many. How much is it right for a man to consume in one lifetime? Wood can be produced indefinitely but GRP comes from oil which is irreplaceable, exhaustible, and being devoured at a rate which alarms far-seeing people. People must live in this world long, long after we have gone.

A basic principle of farming is good husbandry, maintaining the productivity of the land. It is mankind's loss that this elementary principle on a wider, world scale is scorned.

WEATHERING   Nothing lasts for ever. Weather, which wears down mountains, will soon dull the gloss on GRP. Weathering is a slow process which etches and erodes the surface making it rough, pitted and vulnerable to accelerated attack. Eventually the gel coat becomes porous and no longer protects the structural GRP beneath. Normally this takes many years but can occur in only a few years if the gel coat is poor. Weather is the main factor causing deterioration. Maintenance should protect the gel coat from the weather.

Fading will be most noticeable on coloured boats, especially dark blue and green, and least objectionable as yellowing of whites. There are hundreds of shades of "white." At what stage one calls it yellow or grey is largely personal opinion influenced by comparison with a "whiter-than-white" boat alongside. But that boat may be whiter than yours ever was. Only comparison with the shade when new is fair, and this is usually impracticable.

LAYING UP   The boat must be protected from winter weather by putting it under cover or applying a protective coating. Undercover storage is ideal but expensive. There is an old saying, "The more expensive the storage, the more the roof leaks." Better to be in the open than under a leak.

In the open a well fitting cover is the best protection. It should extend well down the sides. Use a woven material for choice. Plastics sheet tends to sweat. The ends should be open for ventilation, but prevent the rain driving in. Elaborate lashings are a curse and discourage inspection and work—and proper relashing. Yet it must not flap for a flapping cover will leave a myriad of scratches in a gale.

If no cover is used protect the GRP with thick polish. Decks, cabin tops and cockpit should be covered as well as topsides. Strippable coatings can be used but check first that they strip from GRP: some do not. Before polishing wash down well and clean off oil stains. Look for and fill cracks and damage, especially anything which may hold water or ice, or which could allow water to seep below.

Boats stored ashore must be well supported. Shores must not be tight or creep can lead to permanent distortion. Check regularly. On soft ground the keel may sink throwing weight on the shores like a man on crutches. Shores should be at bulkheads or frames. Check by tapping. Give the yard specific instructions about this: few appreciate the need. A trailer or cradle must also support the boat properly. Chocks should again be at frames. Long overhangs must be supported to avoid hogging and prevent tipping, especially with a heavy motor aft. Remove outboards from the transom.

It is generally thought that a GRP boat can be laid up afloat without harm. This is not true. GRP very slowly absorbs water leading to osmotic water blisters on the bottom. These are common at ten years if kept afloat continually, especially in fresh water. However, this is a slow process. Little harm will come to a sound boat if left afloat for some years, but it is recommended that at intervals, say five years, the boat is laid up ashore to dry out. Over the years this may prevent the mean level of absorption reaching harmful proportions. Generalisation is impossible. Much depends on the boat's quality, whether it is in salt water or fresh, and the pigmentation. This view is based on survey experience but it is disputed, notably by Tylers. Certainly I would expect least with good quality, unpigmented moulding, but I would not expect any boat to be quite immune.

Boats afloat must be protected from ice. A GRP hull is thin. No one knows what a winter will bring. Once a freeze-up starts it is too late to haul out. Even in Britain ice floes sweep down with the tide of current in moderate winters. Ice can form internally where water has collected in pockets. This is serious in cold climates. Leave no known pockets and drain pipes. Possible places are within keels, behind linings and inside embedding.

Leave plenty of ventilation. There is generally a lot of wood below with little attention paid to avoiding closed spaces or pockets of stale air. It is common to leave gear aboard. This is feasible as a GRP boat is drier than most stores. Mildew can grow on Terylene sails and GRP deckheads, not on the material itself but on the accumulation of dust, dirt, cooking smells or hand stains on it. Ventilation will reduce condensation.

FITTING OUT   Fitting out the GRP side consists of cleaning, making good damage and scratches which were not seen or attended to when laying up, and then polishing. The bottom will need antifouling and woodwork should be varnished or oiled. Both can be done later at leisure. The rest is the same as for any other boat. Even with this amount of maintenance a GRP boat should be afloat at about the time the others start painting.

CLEANING   The state of the gel coat is critical. A smooth, polished gel coat sheds dirt and is easily cleaned. A rough, porous, weathered gel coat marks easily, soaks up stains and is impossible to keep clean. As often happens, maintenance saves maintenance.

Some gel coats appear smooth and glossy but are difficult to keep clean. This can be due to microscratches, multiple tiny scratches invisible to a naked eye, which when dirty look like a dirty stain. Harsh cleaners will cause microscratches all over; so will scourers, including nylon, and even grit on a sponge. Wear or rubbing can leave patches.

Most dirt can be washed off with water, fresh or salt, and a soft cloth or sponge. Cleaners must be approved types (groups A or B). Unapproved or wrongly used cleaners can damage the gel coat and cause crazing, roughness or accelerated weathering.

Group A: Approved cleaners. Subject to safety these may be used hot as well as cold, but should not be hotter than one's hand can stand, about 110° F. (45° C.).

Fresh water   salt water
Any domestic detergent   mild industrial detergents and surfactants (except cationic)
Petrol, gasoline, etc.   diesel fuel, gas oil   paraffin, kerosene, TVO, domestic oil
White spirit   linseed oil, olive oil   glycerine   BCF

Group B: Cleaners approved subject to being used with discretion, washed off promptly, not allowed to form puddles, and used cold or (if safe) up to 80° F. (25° C.). i.e. lukewarm

Ammonia   bleach   weak disinfectant
                              weak acids, vinegar, dilute battery acid, citric acid

Methylated spirits, alcohol, alcoholic drinks   aviation fuel

CTC (carbon tetrachloride)

Naphtha, styrene, toluene, xylene   polyurethane and cellulose thinners, acetone

Group C: The following are *not* approved and should not be used under any circumstances.

Anything in group B used hot or where it can form a puddle.
Abrasives, scouring powders, sand, steel wool, pot scourers.
Caustic soda (sodium hydroxide)   strong alkalis   washing soda (sodium carbonate)
Strong disinfectants, carbolic, phenols   strong acids   methyl chloride
Ether   chloroform   methanol   benzene   trichlorethylene

CBM (chlorobromethane)

Ketones (note: acetone is commonly used under group B).
Anything unknown or doubtful.

A major difficulty is to know what a cleaner is. Labels seldom reveal the true contents, which are usually mixtures and anyway would mean little except to a chemist. If in doubt try on a small area first, leaving it long enough to have effect. Some solvent cleaners safe on GRP may attack or craze other plastics, notably acrylic (Perspex).

Therefore never use cleaners:

1. Unless certain what they are, or that they are sold specifically for cleaning GRP.
2. Where they can form puddles or run into inaccessible places.
3. Where the moulding may be porous, or have cracks or damage.
4. Without removing all traces after use, and preferably using only water rinsable cleaners.

Do not leave detergent or other cleaners in oily bilges for a long time. Pump out within an hour and dilute the residue with water. Repeat if necessary.

STUBBORN STAINS Oil, tends to end up where it is most used, which is around large centres of population. So do yachts. Consequently there are few yachts which avoid getting oil stains along the waterline and topsides. Gel coats have a filial affinity for oil and it soaks in like no ordinary dirt. I have yet to find a cleaner which will really chase it out—and leave the GRP behind. Oil must either be prevented from soaking in by a protective film of polish or paint, which will not itself absorb oil, or the surface must be burnished to remove the stain along with some of the gel coat. Constant cleaning will grind away the gel coat. Roughness and scratches hold dirt. The gel coat, not the stains, may be at fault. Light oils, floating around every harbour, can stain as badly as thick fuel oil. Chunks of tar can be scraped off, using a soft scraper of plastics, wood or aluminium to avoid scratching the surface. Use a steel scraper with great care.

A good mixture for scummy oil is two parts detergent to one part paraffin (kerosene). In the panic following a *Torrey Canyon* or Santa Barbara scale disaster, clean-up gangs may use very powerful cleaners which do more harm than the vilest oil. If possible get GRP boats out of the way and clean them with known cleaners.

SALT Despite fairly low heat resistance, average marine gel coats will normally be affected only by tropical sunlight. But salt crystals can magnify the sun's rays and cause local hot spots, leading to various troubles mostly revealed as blisters. They are the suspected cause of some elusive defects. A defective gel coat with low heat resistance can be affected, even in Britain, on sunny exposed moorings with enough lop to cause a constant heavy salt deposit. Washing down frequently will remove caked salt, but it will be impossible to prevent salt building up on exposed moorings or a long passage.

POLISH Polishing is the main means of preserving GRP. Polish builds up a renewable layer which protects the unrenewable gel coat surface beneath from the weather, and absorbs some of the minor scratches which would bite into the GRP. Not only does the true gel coat finish show through, but by adding gloss and lustre, polish improves it.

The choice of polish is important. It has a tough job. It must be of high quality and weather resistant. An important point is ease of removal. The boat will need repair and resin will not bond to a polished surface. One day the boat must be painted, and the first task must be to remove the polish.

The choice lies between silicone and wax polish. Silicones give a good gloss with little rubbing and are highly water resistant but very difficult to remove. Most car and boat polishes are silicones. Wax polishes are thicker, more wear resistant, and readily removed, but require more rubbing. The best wax is carnauba, which is the base for most heavy duty floor polishes, e.g. "Traffic Wax" used in public buildings subject to heavy wear.

Wax is removed fairly readily by wiping with white spirit or other suitable solvents. Silicone is another matter. Wiping simply transfers it to another place. A suggested technique is to use an unlimited supply of paper tissues on a "wipe once, throw away" principle. This prevents smearing and spreading, but even this is unreliable. The surface must be sanded well to remove the last vestiges of silicone, and wiped again with solvent.

My personal choice is for carnauba wax or "Traffic Wax" because of the thicker protection and easier removal. Silicones make very good polishes except for their great difficulty of removal. An owner may consider that painting is a future owner's headache, and repair the insurance company's; meanwhile the easier to polish the better. For him silicones have the advantage.

Polished GRP is slippery, especially when wet. Walking surfaces should be non-slip, but often essential areas are not. Non-slip polishes are obtainable but difficult to find.

Dull, jaded surfaces can be revived with metal polish. It may seem odd to use metal polish on GRP, but many metal polishes are abrasive and act as fine burnishing pastes. This takes off a surface layer to reveal bright fresh material below, like tearing a page off a calendar. Use the old fashioned abrasive ones (Brasso, Bluebell, jeweller's rouge, etc.), not modern solvent-based easy-clean polishes, which may attack GRP. Alternatively use the finest grades of car finishing burnishing pastes. Coarse grades can be used for scratch removal.

Abrasive polishes remove material and cannot be used indefinitely. The gel coat will become thin and shadowy, or expose the glass below. They are for occasional, not regular, use.

GRIT Grit underfoot causes wear and scratches, especially microscratches. Non-slip surfaces show marks less, but stepping and bracing points and many walking surfaces are commonly smooth and mark easily. Grit can be wind-blown or come aboard on shoes. Non-slip shoes can pick up sand and dirt and hold it like a grinding wheel.

Decks should be swept or washed down frequently. Grit does not show like an oily smear (a few grains are hardly visible), but scratches are permanent and will not clean off.

TRANSLUCENT GEL COATS Immitation wood hatches and metallic flake pigments soon look drab because the translucent gel coat or moulding which covers them gets dull. This is more noticeable than on a coloured gel coat because the detail is seen through it. They must be kept clean and well polished if they are to stay brightly transparent. Varnishing will restore some transparency and gloss, but must be of good quality.

An unreinforced gel coat tends to crack. All cracks and deep scratches must be repaired very promptly or they will let in water. This will attack the pattern and make blank or discoloured patches which will be almost impossible to repair.

METALWORK Use metal cleaners and polishes with caution, particularly solvent types. Runs onto GRP may leave stains, dull streaks or crazing. Be particularly careful that they cannot run under fittings and be trapped, or even seep past fastenings and attack the GRP from within. Other plastics may be harmed, notably acrylic (Perspex). Try the effect on a small area of GRP first. Use masking tape if necessary, to control spreading.

Check all fastenings regularly. Rebed any fittings which work loose, especially if there are signs of seepage or rust stains. Use grease or other protective coatings when laying up.

WOODWORK It is very common to see scratches on the adjoining GRP from careless scraping and sanding of woodwork. Protect with masking tape. Never use a blow-torch. Most paint strippers harm GRP, and runs will mark the gel coat or lodge behind the woodwork to attack at leisure and unseen, or even seep past fastenings to attack the moulding from within.

To reduce maintenance it is common to use teak-type woods which can be left bare or only oiled, without harm or looking unsightly. This does not please those who love bright-work, but the amount is small and looks better than neglected varnish.

SCRATCHES Scratches have a profound effect on the appearance and commonly predominate. They range from gouges deep into the glass to fine microscratches only visible under a microscope, and from single isolated scratches to patches of thousands covering a large area. Often a scratch is mistaken for a crack, and vice versa. The difference is easily seen under a good magnifier. A crack is a deep, sharp canyon, generally with branches. A scratch is shallow, wide, rough, ragged and may cross but never branches.

A scratch makes a whitish scar which tends to blend with white GRP. But dirty scratches show plainly and as most scratches soon get dirty the advantages of white are slight. On coloured GRP both clean and dirty scratches stand out.

Scratches show because they are rough and dirty. One approach is simply to make them clean and smooth without filling, because a clean glossy groove is inconspicuous. Acetone can do this, applied to a single scratch with a fine brush or to a patch by wiping. Varnish, clear resin or polish may be needed as well. Overspill must be wiped and burnished away to leave no smear and confine the repair strictly to the scratch.

Alternatively, colour the scratch to match, by using gel coat, resin or paint applied as above, with any overspill burnished away. Colouring is necessary if the scratch penetrates into uncoloured resin beneath the gel coat. Deep scratches where glass is exposed must be built up with resin putty, finished with matching gel coat or paint, and polished. Matching texture is more important than colour. If both are glossy a moderate colour difference is not particularly noticeable, but a dull or rough patch stands out even if the colour match is good. A repair with a different material weathers differently, the colour fades, the surface roughens and clear varnishes become brown and opaque. Confined strictly to a scratch, these differences can be inconspicuous, but as a smear they will stand out badly and cannot fail to escape a potential purchaser's eye.

The wrong, but commonly seen, way to repair a scratch is to fill it clumsily and leave a wide smear, often of a colour and texture which are widely different from the original. Even given a fair colour match, such a smear is more conspicuous than the original scratch would ever have been. It stands out like the scar of a major repair. I cannot understand how any boatbuilder or handyman can think a clumsy smear is a "workmanlike" repair—or how any owner can accept it. It would never be tolerated on a wooden boat.

CRACKS Gel coat cracks are commonly assumed to be shallow and unimportant, and are ignored. This is wrong. They go right through the protective gel coat until stopped by the glass. They are thus more serious than a shallow surface crack, particularly if under water. Being deep yet narrow, they are difficult to fill with putty. Resin penetrates better. One method is to wipe on thin resin, work it in, then clean and burnish off excess.

Simple gel coat crazing is uncommon now. Every crack tells a story—of damage, impact, movement, hidden stresses, hard spots, distortion, overstrain, fatigue, bad gel coat, etc. As well as filling it, try to work out *why* the crack is there, what other damage or weakness it may point to, and whether strengthening or modification is needed. Interpretation of cracks needs imagination. Few boatbuilders or surveyors can read or even see the signs. Yet the first indications of some of the worst faults have been cracks, apparently innocent and trivial.

GRP class boats are *not* all alike. Apart from mistakes, sometimes very serious, improvements are introduced, as often for manufacturing convenience as better performance, and sometimes with unexpected and dire effects.

CAVITIES Small subcutaneous cavities under an easily broken, eggshell-thin crust of gel coat are very common. It is unusual for even a good boat to be moulded without a few. They are mostly where expected, on features like angles or grooves. Good moulders assume there will be some, and search and fill them. Others complacently assume there will be none, and the owner seldom has long to wait to find they were mistaken.

Cavities are easily filled, but seldom properly. Resin putty can be used as they are not structurally important. As with scratches the repair must be confined to the cavity and all overspill scraped and burnished away. As they are wide enough to be conspicuous in themselves, the resin putty should be finished with gel coat, the original or as near as can be obtained, and burnished to match in gloss and texture. Moulders should supply small quantities of matching gel coat as part of the "tool kit."

It is common to find halo cavities where the original broken area has been filled but no one bothered to see how far the cavity actually went. Always break it open to the fullest extent before repairing. Cavities go in shoals. Where one appears a search will usually reveal others on each side.

The first cavities will probably appear during the guarantee period. It is obviously to the owner's advantage to have them all filled then. Repairmen seem to have little incentive to search: time and again they have not found others within an inch or less. Find and open them all as then there is no excuse for not filling them.

On the other hand, if not under water, where they should always be opened and filled, unbroken cavities are of no immediate harm. The slight blister is far less unsightly than a clumsy repair (some moulders' repairmen are incredibly unskilled). It may be better to leave them and repair only when they break. They can last ten years.

Cavities are usually just under the surface, easily found by tapping and readily opened. Beware of cavities larger than about $\frac{1}{2}$ in. (10 mm.) across. If substantially larger search for more: these are serious, as are numerous small ones. A cavity which does not break readily will be deeper. Cut it open and remould, or inject resin.

From the moulders' point of view carelessness in searching out and filling is very short sighted. Cavities create a very bad impression. Someone must spend an hour or two doing this, and certainly it costs money, but this is far cheaper than having to send a man hundreds of miles to make them good under guarantee later. They are bound to be found, as they are fragile and conspicuous. The trouble and ill will caused are out of all proportion to the trivial nature of the fault, yet often I see boats with a fine crop of flaws in such obvious places that no effort whatever could have been made to search for them. This happens persistently with certain moulders: of some anything can be expected, but others are supposed to be of high repute.

RECOATING WITH RESIN A later gel coat is not now recommended. This is a job for paint. Paints are designed specifically for surface coating, so the colours are dense and they are meant to be used in thin layers. Polyester resins, including gel coat, are designed for thick moulding so the colours are weak. They do not cure properly in thin layers or give a smooth finish.

PAINTING The gel coat finish will not last forever. Sooner or later every GRP boat must be painted, and most cruisers are antifouled from the start anyway.

GRP is durable. How durable we have yet to discover, but it seems reasonable to expect a life comparable at least to a wooden boat, say fifty years, with obsolescence the major factor. The finish of the gel coat will not last more than about ten years, if that, so contrary to the general impression, for most of its life a GRP boat must be painted. Like other things which must look smart and be protected indefinitely, the normal state of GRP is painted.

The early, unpainted, years are more a fortuitous holiday. Nevertheless these no-maintenance years are a major attraction of GRP, and for a first owner intending to sell after a few years, as most do, painting is a worry for future owners. Yet circumstances may decide otherwise. Repair, alterations or a defective gel coat can entail painting prematurely. Builders may paint when new to supply a particular colour or hide defects. Owners have found, to their surprise, that their boats are already painted—and often even an expert is deceived.

Painting is the transition point in a boat's life, with a marked effect on the value due to the prospect of repainting. This is justifiable when premature, but silly when due anyway. The days of annual repainting have gone. Smooth seamless GRP is an excellent substrate. Modern paints can last nearly as long as the gel coat finish, say five years. Wear and tear, not durability, is the limiting factor.

PREPARATION　This is the most important operation as it is the foundation for all paint applied during the rest of the boat's life.

On new GRP, wash thoroughly to remove traces of release agent. Degrease. Key the surface by sanding lightly with fine "wet-and-dry" until all the gloss has gone.

GRP which is not new is usually painted for the first time after years of accumulated use, dirt and polish. Clean thoroughly and remove the polish (see above). Note the difficulties in completely removing silicone polish. Continue cleaning until the surface "wets" evenly. Degrease with white spirit, toluene, xylene, polyurethane or cellulose thinners, or other approved solvent. Key as above.

In both instances apply a special primer designed for GRP. These bond by chemically combining with the polyester. A few paints have a built-in primer, but in general assume that a primer is essential. Follow with the painting sequence as recommended for that paint. Undercoats should be a colour distinct from that of the gel coat, to give warning when sanding that the gel coat has been reached.

As preparation is so important it must be done carefully, and the priming done under the best available conditions (warm and dry) and only on dry surfaces.

PAINTS　A boat should not need painting more often than a seaside house, certainly not every year. It pays to use modern paints, especially polyurethanes.

Polyurethane has an affinity for GRP and is chemically related (it is another kind of polyester). Two-pack polyurethane is more durable and tougher than the simpler one-pack types (this is disputed but seems true generally). Epoxy paints bond well but are not usually so durable. Ordinary oil-based paints will last no longer than on wood. Cellulose paint has been used on new boats, and a good sprayed finish can closely resemble a gel coat. Clear polyurethane has been suggested as permanent protection for the gel coat, but as clear varnishes do not seem to last as well as paint this idea does not yet seem practicable.

Paints vary a lot within types and better ones are developed continually. It pays to follow the instructions. Bad application will nullify the finest paint.

A gel coat is very smooth. Paint must match and show no brush marks. It should preferably be sprayed but this is usually impracticable. On the other hand, brush marks would make GRP look like wood and appeal to people who hanker for the traditional.

ANTIFOULING　Weed, barnacles, sea quirts, tube worms and everything which constitutes fouling will grow well on GRP. Distrust anyone who tries to persuade you otherwise. The only exceptions are worms, teredo and gribble (*Limnoria*), which find GRP "twysteth their dygestions," as was said of some vile compound in olden days. Consequently antifouling is not vital for safety. GRP boats may be kept afloat indefinitely without being eaten away: however wooden rudders, bilge keels, etc., can disappear. Barnacles do no harm in themselves, but when scraped off they may take gel coat with them. On a painted boat they can only take paint. Scraping does more harm than the barnacles.

All GRP boats kept afloat in coastal waters need antifouling. The turbid, effluent-laden waters of popular yachting centres are particularly bad because the light-seeking weed spores concentrate near the surface where boats lie. Most forms of antifouling can be used, and still need annual renewal. GRP does not soak up water like wood and the surface dries quickly, so there is a wider choice of paints which can be applied between tides. Boats kept ashore or trailed must have an antifouling which can stand drying.

There are claims for gel coats which need no antifouling. On conventional ablative antifouling theory nothing could last really effectively for the life of the boat—not just one or two years but fifty. Even ten years would be an interesting development, but I do not believe weed and barnacles will be defeated so easily.

At intervals there arise rumours of something which has developed an appetite for GRP. These could exist—the piddock will eat rock and Singapore is reputed to have a worm with a taste for armour plate—but so far are unconfirmed. Such stories are far more likely to be excuses to explain why a badly moulded boat had holes where it should not. Far more troubles spring from bad moulding than hungry monsters.

REMOVING PAINT Polyester resin is akin to paint. What is destructive to paint is destructive to GRP—often more so—and consequently removing paint from GRP is difficult.

All paint strippers are harmful to some degree but can sometimes be used with discretion. A few are claimed to be safe but should be treated cautiously and the rules below observed. Easily stripped paints, e.g. oil paints, shrivel quickly and a mild stripper may do little harm to the GRP. But the tougher the paint the greater the risk of dissolving the boat and leaving the paint. Two-pack polyurethane is in this class. The toughness of the paint is as relevant as the power of the stripper.

Paint strippers contain caustic soda, phenols or strong solvent, commonly methyl chloride. A nastier lot for polyester resin could hardly be found. The contents are seldom marked on the can and are usually secret blends anyway. Therefore avoid strippers except where nothing else will serve. It they must be used, use the minimum amount for the minimum time, repeating and increasing if necessary to compromise between patience and stubbornness. Use water rinseable types and neutralise at once with plenty of water. Do not use strippers where they can run and form inaccessible puddles, or where the moulding may be porous or damaged. If they do run pour water after them to dilute the puddles. Note that the fumes of many strippers are toxic in a confined space. Do not keep strippers on board. A can which spills, leaks or rusts through could do serious damage before anyone was aware of it.

Never use a blowtorch. This can blister the gel coat and also cause delamination.

On a smooth surface the recommended method is sanding and scraping. But careless scraping can scar badly, and a power sander may bite deeply before the user is aware of it. GRP goes a whitish or greyish colour when sanded and it is sometimes difficult to detect when it has been reached. Scars will show plainly through paint and must be filled. The appearance of scarring is not important under water, but any exposure to water is.

The inside of GRP is commonly painted for appearance but must be cleaned off for repair or attachments. Being uneven, sanding, even if accessible, is impracticable unless one is ruthless enough to sand down to the lowest level and the resulting reduction in moulding thickness is acceptable. Wire brushing can be effective, especially with the cautious use of strippers or acetone. Do not worry if the surface is not 100 per cent clean: 90 or even 75 per cent will give an effective bond particularly if the paint is tenacious anyway. The overlap can be made generous to compensate. It is better to leave boat than to seek perfect cleanliness.

On rough interiors builders should paint with resin, which need not be cleaned off, or use something easily stripped. Only conspicuous parts should be painted anyway. Handbooks should say what the paint is and how to remove it.

SEALING   Replacing a defective gel coat is very difficult, drastic and expensive. As it is usually porous the most practical and cheapest first approach is to try to seal it, to keep out water and weather and prevent further deterioration. Most paints are too permeable. The least permeable, readily available paints are cellulose and two-pack polyurethane. Cellulose generally requires spraying and is impracticable under boatyard conditions. Polyurethane is the more suitable. Apply at least four coats over proper primers and preparation. Polyurethane requires warm, dry conditions, i.e. good varnishing conditions.

A porous or disintegrating gel coat is a difficult problem and a bad substrate for painting. Cure is unlikely. The best hope is that painting will temporarily reduce the trouble, but repainting will be needed later. There may well be better methods and paints.

With some faults the realistic advice is to sell while it is still possible. At least this method will make the boat presentable for sale.

WATER ABSORPTION   Water blisters caused by absorption and osmosis are common on the bottom of boats after they have been afloat fairly continuously for about ten years (often less), most noticeably in fresh water. The blisters have a distinctive aromatic smell, and broken blisters form crescent shaped cracks. Improved materials should reduce this in future, but there is little incentive to cure something which occurs mainly on old boats. Meanwhile millions of boats, most of the GRP boats now built, seem likely to be affected sooner or later as they get old, and only the best will be later.

Ordinary antifouling is permeable and blisters are commonly found behind sound antifouling, the only outward signs being tiny damp patches. Sealing keeps water in as well as out. Enough will have been absorbed to continue the damage and attack any sealing from behind. Remove the antifouling and allow the bottom to dry out for as long as possible before sealing.

Water absorption is cumulative but reversible, although harm may already have been done: e.g. assume a gel coat absorbs at $n\%$ a year (an arbitrary linear rate for simplicity). After ten years continuously afloat it will have absorbed $10n\%$. But if the boat is laid up ashore regularly the amount after each season afloat would be $0.5n\%$. This dries out when ashore so the mean level is $0.25n\%$. In theory this mean level will be maintained, and is much lower than the cumulative level. This example is oversimplified but indicates the trend.

Experience shows that colours and fillers are most to blame although the reasons are not clear. Good practice now calls for all underwater parts to be moulded with unpigmented resins. This gives a marked reduction in water absorption and blisters.

CHAPTER TWENTY-FOUR

Repairs to GRP Boats

GRP BOATS are easy and quick to repair. Minor damage which would immobilize a wooden boat for days or weeks can often be repaired "while-you-wait" or at least in a day or two. Moreover, it is well within the scope of an amateur which cannot be said for replacing planks.

Major damage is harder to repair, but will still be cheaper than serious damage to a wooden boat. Again a capable amateur could tackle it, although it is really a specialist's job. Unfortunately specialists are few. The major difficulty is finding one.

The only real difficulty comes in cases of such serious damage that large areas have to be remoulded, and the moulds are not available for moulding a replacement section. The difficulty in this case is not in handling the materials but in recreating the shape.

Scratches and the almost universal small moulding flaws are covered under Maintenance. In general, minor damage is anything where the shape remains substantially intact, e.g. cracks of any length, small holes 1 to 2 ft. across where there is no complicated shape, chafe, incidental damage, etc. Major damage involves reforming the shape over a substantial area and complex section. Good GRP boats are not prone to damage despite their thin shell. Their natural springiness and light weight bounce them off trouble and their inherent toughness saves them from a lot more. The commonest cause of damage is from impact with sharp objects—but any thin hull, whether GRP, wood or metal, is vulnerable to this form of damage.

Damage is always limited to the area of impact, even in very severe cases. I saw one boat after a dispute with a coaster which had nearly cut her in half. There was a great gaping, crushed hole, where most of one side had been. A conventional wooden boat would have been a total loss, sprung apart and quite beyond economic repair. Fortunately in this case the moulds were still available, and a section consisting of most of one side was moulded and scarfed in place. The cost and time spent in making good the internal work and flooded engine were very much more than the repairs to the moulded hull itself.

Any enterprising yard should be able to tackle minor repairs like small holes or cracks, and so too can the owner, but a large-scale major repair is a job for the specialist. The manufacturers are the obvious choice if the boat is small enough to move on land and they are within reach. This is particularly true if any complex section needs remoulding because a new section can be made in the proper moulds at one-tenth of the cost. Failing the manufacturers, the nearest yard with experience of moulding boats is the best choice. It should be a boatyard, not a purely moulding or boatbuilding factory. The last thing production builders usually want is somebody else's boat, or even their own. Anything which does not fit their production line is an unwelcome disturbance. Also there will be dismantling and repair of woodwork, machinery, etc., which is not moulders' work.

An ordinary boatyard with no experience of moulding should never be entrusted with any major moulding repairs. If there is no experienced yard who can undertake the entire repair, make arrangements for the repair to the moulded parts to be done by outside specialists. If necessary insist strongly that this is done. The builders may be able to send some of their staff along or there are some moulding firms who specialise in outside contract work like this away from their premises. There is no valid reason for the yard to object. The incidental work should keep them happy, and they should be thankful that a contractor is relieving them of the worry and risk of a tricky and unfamiliar job. It is customary for the contractor to render his account through the yard who are entitled to add a reasonable percentage for overheads.

Many yards fight shy of even the smallest repair on GRP. Yet they are not difficult—and are profitable. Unfortunately, when they are tackled they are commonly done in such a clumsy way that the repair looks more unsightly than the original damage, even before a few years' weathering causes conspicuous changes of colour and texture in unsuitable materials.

A good GRP repair is strong and virtually invisible and moreover will remain so. Clumsy repairs are inexcusable. Boatbuilders are traditionally craftsmen, and craftsmen should take a pride in doing a good job. It is utterly wrong to think that craftsmanship died when GRP came along. It matters little what the craftsman is trained in: whatever he tackles will be done well to the best of his ability because that is his nature and training. Craftsmanship is an attitude of mind as much as skill with one's hands.

Therefore GRP repairs are not something to be done by a boy who has "learned a bit about it at night school." They are a task worthy of the craftsman who can pick up the essentials with a good set of instructions and a bit of practice far more quickly than a boy will learn to do a craftsman's job.

MINOR REPAIR   The technique is as follows (Fig. 24.1):

1. Clean up the repair, cut away loose, torn and shattered parts back to firm material.
2. Chamfer the edges to form a sharp "V" all round, so that the repair holds by a "rivet" action.
3. Sand the surfaces to form a key at least 1 in. all round on both sides. Wash down with white spirit, acetone, etc., to remove polish before sanding.
4. Back one side of the hole with plywood or cardboard, bent to follow the curve if necessary, and hold it in position with sticky tape, preferably masking tape, or clamp or wedge it. Wrap the backing piece in polythene to ensure release, otherwise it will stick. On a complex curve it may be possible to mould the backing piece of papier mâché to the approximate shape, or to shape a piece of wood or use flexible polyurethane foam. A crack can be covered with cellulose tape.
5. Lay up a layer of glass mat in the hole (if this is where you have come in, see the appendices at the back for a summary of the moulding techniques, and also the material manufacturers' instructions). Lay on more layers until the hole is full and is proud of the surface. If the hole is deep, pause to allow the resin to set every $\frac{1}{4}$–$\frac{3}{8}$ in. or so. The top layers should overlap the sides of the hole by at least $\frac{1}{2}$ in. except on very small holes.
6. When the repair has set, remove the backing pieces, file and sand smooth, and finish with a coat of resin or paint to match the hull. Burnish and polish.

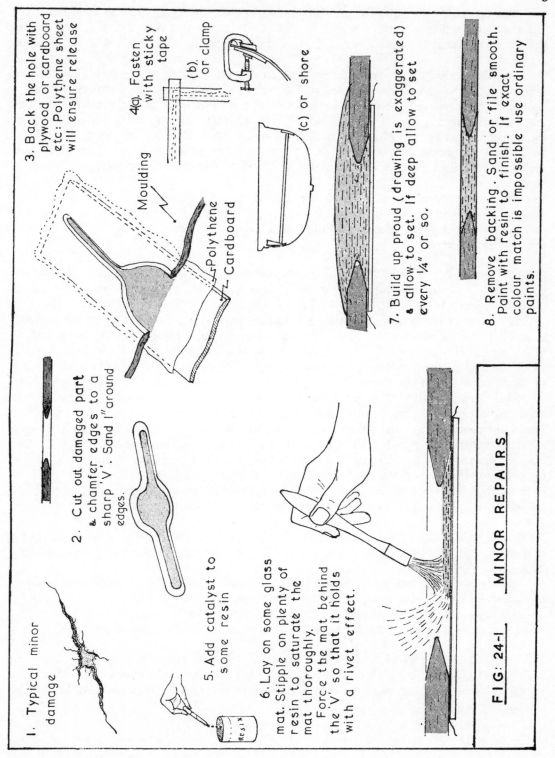

1. Typical minor damage

2. Cut out damaged part & chamfer edges to a sharp 'V'. Sand 1" around edges.

3. Back the hole with plywood or cardboard etc; Polythene sheet will ensure release

Moulding

Polythene

Cardboard

4(a). Fasten with sticky tape

(b). or clamp

(c) or shore

5. Add catalyst to some resin

6. Lay on some glass mat. Stipple on plenty of resin to saturate the mat thoroughly.

Force the mat behind the 'V' so that it holds with a rivet effect.

7. Build up proud (drawing is exaggerated) & allow to set. If deep allow to set every ¼" or so.

8. Remove backing. Sand or file smooth. Paint with resin to finish. If exact colour match is impossible use ordinary paints.

FIG: 24-1   MINOR REPAIRS

The backing piece can be on the "inside" or the "outside" of the moulding; if it has a smooth polished surface and fits exactly, the patch will blend in well and require little further work, but this is seldom so, and the main consideration is usually ease of access.

Polythene sheet laid over the repair when wet, and rolled or squeegeed flat is often recommended to give a smooth even surface, but I have always found it very difficult to do. The polythene tends to form wrinkles as it contracts after the inevitable stretching and working to get rid of air bubbles. These wrinkles form grooves which are much more difficult to get rid of than the original rough surface. A heavy gauge polythene is better, at least 500 gauge (0.005 in., 0.013 cms.), e.g. tarpaulin or cover material, or large sacks, not the light gauge used on small bags. Cellophane and greaseproof paper can also be used.

In a real emergency this sort of repair can be done in a matter of minutes. I have actually done it in ten minutes flat. By adding extra catalyst the setting time of the resin can be speeded up and the smoothing and final coat of resin can be left until a more opportune moment.

RESIN PUTTIES Small repairs can be made quickly and effectively with polyester putties. All contain large amounts of filler, and car repair putties may not be suitable for marine use. There is no way of telling except by trial. The claims are as reliable as television commercials. Epoxy putties are more expensive but stronger, and are available in special marine grades. Putties are good for temporary repairs and sealing, and for filling scratches, cavities, etc. They should not be used where there is movement, e.g. in a split. Certain putties contain glass fibres which give more strength. However the proportions are low and the fibres short. They are not as strong as proper GRP materials.

Unless specifically made for underwater marine repairs (as against claims to mend anything and everything) they should not be used for permanent underwater repairs, especially punctures, as the fillers may not stand continuous immersion. Similarly many putties weather badly. After a few years they discolour, roughen and pick up dirt. Even coloured putties are unlikely to be a good colour match and will fade differently. If used for permanent repairs they should be coated with resin, paint or varnish, confined strictly to the putty. They should be sanded back to the bare extent of the damage and polished, not left as a conspicuous broad smear which will become more prominent as it weathers.

EDGES OUT OF ALIGNMENT Very often the two sides of a crack are out of alignment, but obviously they must be held in position firmly during the repair (Fig. 24.2).

Straight clamps are easily made with two 1-in. wide strips of wood and a screw, or two strips of metal or hardboard and a nut and bolt.

Of course these clamps will get in the way, so "tack" the edges with just enough resin and glass to hold, allow to set, remove the clamps, and complete the repair.

REBUILDING SMALL AREAS A small piece of rather complicated shape, too high to be repaired by a simple patch, too small to warrant a special mould, can be repaired by building up to shape roughly and then forming to the exact profile by filing or sanding (Fig. 24.3).

271

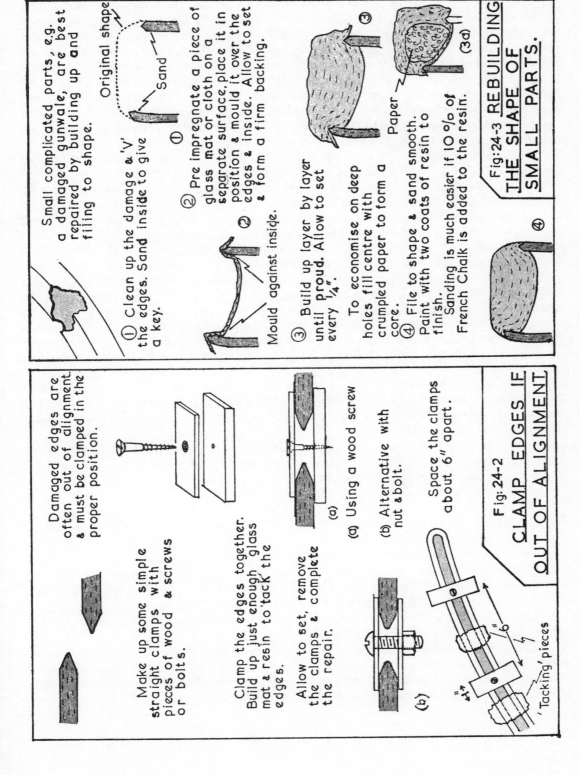

Small complicated parts, e.g. a damaged gunwale, are best repaired by building up and filing to shape.

Original shape

① Clean up the damage & 'V' the edges. Sand inside to give a key.

Sand

Mould against inside.

② Pre impregnate a piece of glass mat or cloth on a separate surface, place it in position & mould it over the edges & inside. Allow to set & form a firm backing.

③ Build up layer by layer until **proud**. Allow to set every ¼".

To economise on deep holes fill centre with crumpled paper to form a core.

Paper

(3a)

④ File to shape & sand smooth. Paint with two coats of resin to finish.
Sanding is much easier if 10% of French Chalk is added to the resin.

Fig:24-3 REBUILDING THE SHAPE OF SMALL PARTS.

Damaged edges are often out of alignment & must be clamped in the proper position.

Make up some simple straight clamps with pieces of wood & screws or bolts.

Clamp the edges together. Build up just enough glass mat & resin to 'tack' the edges.

Allow to set, remove the clamps & complete the repair.

(a) Using a wood screw

(b) Alternative with nut & bolt.

Space the clamps about 6" apart.

'Tacking' pieces

Fig:24-2 CLAMP EDGES IF OUT OF ALIGNMENT

A typical case is the corner of a transom or the gunwale of a dinghy, well defined, prominent shapes and often with difficult access behind. As always the first requirement is a firm backing. A piece of pre-impregnated glass mat, wetted out on a convenient nearby surface, laid in the hole and allowed to set will make a badly moulded, porous backing but it will be firm enough for laying up the subsequent layers. Build up the shape roughly with layer after layer of mat until it is proud. Allow it to set every $\frac{1}{4}$ to $\frac{3}{8}$ in. or so to prevent the excessive heat which is developed when the resin sets in a thick lump, heat which can set up distortion and cracking. The smaller amounts are also easier to control because a thick layer of "wet" mat will slide around like a dollop of mud. To avoid wastage mix only small quantities of resin, an ounce or two at a time.

On a deep repair a core of crumpled paper will reduce the amount of expensive resin and glass required, but this should not extend so far that it reduces the finished thickness to less than the thickness of the original moulding. Resin-glass putty can also be used, or flexible polyurethane foam.

When enough has been built up, allow it to set and if time permits leave it a week or so to cure partially and lose some of its tackiness. (Many modern resins, however, are nearly tack-free.) It may be possible to do some quick, rough trimming with a sharp knife during the short critical time it is in the rubbery stage immediately after setting. A pattern such as a non-slip pattern can be cut in with a knife and straight edge at this stage. However, this stage does not last long and if too soon there is a danger of the material coming away in lumps.

File it to shape with a coarse file. The perforated metal files like the Surform are very effective. If there is enough room, a power sander can be used, or a rotary file or burr in an electric drill, although an ordinary electric drill is seldom really fast enough.

All tools will clog badly and persistently unless some french chalk (talc) is added to the resin. 10 to 20 per cent will do little harm, but will make a world of difference to the workability, and practically eliminate the tendency to clog. Clogged files and sanding discs can be cleaned in acetone.

Using the proper glass mat and resin in this way is much stronger than using a resin-glass putty and is preferable on any hole more than an inch or so across, or below the water-line where reliability is important.

ONE SIDE INACCESSIBLE The repair is made awkward where one side is inaccessible (Fig. 24.4). This is quite common and becoming more so. Access on a cruiser is generally restricted with absolutely no regard given to the possibility of repair, e.g. by large, elaborate internal mouldings bonded-in or by woodwork glued so that it cannot be dismantled; or the damage may be under an engine which cannot be disturbed, or to a hollow sealed keel, or simply out of reach in the bilges.

The main difficulty lies in getting the initial firm backing. Once a backing piece of some kind is in position the rest is easy.

The important difference compared with the ordinary repair is that the backing piece cannot be removed afterwards. It is there for good. It must not be treated with release agent or wrapped in polythene, or it will rattle ever after! If it is untreated, and of suitable material, the resin of the repair will bond it on.

In many cases the reverse side is inaccessible, e.g. in way of buoyancy tanks & double mouldings, & the repair must be done from one side only. It is not easy to obtain the initial firm backing but these dodges will make the repair possible; ingenuity may devise others.

(la) Slide the backing plate between the two skins holding it by a screw eye or tack.

(lb) Retain in position with string, or,

(lc) With temporary straight clamps.

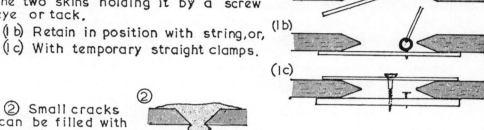

(2) Small cracks can be filled with resin / glass putty.

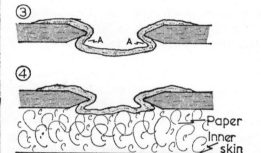

(3) Pre-impregnate some glass mat on a separate surface & carefully transfer it to the hole. Work it well behind the V edges (A) & allow to set. It will be a bad, porous moulding but strong enough to form a firm backing for the rest of the repair.

(4) Where the other skin is close the space between can be filled with crumpled paper to give some support to the first pre-impregnated layer.

(5) A pre-moulded section of approximate shape, plastic or papier-maché can be slid inside & retained temporarily with thread or fine wire.

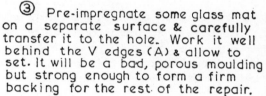

Inner skin

(6) To give access for a large or difficult repair, trepan a section from the inner skin & bond back in place afterwards. Note the bevel edge.

NB No release agent should be used when the backing plate is left inside. It must bond on otherwise it will break loose & rattle!

Fig: 24·4 REPAIR WHEN ONE SIDE IS INACCESSIBLE.

Various dodges can be used. They fall into three categories:

1. Backing pieces slid in and retained by various ingenious means.
2. Laying on a pre-impregnated first layer and allowing this to set hard to form the backing for the following layers.
3. Opening up the inner skin to give access, replacing the cut-out portion afterwards.

1. Damage to a plastic boat is usually in the form of a crack, longer than it is wide, so that one can generally slide in a backing piece, or pieces, and wriggle it into position.

A screw-eye and a piece of string will retain it in position quite effectively. Rather more elaborate is a clamp and screw, but it is quite likely that the edges may need clamping anyway to keep them in alignment. A "saddle" of masking tape is also quite effective but it is important that the masking tape is not left on the outer surface as this would interfere with the bond. It should be cut off short as soon as the backing piece is stuck to the rest of the patch.

The backing piece can be "stitched" on with thread or fine wire. This is a good method on curved parts where it may not lie snugly.

On a simple curve the backing piece can be just bent to shape, but on complex curves it should be moulded or be in strips. The shape need not be exactly right, but it is very important that any divergence from the proper shape must make the thickness greater, not weaker. An adjoining section may provide the shape nearly enough, or sometimes the other side of the boat; perhaps a sister-ship is available. The backing piece will be accurate enough if moulded against the outside. It need not be moulded from GRP. Papier maché (newspaper and Polycell), plaster, fire cement, silicone rubber, heat-formed thermoplastic sheet, rigidised flexible foam, etc., are other possibilities with or without reinforcement of glass or rag.

2. An effective backing is formed by pre-impregnating some glass mat on a separate surface, carefully transferring it to the hole, laying it in position and allowing it to set. From the purely moulding point of view it will certainly be a very unsatisfactory, porous bit of moulding, but it will at least set stiff enough to form a satisfactory backing on which to build up the main layers of the patch. It has the advantage of leaving no loose backing piece inside.

To preserve the "rivet" effect or grip on the "V" edges this pre-impregnated material must be worked behind the V as far as possible while it is still wet.

The middle will sag uncontrollably under its own weight. Little can be done about this. Glass mat may even pull apart, and on a long span the stronger glass cloth or woven rovings will have to be used, but it is not so easy to work these materials behind the "V"

The backing does not have to be glass-fibre. If no glass cloth or rovings are to hand use thin rag (thick rag will be unmouldable). After the resin has set it should be trimmed back behind the "V" to roughly point A in Fig. 24.4(3) before laying-up the glass so that it does not come between the repair and the GRP edge. This would form a barrier which would rot in time and cause leaks.

Sometimes the other skin is only an inch or two behind, perhaps too close to insert a backing piece. In these cases the space between can be filled with crumpled paper to give support for the wet pre-impregnated glass mat.

3. In cases of extensive damage, or a tricky repair, the inner skin can be cut away

to give access. A neatly trepanned section, cut with a sharp bevel edge can be bonded back in place afterwards fairly inconspicuously. With cunning the cut might coincide with natural features. An inner moulding ought to be bonded firmly to the hull so that separation is impossible. If force is used the inner moulding will be damaged and the hull weakened although this may not be apparent. It may be possible to saw the inner moulding away neatly around its glass angles and replace it by new angles, but this will depend on access and what else is involved. It needs very careful preplanning.

It is important to maintain a sense of proportion. The inner skin is always the less important; the boat, the hull proper, is the main thing, and so I do not advise cutting away part of the outer hull to give access for a repair to the inner skin.

TRAPPED WATER Water will get through any hole in the bottom. It will also get into the slightest crack in the deck. In both cases the hole may be anything from a gaping gap to a tiny crack or pinhole which may not even have been noticed. Inside the boat there are waterways and seepage paths behind frames and joins and within patches of poor moulding. Water will follow them to lodge in pockets or fill closed inaccessible spaces such as the inside of keels, behind interior mouldings, in buoyancy spaces, etc. Obvious external damage can be repaired but trapped water remains, perhaps far away.

Seepage paths revealed during repair must be followed up to see where the water has got to. Trapped water leads to decay. The inside of a cavity is bound to have exposed fibres and is often badly moulded. Wood may be embedded. It is easy to get water in but very difficult to get it out. Water flows downwards and there is commonly a weir effect. Leaks, especially deck leaks, will not get out the way they came in. The usual course is to drill drain holes in likely places (the holes must be plugged afterwards). A sub-surface moisture meter (Aucon) helps to locate pockets.

MAJOR REPAIR Serious damage, e.g. an area of several square feet, would have to be remoulded. If it is a flattish shape or a simple curve you may be able to make a simple mould or shuttering by using thin wood, metal, hardboard or cardboard to form the mould. The neatest result will be obtained by placing the shuttering tightly against the outside and working from inside, but this presupposes good inside access; this is uncommon, and it is more usual to have to work from the outside, which requires much more sanding and grinding to get a smooth surface.

A generous overlap inside must be arranged to give a strong bonding area. If working from outside it may be necessary to mould butt-straps over the inside join afterwards, or, where access inside is quite impossible, to rebate the patch into the moulding, or grind a wide "V" edge. 12 in. overlap would not be too much.

A damaged part which is a complex curve of large extent is best repaired by the makers, who will be able to make a replacement section from their moulds. If co-operative they could mould a section at their works which could be trimmed to shape and attached by a local yard or contractor. This will be essential if the boat is too large to move easily or is too far away. It is a fairly simple matter to cut it to shape and mould over the join to make it fully part of the boat.

When the manufacturers have gone bankrupt, or if the model has been discontinued and the moulds destroyed, the repair starts getting more difficult, as it is also necessary to recreate the original shape. One way is to reconstruct the boat with plaster. It is possible to construct a female mould direct, but this is not recommended. If you reconstruct the boat in plaster, making in effect a male pattern, you can visualise its shape, and spot and correct any irregularities in a way which is impossible with a direct female mould (Fig. 24.5). The method of making moulds are described briefly in Appendix III. If the boat is a popular class it may be possible to find a co-operative owner of a sister ship off which a mould of the damaged part can be taken. This is far quicker than trying to recreate the shape directly. For an emergency repair to make the boat watertight temporarily, it would be necessary to accept a simplified shape which could be built up quickly with wood, canvas, plastics sheet, etc.

PREVENTING FURTHER DAMAGE   Much damage is due to bad design or bad fitting out, including later attachments by the owner or a yard, e.g. a fitting which works loose and leaks due to no backing. When making a repair one should consider *why* something failed and make sure that the repair is stronger and attachments made properly. Straightforward replacement is wrong. Moreover, if one part has failed there are probably similar parts or fittings elsewhere which should be strengthened before they also fail. Class boats commonly have certain weak features. An owner should keep an eye open for what happens to other boats in the class and correct his own before that too fails.

It is common to dismiss impact damage as being entirely due to the impact. The fault is often bad design, i.e. the boat failed when it should not have done, or damage was worse than need be. This is commonly due to hard spots, and repair should include modification to correct these and similar places. Such damage often occurs away from the actual point of impact, which may leave no more than a scratch.

COLOUR AND TEXTURE   Exact colour matching is very difficult even if the original gel coat is used, because the boat will have faded. A large repair or extensive patch of minor repairs will almost certainly mean that the whole boat must be painted. Every GRP boat must be painted one day, but the aim is to postpone this as long as possible. A painted boat is suspected and considered of lower value. If premature painting is needed there could be grounds for damages or insurance claims.

As important as colour is texture, the surface finish. Many repairs show plainly, despite good colour, as matt patches on a glossy surface or sometimes as over-polished patches. Repairs often weather badly and after a few years stand out as conspicuously rough patches.

If painting overall is unacceptable the repair should be finished with gel coat with as good a colour match as possible, and burnished and polished to match the finish. Gel coat will keep its matching colour and texture better than a different material like paint. There is no excuse for leaving a repair, even a small one, in a conspicuously different colour and texture, especially as a clumsy smear. It is a boat, not a barn.

MISCELLANEOUS REPAIRS   Glass angles commonly break away from wood. It is unsatisfactory to rebond them because the angles will be dirty behind. Screw or bolt them back. Angles rarely break away from GRP. If they do it means the surface was bad to start with. Cut the angle away, clean and key the GRP, and remould.

Panting or flexing, often in flip-flop fashion, is alarming and dangerous, leading to rapid weakening through fatigue and overstrain particularly at nearby hard spots. Mould

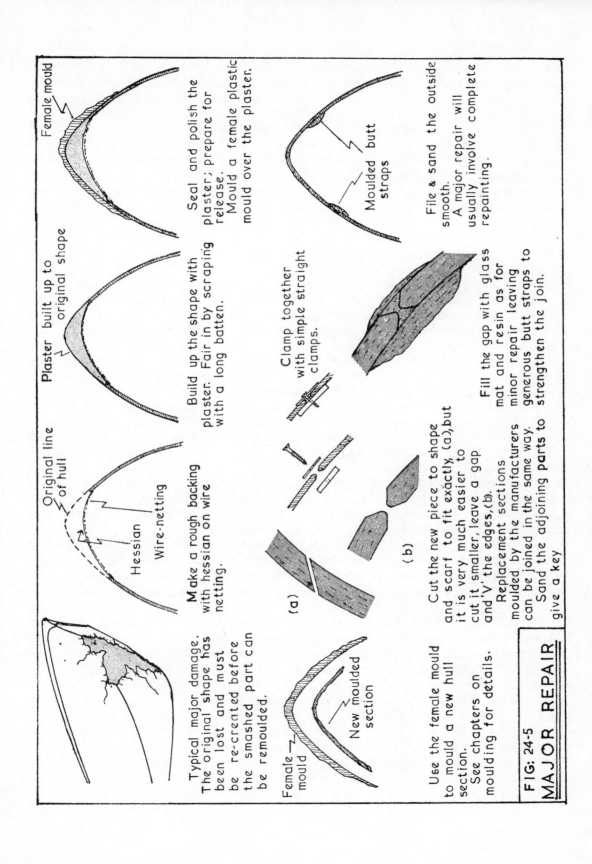

Female mould

Plaster built up to original shape

Original line of hull

Hessian

Wire-netting

Seal and polish the plaster; prepare for release. Mould a female plastic mould over the plaster.

Build up the shape with plaster. Fair in by scraping with a long batten.

Make a rough backing with hessian on wire netting.

Typical major damage. The original shape has been lost and must be re-created before the smashed part can be remoulded.

Moulded butt straps

Clamp together with simple straight clamps.

File & sand the outside smooth.
A major repair will usually involve complete repainting.

Fill the gap with glass mat and resin as for minor repair leaving generous butt straps to strengthen the join.

(a)

(b)

Female mould

New moulded section

Use the female mould to mould a new hull section.
See chapters on moulding for details.

Cut the new piece to shape and scarf to fit exactly, (a), but it is very much easier to cut it smaller, leave a gap and 'V' the edges, (b).
Replacement sections moulded by the manufacturers can be joined in the same way. Sand the adjoining parts to give a key

FIG: 24·5
MAJOR REPAIR

extra thickness to restore lost strength and reduce the panel area with frames or stringers. If the gel coat has cracks assume 50 per cent weakness. This is very difficult to prove (or disprove!) but justified by theory. This movement is also called "oil-canning".

Ninety per cent of sandwich mouldings delaminate, many extensively and very early. This is difficult to detect but serious. As well as causing structural weakness, water will soon find its way in and cause decay in the GRP and deterioration of the core. If detected early one can try to bond the skin back by injecting epoxy (not polyester), but it must be assumed that the bond is weak all over and delamination is more extensive than can actually be detected. Rebonding is impossible once the core gets wet. There is only one satisfactory answer: claim if you can, sell if you cannot.

Some faults are obscure. Always look for the root cause. The average boatyard is good at superficial repair without curing the real trouble. Get expert advice: doctors do.

HINTS FOR PRACTICAL CONDITIONS   Ideally, permanent repairs should be done in a heated workshop. But a cruiser cannot be trundled around like a wheelbarrow, although the more serious the repair the more important this is and the less, in proportion to the repair cost, will be the cost of moving the boat. For modest repairs a heated workshop is not necessary. They can be done in the open provided commonsense is used in waiting for reasonable weather. Pick a fine day for the actual moulding work—good varnishing weather is just right. Damp is worse than cold. Everything must be quite dry. Keep strong wind off setting resin, e.g. lay polythene over it.

When the devil calls the tune there is little choice. Polyester resin can be made to set in cold conditions by increasing catalyst up to 5 per cent. In freezing temperatures boost the resin with 1 per cent of amine accelerator (Scott Bader accelerator D). Repairs done under really cold or damp conditions should be considered temporary, to be done again under better conditions later.

Extra heat will help a lot, and a tent of some kind will conserve it. In civilised surroundings use radiant fires. Up the creek ingenuity is needed. Play a blowtorch on a metal sheet placed against the repair, or preheat it. (*Never* play a flame directly on the repair or heat it over a fire. Polyester is inflammable.) No part should get too hot to touch; about 120° F. (50° C.). Other suggestions are to hold a hot water bottle against it, with a layer of polythene to prevent sticking; warm the other wide; or sit on it (with appropriate anti-stick precautions). Cold resins are thick and difficult to mould with. Warm them before use by standing the tin in hot water (not directly on a stove) or storing in a warm room.

EMERGENCY REPAIRS   There is nothing special about a GRP boat when it is sinking. Use your head. If water is coming in fast stuff something in the hole: rags, socks, your wife's unmentionables, anything you can lay your hands on. With so much of the average GRP hull out of reach inside do not scorn the old sailing ship trick of pulling a sail against the outside. Polythene sheet clings well to a smooth wet surface. There are epoxy putties which can be used under water, but ordinary polyester resins and glass can not. In any case the inrush of water must be stopped first.

The best method is to dry out and use a GRP repair kit, although this is scant comfort far from land. Ideal moulding conditions are unusual in emergencies. If the resin sets at all it will serve, and it need not be disastrous if the tide rises too soon. Polythene stuck on over the outside will keep most of the water out.

If a repair kit is not available resort to the traditional canvas and tar, or the cleaner modern paints and glues. Paint will effectively waterproof canvas or rag. Polythene is waterproof but difficult to stick reliably. A plywood or metal patch, well bedded in paint or sealant, can be bolted, screwed to backing pieces, or secured with self-tapping screws although the latter are unreliable. Strong PVC tape sticks well to GRP provided the surface is wiped dry. Tape should not be used where there is movement unless the edges are clamped. Remember, everything must come off again before a proper repair can be done.

Emergency repairs should keep the boat afloat, but they will not restore strength. Nurse a makeshift repair. Reduce speed and exercise caution: the more makeshift the repair the more the caution.

Get a proper repair done as soon as possible. Temporary repairs *must* be temporary. They have a very strong tendency to become permanent. Next fitting-out time may not come!

REPAIR KIT Only best quality materials suitable for marine use should be used. Car repair kits are seldom good enough. The kit should contain the following:

Polyester resin, pre-accelerated	3 lb.	1·5 kg.
Gel coat resin, pre-accelerated, topsides colour*	½ lb.	0·25 kg.
Gel coat resin, pre-accelerated, deck colour*	½ lb.	0·25 kg.
Tubes of catalyst paste (double for cold weather)	3 × 1 oz.	3 × 25 g.
Dropper bottle of cold weather booster	1 oz.	25 ml.
Glass cloth, about 7 oz./sq. yd. (250 g./m.²)	1 sq. ft.	0·1 m.²
Glass mat, 1 or 1½ oz./sq. ft. (300 or 450 g./m.²	9 sq. ft.	1 m.²
Resin putty with hardener	½ lb.	0·25 kg.
Acetone**	½ pint	250 ml.

* Alternatively uncoloured resin and colour paste.
** Obtainable from local chemist.

Tin of polish, tin of fine burnishing paste, wet-and-dry sandpaper (1 medium, 1 fine), 12 cheap paint brushes ½–¾ in. (10–12 mm.), 12 paper cups (not plastics) and stirrers, resin measure, 3 medium gauge polythene bags, small roll adhesive tape, cardboard for backing, tin of talcum powder, scissors, trimming knife, Surform file, pad saw, old chisel.

Instructions, including instructions for mixing resins and putties.

For emergencies:

Underwater setting epoxy with hardener
2 tubes of sealant
1 roll strong PVC adhesive tape, about 2 in. (50 mm.)
Half quantities are appropriate for small cruisers. Two kits should be carried on large ones.

With reasonable storage in temperate climates resin and catalyst will last at least a year, probably two, possibly three or more, but less in hot climates. Ideally they should be renewed every year whether used or not. The time to find out is *not* in an emergency! The other components will last indefinitely. The glass should be in a sealed bag to keep it dry.

The resins should be quicker setting than normal moulding resins, which is easily arranged by increasing the accelerator. Repairs will usually be small but wanted quickly. Marginal temperatures are probable.

The instructions, particularly the resin mixing instructions, must be clearly written and readable with your sailing spectacles in poor light. Open the kit at home, work out the mixing instructions, and write them boldly on a card kept with the kit. Make sure they relate to the kit's crude measuring equipment. Do not wait for an emergency to find out how it works. Get some extra materials and try them out—and READ THE INSTRUCTIONS.

DECAY To speak of decay in a GRP boat may seem blatant heresy which in a less tolerant age would have led straight to the stake. There are many experts who do not believe it and innumerable owners blissfully unaware that their boats are decaying under their feet. But "today's heresy is tomorrow's gospel."

This is not another scare story (GRP has been plagued with them since its early days), nor is it an irrelevant laboratory finding. It is based on many surveys of GRP boats of many types, makes and ages; dispassionate, careful, detailed inspection of what actually happens to GRP boats.

What is decay? It does *not* mean rot: that is just one narrow form of decay. As yet there is no known fungal or bacteriological organism which thrives on a diet of GRP. Decay is a wide term. Stonework crumples, mountains erode, mighty empires fade. Nothing lasts for ever. We live in a world where everything either grows or decays.

However there is a distinction between the normal rate of deterioration, which commonsense owners know must happen whatever salesmen claim (gullible owners find out the harder way), and an abnormally rapid rate of decomposition. It is the latter which is here termed decay.

It is important to keep a sense of perspective. Decay is slow, after years not weeks. There is no "doomwatch" agent which gobbles up a boat before the owner's horrified gaze—or even while is back is turned. Decay is *always* caused by some abnormality from which bad moulding in some form is never far away and bad fitting out practice comes close. Well moulded, well fitted out, well maintained boats do not decay.

Decay will not occur without water. The most destructive agent is stagnant water; not stinking water but water which collects and remains in pockets. Water dissolves salts out of the glass and resin. The process is self-accelerating. As the concentration builds up, as it will if the water is stagnant, the rate of attack increases. Given the opportunity, both glass-fibres and resin *are* attacked by water. Claims of indestructibility are not fulfilled in practice.

Water has to get there. The rate of permeation into sound, solid moulding is very slow although it does happen steadily. But if the moulding is poor, if there are voids, bubbles, cavities, "dry" resin-starved areas, exposed fibres, seepage paths, waterways, etc., water will penetrate into the heart of the moulding and attack it from within. Entry may be from damage, cracks, gel coat flaws, seeping fastenings, unsealed edges and holes, poorly sealed joins, leaks past embedded fittings, porosity (especially on thin, awkward moulding), resin starvation, poorly bonded angles, waterways in angles and frames, delaminating sandwich, plain bad moulding and other routes. Combinations of these can form most devious, elusive seepage paths running from end to end of a hull.

Water can come equally from below or above, inside or out, from sea (or fresh) water or weather, from bilge water or condensation. Every external scratch, crack, damage area or flaw should be sealed promptly to keep out water. Shallow scratches are less important, but deep scratches exposing glass must not be left. The common and generally ignored gel coat cracks penetrate beyond the gel coat to the glass and allow water to lodge in contact with glass-fibres, the very condition to be avoided.

Decay in GRP is always local. It must eat forward steadily: it cannot go where water cannot penetrate. But note that once water gets into a waterway or seepage path "local" decay means anywhere this water can get to, including capillary movement or wicking up exposed fibres. The only decay which is visible is that which is eating its way in at an obvious entry point. Decay eating its way *out* from an internal pocket is not seen until far advanced, and by that time the moulding is severely weakened.

There is no "cure" for decay, such as pumping in preservative. The *only* protection is sound moulding and sound fitting out. If the moulding is sound, decay is strictly local, no water is trapped in hidden pockets and it can be treated as minor damage. But if the moulding is poor and the boat is badly fitted out there is absolutely nothing that can be done—or is worth doing. The boat's life will be short.

Decay takes years to show. Only serious cases are apparent before ten years, but there have been cases of boats eaten right through or weakened sufficiently for local failure before that age, e.g. a hull/deck joint failure at four years due to seepage via a delaminating sandwich deck. There is no doubt that decay, and even more the need to prevent it, is going to be a serious matter in the future.

INVISIBLE DAMAGE GRP does not fail suddenly like steel but progressively from as low as 20 per cent of its theoretical ultimate strength. Unlike metals GRP is not ductile. It cannot yield to relieve or redistribute stress but breaks down progressively, more like reinforced concrete. First the resin/glass bond fails, then the resin or glass-fibres locally. At every stage the GRP is left permanently a little weaker, more flexible, and therefore more prone to further damage. *All* damage is permanent. There is no recovery. At low levels damage is invisible or, at best, revealed by faint gel coat cracks which need experience and imagination to interpret.

The three principle causes are overstrain, fatigue and creep, all of which will produce failure at well below the theoretical strength, and weaken the structure long before that.

Fatigue is dependant on design, stress level, number of cycles, conditions and other factors; a complex subject and very difficult to predict. All factors must be considered in each case. Laboratory tests have shown a reduction to 70 per cent of strength after 1,000 cycles and 50 per cent after 10,000 within the normal working stresses, and complete failure after 100 cycles at 50 per cent of theoretical strength. Fatigue life is less under wet or hot conditions. These figures are not directly applicable. They could be better but there are many factors which will make them worse. Such time cycles can easily be achieved in a few seasons' sailing or even one long hard thrash to windward, or indeed any rough passage under sail or power. Fatigue must not be ignored.

Creep, i.e. distortion caused by sustained load, must happen by internal movement and that means internal damage. The load causing creep will be well below the theoretical strength. There may be little or no distortion at first. A common example is a tight shore left all winter.

The only obvious signs of internal damage are distortion, unusual flexibility, or stress cracks, especially parallel cracks roughly enclosing an area or associated with some feature. It must be assumed that the moulding has already been weakened, but proving or disproving this, or quantifying it, is very difficult.

Invisible damage is unlikely to lead to immediate failure without further and more obvious signs. Nevertheless it is important to realise that GRP does weaken and fail progressively. The factor of safety can be steadily eroded so that eventually it fails at a stress level which it had sustained many times before. GRP boats should not be designed to anywhere near the limit of their theoretical strength except where a short life is acceptable, as in top racing boats. Special care must be taken to avoid high local stresses which will cause premature local failure. This is the insidious danger of hard spots.

Even if indicated it is impossible, without elaborate equipment, to prove or detect the extent of invisible damage. The practical course is to wait until it gets more obvious, or reinforce the likely extent as a precaution. Note that the damage may not be where the cracks show (Chapter Two, Hard spots). It needs imagination to visualise where the actual stresses have been and what has caused them. Good design, understanding of hard spots and stresses, and proper fitting out initially and subsequent additions are the only ways to reduce them. Nevertheless much overstrain and fatigue must remain undetected. I must apologise for leaving the reader with such nasty thoughts to keep him awake in the night watches when the boat is creaking and bumping as she batters her way through a dirty night.

"997 . . . bump . . . 998 . . . bump . . . 999 . . ."

"Lovely morning skipper. Your watch."

Even if indicated it is impossible without elaborate equipment to prove invisible damage. It is equally difficult to disprove it, but the onus of proof generally lies with the owner, not the moulder blandly asserting it is sound.

Crude penny tapping will not detect faults deep within the moulding unless they are massive. Ultrasonic testing will reveal much more, deep flaws, including patches of small discrete flaws, breakdown of resin/glass bond, failure of resin or glass, delamination and thickness variation. It is non-destructive but expensive and not simple. Most instruments are designed for metal and GRP does not transmit ultrasonic energy nearly as well. Attenuation is high and, GRP being a composite material, specular reflection is excessive. But if one is not seeking a performance as on steel it does yield very useful information in the hands of a surveyor experienced in GRP. X-ray testing cannot indicate depth and is not suited to finding the laminar-type flaws of GRP. Other methods may be developed. Efficient non-destructive testing is a specialist field and, because of the expensive equipment, likely to remain so.

However this invisible damage is not likely to deteriorate suddenly. Catastrophe comes later as the factor of safety is eroded by progressive failure and it is probable there will be obvious signs well before failure. A practical approach is to wait for it to become obvious—but nevertheless exercising caution, keeping an eye on suspected parts and reinforcing as a precaution. A great deal of invisible damage must undoubtedly go blissfully unsuspected, and even when there are signs few owners can be expected to read them aright and most will not even notice them.

Appendices

THESE appendices cover the materials used and the technique of moulding very briefly; they are intended for the non-technical reader, or the reader without much previous experience of plastics, who is faced with the problem of fitting out or repairing a hull moulded by someone else. Of course anyone who has already moulded the hull will know all about moulding and will have learnt the dodges the hard way.

This brief description supplements the supplier's instructions, it does not supplant them, but it will explain what moulding is all about in the preliminary and planning stages before the suppliers' instructions have been received and confidence has been gained by actually using the materials.

However, I find that suppliers' instructions are apt to be contradictory, and none of them look at the moulding as a whole. Many sets of instructions, too, seem to be intended for working in a well-equipped laboratory or at least in a first-class workshop, and they usually expect you to have a scientific background. The practical conditions in most boatyards or backyards are quite different and far from ideal. Yet the impression given by many resin suppliers is that it is quite out of the question to work outside a well-built laboratory, or without a degree in chemistry.

This is definitely not so. Working under practical yard conditions is quite feasible, even when conditions are theoretically far from ideal; and the mouldings made under those conditions are reliable. Moreover a degree can be a definite hindrance—the only people I have found who have made a complete muck of things, have held high academic qualifications. I think ordinary folk at least read their instructions.

Some extra care is needed under yard conditions, and Appendix 5 shows how it can be done.

Most of the worst mouldings are made under good conditions. It is good men, not good conditions, that make good mouldings.

The Materials

THE chief materials used are glass-fibre and polyester resin. Glass-fibre (fibreglass or fiberglass are just the same) was known to the ancient Egyptians, and natural resins in the form of amber were demanded for jewellery, ages before women found that gold was more expensive.

There is little startlingly new about the materials or the principles. It just needed modern technology to make them workable and economic. Now all that remains is for them to be used.

GLASS-FIBRE Glass-fibre consists of very fine fibres of glass, one-tenth of the thickness of a hair, made up into strands of some 200 fibres.

The usual form in which it is used is as chopped strand mat, woven cloth or rovings.

In chopped strand mat the strands are chopped into short lengths of about 2 in. long and rolled into a loose random mat, like straw spread out on a floor and rolled down. A binder, which dissolves later in the resin, holds it together until it is used, so that it is firm enough to handle. This is the general-purpose material, comparatively cheap, easily formed and bulky so that it builds up a thickness quickly.

Alternatively the strands are used as continuous lengths, not chopped, and are woven into a cloth. This is not often used in boat work because it is expensive, but it is the strongest form, and is occasionally used in a shape where its high strength can be employed economically. It is more commonly used as a tape, as it is the only material which can be handled in narrow widths.

A common compromise is woven rovings. Rovings are bunches of strands, typically about 60, as thick as codline, and they form a thick, loose fabric. It combines the bulk and lower cost of mat with the higher strength of a woven material. It is often used sandwiched with mat for higher strength. Single strings of rovings are often used on their own as a binding (e.g. for tubes) or to fill in difficult corners.

POLYESTER RESIN The common resin used is a cold-setting polyester resin. As supplied for use it is a syrupy liquid, in which form it is stable for a year or two. However, once a hardener is added it will become solid in a short time. Moreover, this is a strictly one-way reaction. Once set it will never again become liquid even if heated. This is known as a thermosetting resin as opposed to the thermoplastic type which can be melted and solidified any number of times. (Polyester resin may soften if heated, but only a little, and it will not melt even if on fire.)

For convenience a cold-setting resin is used. Cold-setting is a comparative term and only means that it sets at room temperatures, instead of having to be heated to 300° to 400° F., as is the case with most other plastic materials. It does not mean that it must be frozen; far from it, for a working temperature of 60° F. (15° C.) is still considered desirable. (See Appendix 6).

Polyester is a wide term and covers many things. Terylene (Dacron) is one. It is always as well, when ordering for the first time, to state what it is intended for, in particular to state that it is for use on boats.

It is usually better also, particularly in the early stages, to tell the supplier what you are going to do and rely on him to send the right materials, rather than make a blind guess or select one with a pin from a catalogue of incomprehensible specifications.

Polyester resins will not remain liquid indefinitely and will solidify with age. (See Shelf Life, Appendix 4.)

HARDENERS   Polyester resins are basically three-part (three-shot) resins, i.e. two additional components must be added to make them set, commonly known as accelerator and catalyst. Catalyst is the one which makes it set, accelerator makes this happen at room temperature.

The trend today is to using resins with the accelerator already mixed in so that they are two-part (two-shot) resins. This is much simpler and also safer (see Appendix 7) and is to be recommended very strongly wherever possible, particularly for anyone reading these notes.

It is as well to check whether your resin has already got accelerator in it or not. If necessary test a small amount and see if it sets.

CATALYST   All catalysts for polyester resins are peroxides. To most people a peroxide is only a way of turning a clever brunette into a dumb blonde or rocketing her to the moon, but these catalysts are special peroxides and they must be handled with caution.

Catalyst is essential to make the resin set and it must *never* be forgotten. It is easy enough to forget or overlook it in the heat of the moment with so many other things to worry about, but it will only waste materials and time if you do and one small quantity of resin which escapes the catalyst and is not detected can ruin an entire boat. If in doubt it is safer to add more than to chance it.

The commonest catalyst is a liquid, MEKP (Methyl Ethyl Ketone Peroxide). Some manufacturers may give it a fancy code-name like Catalyst M, but it is always the same peroxide. As a liquid it is easy to measure volumetrically in small quantities with considerable accuracy. Other peroxide catalysts are also used, but these are usually in the form of a paste or powder which is harder to measure. Never use anything else even if you have run short. Waiting will not hurt the moulding; the wrong peroxide, or "something from the chemists" will ruin it.

All peroxides give off oxygen when heated and therefore they will assist a fire. There is, however, a powder form which is non-inflammable and safe under all conditions. Catalysts will also harm the eyes if any gets into them and should not be allowed to remain in contact with the skin. (See Appendix 6, Safety.)

Peroxides can lose their strength with age, and old catalyst should be treated with suspicion. If necessary a larger proportion must be used, and certainly a small quantity should be tried first. If they smell the same it is a fair chance that the liquid catalysts of two different manufacturers are interchangeable, but remember that the strength could be different. Test it on a small amount of resin first.

EPOXIES Epoxy resins are sometimes used. They are similar to polyesters, similar that is to anyone who is not a chemist, but they are stronger and more expensive. They are excellent adhesives, which polyester resins are not.

The commonest use is as a plain glue, but they may also be used for moulding where very high strength is important or the conditions are particularly arduous. It is usually uneconomic to use them with glass mat and they are more suitable for those extreme cases where cloth is called for.

A "wet" epoxy can be applied over a "dry" polyester and *vice-versa*, but they must not be used while both are "wet". The first must always have set hard.

Only one hardener is used, in unchangeable proportions. There is no control over setting time but they are less critical about how long this may take. Special hardeners can be used under freezing conditions and even under water.

Some of the hardeners have a strong dermatitic quality, worse than anything to do with polyesters, but these are now going out in favour of non-dermatitic hardeners.

THIXOTROPIC RESINS A thixotropic resin is one which still brushes readily but does not tend to run on its own, like a lazy boy who only runs when he is beaten. It is essential to use a thixotropic resin when moulding on a vertical or sloping surface, otherwise the resin will tend to drain out of the glass before it has set. The effect is to have a thin, starved area at the top, full of air bubbles and exposed fibres, and a thick puddle of resin at the bottom. A thixotropic resin will not prevent this altogether but it will reduce it substantially.

Thixotropic pastes can be supplied by most resin suppliers for mixing into the resin, but it is much better to buy ready mixed resins which are thixotropic already.

COLOUR Resins can be supplied ready coloured or they can be coloured by mixing in colour pastes. These colour pastes are colours mixed by the factory and dispersed in a carrier, usually a form of polyester resin, which will mix easily into the resin.

It is not worth using anything but proper colour pastes made for the purpose. Powders are much more difficult to mix in, and many colours are seriously affected by some of the constituents of the resin, particularly the catalyst. Worse still, some colours will poison the resin and affect its strength. A proper colour paste supplier will know this.

FILLERS Fillers are powders mixed into the resin to give improved properties. Like drinking alcohol they can have an excellent effect in moderation, but are ruinous in excess.

These powders are usually cheap, a lot cheaper than the resins. They have therefore been added in the past to cheapen the resin. This leads to excesses and abuse and is the wrong approach. The right powders in the right proportion can give improved properties such as abrasion resistance, better workability, denser colour, reduced shrinkage and other good effects. Excess will lead to bad weather resistance, surface crazing, loss of strength and poor finish. (See Appendix 4.)

Common fillers are:

Slate flour, quartz, silica—for good abrasion resistance and hardness;

China clay, chalk—for reduced shrinkage;

Talc—for better workability.

Coarse sand, quartz—non-slip effects.

It should be noted, however, that many of the properties are incompatible, e.g. good abrasion resistance and better workability cannot be achieved together.

CURE Hardening of both polyesters and epoxies is a two-stage affair of quick setting followed by slow progressive cure, not unlike concrete. They set quite soon after adding the catalyst (hardener for epoxy), sometimes with disconcerting suddenness. At this stage they are rubbery. Hardening is very marked over the first few days but becomes progressively slower, the rate being exponential towards the theoretical state. A typical time scale might be: soft 5 min., rubbery 1 hour, "green" 1 week, substantially cured 3 months, "fully cured" 1 year, theoretically cured—never.

Some people (I am one) believe that in practice GRP never attains the full state of theoretical or laboratory cure. But as testing is destructive and difficult this is hard to prove. For practical purposes the question is academic: GRP reaches the state it is designed to reach and which is expected of it, and that is good enough. Any difference is marginal.

Certain factors speed or delay cure, notably temperature, damp and workmanship. If properly moulded GRP will cure in time largely regardless of the conditions during curing, although these will affect the rate. But bad conditions during moulding may prevent the moulding ever curing properly later; too hot can be as bad as too cold.

GRP contracts slightly during cure. This can affect the finish and stress points. Figures are unreliable owing to the influence of shape and elasticity in the early stages, and the effect of different materials and standards of workmanship.

THICKNESS In theory only the glass content determines strength, not the thickness. In practice the only quick check on glass weight is to measure the thickness. As resin content should be within well defined limits this is a fair guide. The inside is rough but should not cause more than 1 mm. error.

With glass mat the accepted figure is 0·7 mm. per oz./sq. ft. of glass (2·3 mm. per kg./m.²) plus up to 0·5 mm. for gel coat and something for inner coats. A rougher guide is 32 oz./sq. ft. per inch thickness, or approximately $\frac{1}{32}$ in. per oz.

Woven rovings should be somewhat thinner. A single figure is unreliable as more depends on the grade and workmanship, but for average moulding the above figure is not far out. With both mat and rovings, high strength, low resin ratio mouldings will be markedly thinner. The onus of proof should lie with the moulder. It is too easy to claim it as an excuse without justification. Some moulders are consistently thin, more are thick. Resin/glass ratio can be checked destructively by burning a sample.

The common way to measure thickness is to drill a hole. This is pure hit or miss. Even on good moulding nominally equal thicknesses can vary by 10 per cent. On poor moulding they can vary 100 per cent. (This figure may be disputed. I have measured more, even ten to one!) Destructive testing, which includes drilling holes, must not be done without the owner's consent and must be made good inconspicuously and soundly.

Electronic thickness testing is non-destructive and not hit or miss. Measurements can be made over a wide area, virtually all over the boat. Ultrasonic testers are very expensive. The du Plessis-Mec tester is simpler and cheaper.

APPENDIX 2

Method of Use

As far as we are concerned glass-fibre is *never* used without resin; resin can sometimes be used without glass-fibre, but the glass-fibre is never far away, and it is just used as a primer or coating for GRP that has just been moulded or is about to be moulded. In general they are always used together and together they form reinforced plastics, a material far stronger than either by itself.

Unless obvious from the context it can be taken that whenever glass fibre or mat, rovings or cloth are mentioned in this book, they are being used with resin in the proper way.

The basic idea is to saturate the glass-fibre with resin so that when the resin sets the whole lot becomes hard and firm. When "wet" with resin the glass-fibre has as much natural shape and form as a wet blanket. Consequently some form of mould is essential to hold it while setting. Once set it will retain not only the shape of the mould but also its finish. If this is good very little further work is needed on the moulding, no painting, no preparation—a great time-saver compared with conventional materials, which offsets a higher material cost. Another advantage is that once the mould has been made there is very little time and trouble spent in shaping the material. The piece is moulded directly in the right shape, and it is right first time. No other material offers this advantage except perhaps concrete—which is hardly a common boatbuilding material.[1] Wood may be cheaper, but look at the time spent in cutting it to shape, fitting and trying; look, too, at the wastage, the offcuts and piles of shavings. The same applies to steel and aluminium.

In fitting out operations the piece is often moulded in position, so that it immediately takes the shape of that part of the boat and there is no need even to make a mould. This is a tremendous time-saver and convenience.

Release from a mould presents little problem if you use the right techniques. When moulding in position, however, you do not often need release, and the piece is intended to bond on. If nothing is done to ensure release it will bond naturally.

"GOOD" FACE AND "ROUGH" FACE Hand lay-up mouldings always have one "good," resin-rich face, a smooth, solid, glossy face, made by being in contact with the mould and reproducing the mould finish (for good or bad) in great detail. The other side is always rougher and uneven as it is not controlled by the mould. It may be considered the "natural" surface. If well made it will be undulating, but still solid and glossy. Some fibres will be visible but they will be firmly embedded.

For this reason a boat is always made in a female mould so that the "good" face,

[1] Written in 1963 when wood was still traditional, GRP new, and ferro distinctly uncommon. Now GRP is traditional and already ferro is making it old fashioned!

made by being in contact with the carefully prepared surface of the mould, is on the outside, and the less conspicuous inside is the rough side.

This inside finish, however, although described as "rough" for the sake of contrast, is not unattractive. It should definitely not be hairy or look like a doormat. That is bad moulding; it will trap dirt and soon break up, and so, probably, will the moulding. It must be just as solid as the "good" face despite any unevenness.

"WETTING OUT" "Wetting out" is the basic moulding operation, the impregnation or "wetting" of the glass-fibre with resin. This stage is also known as the lay-up or laminating stage.

It sounds easy enough to soak the glass-fibre with resin, and so in principle it is. But a good or bad moulding is mainly distinguished by the care and skill with which this is done.

Initially the glass-fibre is a loose collection of fine fibres surrounded by air. All the air must be driven out and replaced with resin so that resin surrounds and bonds to *every* fibre in *every* strand. This ideal can seldom be achieved absolutely, but the aim is to approach it as nearly as possible.

Bubbles and pockets of air are flaws and mean weakness. They are always undesirable, but may be considered negligible or potentially serious according to their size, position and number.

The common way to "wet out" is by stippling with a paint-brush. Stippling is a short jabbing action, a stencilling action, instead of a sweeping painting stroke. This forces the glass down into the resin and compacts it, rather like a herd of cows trampling straw into mud.

To "wet out" the glass-fibre lay it on the mould surface and stipple resin into it with a paint-brush. Ample resin is vital—at least two and half times as much resin as glass, probably three times as much, and even more on difficult bits. These amounts are by weight. Throw away your ideas about painting; think of the brush as a shovel. A lot of the resin can actually be poured on. Do not stint resin wherever the glass looks "dry," even though it may have already had more than its theoretical share.

The moulding is essentially a resin moulding, a plastic moulding not a glass-fibre one. (It is unfortunate that popular usage emphasises the glass-fibre or fibreglass part. In comparison, reinforced concrete is known loosely as concrete, not steel.) The glass-fibre certainly plays a very important and a most essential part, but it is the backroom partner. The resin is the glamorous partner which gives the smooth solid appearance and a bright shiny finish. The glass-fibre can only do its job if completely embedded in the resin. From the outside a moulding will look substantially the same whether it contains glass-fibre or not, and it is quite feasible to make a nice rigid boat-shaped object of resin alone, and it would float, but without glass-fibre it would soon break up. A boat made of glass-fibre alone would not even look like a boat; it would have no rigidity or shape and would certainly not float. Moreover without resin to bind the individual minute fibres into a composite block it would not even be strong.

But embed the glass-fibres in resin and the combination forms a very strong, rigid and solid moulding. A simile is the steel in reinforced concrete. A better example is the fabric in a good rubber hose or the reinforcing cords in a motor tyre.

The resin, therefore, must extend right through. There must be no sandwich effect of resin skins and unimpregnated glass-fibre between, nor must the resin be skimped so that the moulding looks fibrous like a doormat. Enough resin must be worked into the mat to make it thoroughly "wet" right through and leave the surface really looking wet.

Too much resin is undesirable if extensive, but it is not serious. Too little will not embed the glass-fibres, so that it will be impossible to use their strength. Remember that individually the fibres are too fine to contribute much useful strength. They can only work collectively in their thousands, but to do this they *must* be well embedded in resin. "United we stand, divided . . ."

There is a grave tendency for beginners to skimp the resin, which, if they are paying for it themselves, is quite understandable. Comparing it with paint such quantities of resin seem terribly extravagant. But forget all about paint at this stage. You are actually building the boat of resin; think of concrete, plaster or wood *but do not think of paint!*

The glass-fibre will "wet" out more readily if a generous layer of resin, about half the amount needed, is slapped on to the mould first, spread around with the brush, then the glass-fibre spread over this and left for a minute or two to soak up resin. The glass-fibre must be put down immediately after the resin because without the glass to hold it a thickish layer of resin will start to flow.

The main skill lies not in "wetting out," which can be picked up more quickly than it takes to read about it, but in the manipulation of the glass-fibre fabrics. Flat and regular shaped parts are easy enough, but boats are not simple shapes. Grooves, angles, ridges and edges all need special care, and the skill lies in making sure that the glass really gets down into every corner.

Obviously any woven fabric retains some cohesiveness and tends to resist being pushed into intricate shapes. So, too, but to a lesser extent, does mat. Thus the reinforcement tends to "bridge" grooves and angles instead of going right down into them. Yet it must go right down into them or there will be cavities and flaws at the bottom which, by their position, are likely to be vulnerable and conspicuous places. This is where particular care is needed, and skill and experience tell.

GEL COAT   A good surface finish is not obtained by accident. The outside of a moulded boat is a "resin rich" finish, a thick layer of resin applied to the mould surface and allowed to set before the main lay-up starts.

This layer of plain resin is called the "gel coat," and its purpose is to take up the surface finish of the mould, to protect the fine fibres and prevent them appearing on the surface. A "plastic" or resin finish is wanted, not a fibrous one; this is only obtained by a good, carefully applied, layer of resin in the gel coat.

MANIPULATION OF THE GLASS   Cut out all the glass you need before starting to mould. The pieces can then be tried out for shape on the mould; obviously this is impossible once the mould is sticky. Paper templates may make it easier to cut out awkward parts. Mark each part clearly to avoid confusion.

All joins must be made by overlapping. Butt joints do not give any continuity of strength. Joints should be staggered so that they do not build up appreciable extra thickness. An overlap of 2 in. (5 cms.) is generally sufficient.

Accuracy in cutting is not necessary or even desirable. The glass-fibre will move around while being "wetted out" and will change shape. This will upset careful tailoring

A large overlap will do no harm. It uses a little more material, but it would probably have been wasted otherwise, and it avoids the need for careful cutting out.

Mat will usually break up to follow a difficult contour; fabrics will need more tailoring. Remember, however, that if mat breaks up it is likely to be thin along the line of the angle and create a weak line. Extra pieces will be needed as patches to compensate for this. Similarly small patches may be needed to cover gaps caused by tailoring.

All pieces bond together to form part of the moulding. Properly done they are quite inseparable so that the whole moulding can really be considered as being in one piece. Note that this one-piece moulding does not have to be all the same thickness. It can be built up layer by layer to any thickness anywhere. This means that where strength is wanted it can be made as thick as necessary but where there is no need for strength it may be kept quite thin. Thus although the materials are expensive they are used very economically, and there is little wastage and weight is kept to the minimum.

Every other material has to be much thicker than necessary, all over, to provide adequate thickness in the few places where it is really needed. This means extra expense, weight, and cost.

ROLLERS Special rollers are often used for "wetting out" to force the glass into the resin. Various cunning shapes are used to reduce pick-up of the glass strands and increase the pummelling action. They serve a useful purpose but are not essential with the modern easy-wetting materials. A 2 in. or 3 in. paint-brush will work nearly as quickly.

The roller must always be used "wet" with the resin acting as a lubricant. Start on a small patch, moving the roller only a small distance, gradually extending the patch as it wets out. If you take long strokes on dry mat you will have such a bird's nest in less than a minute that it will make a weaver-bird look like a bricklayer's mate.

RELEASE A mould is essential to give shape and form. But we are applying a sticky substance, a moderate glue, and it is obviously desirable that it should come off afterwards. This is not difficult to achieve, but very important, because if it sticks not only will the moulding be ruined but the mould too. A ruined moulding is a comparatively small loss, although heart-breaking at the time, but the mould may represent a very great deal of trouble and expense. Moreover, the moulding cannot be replaced until a new mould has been made and this may take a long time.

The first step is to polish the mould face as much as possible with a good wax polish. As well as aiding release this will give a good surface finish on every moulding. A porous surface will need sealing before it can be polished. Use shellac or proprietary sealers. Ordinary paints will be attacked by the resins but not two-pack polyurethane, or epoxy.

Shortly before moulding apply the main release agent. This is most commonly a PVA (poly-vinyl-alcohol) emulsion which is painted or wiped on very thinly. It dries to form a thin protective skin all over, thick enough to give protection but not too thick to mask detail and the finish. It must be dry before starting to mould and it is very important to inspect it carefully to make sure no little bit has been left out.

This method provides two release agents. The PVA is the main release agent, but the wax polish is an insurance. Once the mould has been "broken in," i.e. after about five mouldings, it is common to use the Mirroglaze system based on polish alone.

BONDING   In much of the work described in this book it is not release that is required but bonding, particularly when a piece is moulded in position.

Bonding is covered in Chapter One. In general a "wet" moulding will bond unless the other material is treated for release. The strength of the bond will depend on many factors but it can be taken for granted that any "wet" moulding, i.e. one being laid-up, is liable to stick unless precautions are taken to prevent it. This is important if there are adjacent parts to which it must *not* bond. A moulding can spread further than expected and, in particular, resin can, and usually will, run and drip on to another surface. Such drips will stick.

TRIMMING   Mouldings can be trimmed with a hacksaw after they have set. This is best done after release from the mould to avoid damage to the mould.

Alternatively, a thin moulding can be trimmed with a sharp knife at the rubbery stage just after the resin has set. This is considerably easier but as this rubbery stage does not last long, about a quarter to half an hour, it is not always easy to hit on the right moment. If you start too soon the resin will not have set properly, and the act of cutting may result in enough movement to cause permanent distortion, too late and it will be too hard to cut with a knife.

Beginners would do better to wait and trim it with a hacksaw. Although more tedious there is less likelihood of causing inadvertent distortion.

Edges are difficult for beginners to mould solid right to the end. The last inch tends to be porous, full of air bubbles and badly moulded. When designing and making the mould beginners would do well to allow an extra inch or two and trim back to firm material afterwards. If the designed edge is marked with a scribe line on the mould it will be reproduced as a guide line for trimming on the moulding.

SUMMARY OF MOULDING

1. Prepare the mould, seal and wax polish.
2. Cut out the glass-fibre and tailor it to shape.
3. Apply a thin coat of PVA release agent.
4. Inspect the release agent and touch up as required.
5. Paint on the gel coat and allow to set.
6. Paint or slap on a thick layer of resin. Immediately lay on the glass-fibre and press down by hand. Leave to soak up for a minute.
7. Stipple resin on to the glass-fibre and work it into the underlying layer of resin to "wet out" the glass thoroughly. Keep on stippling in resin until the whole surface appears "wet." Add more resin wherever it looks "dry."
8. Continue round the moulding, overlapping all joins by at least 2 in.
9. Allow this first layer to set, although this is not essential.
10. Repeat with the second layer as in (7) and (8). Joins should not occur in the same places as on the previous layer.
11. Continue with the third and following layers. These may be applied "wet" on "wet" without waiting for the under layer to set.
12. Allow the moulding to set, and clean out brushes and tools.
13. Sand down high spots, lumps and upstanding whiskers.

14. Apply one or two thin coats of resin to even up the surface.
15. Release from the mould.
16. Trim edges. (This can also be done at the rubbery stage between (12) and (13) just after the resin has set.)
     Stages 15, 16 and 13, 14 are interchangeable.

N.B.—Whenever resin is mentioned it is assumed that it has been properly activated by adding catalyst.

SPRAY-UP In spray-up moulding glass rovings are chopped and blown onto the mould in a stream together with a spray of catalysed resin. Certainly it is quicker than hand lay-up, but it is not a one-man process. It still needs a gang to roll it. Like most modern progress it creates several new problems for every one solved.

It is wrong to assume that it produces better mouldings. In most cases it does not. Instead of relying on the collective skill and integrity (or lack of them) of a gang, everything depends on one key man, the operator. He may or may not be good. He may or may not have the high degree of honesty and integrity needed. When he has a hangover or a cold all the company's moulding suffers, not just a small part of it. If he gets sick moulding stops or someone less skilled has to take over. Production also depends completely on the machine: when it stops, moulding stops. Down time is often excessive. In the past some equipment has needed a mechanic standing by.

It has been found from experience that spray moulding tends to produce uneven thickness. It may average out over an area, but on a local scale the surface generally has waves giving on average about 25 per cent variation in thickness, sometimes as much as 50 per cent. Distribution can be more widely uneven: I once measured a boat with sides differing in average thickness by 50 per cent. Mouldings often have a high bubble content.

For high quality, hand lay-up is better than spray-up, and is essential when woven rovings are needed. Spray-up is more suitable for thick, quick, rather crude mouldings where strength is less important than speed of moulding.

These comments will be disputed and in some cases were undoubtedly due to lack of care, experience or supervision—which all goes to show how vitally the spray-up method depends on a high degree of skill and integrity in the operator. Some moulders have mastered the art of spray moulding. But from the boats I have seen, many have not.

HIGH PERFORMANCE MOULDINGS Highest strength with least weight is achieved by using woven rovings, occasionally cloth, and careful control to keep the amount of resin low. A low resin ratio is not achieved just by cutting down on resin: that leads to resin starvation, bad moulding and a lot of trouble. The resin must be distributed evenly, and thorough, hard rolling is essential to ensure that the glass is wetted out by being pushed down tightly into the resin rather than the usual way of letting it swim in a sea of resin. This requires skill, patience and takes a long time. It is essential to keep a careful check on weights at all stages to make sure the moulding is on target. It is no good trusting that it will be within the specification when it is finished.

The Mould

SOME form of mould is essential. "Wet" glass-fibre is soggy and shapeless. It must be supported while setting. The mould gives shape to the moulding, but it also gives the finish—good or bad.

MALE OR FEMALE MOULD Moulds can be of male or female type. The choice depends on which side needs the best appearance or most accurate shape. One side of the moulding, the side laid up against the mould, will be the exact reproduction of the mould both in shape and finish, but in reverse of course. The other side is the uneven, natural finish.

A boat always has a good outside finish and is therefore made in a female mould; a cockpit, on the other hand, would need a good finish on the inside and is therefore made on a male mould. Remember the best and most accurate face of the moulding must always be the side which is in contact with the mould.

It is not easy to make a mould direct, male or female. It is difficult to visualise the object inside-out, so the mould is usually made from a master-pattern giving a positive pattern/negative mould/positive moulding sequence. In this way, too, the pattern can be a material which is easily worked but not strong enough for a mould, and the mould can be itself a fibreglass moulding giving the necessary toughness and finish, but impossible to form to shape except over a pattern.

DESIGN All moulds must be designed so that the moulding can come away cleanly. Undercuts will cause it to jam and there must be adequate taper or draw. This is very important, and there is no doubt that simple moulds are easiest to release and last longest.

A complicated mould, or a mould which is clearly going to jam, will require a split mould in two or more pieces. It is just as important to ensure that every piece will come away cleanly. A split mould allows much more elaborate mouldings and also does not restrict the design of the piece to something which can be made in a one-piece mould. A split mould, too, will usually release more easily than a one-piece mould with a straight draw.

Arrangements must be made to bolt the parts together; this can be done by moulding flanges on both parts and simply bolting or clamping them.

Some taper should be allowed to the sides; 10 degrees on a long deep draw, but a short draw can be nearly parallel. Sides release easily, but corners are inclined to stick, particularly sharp right-angled corners. All corners should be well radiused. It is quite simple to radius the corners of a simple box-mould by filling them with plaster or filler or special wax fillet, as well as the more expensive yacht fillers; alternatively a cove strip can be used.

It is often quite simple to mould in some feature as a bulge or dent which would otherwise require a fitted block or woodwork. This should be done with caution, particularly on prototypes, as once it is moulded in its position cannot be altered or the fitting changed. Elaborate moulds are better left to the later stages of development when the snags have been ironed out and one is sure that every fitting is in the right place, of the right kind and is really wanted.

PATTERN The usual practice for more than one or two mouldings is to make a master pattern first of wood or plaster and on this is moulded the fibreglass mould. The choice of material depends mainly on what the mould-maker is used to using. A boat-builder naturally thinks of wood, others may prefer plaster. Both of these need accurate and careful work and, particularly with plaster, a lot more skill than is fondly imagined. The shape and dimensions must be *exactly* right for all the production mouldings will have that shape. If the pattern is wrong, all are wrong, no matter how well moulded. Hulls really need the smooth lines of wood. Plaster moulds tend to be wavy.

THE FINISH OF THE PATTERN The finish of the master pattern determines the finish of every moulding. It is worth taking great trouble to get a first-class finish, because that finish will be imparted to the mould, and then every moulding will have a good finish as it comes from the mould. No additional work will be needed, which is obviously a tremendous saving of labour, as the amount of time spent in sanding and painting a wooden boat is substantial.

The first stage in preparing the pattern for use is to fill and sand it down. This is followed by coats of sealer well rubbed down. The finish is obtained by painting, applying a number of coats and rubbing down well in between. Ordinary paints should not be used as they are marked by the resins. Two-pack polyurethane or epoxy paints are unaffected by the resins and give a very high gloss finish when burnished and polished.

The more care spent on this stage, the better the final moulding will be. After all it is only done once, not on every boat as in other forms of boatbuilding, so it is worth taking a lot of trouble over it.

THE MOULD The mould is usually a fibreglass moulding also. No other material at a reasonable price is tough enough for moderate production, has a first-class finish and is easily formed to shape—assuming there is a shape to form it on, for that is the real problem.

Other materials can also be used for a mould, such as plaster, wood, hardboard, cement, etc. However, these are more suitable for one-off or short-run moulding, as they are not tough enough for production and will need continuous touching up. They are useful for cheap, simple moulds for a single moulding. Plaster is particularly good where a complicated mould must be broken up to get the moulding out. Sometimes the moulding can be simplified so that wood or hardboard can be used.

SIMPLE MOULDS In fitting out work the requirement is often for a single simple mould and the finish is unimportant, e.g. to form a web or flange. Such parts will usually be in an inconspicuous position and being on the "rough" side anyway the contrast is less noticeable.

A simple "shuttering," similar in idea to formwork with concrete, is sufficient and is easily cut out of cardboard, plywood or hardboard. Hardboard is particularly good because it has a naturally smooth surface which gives easy release and a reasonable appearance, but this can also be obtained with any of the others by wrapping them in polythene; this is quick and cheap. In most cases the piece will be formed in position using the boat itself as part of the mould. This ensures an exact, intimate fit.

It is useless to spend a lot of time on making a mould for a single moulding. If work is required it might as well be done on the moulding itself. A mould for a single item which costs ten times as much as an acceptable alternative in wood or metal requires a lot of justification. A sense of perspective is essential.

However, by accepting a rougher finish and a simpler shape it is often possible to use plywood or hardboard to make a cheap mould and thereby obtain the advantages of a moulded piece at reasonable cost. A positive mould is often easier to make, but as this puts the rough side of the moulding outwards considerable smoothing is needed later.

Ingenuity is the most valuable aid. Often common everyday objects can be used, polythene ware from the kitchen or nursery is excellent, and so are treasures from the gash box. A collection of shapes is a valuable standby and can be kept well supplied by intercepting things on their way to the dustbin.

Plaster and wood can be used in combination, using wood for the easy parts and plaster for the difficult.

There is scope too for composite construction on the boat combining moulded pieces for small difficult shapes, made on plaster moulds, with panels of marine plywood.

Easily formed materials like papier mâché, cardboard, plasticine, modelling clay and even sand can all be used with little cost or trouble where a good finish is not essential. Sand will need to be stabilised by spraying or painting on a coat of resin or some other sealer.

There is plenty of scope for disguising a poor finish when fitting out. Below decks most things will be hidden or can be painted. Above decks everything will be conspicuous and must match with the well finished hull and upperworks. But even so the rough finish of a moulding can be tidied up and painted with resin to match. This will, of course, take time and trouble, but the alternative is to make the piece in wood or metal which will also take time and trouble, and further trouble later in maintenance.

Moulding is primarily a process for reasonable quantity production, but with ingenuity, common sense and strict sense of proportion, even a one-off moulding can frequently be a reasonably economical alternative to making the piece in wood, requiring a comparable amount of work yet having the superior properties, lightness and low maintenance of a moulding.

For serious production, proper sub-mouldings would be used, made with a good mould and pattern. However, anyone making boats on a production scale will not be reading these appendices, which are intended more for a beginner, amateur or professional thinking in immediate terms of one boat. For a one-off moulding to be worthwhile it is essential to use ingenuity and simplicity—but it can certainly be done, and economically too.

RELEASE Proper preparation, as described in the next appendix, and sensible mould design will ensure certain release.

However, no moulding drops out of the mould. It must be eased out, as there is a substantial vacuum behind it and very intimate contact with the mould.

A simple moulding can be eased away all round, using the natural springiness of the moulding and the mould, until it is free. Usually there is a bang after part has been eased and the whole moulding comes away quite cleanly.

In stubborn cases, thump the reverse side of the mould gently with the fist or a soft mallet, or drive thin strips of hardboard between the mould and moulding. Hardboard will not scratch the moulding (or, more important, the mould); metal or wood will.

Do not despair if it is difficult to release. Persevere with the methods a little more firmly, and it will usually come out in the end. Complete failure, i.e. a moulding stuck irrevocably to the mould, is rare, even when a release agent has been applied carelessly, and the difficulty is usually only a case of getting at the vacuum to release it. In some cases compressed air-lines are let into the mould to blow the moulding off but these must be situated with care or the moulding may bulge and burst before an awkward corner lets go.

Modifications to the mould are advisable, if it proves very stubborn, in particular turning it into a split mould rather than a single-piece one.

BONDING The commonest requirement when fitting out a boat is to mould something in position. In this case the boat acts as the mould, with or without the assistance of releasable "shuttering" to give further shape.

Chapter One describes the methods of making sure the new moulding bonds to the old or to other fitments such as woodwork.

Moulding in position can cover a wide field from a simple butt-strap, which is just a flat strip, to an elaborate built-in tank. These are all described in the main body of the book. The main thing is to realise that one can mould with the idea of bonding on to the "mould," in this case the boat, as well as moulding a separate object which must be released from the mould afterwards. There is no difference in the basic moulding technique, except that no release agent is used, of course, and as there will be no "good" side, because it will be bonded on, there is no need for a gel coat. In some cases, however, a primer will be needed.

MOULDLESS CONSTRUCTION Actually, a mould is used but it is incorporated in the finished moulding. This obviously means it is a once-only mould. A good example is mouldless sandwich. The structure is built with sheets of plastics foam on a framework. The outside is covered with GRP to a suitable thickness, the structure turned over, framework removed and the inside covered with GRP thus forming a sandwich moulding. Obviously both sides are rough but as it is a one-off it justifies some work to finish it. The natural surface can be improved by finishing with gauze or light cloth and sanding. Then if paint can turn rough wood into a yacht finish it can do the same for GRP.

This method has been used successfully by Derek Kelsall and others to make large one-off GRP boats, for which heat-formed Airex foam PVC has been found most suitable. Other cores can be plywood, balsa, chipboard, polyurethane foam (rigid, flexible or flexible rigidised with resin) according to the purpose, but not polystyrene with polyester resin unless protected.

Moulding Hints

SETTING TIME Once the catalyst has been added the resin will set, and practically nothing will stop this. The time taken, however, the setting time, is affected by various factors. The main ones are: temperature, quantity of catalyst, quantity of accelerator, and type of resin.

The last two are usually fixed features. Even if the accelerator has to be added before use, and not by the manufacturers, a bad practice but regrettably common, it will be done in bulk and will not be suitable for short term adjustment. It may, however, be used for seasonal adjustment or for adjustment between a hot job and a cold one.

The temperature has considerable effect on the setting time. It may or may not be under control. Higher temperatures will cause quicker setting, low temperatures will delay it.

The proportion of catalyst is the main means of controlling the setting time and, in particular, to compensate for changes in temperature or abnormal working conditions. More catalyst means quicker setting, less will slow it down. An average quantity is 2 per cent but this can be varied from 0·5 per cent to 5 per cent without noticeable ill-effect.

Hot conditions such as in the tropics—and even during a British summer if working under a hot roof—will call for reduced catalyst to keep the setting time long enough for unhurried working.

Very cold conditions require extra catalyst, and possibly extra accelerator too. Cold conditions are usually considered to be out of the question. This is by no means the case, particularly with the modern hardeners (I have worked successfully, but uncomfortably, in a cold store.) The danger with cold conditions lies in not taking sufficient precautions (or not knowing how) to ensure that the resin sets within a few hours. Cold conditions can delay setting time so long that secondary effects such as absorption of condensation cause serious loss of strength and other properties. There is a lot of condensation under cold, frosty conditions. 1% of tertiary amine accelerator has a synergistic boosting effect.

Without precautions this delayed setting time could be a matter of several days, but such a delay would definitely be due to the fault or inexperience of the moulder. Really cold conditions are not for beginners, who should make an effort to obtain moderate temperature.

If the workshop is heated the heat should be left on all night, or at least long enough after work has stopped to ensure that all that day's moulding sets within the proper time. Otherwise it may still be "wet" the next morning.

It is quite simple to experiment with different proportions of catalyst to establish a convenient working time. Using small quantities there will be little wastage. The section "Measurement" gives hints for working with small quantities.

Remember the control is easy and lies in your hands. Too quick, cut down catalyst; too slow step it up.

WORKING TIME   A slow setting time, provided it is not unduly prolonged, will cause little harm; a quick setting time may spoil the project.

A setting time that is inconveniently quick, e.g. 15 minutes, will mean rushed, skimped work with a real danger of unfinished wetting out if the resin sets too soon. There will be a continual nagging fear, a quite justifiable fear, that the resin will set before that piece has been finished.

But a setting time of one or two hours will give ample time for calm unhurried work, and that is very important, for the most important thing is to ensure that the glass is thoroughly "wetted out" and that it is worked right into every angle and groove. This is very much more important than bothering about the exact setting time of the resin. If it takes a day to set, that is a lesser fault than bad lay-up with cavities and bubbles trapped in it. *This will certainly happen if the work is rushed.*

I find that many suppliers recommend far too short a setting time, a time as short as 10 minutes. 1½ hrs. should be the absolute minimum for a beginner. Resin manufacturers are usually more concerned with marginal factors which secure optimum resin performance and do not give enough consideration to the practical problems of wetting out. The most perfect resin is useless if not combined properly with the glass-fibre.

Obviously the larger the section being moulded, the longer the setting time needs to be. Do not try to mould a whole boat in one piece and all at once; 1 sq. yd. (say 1 sq. m.) is a convenient size of piece to handle, and uses around 2 lb. of resin (1 kg.), which as two batches of 1 lb. is the sort of amount to make up at one time. You can overlap and go straight on with the next piece so that it is just as strong working with two pieces of 1 sq. yd. as working with one large piece of 2 sq. yds. The smaller pieces are a lot easier to handle and there is less chance of wastage due to the resin setting before the piece has been fully "wetted out."

The resin will not wait for interruptions, tea breaks, meal-times, chatty friends, or the telephone. Once the catalyst has been added it is like a time fuse. Consequently it is important to work with pieces which you are sure can be "wetted out" not only within the setting time of the resin but also within the time you have available. Anyone who drops his tools the moment the whistle blows is not wanted on this job. Once you have started you must carry on as long as there is glass on the mould to be "wetted out," and catalysed resin in your pot.

SHELF LIFE   Polyester resin needs a hardener added to make it set, but even without this it will not remain liquid indefinitely. The liquid stage is only a half-way stage in the chemical reaction. The final stage is a solid and it is bound to go solid with age even if not used.

The normal shelf life, i.e. the time it is liquid and still usable, is at least one year and usually two or three, although it often tends to get rather thick and difficult to use towards the end. Storage under warm conditions, e.g. near radiators or in the tropics, will shorten its useful life. It must therefore be stored under cool conditions. In Britain and other temperate countries an unheated store is quite adequate. Storage below 70° F. (21° C.) is all that is needed for a long shelf life even in the tropics, i.e. an air-conditioned room or store, not expensive cold storage.

Note that a limited shelf life does not imply any limitation in the life of the moulding. The resin in a moulding is hardened on purpose and will last indefinitely, so will the resin which goes hard in the can, as a solid is its final stable state. The shelf life only refers to the time it is liquid and therefore in a condition for moulding.

Addition of the common accelerator either by the manufacturer or by the user will, with one exception, have negligible effect on the storage life. The exception is Dimethyl Aniline but it is not so common. The usual purple cobalt accelerator has no effect on the shelf life. N.B.: A few resins, notably Crystic 189, cannot be pre-accelerated far ahead.

Old resin is as good as new, except for any thickening towards the end. As a general rule if it pours it is usable, there is no hidden deterioration and the instruction to use it before a certain date is an indication of its useful shelf life, not a limit.

Remember, however, that catalyst can lose its strength with age.

Glass-fibre, if kept dry and protected from mechanical damage, is likely to last as long as any other glass, and judging by the bottles which litter our countryside, that is a long time.

READY-MIXED RESINS Nowadays the trend is towards buying ready-mixed resins with colour, fillers, accelerator all added by the manufacturer leaving only catalyst to be added by the user immediately before use.

There is no doubt whatever that this is a very much more convenient way to use resins and moreover the resin is better. All those items just cannot be mixed thoroughly when doing it in a bucket with a stick or even a power mixer, but they can in a factory with proper ball mills and equipment. When did you last mix up your own paint—not just adding a colour tint but mixing up the basic ingredients? It is never done today because factory made paint is so much better and more convenient.

A wide range of blends and grades of resin is now available which will cater for all normal requirements and there is a considerable range of colours. It means sticking to a standard range of colours, but at least that colour can be repeated which is not so if adding colour oneself.

To supply a lot of separate components and expect the user to mix them laboriously by hand as is done by many suppliers seems terribly primitive and fraught with error. Moreover, it distracts the user and gives the impression that the secret lies in the mixing. This is not so. Provided they are good resins and suitable for the purpose, the exact composition matters little. It is the way it is used which is important. Which is more important in a wooden boat, the quality of the wood or the way it is built? Surely it is the way it is built, for many tough old fishing-boats were built for their present owners' grandfathers out of cheap timber and the rejects of expensive yachtyards; careful workmanship can make a strong boat out of old orange boxes. It is just the same with resins; honest workmanship is better than perfect materials. The result may not be first class, but can certainly be a good second class, and just as with wood, it is unlikely anyway that anyone will achieve a really first class result until they have had a lot of experience.

There is no magic about plastics, particularly glass-fibre and resin. They are only materials to be used just as wood and metal are only materials to be used, and are not an end in themselves.

The boat is the important thing and we are building boats, not playing with a chemistry set. The simpler the materials are to prepare, and in particular the less thought and worry that is needed to prepare them, the more thought and care can be given to using them properly to make a good boat. No man can concentrate on good workmanship if he is worried about being blown up if he does something wrong.

ACCELERATOR Sometimes the accelerator for the resin is supplied separately and has to be added as well as the catalyst before the resin will set. I dislike this practice when resins are supplied **to** ordinary people with no scientific background. As well as introducing another thing to be remembered (or forgotten), another distraction from the basic task which is moulding, it has always seemed to me to be much too dangerous, because if the accelerator is allowed to come into contact with the catalyst, when both are neat and not dispersed in the resin, they can react violently; that is just a salesman's way of describing an explosion violent enough to cause serious injury and damage.

Separate accelerator adds an unnecessary anxiety and worry for ordinary unscientific people, working under practical workshop, not laboratory, conditions and with their puzzled minds preoccupied with an unfamiliar and somewhat distrusted process.

The only safe course is to buy resins with the accelerator already mixed in; dispersed in the resin they do no harm as the catalyst can never come into contact with undiluted accelerator, and cause a "reaction" vigorous enough to take the roof off.

There is no disadvantage in supplying accelerated resins like this, and there are very definite advantages. It may reduce the range of operating temperatures, but there will still be a sufficiently wide range for a beginner and no one should try to work well outside the normal temperatures, until he has had experience in any case. By that time it will no longer be a mystery and it may be safe to trust him with a little accelerator to pep up the resin at low temperatures.

If, by some misfortune, you do find accelerator has to be added separately, the following points should be observed:

a. Mix in the accelerator in bulk, i.e. into whole drums or bucketfuls, before starting work. If possible mix it into all the drums and then lock up the accelerator and everything used to mix it.
Mark the cans so there is no mistake. By mixing large quantities at a time measurement is much simpler.

b. Keep separate measures and mixing containers for catalyst and accelerator. Mark them boldly, keep well apart (separate buildings for choice), and never use any measure for both accelerator and catalyst.

c. If you want trouble, keep the accelerator and catalyst bottles side by side, use the same measure for each and add your few drops of accelerator and catalyst to each small batch of resin as you need it. If you do this I advise you to count your fingers every night and make sure the doors and windows will blow out easily—you might want them out of the way in a great hurry.

Very few suppliers of resins with separate accelerators give enough warning against such a practice, which to me seems suicidal. A warning adequate for a scientist is not sufficient for a workman; it is better for the danger to be impossible.

My very strong recommendation is to refuse to buy any resin which is supplied with separate accelerator. It is dangerous for a beginner and a waste of time for the experienced. Note, however, that some new kinds of catalyst and accelerator can be mixed but it is still safer to refuse first and ask afterwards.

COLOURS Normally coloured resins are used and these will require no painting—at least not in the fitting out stages. Colour may be mixed in by the user or the resins can now be bought ready coloured.

Colour match is always a problem. Any part added after moulding, such as a sub-assembly, a moulded-on fitting or a repair, must be made with exactly the same resin as the original moulding. This will not present much difficulty if using factory coloured resins but where the colour is mixed in by the moulder, perhaps a bucketful at a time, it is almost impossible to repeat it exactly. It is important to colour up all the resin needed for a moulding in one batch, and if there are to be matching sub-mouldings to leave enough over for these. Otherwise the moulding will be noticeably piebald. It is most noticeable of course on the gel coat and therefore it is essential that all this is coloured in one batch. The colour of the lay-up resins is not nearly so important.

Colours will fade slightly with age so that it is almost impossible to match the colour on an old moulding, e.g. for repairs or additions to a boat that is several years old. This usually means that the whole boat may have to be repainted. The problem is just the same on cars where a minor repair usually involves a respray—even if the insurance company is not paying.

FILLERS Much rubbish is written about fillers, i.e. a cheap powder added to the resin.

Use of filler is not harmful provided it is the right filler in moderate proportions. Fillers can impart extra properties to the resin, e.g. improved hardness, abrasion resistance, reduced shrinkage, better workability, denser colour and, in fact, a filled resin can be a lot better than an unfilled one. (See also Appendix 1.)

On the other hand, loading the resin with excessive amounts of filler with the idea of diluting and cheapening the resin, will seriously weaken it and ruin its weather resistance. It is this practice, or the fear of it (for it undoubtedly has existed in the past and I could mention one or two well advertised, "popular" makes of boats even now) which has brought the idea of fillers into disrepute. However, its prevalence is grossly exaggerated and so is the cheapening effect; the extra difficulty of working with such a thick resin will offset the hoped for cheapening and it will be plainly obvious in the finished moulding. Moreover a moulder who adopts this practice is not going to spend money in touching up the moulding, so the defects caused by excess filler will be there to see.

It is difficult to lay down hard and fast rules as to a reasonable amount of filler. It depends on the type of filler, the resin and the purpose of the filler—for it should always be used with a purpose. In general up to 15 to 20 per cent for a soft filler (china clay, chalk, talc, etc.) and 20 to 30 per cent for a hard, heavy filler (quartz, slate) will be beneficial rather than harmful.

Colour and usually thixotropy are obtained by using "fillers," i.e. something added to the resin—yet few boats whose makers boast they are made with "unfilled" resins are uncoloured and all must be made with thixotropic resins!

A very large filler content, 70 to 90 per cent of the total, is often used to make putties and this is definitely done for cheapness. But it is more correct to consider these rather as cheap powder fillers bound together with a little resin to form a putty, than as resins loaded with filler to cheapen them.

Putties like this are perfectly acceptable provided they are definitely used as putties and not as structural resins. They are a convenient and cheap way of filling awkward spots, or doing simple repairs.

SELF-EXTINGUISHING RESINS It is impossible at the present time (although a lot of research is being devoted to this point) to make polyester resins fireproof. However, a lot of polyester resins are self-extinguishing or can be made so with simple additives.

Self-extinguishing means that the resin will cease to burn as soon as the flame is removed, i.e. put out the fire in the engine and the boat, which until then will have been burning steadily but reluctantly, will stop burning on its own.

The usual additives are antimony oxide ("Timinox") and "Cereclor" a chlorinated wax made by I.C.I. There are others, however, and I am sure there will be more before long.

"Het" acid resins, a form of polyester resin, have better self-extinguishing properties than any others. Unfortunately their weather resistance is not so good as the normal polyesters.

Many self-extinguishing resins give off dense smoke, and in some cases fumes, and may be a mixed blessing. (See also Chapter 21.)

ALWAYS ADD CATALYST BEFORE USE Always remember to add catalyst before use to every batch of resin. It is easy enough to forget in the heat of the moment or to have doubts. The only safeguard is a very strict routine.

If in doubt add more, perhaps half quantity and be prepared to work faster. Extra catalyst will cause no harm other than quicker setting but no catalyst means that the resin just will not set and that will ruin the job.

If you find this has happened the only thing to do is to rip it off even if there are later layers on top which have set. There is no certain way of getting catalyst dispersed through "wet" mat once it has been put on and therefore it will never set properly. Brushing or spraying on catalyst will never set off more than a crust.

Some wasted material is better than a spoiled boat even though it may be heart-breaking at the time.

MEASUREMENT All resin suppliers skip lightly over the means of measuring the proportions of resin and catalyst, assuming apparently a well equipped laboratory and staff used to handling small quantities with accuracy.

Under practical boatyard or backyard conditions the measurement of quantities of catalyst of the order of 1 to 2 per cent of the resin can be a tricky operation. Yet accuracy is essential if results are to be consistent and reliable.

The resin is easy enough to measure. Kitchen scales will weigh quantities from $\frac{1}{4}$ lb. upwards with adequate accuracy. However, to preserve domestic bliss I strongly recommend buying a separate set of scales. An alternative is to borrow the kitchen scales for an hour, and, with the most elaborate precautions over cleanliness, calibrate a measure or standard mixing container on a volumetric basis (a cheap kitchen polythene measuring jug is suitable). Otherwise after a few days' use you will not dare to return the scales and will have to buy her some new ones anyway.

The difficulty of measuring the catalyst is apparent if you consider the actual quantities involved. 1 per cent of 1 lb. (500 g.) is about one-sixth of an ounce (5 gr.—how delightfully easy the metric system is), or the weight of two cigarettes. Moreover the tolerance, assuming it is as much as 10 per cent (pretty crude as measurements go), is then once-sixtieth of an ounce (0·5 gr.), the weight of a couple of matches.

Matches and cigarettes are common enough and could be used as weights, but kitchen scales are not nearly sensitive enough to weigh a cigarette or a match; they might detect a change of $\frac{1}{4}$ oz. in good light, and even a sensitive letter balance would hardly record a change in weight of a few matches.

In any case there is no time for such fiddling measurements and some sticky resin transferred to the scales will very soon throw the measurements right out.

Of course laboratory balances could be used but they are expensive and are quite definitely not workshop instruments.

Fortunately there is a very simple way out if using liquid catalyst and it requires a piece of equipment which costs pennies at any chemists. The method is to measure volumetrically using a medicinal eye-dropper and count the drops. This sounds crude, but it so happens that one drop of a liquid is remarkably constant. 1 per cent of 1 lb. is of the order of 160 drops of the common liquid catalyst MEKP. 1 per cent of 1 oz. would be 10 drops, so that it is possible to measure, accurately, the amount of catalyst for quantities of resin which themselves need quite a sensitive balance for a workshop. As 1 drop of catalyst is about 1/1,000 oz. it is obvious that this method is very much more sensitive than kitchen scales or even quite expensive balances. Moreover, it is robust enough for a workshop, cheap enough to throw away if someone steps on it and needs no skill as long as the chap can count.

It will be necessary to calibrate the drops in each case. The figures quoted above are typical but the size of drop is different for every liquid and they may not be the same for yours.

Calibration can be done by scaling up to a measurable quantity on your larger scales. Drop catalyst into a small container (of known weight), counting the drops until the scales show a figure which can be read reliably. (The limitation may well be the quantity of catalyst available.) This will be tedious on kitchen scales as it may be several thousand drops. A short cut is to use a letter balance. From this is it easy to scale down to give the number of drops for 1 per cent of 1 lb. or whatever convenient weight represents the normal working batch of resin.

When working it is tedious and time-wasting to count out more than 50 drops or so —and unreliable, for it is easy to lose count. It is accurate enough if the dropper is calibrated in units of, say, 10 or 20 drops. Typically 1 per cent of 1 lb. would be 4 dropperfuls of about 40 drops each. Consistency of measurement is much more important than known accuracy, and you will soon establish the number of "squirts" per standard containerful.

The size of drop will vary with temperature and pressure, but it is of secondary importance and within the tolerance of practical workshop measurement. Beware, however, of a thickening with age although I have never known it happen with a catalyst.

Paste or powder catalysts are much more difficult as they have to be weighed, but pastes are sometimes supplied in tubes like toothpaste so that the amount needed can be expressed in length squeezed out.

Above all, never guess the catalyst. With experience the volume of resin can be guessed; it will usually be a standard mixing container, or a guessable proportion of one. But it is courting disaster to guess the small proportions of catalyst.

Work with small batches, say 1 lb. (½ kg.) at a time adding catalyst each time immediately before use. 1 lb. is a convenient quantity to work with. If it sets prematurely it is no great loss; to add catalyst to a whole large bucketful will result in expensive wastage and considerable anxiety in trying to use it all up before it sets. Rushed, skimped work will be the inevitable result.

Plenty of throw away mixing containers will be needed. ¾–1 lb. is a convenient quantity for waxed cartons or cleaned out food tins. If the container is always the same size the resin need not be weighed or measured for each batch and this will save a lot of time.

For continuous moulding polythene containers are worthwhile as they can be cleaned out. Banging the outside will break up the resin inside. Polystyrene containers will be dissolved; unfortunately this rules out the plastic throw-away cups.

CLEANING AND KEEPING CLEAN Some people get very discouraged by the sticky mess which at first seems unavoidable. (Personally I dislike the oily mess inseparable from engines.)

However, there are simple techniques for keeping clean and there is no need for anyone to get dirtier than when painting. It is just a knack. When a child, and quite a few grown-ups too, antifoul the bottom of a boat it is hard to tell painter from boat, but the professional painter will hardly dirty his hands.

Attention to the following points will leave your hands at the end of a working day clean enough to go to a society ball:

1. Before starting work rub in barrier cream (Rosalex 9, Kerrocleanse 22). If working in a confined space apply it to your face, neck and arms too. Repeat this every few hours, say after every meal-break. Cover your finger-nails well as resin adheres better to them than to skin.
2. Have a plentiful supply of clean rags and wipe your hands frequently.
3. Dust your hands with talcum powder at frequent intervals, e.g. whenever you wipe them. This prevents resin building up and reduces the stickiness. (Perfumed bath powder is expensive. Baby powder is cheaper, but better still is to buy a loose bagful from a local chemist.)
4. If working in a confined space, wear a hat or scarf over your hair. A piece of polythene may look odd as a headscarf, particularly on a man, but it is cheap and expendable. (It is dangerous to put one's head inside a polythene bag.)
5. When you finish work, clean off the resin with an emulsion hand-cleaner (Kerrocleanse GP or Swarfega). It is important to use an emulsion hand-cleaner as this acts as a lubricant and eases the muck away kindly by getting behind it. An abrasive type grinds it away, skin and all, and leaves the hands rough. The housewife's dream, soft smooth hands, is not cissy but common sense in this business, for resin will not stick to a smooth cream-covered hand just as it will not stick to a smooth waxed mould.

Never use solvent on your hands. This dries up the oils in the skin leaving it hard and coarse, and next time the resin sticks very much better. It is also removing the natural protection against dermatitis. Any solvent strong enough to dissolve solidified polyester resin will usually take flesh and blood in its stride, and some of these solvents are particularly powerful.

If you cannot get the resin off do not despair (unless you have an important date that night or your hands look as if you have just committed a murder). Due to the natural oiliness and sloughing action of the skin, it will all fall off in a few days. Picking it off is not recommended as it may take some of the skin off too but the temptation will probably be irresistible. Anyway it will do much less harm than using solvents or harsh hand-cleaners, and at least it gives satisfaction.

The skin will clean itself provided its natural oiliness can be preserved but this does not apply to finger-nails. Resin will bond to these until it grows out. Plenty of barrier cream first is the best answer.

Rubber or polythene gloves are often used, but they are of less benefit than one might imagine. They soon become stiff and hard with solidified resin and I always find that putting them on and off gets resin inside the wrists which is more uncomfortable than having no gloves. They can only be recommended in cases of dermatitis risk. Anyone used to working with his hands and who likes to feel things will be more comfortable with plenty of barrier cream, and anyone who is a dermatitis risk should be on other work.

CLEANING BRUSHES The consumption of brushes will be phenomenal unless a strict routine of cleaning is adhered to.

Whenever you stop work or pause, put the brush in the cleaning tin at once, before anything else, and also give it a clean-out frequently during work. The suggested routine is to have at least two brushes, and every time a fresh batch of resin is mixed up, put one brush in to clean and take out another. Once resin sets hard in a brush nothing will shift it and the brush is ruined.

Acetone is the most effective cheap cleaning solvent but it is inflammable and certainly introduces a fire risk. The alternative is a strong non-oily detergent. This has no fire risk, but the brush must be dried out very thoroughly otherwise it will introduce water into the moulding; this is undesirable. Traces of acetone, however, are compatible with the resin. (It is a solvent but not a destructive one). Styrene is also good and traces are highly compatible (it is a constituent of the resin anyway) but it is more expensive and not generally available. Toluene and cellulose thinners can be used if nothing else is available.

A compromise with less fire risk is to use a small quantity of acetone for initial cleaning and also to get rid of the water immediately before use and to store the brushes in detergent.

Overnight and after use, brushes should be left standing in acetone or detergent. Acetone will evaporate unless it is in a closed tin. A polythene bag tied over the top of the tin is a useful alternative. Keep the brushes off the bottom of the tin because a resin sludge will collect at the bottom and slowly solidify.

Acetone as sold in small fancy bottles for removing nail varnish costs £25 per gallon. However, a local chemist should be able to supply a pint or two for 10–20p and a wholesale chemist can supply it by the gallon at about 50p per gallon. The large chemists can usually obtain gallon quantities to order.

USE MARINE MATERIALS Always insist on having materials of the highest quality for only these are suitable for marine use. They will be more expensive, of course, but cheaper materials prove more expensive in the long run. Good materials will make the difference between lasting indefinitely and lasting for only a year or two.

Do not use "garage" materials. What is suitable for a car is not suitable for a boat. Many of the suppliers of small quantities, the few pounds of resin and yard or two of glass, come into this category.

For marine work, go direct to the manufacturer whenever possible. Hunt around until you find one who will consider small orders. At least you will collect useful literature and will be in a position to demand a definite grade of material from a local agent instead of being fobbed off with his own cheap brew.

The important points to demand are these:

1. Use the better quality "E" glass-fibre (alkali-free) not the cheaper "A" glass (alkali glass).
2. Use resins approved for marine use; only the manufacturer can tell you this.
3. Filler content must be moderate and of a type approved for marine use. A well-known manufacturer's recommended mixed resin will be reliable, but demand the formula if it is a kit supplier's own brew.
4. Insist on light fast colours and non-yellowing translucent resins.
5. If you do not know the manufacturer, or it is not a well-known company, insist on a guarantee that the materials are suitable for boats.

QUALITY CONTROL The single factor responsible for more trouble than anything else is bad quality control during moulding. GRP boats seldom develop faults. They are built with them. Faults can be corrected easily and cheaply during moulding, but it is very difficult and expensive later. Quality control demands two things: quality conscious management and an eagle-eyed foreman. All else follows. Only the foreman can spot faults and correct them before it is too late, but QUALITY STARTS RIGHT AT THE TOP—NOWHERE ELSE.

No visiting surveyor can replace the man who is on the spot all the time. The best a surveyor can do is inspect the moulding carefully and thoroughly afterwards, and pass or reject the whole—which usually becomes a lengthy legal affair.

On a practical level, use uncoloured resins for all moulding except the gel coat. Not only can the foreman see the flaws but also the worker. Do not paint GRP inside except where it is conspicuous. Different coloured markings on the layers of glass give a quick check on thickness. Keep and mark cut-outs, also samples of all materials used. Keep good records showing types and makes of materials used, workers, weather and anything else significant. This is essential for checking back. Otherwise faults will remain mysteries.

Every moulding must be inspected carefully. This must be someone's personal responsibility. To allow small, easily detected flaws to pass, as is so commonly the case, is inexcusable. It gives the moulder a bad name and one wonders what else has not been seen.

Working Under Practical Yard Conditions

WHEN faced with the problem of working under practical conditions it is a help to know that the working temperature of 60–65° F., so often quoted as the minimum, is only the ideal. There is no question of the resins "not working" below this temperature.

Certainly they will take longer to set and cure if it is a lot colder, but if this is realised, and extra catalyst added to compensate, they will set in the normal time and cure reliably. The curing is largely a cumulative process and goes on for months. Below the ideal temperature it may never achieve the 100 per cent theoretical cure, but it will be quite near enough for a boat. In any case the exact state of cure is difficult to define and even more difficult to test non-destructively. It is probable that no boat is ever fully cured by laboratory standards, even those moulded under ideal conditions—but no good fibreglass boat has yet fallen to pieces.

Any decrease in strength or properties due to lower temperatures will be gradual. There is no question of a boat being perfect if moulded at 60° F. and a wreck at 59° F. The conditions need to be really bad, and very damp as well as cold, before there is any appreciable difference. Damp is more serious than low temperature.

We are not designing and building to the limit as in aircraft; we are building boats and there should be a generous factor of safety in any case, certainly enough to take care of a strength reduced to, say, 90 per cent because of bad conditions. Ninety per cent strength more than covers discrepancies due to practical conditions of temperature, even under unfavourable weather conditions—although not conditions which are bad or extreme for the British Isles, nor for continental winter conditions.

Other factors will have a much greater influence than temperature, particularly inexperienced workmanship; even an experienced moulder should make a greater allowance than this for mistakes and average production flaws. (Only the most conceited will deny their existence—although many will not realise they are there and that goes for wooden boatbuilders too.)

If you think this sounds serious consider the scope for error in a wooden boat (and the scope for painting and puttying over bad workmanship); apprentice labour, hidden flaws in the wood, cracks when it dries out, swelling when it takes up, hundreds of separate pieces held together by thousands of fastenings and they have all got to be good. The possibilities of weakness are infinite. They are, of course, allowed for by empirical, traditional methods which consciously or subconsciously rely on a high factor of safety. No one thinks this at all unusual!

Figures of strength must always be kept in perspective, bearing in mind that they are usually laboratory figures and will seldom be achieved, certainly not achieved consistently, even by exprienced moulders working under good conditions. (I do not say that their differences will be nearly as great as an inexperienced worker under bad conditions.) Boats must always be built with a high factor of safety by the very nature of their calling. (See also page 281 on progressive failure.)

Wood and metal boats have the advantage over plastic ones in that they were built, and used for generations before anyone analysed the materials they were made of. Laboratories came later. Fibreglass boats have been bedevilled because their materials were developed in laboratories. They are surrounded by an aura of mystery still to which it is thought only chemists have the key. That is quite wrong. It may need a chemist to develop the resins but it needs a boatbuilder or a practical engineer to make the boats. A chemist can no more build a boat than a laboratory metallurgist build a ship. A wooden boatbuilder does not make his own wood, nor does a shipbuilder smelt his metal, and seldom even rolls his own sheet.

Modern technology demands that the materials are developed in laboratories—but this is only the start of the teamwork. It needs broad minded, experienced practical men to make them work.

Resin and glass-fibre are materials to be used. There is nothing to be frightened about and it needs no great skill to use them, far less skill in fact than in using conventional materials.

Too much importance is placed on the materials and the chemists have laid too much stress on optimum conditions which give only marginal differences. No one stands back and looks at the job as a whole, as a boat being built by practical men under practical conditions. No wood or steel boat is built under ideal conditions but this is allowed for by their normal factor of safety.

I do not say fibreglass boats should be moulded seriously under bad conditions, but we are more concerned here with fitting out and given reasonable precautions polyester resins can be used under similar practical conditions as, say, glue or even paint, and certainly varnish—all common traditional materials.

COLD CONDITIONS The usual hardeners used in greater proportion (which should be allowed for when ordering) will work satisfactorily at 45° F. (7° C.). This temperature covers attainable conditions in Britain throughout most of the year, assuming really cold spells can be avoided. Little excuse will be needed to avoid working below such a temperature.

If work has to be done much below this temperature, it is better to use a booster or special catalyst/accelerator combinations which can be used at freezing temperatures.

If your supplier or manufacturers say it cannot be done try another, because it can—with care. The supplier too can fortify a pre-accelerated resin with extra accelerator for cold conditions. Note that at normal temperatures less catalyst will be needed.

One per cent of tertiary amine accelerator (Scott Bader accelerator D), normally used as the accelerator for benzoyl peroxide catalyst, has a synergistic effect with the common purple cobalt accelerator and acts as a booster in cold weather.

The most important thing when working under cold conditions is to ensure that the resin sets in the usual time. It is then fairly safe from contamination by damp or condensation and can cure at its leisure. If hanging around for a long time in cold, frosty conditions, which are usually damp from condensation and mist also, the surface will certainly be affected and this may penetrate into the moulding for quite a long way.

The proportion of catalyst can be increased safely to three times the amount at normal temperatures, say, from 2 to 6 per cent. Any undesirable effects caused by the larger amount of catalyst will be of small importance compared with the dangers of prolonged setting time. Try small amounts of resin to establish a convenient proportion. Even at freezing point the ordinary hardeners will give a very quick setting time when well stepped up.

Any heating which can be used to ease the conditions will be well worthwhile. (See under Heating, page 312.)

Beginners should not work at these low temperatures. Too many things can go wrong and give bad results which will be confusing because the causes will not be clear. If you have never used the materials before it is much better to wait until the temperature is at least 50° F. (10° C.).

Cold resin is thick and difficult to use. Air bubbles will not be able to get out before the resin sets. Warm cold resin before use by standing it in a tin of hot water. N.B.: Do this before adding catalyst, otherwise it will set as the resin warms up. It is the resin temperature, not the ambient temperature, which matters. Do not use resin brought straight indoors from a cold outside store.

There is no doubt that if the moulding can be left until warmer weather it will be much easier and probably better done. These hints are intended only for those occasions when the work *cannot* be put off until the temperature is above 50° F. (10° C.).

The extra time taken for the moulding to cure means that it will be "green" and rubbery for a longer time.

Extra care will be needed to ensure that it is not distorted by bad support and handling. Being more flexible it can move, but it is hardening all the time. Therefore, if supported in a distorted position for a prolonged period, it may take up a permanent set.

NEED FOR DRY CONDITIONS It is far more important to work under dry conditions than warm. Most boatyard sheds are open and exposed to all the mists rising from the river, often the work must be done in the open, ashore or afloat. Boats are seldom far from their native element and it is difficult to avoid a certain amount of damp.

Any watertight roof, however, will serve to keep out the rain. Mists and dew are best avoided by suitable timing and where possible by not working on really damp, muggy days.

Out of doors it is usually possible to rig up a cover to form a tent. Polythene sheet gives better illumination. If an ordinary cover is being used, and rolled back for working, it is essential to avoid working on wet days, and in showery weather be prepared to cover over quickly.

Good varnishing weather is good moulding weather. If conditions are not suitable for varnishing or painting they are going to be difficult for moulding. Just use common sense.

This susceptibility to damp only really applies to the "wet" resin. Once it has set it is virtually unaffected except actually on the surface. As it cures it becomes highly resistant to water, but there is a period in the early stages of curing, about the first day or two, when prolonged contact, such as immersion or a puddle, will leave the surface marked and blotchy and perhaps permanently slightly tacky. The blotchy marks can be burnished away afterwards, but such prolonged contact should be avoided until it is cured. Note that this will depend on the temperature.

TROPICAL CONDITIONS In Britain cold damp conditions are usually the problem—winter and summer—but in the tropics, heat and high humidity can cause as much trouble.

However, there are times, even in Britain, when conditions can be too hot for moulding. Working out of doors in summer sunshine can give a deck temperature high enough to set resin off very quickly. So, too, can an uninsulated tin roof.

Reduced catalyst will be needed to extend the setting time. The proportion can be reduced safely to 0·5 per cent. Accelerator too can be reduced and if resins are regularly used under hot conditions they should be supplied with a reduced proportion.

High humidity will impose a limit to the length of setting time that is desirable. Three hours should be considered the maximum in high humidity. Longer than this the resin, and even the glass can absorb moisture. The glass should be handled as little as possible with bare hands. Sweaty hands will leave grease marks and prevent the resin bonding. Styrene evaporation will make the resin thicken quickly. Add 5–10 per cent of styrene to compensate (as this makes the resin set quicker reduce the catalyst a little).

Obviously all cans must be kept well sealed and nothing left exposed to the air.

The range of temperature may be very large, particularly when exposed to the sun or in a hot roofed shed. Apart from a shortened setting time a rising temperature will not cause much trouble, but a quickly falling temperature will delay the setting and simultaneously produce a lot of condensation, e.g. a resin catalysed for a temperature of 100° F. (38° C.) will take a long time to set if the temperature falls quickly to 60° F. (16° C.). It is as well to stop work when the temperature starts to fall quickly.

Hot storage conditions will shorten the life of the resin. The storage conditions are under the control of the moulder once they have arrived, but unfortunately the transport conditions are not. I have known cases where resins have been sent from Britain as deck cargo (Ministry of Transport regulations prevent it travelling in a hold on passenger ships because of the low flash point) and have been practically solid on arrival. The shipping company if informed of the need will keep it under cover, out of the sun, but it will often sit around on a dockside for a month or more before the local officialdom are finally satisfied that they have done their worst.

It is possible for the resins to be supplied with extra inhibitor (the component added by the manufacturer to delay setting until required for use). This will prolong the storage life under adverse conditions and is well worth while for any resins shipped to, or even passing through, the tropics. Extra catalyst and probably accelerator will be needed for such resins.

CONDENSATION ON GLASS-FIBRE Moisture will condense on glass-fibre just as it will on a window-pane. A film of moisture on the fibres will prevent the intimate resin-glass bond which is such an important feature.

In damp or frosty weather the glass-fibre must be dried out before use. It does not take much to do this, warming in front of a stove or under a heater is sufficient. The high humidity of the tropics will also cause condensation on the glass.

When not in use the glass should always be kept sealed in a polythene bag.

Condensation can also occur when glass-fibre is brought into a warm workshop from a freezing store. It should be allowed to warm up to room temperature, say for several hours, before use. Inner layers will be insulated by the outer and will take time to warm up.

HEATING Heating an open shed is obviously impossible—and not necessary. A radiant electric fire, a pig lamp, or, if no power is available, a bottled gas-fire or radiant paraffin heater will raise the temperature of the actual working surface of anything it is beamed on quite enough to satisfy the most temperature-conscious moulder. This sort of heating is extremely flexible as the heat can be put right where it is wanted; it is easy to control the temperature by the distance off and little heat is wasted. A small electric fire will be about as much use as a candle in a barn for heating the average open boat shed, but it will warm up several square yards of boat hull.

There is considerably less fire risk in using a radiant electric fire than with an open stove, an important point in a shed full of shavings.

The fire can be used on either side of the boat's surface, e.g. the fire can be placed outside while working inside.

I have even heard of hot water bottles being used.

A radiant fire must be used with discretion. It is easy to "cook" the surface if placed too close. When the surface is too hot to touch or smells it is a fair guide that the fire is too close.

LIGHTING Moulding calls for good lighting. It is important to be able to see what you are doing, otherwise you may find there are a lot of flaws later.

Below decks a wander-light is essential. A lot of fitting-out work will be in cramped positions and places difficult of access. Awkward working positions call for particular care when moulding, and bad lighting must not be an additional handicap.

VENTILATION In a confined space the smell of the resin will be strong. Some people are troubled by this and get headaches and nausea, and even if not affected it is wise to ensure as much ventilation as possible. Certainly keep all the hatches open; a fan or blower may be necessary in a very confined space. Girls are particularly affected by the fumes.

WORKING IN A CONFINED SPACE Working in a confined space is not easy whatever you are doing. With sticky materials it can be very trying.

Resin will tend to get everywhere. Scrupulous cleanliness is difficult but essential. Drips should be mopped up as soon as possible, otherwise you will sit in them and transfer resin to other places where it is not wanted. If in one position long enough for the resin to set you may even get stuck!

Wear a hat or some form of head-covering. If working above your head, goggles will be needed too. A dollop of resin in one's eye is not pleasant.

If you have to lie or lean on newly moulded parts, put down polythene sheet to protect it and to prevent yourself or your clothes sticking to the sticky surface. This will also keep it clean if there is more moulding to follow.

Overalls are obviously essential. It is better if they are not fluffy as otherwise a layer of fine fluff will be left every time you lie or lean on anything still tacky. This will interfere with any subsequent moulding.

Dirty footmarks will prevent subsequent layers from bonding properly. Shoes sticky with resin will pick up all the dirt in reach so that walking about inside a moulding soon makes it very dirty. This must be avoided as much as possible by putting down polythene. A lot of fitting-out may be done before the moulding is absolutely finished and finishing coats at least will be applied to cover up marks. Dirty greasy foot marks will prevent this bonding properly and probably show through.

CLEANLINESS When doing a minor job below to a finished boat be careful to confine resin strictly to the part where you are working. This is very important if the boat is in commission.

Obviously the first thing is to remove or cover any furnishings in the vicinity while your hands are still clean.

Once your hands are dirty and sticky be very careful what you touch. A sticky finger-mark on a polished, moulded cabin top will be difficult to remove, and moreover, un-skilled attempts to remove it will only leave an even more conspicuous mark.

On an expensive cruiser it pays to take very elaborate precautions. This, of course, is all just common sense—but forewarned is forearmed.

SUMMARY The following points will make the job easier and better when working under practical conditions which are far from ideal:

1. Arrange for the boat to be kept dry, either under a roof, tent or boat cover.
2. Avoid working under very cold conditions or during a spell of very cold weather.
3. Increase or reduce catalyst to maintain a setting time of around 1 to 3 hours regard-less of the temperature. Accelerator may need adjustment also.
4. Use local heating, electric fires, gas fires, even hot water bottles to raise the surface temperature of the actual area where you are working. These should be kept on until the resin has set.
5. Do not design to the limit. Allow a generous factor of safety to cover working condi-tions, normal moulding tolerances, possibly inexperience too. The normal factor of safety used in designing a boat will take care of most of this, except extreme condi-tions.
6. In cold weather allow a longer time for adequate cure. Remember the boat or moulding will be "green," uncured and more flexible for longer time. Do not use or highly stress it too soon. Any long maintained distortion is likely to become per-manent.
7. Cleanliness: Resin is sticky and boatyards are dirty. Take extra precautions par-ticularly over footmarks.
8. Fire risk: Store resins and solvents away from shavings and timber, preferably outside.
9. In damp weather dry the glass-fibre before use to drive off condensation. This is most severe in cold, frosty or misty weather, and high tropical humidity.

I fully realise that many of these suggestions will be rank heresy to anyone who is accustomed to working under good conditions. But they have probably never had to work under rougher conditions.

If the mountain will not come to Mohammed, Mohammed must come to the moun-tain. If plastics are to be used on boats seriously, they can only pick and choose their conditions in a well-controlled production building shed. After that they must take what-ever comes, and if they cannot be used under average yard conditions then all moulded boats must return to their builders' heated, air-conditioned factories for every bit of maintenance and repair. This would be an intolerable handicap.

Whenever a moulded boat is fitted out in another yard, or by the owner, or when it is repaired, or just wants routine maintenance, it is usually a question of working under conditions theoretically impossible—or not at all. First and foremost fibreglass boats are boats and it must be possible to treat them more or less like other boats.

I do not claim that these suggestions give better results, or even as good, as those obtained in a first class workshop under carefully controlled, ideal conditions. But they do allow work on boats under conditions which the earlier books, and quite a few current ones, state, categorically, were quite impossible. And they do give adequate strength bearing in mind the sensible factor of safety which should be built into every boat.

The fact is that the theoretical ideal conditions have been, and certainly will be, overtaken by newer developments and methods, and the future will see many more such developments. Improved hardeners are here already and so are improved resins. Even more important is a progressively more practical outlook, as more and more people away from the laboratories find out what actually can be done.

The often-quoted ideal temperatures of 60–65° F. (16–18° C.) is not any critical figure, above which it works, below it does not. It is only an optimum, and a flat optimum at that, with performance falling off gradually as the temperature is reduced (and even that is problematical).

These tips are based on my own practical experience, and that of my staff, gained by working under indifferent boatyard conditions over a period of many years. It goes back to quite early days when the resins really were tricky and temperamental. As well as working around my own boatyard, where only the moulding workshops could possibly be heated, we worked in other yards up and down the country, and in other places like building sites which are far worse than any boatyard.

In theory such conditions were impossible—but flying was impossible to our grandfathers and only lunatics talked of lunar travel. Heresies become the gospel for the next generation, and martyrs become saints.

There are some good moulders working under primitive but cleverly adapted conditions, and there are plenty of moulders with first class conditions producing very bad mouldings. Good conditions help, but above all it is the man, not the conditions, which count.

DRUGS AND ALCOHOL Drugs are a world-wide modern problem. The combination of polyester fumes and drugs produces hallucinations, generally of grandeur. To a lesser extent the same applies with alcohol. Some very serious, inexplicable faults could be attributed to this. Employers and managers should be on the watch for staff with a taste for drugs or alcohol, and the moral for amateurs is obvious.

HUMIDITY Where some control of conditions is practicable relative humidity should be maintained at less than 80 per cent. This figure is exceeded out of doors on two days out of three on the South Coast of England, more inland. It is soon reduced by workshop heating but this may entail some heat even on certain summer days. Note that cooling will increase humidity.

A hygrometer is more useful in a moulding workshop than a thermometer.

Safety

ON the whole the materials used are reasonably safe but they must be treated with some respect. This, of course, applies to most common materials.

FIRE RISK

a. Resins

Polyester resins are inflammable. Even self-extinguishing grades will burn when liquid.

They are not dangerous although the flashpoint, 87°F. (31°C.) is on the low side. The main danger lies in the quantities used and stored. A production moulder may well have tons in store and even a small amateur project may have 100 lb. This would be a lot of paint which is a comparable hazard.

If it does burn the dense smoke will hamper fire-fighting. Foam is advisable. Resin sinks in water but may flow or be washed around.

b. Catalyst

Peroxide catalysts can explode if heated violently, e.g. in a fire. If it ever does start burning vigorously, clear out—quickly.

Before that stage is reached, the oxygen liberated by the catalyst will feed the fire. Burning peroxide, or any fire where a quantity of peroxide is involved, cannot be smothered. Water is the correct action as this cools the fire and dilutes the peroxide. Any peroxide in the vicinity of a fire, but not actually involved, should also be kept cool with water.

Catalyst-soaked rags should be put in a bucket of water or kept damp. They can smoulder and ignite spontaneously if dry. Obviously a waste-paper basket, or a bin of moulded off-cuts, is not a suitable place.

Never keep peroxide catalyst in a metal container. Spontaneous explosions can occur after prolonged contact with metal. For the same reason do not leave metal in catalyst jars, e.g. metal measures, stirrers, spoons, etc., and use a jar with a plastic lid. Explosion from this cause is more likely at higher temperatures. It is unlikely below 65°F. (18°C.). Extra precautions are needed in summer.

There are new high-flash point peroxide catalysts which are much less inflammable or prone to explode, and also powder catalysts which are completely safe. Paste peroxides need the same care as liquids.

c. Solvents

Solvent fires should be attacked with foam. Acetone is highly inflammable; the vapour is heavy and can roll along the floor towards a stove or cigarette end. If acetone is used inside a boat, treat its vapour with the same respect as petrol vapour.

No Smoking should be the rule when moulding. This may at least discourage those friends who only talk and waste your time while the resin sets too soon.

STORAGE The quantities of resin, catalyst and solvent stored in the workshop should be kept to the minimum, preferably no more than is needed for the day's work.

Ideally, separate fireproof stores for each material, well away from other buildings, should be used. This is obviously too much to expect for amateurs and small-scale work, but a suitable alternative is a simple open shelter.

The important thing is to keep the bulk storage away from other buildings, or anything else of value. This is most important for the solvents, followed by the catalyst and then resin. Resin, however, is the easiest as unopened drums, and even well-sealed part used ones, can be left in the open. In the tropics, however, they need to be in the shade.

CATALYST Peroxide catalyst in the eyes will harm them. Be careful not to splash your face with catalyst, which is quite easily done particularly when dispensing from large heavy containers. Goggles are suggested but are likely to be too cumbersome for normal work.

If any does get into the eyes, get medical attention *at once* and say what has happened.

For immediate first-aid wash copiously with water, or better with "Optrex" which contains a weak antidote.

Catalyst should not be allowed to remain on the skin but should be washed or wiped off at once.

DERMATITIS Polyester resins can cause people with sensitive skins to develop dermatitis; so too can some of the hardeners used with epoxy resin.

If susceptible to dermatitis there is only one sensible solution—stick to wooden boats. Rubber gloves and barrier cream are only a partial solution if susceptible—and if not susceptible there is little risk anyway.

Cases of dermatitis are not common. I only know of two. The first, one of my own staff, had contracted it already from working with strong plating solutions. It got no worse but was painful because cleaning off hardened resin opened up the old sores. In the other case the victim, who was not even employed on moulding, came out in a rash whenever he passed the open door of the moulding shop!

In general, barrier cream (Rozalex 9, Kerrocleanse 22) gives adequate protection and it is advisable anyway as it makes cleaning one's hands much easier and kinder. Few people are really susceptible and, if they are sensible, they will avoid using these materials.

CHILDREN These materials are not suitable for children.

There is nothing actively poisonous about any of them, but they will do no good if swallowed. In particular, if resin sets "in the works" it will cause a serious blockage. Catalyst will cause definite harm, particularly in the eyes.

Any child which gets covered with resin, particularly its hair and clothes, is going to have a long and very painful clean up. This also applies to animals, and it must be remembered that their skins, under the hair or fur, is much more sensitive to solvent than a human skin, and this causes real pain—ask my dog, he often came into the moulding shop and sat down to scratch in a puddle of resin!

Glossary and Terms

A

"A" Glass   Cheaper glass-fibre made from glass containing soda. Not recommended for marine use.

Accelerator   Component added to polyester resin to initiate setting at room temperature.
N.B.—For convenience and safety this should be added to the resin by the manufacturer.

Acetone   Commonly used as a solvent for cleaning tools and brushes.

Activate   To initiate the setting of a resin by adding catalyst or hardener.

Aerosil   A very finely powdered silica used to impart thixotropic (q.v.) properties to a resin.

Ageing   Alteration of properties with age, for better or worse. Sometimes used to describe curing.

Air inhibition   Setting of resin affected by contact with air. Usually gives a hard but tacky surface.

Antimony oxide   A white powder commonly used as an additive to make a resin self-extinguishing.

Ambient temperature   The temperature of the surroundings, e.g. room temperature.

B

Barrier cream   Protective cream to protect the skin, particularly a sensitive skin, from possible harmful effects of contact with resins and guard against dermatitis. It also helps to keep hands clean.

Benzoyl peroxide   A peroxide catalyst for use with polyester resins. Catalyst B.

Binder   A weak adhesive, soluble in resin, used to bind glass-fibres together to form glass mat and keep it in a handleable form until wetted out in the mould.

Blister   A moulding flaw where an air pocket is formed between laminations.

Burnishing paste   Fine abrasive polish used to get a first-class finish on a pattern or moulding.

"Bucket and Brush" moulding   A derogatory name for hand lay-up moulding.

C

Capillary attraction   Ability of a liquid to creep up the surface of a fine fibre or tube due to surface attraction.

Carnauba wax   A high quality hard wearing wax used as the base for the best polishes.

Catalyst   The component which must be added to a polyester resin to make it set. The term is used loosely.

Cavity   A moulding fault where the first lay-up does not follow the mould contours and forms a cavity behind the gel coat.

Chain molecule   Long molecules formed by chains of simple repeating groups of atoms.

Chalk   Calcium carbonate used as a filler in resins. Normally made chemically rather than quarried and ground.

Chamfer   To taper off an edge.

China clay   Aluminium silicate, an off-white powder used as a filler for resins.

Chloro-bromethane   A fire-extinguisher fluid which dissolves polyester resin. Not to be used on fibreglass boats.

Chopped strand mat   A mat made of glass-fibres chopped into short lengths and held together with a soluble binder. The commonest reinforcement for mouldings.

Close weave   A cloth woven tightly with the strands almost touching.

Cobalt naphthanate   A purple liquid, the common accelerator used with polyester resins. WARNING: Explosive if mixed directly with peroxide catalyst. Only safe if supplied already mixed into the resin.

Cold moulding ⎫ Moulding with resin which normally sets at around room
Cold setting resin ⎬ temperature, say 50° to 80° F. (10° to 26° C.) as distinct from a resin which must be heated to make it set. Does not mean moulding under freezing conditions although these are not eliminated.

Colour paste   Colours for polyester and epoxy resins used in paste form, to give easy dispersion.

Compression moulding   Moulding under pressure in a press.

Compressive strength   The ability of a material to withstand compressive loads, i.e. pressure.

Contact moulding or laminating   Another name for hand lay-up moulding.

Core   A different material, usually cheap and light, between two moulded skins to space them apart and so give greater stiffness. Also applied to a former over which a stiffening rib or frame is moulded.

Crazing   A fault on the surface of a moulding producing a mass of tiny cracks and star patterns.

Cure   The process during which a moulding develops its full strength. It starts as soon as the resin sets and normally takes a much longer time.

Cure time   The time taken to cure.

Cyclo-hexanone peroxide   A catalyst for polyester resins. Catalyst H.

Cycle   The operation of an entire moulding process from the start of one moulding to the start of the next.

D

Delamination   A serious fault where the layers of the moulding separate.

Depositor   The part of a spray-up equipment which chops and puts down the glass-fibres.

Di-butyl-phthalate   A liquid very compatible with polyester resins; used as a carrier for colour pastes, accelerator, catalyst, etc.

Die   Polite name for a female mould, although usually refers more to a steel mould.

Disc Rollers   Special rollers made of thin discs used in hand lay-up moulding.

Drape   The ability of a fabric to conform to curves due to the looseness of the weave and elasticity of the material.

"Dry"   Describes a moulding which has set, as opposed to one which is still liquid. Also to work or fitting out on a moulded boat without using moulding materials.

E

"E" Glass   The better quality glass-fibre made from glass with a low alkali content; recommended for boats.

Emulsion hand cleaner   A hand-cleaner which eases and lubricates away the dirt as opposed to abrasive kinds, which scrape it away.

Epoxy resin   A resin, stronger and with better properties than polyester but a lot more expensive. Also known as epoxide.

Exotherm   Heat given off by the chemical reaction when a resin sets.

F

Female mould   A mould in which the moulding is done on the inside. The outer face of the moulding is against the mould and is smooth.

Fibreglass⎫
Fiberglas⎭   The trade names for glass-fibre supplied by Fibreglass Ltd. or Owens Corning Fiberglas Corp. Both terms are very commonly and popularly used instead of GRP. (See Introduction.)

Filler resin   Thick resin similar to a filler paint or brushing cement. Used to produce a smooth surface on the "rough" side of a moulding or when sheathing.

Fillet   A method of joining two pieces together with a moulded angle between the two.

Fire retardants   Compounds mixed with the resin to make it less liable to burn.

Flexural strength   The ability to withstand a bending or flexing load.

Foam   A lightweight plastics material containing air or gas-filled cells.

Foam-in-place   Plastics which is poured or sprayed as a liquid and foams up in position.

Filler   An inert powder or other substance added to resin to impart special properties.

Foam core   A core between two moulded skins consisting of a plastic foam.

French chalk   Talcum powder, magnesium silicate. Used as a filler when lubricating or anti-clogging properties are needed. Also used for keeping hands clean when working.

G

Garan treatment   A treatment applied to a glass-fibre to improve the bond of polyester resin to glass-fibre.

Gelling   The action when a resin changes from a liquid to a solid, i.e. polymerises.

Gel time   The time the resin takes to set or gel after the addition of catalyst or hardener.

Glass   In this book it is commonly used as an abbreviation for glass-fibre.

Glass-fibre   Glass drawn out into very fine fibres. The basic reinforcing constituent of GRP.

Glass mat   See "Chopped strand mat."

Goo Slang expression for liquid resin.

Good side The side of a moulding laid up against the mould face so that it takes up the smooth surface of the mould.

"Green" Resin which has just set and is still rather soft and rubbery; by analogy with concrete and wood.

GRP Glass reinforced plastics. Generally based on polyester resin. See Fibreglass.

Gunk A former term for dough moulding and the resin dough used.

H

Hardener A substance added to a liquid resin to make it set into a solid, i.e. to polymerise. In this book it is restricted to the activating agents for epoxy resins and synthetic glues.

Heat distortion point Temperature at which a resin starts to soften and its strength starts to decrease.

Het-acid resin Polyester resin with exceptional fire-proof qualities.

Homogeneous Of uniform quality and consistency.

Honeycomb Strips of paper, cloth, metal, etc., joined together to form a honeycomb pattern. Used as a lightweight core in sandwich mouldings.

Hot-setting resin A resin which must be heated to make it set.

Hygroscopic Tending to absorb moisture from the air often with permanent change of properties.

I

Impregnate To saturate with resin.

Inhibitor A substance added during manufacture to delay a resin polymerising or setting into a solid.

Injection moulding Moulding by forcing a liquid plastic into a mould under considerable pressure and heat.

Insert A piece of some other material such as wood or metal put in during or before moulding to serve a definite purpose such as strengthening or to take a fastening.

Intumescent Fire-retardant paint or gel coat which foams up when exposed to heat.

Isophthalic A form of polyester resin with better flexibility and wear resisting properties.

In situ In the position which it will finally occupy, e.g. moulding or forming foam.

J

Jig Any arrangement for holding parts in position, while joining them together or to maintain their shape.

Jigsaw Small saw with reciprocating action used for trimming mouldings. Usually power-driven.

K

Keene's cement "Pink" cement, a hard plaster which cures slowly and remains workable for several days after setting.

L

Lacuna A general term for moulding flaws like cavities, blisters, pinholes and pockets.

Laminate To mould in a series of layers. Also used as a term for a moulding so made.

Lamination A single layer of a lamination and also the process of moulding in a series of layers.

Layer A single stage of a lay-up or laminate.

Lay-up The process of moulding where glass-fibre and resin are applied in layers and consolidated. Commonly used also to refer to the individual layers, first lay-up, second, etc.

M

Male mould A mould where the moulding is made over the outside so that the inside face of the moulding is against the mould face.

Marco process An early method of moulding plastic boats using a rubber bag and vacuum to suck in the resin.

Marginal temperatures Temperatures outside the optimum range for working with resins.

Masking tape A strong adhesive tape which is readily removed without leaving marks, used to protect a surface while painting and to limit the area.

Mat See "Chopped strand mat."

Matched moulds Two or more moulds arranged to surround the moulding completely as a male and female mould. Normally used in a press.

Matting-in Joining two members by moulding an overlapping angle fillet or butt-strap.

Methyl-ethyl-ketone peroxide A liquid catalyst, the commonest catalyst for use with polyester resins. Usually abbreviated to MEKP. Sometimes called Catalyst M.

Microballons A very light powder consisting of minute phenolic bubbles. Used as a filler or paste and the basis of syntactic foam.

Mohair rollers Best quality paint rollers made from mohair, a form of wool.

Monomer One of the constituents, usually styrene but sometimes an acrylic, of a polyester resin which plays an important part in the cross-linking action of polymerising or setting. It is also used as a thinning agent.

Mould The former, in or on which a moulding is laid up. It is normally the exact opposite or negative of the proposed moulding.

Moulding The process whereby an object is formed to shape in a mould. Also describes an object so formed.

N

Needleloom A form of chopped strand mat where the strands are held in place by "needling" or very loosely stitching on to a gauze instead of bonding with a soluble binder.

Neoprene A synthetic rubber.

O

Open weave   A woven material with considerable space between the strands.

Orange peel   A wrinkled effect looking literally like orange peel, a common fault on surface finishes.

Orbital sander   A mechanical sander which uses a flat sheet with an orbital motion similar to hand-sanding, i.e. every part of the sheet moves the same distance as opposed to a disc rotating at high speed about a central point.

P

PVA   Polyvinyl Alcohol. The commonest primary release agent. Forms a very thin protective skin over the mould.

Pattern   The accurately made and very carefully prepared master-pattern from which the mould is made. It is usually a positive, i.e. the shape of the final moulding.

Pinholes   A moulding fault consisting of groups of tiny holes like pinpricks on the gel coat. Also formed in the interstices of woven reinforcement.

Plain weave   A simple over-and-under weave.

Plastics   A general term covering synthetic, man-made materials, of large molecular structure which can be formed, moulded, or extruded into shapes or coatings.

Plastic boats   In this book plastic boats is used as a short form of reinforced plastic boats, otherwise known as glass-fibre, fibreglass or fiberglass boats.

Plasticiser   A compound added to a resin to improve flexibility and reduce brittleness.

Plug mould   Polite description for male mould.

Polyester resin   The common resin used in moulding fibreglass boats.

Polymer   General term for long molecular chain plastic materials which can be moulded under the influence of heat and pressure or by the addition of an activating agent.

Polymerise   The setting or gelling of a resin, the action whereby long chain molecules link up with one another or with an intermediate agent as the resin changes from a liquid to a solid.

Polystyrene   A common plastic material. In boat use normally limited to the very light expanded polystyrene used as a buoyancy material. Attacked by polyester.

Polyurethane   A plastic used for a tough and durable paint and also as a plastic foam either rigid or flexible.

Pop-rivet   A rivet flattened by the head of an internal spindle which breaks off on further pulling. (See Fig. 1.15.)

Post heat }
Post cure }   To heat the moulding after the resin has set to speed up the curing time.

Potlife   The length of time between adding catalyst or hardener and the resin setting. The usable working time.

Pre-impregnate   To impregnate a glass fabric with resin before placing it in position.

Primary release agent   The most important release agent, if two are used, and the one in contact with the resin. Usually PVA.

Primer   Used to secure good adhesion to wood or metal or to insulate a resin from the harmful effects of contact with the material underneath.

Promoter   General name for hardeners, catalysts or accelerators which initiate or promote setting.

Putty A dough made by mixing resin with large proportions of filler. Glass-fibres can be added for strength.

Q

Quartz Used as a filler; very hard and gives good wear resistance. A coarse quartz grit makes a non-slip surface.

R

Release The process of easing a moulding out of the mould.

Release agent Substance applied to the mould to prevent the moulding sticking to the mould.

Resin Syrupy liquid, usually polyester or epoxy in boatbuilding which forms the major part of a reinforced plastic moulding.

Resin putty See "Putty."

Resin rich With an abnormally high proportion of resin.

Resorcinol One of the strongest and best synthetic glues. Phenol base.

Rough side The side of a moulding not laid up against the polished mould face. The "natural" or inside finish on a boat.

Rovings Continuous glass-fibres bunched together into a thick loose string and often woven into a fabric.

Rubbery stage A stage of short duration immediately after a resin has set when it is still flexible and rubbery; it quickly gets hard.

S

Sandwich moulding A form of construction using two reinforced plastic skins with a spacing core between made of some other material, usually light and cheap.

Satin weave A weave where a strand passes under one strand and then over several others.

Secondary release agent The less important release agent when two are used, usually a wax polish on the mould face.

Self-extinguishing Ceases to burn when the source of flame is removed.

Self-tapping screws Hardened steel screws which cut their own thread as they are driven home.

Scrim Loose very open weave cloth, often incorrectly applied to any glass cloth.

Sheathing The process of covering a boat, tank or anything else with a plastic skin, usually of glass-fibre.

Shelf life The length of time a material will remain usable under reasonable storage conditions if not used.

Setting time The time taken for a resin to set after the addition of catalyst or hardener.

Silane treatment Special treatment for glass-fibres to give better resin-glass bond.

Size A lubricant applied to a strand to make it possible to weave it into a cloth. It must be removed before moulding as it interferes with the resin-glass bond.

Slateflour Hard powder imparting abrasion-resisting properties and dark colour, used as a filler for resins.

Softening temperature   Temperature at which resins soften and become too weak to be satisfactory.

Speckle paint   A paint made of several different coloured compounds which do not mix together. When sprayed under the correct conditions it produces a speckle effect, very effective in disguising the rough inside of a moulding.

Split mould   A mould made in two or more pieces which separate to release.

Spray up   Mechanised form of lay up. Glass-fibres are chopped and sprayed on to the mould together with a stream of catalysed resin.

Square weave   A simple under-and-over weave.

Starring   A fault where the gel coat develops an extensive pattern of fine cracks, often in star pattern.

Stipple   To paint with short jabbing strokes, not a sweeping painting action. Used to impregnate glass mat.

Strand   A bunch of fibres tightly twisted together, the smallest usable unit.

Styrene   The usual monomer in polyester resins. Can also be used as a thinner for polyester resins.

Stove cure   Heating to obtain a better and faster cure.

Sub-moulding   A portion of a boat or moulding which is moulded separately and fitted in later.

Surfacing gauze   A very fine open mat made of gossamer thin strands of glass-fibre. It is intended to hold a good layer of resin to improve the surface finish either inside the moulding or to back up the gel coat.

Swedging   The moulding of ridges, grooves, depressions, corrugations, raised panels, dents and other alterations to the shape of a predominantly flat panel with the idea of increasing the stiffness.

Swirl mat   Glass mat made from continuous strands laid down in a loose random circular or S-shaped pattern.

Syntactic foam   A lightweight resin, or resin-glass, putty, made by using a very light "bubble" filler.

T

Tack-free   A surface which is never sticky when it sets.

Talcum powder   See under "French Chalk."

Tapping   Cutting a screw thread.

Tensile strength   The ability of a material to withstand tensile loads, i.e. pulling.

Thermoplastic   A material which softens and melts on heating but solidifies on cooling with no change of properties.

Thermosetting   A material which polymerises and undergoes an irreversible change on heating, with or without the aid of hardeners or catalysts. Also applied to materials like polyester and epoxy resins which undergo an irreversible change at room temperature after the addition of hardeners or catalysts.

Thixotropic   A material which, like a lazy boy, is reluctant to run on its own, yet moves readily under compulsion such as brushing (or beating).

Thixotropy   The degree of thixotropic effect.

Thixotropic paste   A thick paste which imparts thixotropic properties when mixed with an ordinary resin.

Tissue A fine gauze or mat made with very thin strands or single fibres.

Translucent Permits a proportion of light to pass but not optically clear like window glass.

Two-part mixture A material which is formed or sets by the mixing of two components.

U

Unidirectional Strength lying mainly in one direction. A glass cloth can be woven to give greater strength in one direction than another.

V

Vacuum bag moulding A method of moulding where the moulding is covered with a bag and the resin sucked in under a vacuum.

Vinyl hot melt compound A rubbery thermoplastic which is melted and poured over a pattern to form a flexible mould. More suitable for small moulds but its flexibility allows undercuts and parallel draws.

Viscosity A measure of the "thickness" or pourability of a liquid. A viscous liquid does not pour freely.

Void-free A moulding containing no cavities, blisters, lacunae or air spaces, etc.

Volane treatment A chromium based treatment for glass cloth giving improved resin to glass bonding with polyester resins.

W

Warp The crossways strands of a cloth.

Water absorption The amount of water which a laminate will absorb. The effect is usually detrimental.

Weave Description of the construction of a cloth.

Weft The lengthways strands of a cloth.

"Wet" Resin which is still liquid (as opposed to "dry" resin which has set). Also used to describe a moulding or glass fabric before the resin has set.

Wet-and-dry A form of sandpaper which can be used wet as well as dry.

"Wet-on-dry" Laying up a layer of a moulding where the underlying layer has already set hard.

"Wet-on-wet" Laying up a layer of a moulding before the underlying layer has set.

Wet strength The strength of a moulding when thoroughly wet.

Whiskers Loose or upstanding strands of glass-fibre, usually solidified with resin; also the ragged edge of a moulding.

"Wetting-out" The action of soaking a glass fabric with resin. Also a measure of the readiness of a fabric to soak up resin. For proper wetting-out every fibre must be completely surrounded or "wetted' with resin.

Wood primer A thin resin which soaks into wood to ensure a good physical bond.

Woven rovings Fabric woven from strands of rovings, usually a thick bulky fabric giving the bulk of a mat with the strength of a woven material.

Wrinkles A gel coat fault due to softening of the gel coat by the resins of the subsequent lay-up.

Y

Yarn Strands of glass-fibre from which a cloth is woven.

Conversion Factors

British		Metric	Metric	British
1 inch		= 25·4 mm.	1 mm.	= 0·039 in.
1 foot	= 12 in.	= 0·305 m.	1 cm. = 10 mm.	= 0·39 in.
1 yard	= 3 ft.	= 0·91 m.	1 m. = 39·37 in.	
			= 3·28 ft.	= 3 ft. 3·4 in.
			= 1·09 yd.	
1 square inch		= 6·45 cm.²	1 cm.²	= 0·155 sq. in.
1 sq. ft. = 144 sq. in.		= 0·093 m.²	1 m.²	= 10·76 sq. ft.
1 sq. yd. = 9 sq. ft.		= 0·836 m.²		= 1·196 sq. yd.
1 cubic inch		= 16·39 cm.³	1 cm.³	= 0·061 cu. in.
1 cubic foot		= 0·028 m.³	1 litre	= 61·03 cu. in.
1 cubic yard		= 0·764 m.³	1 m.³	= 35·32 cu. ft.
				= 1·31 cu. yd.
1 ounce (oz.)		= 28·3 gr.	1 gr.	= 0·035 oz.
1 pound (lb.) = 16 oz.		= 0·454 kg.	1 kg.	= 2·2 lb.
1 hundredweight (cwt.) = 112 lb.		= 50·8 kg.		
1 ton = 20 cwt. = 2,240 lb.		= 1,016 kg.	1,000 kg.	= 0·98 tons
1 pint		= 0·568 litres	1 litre	= 1·76 pints
				= 0·22 gallons (Imp.)
1 gallon (Imp.)		= 4·55 litres		
1 gallon (Imp.)		= 1·2 gallons (U.S.)		
1 gallon (U.S.)		= 0·83 gallons (Imp.)	1 litre	= 0·26 gallons (U.S.)
		= 3·8 litres		

Mat and resin	Cloth and rovings	
1 oz./sq. ft.	= 9 oz./sq. yd.	= approx. 300 g./m.²
1½ oz./sq. ft.	= 13·5 oz./sq. yd.	= approx. 450 g./m.²
2 oz./sq. ft.	= 18 oz./sq. yd.	= approx. 600 g./m.²
3 oz./sq. ft.	= 27 oz./sq. yd.	= approx. 900 g./m.²

Temperature Centigrade	Fahrenheit
− 40	− 40
0	32
15·5	60
20	68
100	212

$\frac{1}{16}$ in. = approx. 1·5 mm.
$\frac{1}{8}$ in. = approx. 3 mm.
$\frac{1}{4}$ in. = approx. 6 mm.
$\frac{3}{8}$ in. = approx. 9 mm.
$\frac{1}{2}$ in. = approx. 12 mm.
$\frac{3}{4}$ in. = approx. 18 mm.
1 in. = approx. 25 mm.
2 in. = approx. 50 mm.

Conversion from one scale to the other:

C. to F.
Add 32, multiply by nine fifths

F. to C.
Subtract 32, multiply by five ninths

There is a simpler conversion based on the fact that: − 40 °C. = − 40 °F. The adding and subtracting are the same in both cases, which is easier to remember and avoids uncertainty.

°C. to °F.   Add 40, multiply by nine fifths, subtract 40.
°F. to °C.   Add 40, multiply by five ninths, subtract 40.

Index